# Collecting and Investing Strategies for Barber Dimes

## By: Jeff Ambio

# Dedication

*To my father, Louis Ambio, who has always supported my passion for coin collecting and numismatic research. Our father-and-son trips to the local coin shop will always have a special place in my memories.*

# Collecting and Investing Strategies for Barber Dimes

By: Jeff Ambio

Copyright © 2009
ZYRUS PRESS INC.

Published by:

ZYRUS PRESS INC.
PO Box 17810, Irvine, CA 92623
Tel: (888) 622-7823 / Fax: (800) 215-9694
www.zyruspress.com
ISBN# 978-1-933990-22-4 (paperback)

Coin images © Bowers and Merena and David Lawrence.
Cover art © 2009, Zyrus Press by: Bryan D. Stoughton.

# About the Author

Jeff Ambio holds a Bachelor of Arts in History from Cornell University and a Masters of Business Administration from Pepperdine University. Upon graduating from Cornell in 1998, Ambio decided to turn a life-long passion for coin collecting into a full-time career. Over the past 10 years, his career has developed into a successful and rewarding profession. Today, few other professional numismatists can lay claim to so prolific a career in so short a period of time. Ambio's numismatic resume reads like a directory of America's most prestigious rare coin auction houses and dealerships, and his writings provide collectors, investors and even other dealers with many of the tools and knowledge that they need to build significant collections and conduct successful businesses.

Ambio's first position as a professional numismatist was as a Cataloger and, later, Catalog Production Manager for the U.S. coin division of Heritage Numismatic Auctions (now Heritage Auction Galleries) in Dallas, Texas. During his tenure with Heritage, Jeff handled thousands of rare coins, produced dozens of catalogs and designed many of the marketing pieces published by the firm.

In 2003 and 2004, Ambio served as a Cataloger for Superior Galleries of Beverly Hills. He relocated to California in 2004 and accepted the position of Director of Numismatics for Bowers and Merena Auctions of Irvine. Jeff also served as Vice President of Numismatics for Rare Coin Wholesalers of Dana Point, California.

In addition to extensive cataloging and marketing experience, Jeff is a widely read numismatic author. His writings and articles are credited with ground-breaking work in the field and have appeared in numerous publications, including *Rare Coin Investment Trends*, *The Gobrecht Journal*, *Numismatic News* and *Coin World*. Ambio is the author of the books *Collecting & Investing Strategies for United States Gold Coins* and *Collecting & Investing Strategies for Walking Liberty Half Dollars* (part of the Strategy Guide series), and he also completely revised and updated David W. Akers' classic book *A Handbook of 20th-Century United States Gold Coins: 1907-1933*. His fourth and most current book, *Collecting & Investing Strategies for Barber Dimes*, is the first comprehensive book published on this important series in nearly 10 years.

Early in his career, Ambio's achievements as a numismatist were honored with a scholarship to attend the American Numismatic Association (ANA) Summer Seminar. In 2007, Jeff came full circle, this time returning to the ANA Summer Seminar as an instructor and originator of the course "Attributing United States Coins." He plans to teach classes on Walking Liberty Half Dollars and Silver Dollars at future sessions of the ANA Summer Seminar. In addition to several local and regional organizations, Jeff is a member of the ANA and the NLG.

In 2007, Ambio returned to his lakeside home in Texas, where he now works as a technical and marketing consultant for rare coin auction houses, dealerships, brokerage firms and private collectors/investors across the United States. His recent cataloging work has expanded to include United States currency as well as Ancient and World coins. Shortly after relocating to Texas, Jeff founded his own rare coin dealership – Ambio Rare Coins (ARC).

# Foreword

When Jeff Ambio approached me about writing a foreword to his new reference book on Barber dimes, I first wondered if there was a need in the marketplace for such a reference. After all, my father wrote the first authoritative reference on the series back in 1991, a work which has been followed up by a few other guides to the series. How much more is there to write?

It took just a few, short minutes to dispel any trepidation. Once I dove into this book I quickly realized the Jeff has done a wonderful job with this topic. Every date is researched with exhaustive detail, relative rarities explored, auction records noted, and values accurately estimated.

Other chapters go a long way to discuss the greater issue of collecting strategies and an overall history of the series. If you are a serious collector of Barber dimes, you must have this book on your desk for handy reference. If you are thinking of collecting Barber dimes, you should read through this book before you get started. I would further add that the strategy chapters would apply well to any collector of coins.

In this day and age of the Internet, a great resource like *Collecting & Investing Strategies for Barber Dimes* is a vastly underrated resource. Thank you, Jeff, for taking on this huge task and bringing it to the collector!

*John Feigenbaum*
*John Feigenbaum is a life-long numismatist who followed his father's footsteps into the coin business and works at many levels to make coin collecting more accessible to collectors. He is President of several numismatic companies, including: David Lawrence Rare Coins, Dominion Grading Service & StellaCoinNews.com.*
*May 2009*

# Preface

The idea to write a book on Barber Dimes first came into my mind 10 years ago when I launched my career as a professional numismatic cataloger, researcher and writer. Contrary to many other series, Barber Dimes—and Barber coinage as a whole, for that matter—has received remarkably little attention in numismatic literature. I will never forget that day in the spring of 1999 when I first walked into Chief Cataloger Mark Van Winkle's office at Heritage Numismatic Auctions and was confronted with a comprehensive numismatic research library the likes of which I had never even imagined could exist. Numerous books on series such as Bust Half Dollars, Morgan Dollars, Saint-Gaudens Double Eagles and classic Commemoratives were waiting to help me expand my knowledge on rare coins and hone my skills as a numismatic writer. Some books, like *United States Early Half Dollar Die Varieties: 1794-1836* by Al C. Overton, are highly detailed attribution guides that seek to offer very specific information for a specialized audience. Others, such as *The Morgan and Peace Dollar Textbook* by Wayne Miller, while no less detailed, seek to reach a wider audience by providing information that ranges from striking characteristics to diagnostics of branch mint proofs. Both types of books are invaluable to the numismatic scholar.

I was surprised to learn, however, that there were very few books in Mark's library that dealt with the Barber Dime series on any level. This is, after all, an important series. Not only does it number within its ranks the proof 1894-S—one of the "100 Greatest United States Coins," as defined by Jeff Garrett and Ron Guth in 2005—but it is riddled with many other scarce-to-rare issues from both the main coinage facility in Philadelphia and the branch mints in Denver, New Orleans and San Francisco. As of 1999, however, only three significant numismatic books had been published that dealt with the Barber Dime series in any capacity.

The earliest of these is *Walter Breen's Encyclopedia of United States and Colonial Proof Coins* (1977). Using capsule entries, Breen provides mintage figures and brief diagnostics for each proof Barber Dime. He also discusses the branch mint proof 1894-S and provides what (at that time) was an up-to-date census of the known examples. The 1988 follow-up work Walter Breen's *Complete Encyclopedia of U.S. and Colonial Coins* is expanded to also include mintage figures and diagnostics for the business strike Barber Dimes, as well as a brief history of the series. Both of those books, however, dealt with the U.S. coinage family as a whole and, by necessity, could only give limited attention to each individual Barber Dime issue.

The first book devoted exclusively to Barber Dimes is David Lawrence's *The Complete Guide to Barber Dimes* (1991). Groundbreaking for its time, the Lawrence reference is the earliest that sought to analyze the Barber Dime series from a variety of angles. In addition to mintage figures and variety information, Lawrence's book provides a history of the series, grading criteria, certified population data, pricing data, rarity estimates and brief comments concerning strike, luster and other characteristics.

In the years since 1999, the attention paid to Barber Dimes by numismatic scholars has not improved to an appreciable extent. David Lawrence returned to the subject in 1999 with the book *The Complete Guide to Certified Barber Coinage*, which was co-authored by his son John Feigenbaum. Certified population data, pricing data and rarity estimates were revised in that text but, since it also included the Barber Quarters and Barber Half Dollars, there was little room to delve into a highly detailed analysis of each individual issue. Of particular importance in the Feigenbaum and Feigenbaum reference are price indices for each issue in grades of MS-63 and MS-65. An important predecessor to the Investment Potential Ratios that I have developed for use in the current book, the Feigenbaum Price Indices represent what, in my opinion, are the first attempt to analyze and rank each issue in the Barber Dime series as a function of both population and value.

Kevin Flynn's book *The Authoritative Reference on Barber Dimes* made its appearance in 2004. Every major and minor die variety in the Barber Dime series known to researchers is highlighted in that book, providing an incredibly detailed view of one aspect of the Barber Dime series. The Fourth Edition, Volume II of the book *Cherrypickers' Guide to Rare Die Varieties of United States Coins* by Bill Fivaz and J.T. Stanton (published 2006) provides a more focused view of Barber Dime varieties by presenting only those that are of the greatest interest to collectors. The Fivaz/Stanton work covers all U.S. coin series from Half Dimes through Double Eagles, as well as Commemoratives.

Numerous articles, and a few other books, have been published over the years that deal either in whole or in part with some aspect of the Barber Dimes series. Many of those works give coverage of only one issue in this series—the 1894-S is a favorite—or provide a glimpse into only one facet of collecting or investing in Barber Dimes. Additionally, numismatic catalogers have provided much information on individual issues and coins in the Barber Dime series. Their work, while often including new information based on personal observation and/or critical research, is widely scattered throughout countless auction catalogs and, as such, is not readily accessible to the average collector or investor. Catalogers also spend much of their time working under extreme pressure imposed by auction production deadlines. As such, the only Barber

Dimes that are likely to receive in-depth research prior to the completion of a catalog description are an 1894-S and, perhaps, a high-grade example of a key-date issue like the 1895-O.

My experience as a numismatic researcher, as well as time spent sharing thoughts and views with other professional numismatists and private collectors/investors, has convinced me that the market is sorely in need of a single reference on Barber Dimes that provides a highly detailed, analytical study of all the critical aspects of this series. This, therefore, is the niche that this book seeks to fill. My hope is that whether you are a collector, an investor or a little bit of both, *Collecting & Investing Strategies for Barber Dimes* will equip you with all of the tools you need to buy and sell Barber Dimes with confidence in the dynamic and ever-changing rare coin market of the 21st century.

Jeff Ambio
Texas, January 2009

# Acknowledgements

S everal firms and individuals were instrumental in the publication of this book. I owe a special debt of gratitude to my publisher **Bart Crane, Jessica Mullenfeld** and the entire team at Zyrus Press. Bart and his team have been overly generous with their time and resources in the production of this book. Without their expertise and dedication, this project would never have been possible. Thank you, Bart and Jessica.

I would also like to acknowledge **Elaine Dinges, Ceilia Mullins, Ron Castro** and everyone at Bowers and Merena Auctions for furnishing many of the Barber Dime images used in this book. Ceilia, in particular, spent many hours gathering these images and ensuring that they were in print-ready format. **Bryan Stoughton**, Creative Director for Bowers and Merena Auctions, also deserves special recognition for designing the cover for the entire *Strategy Guide* series.

Allow me to also thank **John Feigenbaum**, President of David Lawrence Rare Coins and DLRC Auctions and **Kim Ludwig**, Marketing Supervisor for DLRC for providing images of the Barber Dimes from Part III of the fabulous Richmond Collection. Additionally, John graciously agreed to write the Foreword to this book. The reputation and level of expertise that John and his father, the late David Lawrence Feigenbaum, have attained in the market for Barber coinage is unsurpassed in the rare coin industry of the 21st century. Thank you, John, for sharing some of your perspective on Barber Dimes—it has helped make this book a more complete and meaningful work.

Several other individuals also gave freely of their time by providing critical research information for various sections of this book. **John Dannreuther**, Co-Founder of PCGS, provided detailed attribution information regarding the proof and business strike 1893/'2' Barber Dime. **David Lange**, NGC Research Director, also provided attribution information regarding the 1893/'2' Barber Dime. **Steve Roach**, Director of Marketing for Certified Collectibles Group—NGC, made available important archived NGC Census data on the 1893/'2' in both proof and business strike format. **Mark Borckardt**, Senior Cataloger for Heritage Auction Galleries, challenged me to develop a formula that would help determine whether individual U.S. coin issues are underrated or overrated relative to current market values. Mark also shared information, as well as his personal thoughts and observations, regarding the pedigrees of individual examples of the 1894-S Barber Dime. **Karl Moulton** graciously provided old catalogs and prices realized listings (many at no cost to the author) that were invaluable in establishing and tracing pedigrees for some of the finest Barber

Dimes known to exit. Karl also shared some of the results of his research on the 1894-S Barber Dime, especially the pedigrees of individual examples. Finally, **Laura Sperber** of Legend Numismatics related important information about the 1894-S Barber Dime that she handled in 1990.

# Table of Contents

# *Introduction*

The bulk of this book is devoted to a detailed analysis of every proof and business strike issue in the Barber Dime series of 1892-1916. I encourage you, however, to read the introductory chapters before delving into the date and mintmark analyses. The Introduction, in particular, is invaluable to discerning my methodology on researching and writing this book, as well as understanding the parameters of this study and how to interpret the information that I have gathered on this important series.

In Chapter One: "Popular Collecting and Investing Strategies for Barber Dimes", I suggest several methods through which you can build a meaningful collection or investment portfolio comprised either in whole or in part of Barber Dimes. Chapter Two: "Considerations for Buying Barber Dimes", outlines several key factors governing the nature of the market in which these coins trade. Particularly important aspects of that chapter are observations on third-party certification and suggestions on how and where to acquire Barber Dimes. Finally, Chapter Three: "A Brief History of the Barber Dime Series", details the birth of this series and broad themes affecting yearly mintages and/or distribution of the coins.

Chapter Four begins the main issue-by-issue analysis of the Barber Dime series. The information presented on each proof and business strike issue is based on the thousands of Barber Dimes that I have cataloged for auction, bought and sold or otherwise studied over the course of more than 10 years as a professional numismatist. Other books such as *A Guide Book of United States Coins, 62nd Edition* by R.S. Yeoman, *The Complete Guide to Barber Dimes* by David Lawrence and *Walter Breen's Complete Encyclopedia of U.S. and Colonial Coins* were consulted only to verify facts such as mintage figures, attributions for significant die varieties, etc.

I have limited my discussion of the business strike issues in this series to Mint State coins. While this decision may come as a shock and/or disappointment to some readers, realize that it has been made after serious consideration and thorough reflection. The U.S. rare coin market of the 21st century is fixated on technical quality. With the exception of costly key-date issues, some of which are unknown in Mint State anyway, the lion's share of the money that changes hands in any given year of numismatic trading concerns coins that grade Proof-60/MS-60 or finer. These are certainly the levels at which the typical numismatic investor is likely to spend the majority of his or her money.

Conscious of current and future demand for the coins that they buy, more and more collectors are also coming to the realization that they have to acquire the finest in technical quality that they can afford in order to best protect their investment in numismatics. In fact, ever-increasing prices for rare and desirable United States coins have largely forced the transformation of the pure collector into a collector-investor. This new breed of numismatist is still a collector at heart who is drawn to coins because of their historical significance, artistic beauty or some other innate quality that the coins possess. Unlike the pure collector, however, the collector-investor views their collection not so much as a family heirloom to pass on to children and/or grandchildren, but as an integral part of a well-rounded investment portfolio. Whether this portfolio is meant to provide short-term tax benefits or long-term security, the collector-investor embarks on their pursuit of rare coins with the intention of selling all or part of their collection within their lifetime.

The Barber Dime series is one of many in the U.S. coinage family for which unimpaired proofs and Mint State examples have attracted much of the collector and investor interest in coins of this type. Unlike other series in this group, however, Barber Dimes still continue to see appreciable collector interest in circulated grades. This is particularly true for key-date issues such as the 1895-O and 1901-S that are rare and costly in Mint State. Additionally, the Barber Dime series as a whole is quite scarce in Mint State, and it is much rarer at that level of preservation that more widely collected U.S. coin types such as the Walking Liberty Half Dollar and Morgan Dollar. Even so, the largest percentage of money that collectors, investors and dealers have assigned to the Barber Dime series is devoted to coins that grade Proof-60/MS-60 or finer. Consequently, the Barber Dimes that garner the most attention and greatest exposure in numismatic circles are unimpaired proofs and Mint State coins. Finally, and by extension, the Barber Dimes that I believe have the greatest potential for future price appreciation are those that grade at least Proof-60/MS-60. In this sense, the Barber Dime series is akin to most others in the U.S. coinage family, whether we are talking about rarer coins such as Capped Bust Half Dimes or more common coins the likes of Peace Dollars.

Within the analysis that I have provided for each proof and business strike issue in the Barber Dime series, you will find several sections that include valuable information for the collector and investor. These are:

**Mintage:** A statement of the number of coins struck. The Barber Dime series was not subject to widespread exportation and/or melting like other U.S. coin types such as the Seated Dollar, Morgan Dollar and Saint-Gaudens Double Eagle. As such, mintage figures are a fairly accurate indicator of assessing relative rarity in Mint State for many issues in this series. You should bear in mind, however, that many of the earlier issues of this type saw far greater circulation than some of the late-date issues.

**Rarity Rankings:** I have sequentially ranked the proof and business strike issues in this series in terms of overall rarity in Proof/Mint State and rarity in high grades (Proof-65/MS-65 or finer). The results of this study are located at the beginning of each date and mintmark analysis, as well as in the appendices at the end of this book. For each issue, I have provided its rankings within the context of the entire Barber Dime series and, for the business strikes, the issuing Mint.

My decision to include rarity breakdowns for this series by Mint is based on two factors. First, the forces governing the rates of survival of Mint State Barber Dimes can often be analyzed within the context of the issuing Mint. As a whole, New Orleans Mint issues saw extensive commercial use, while Philadelphia Mint issues tended to be saved in greater numbers beginning in the year of production. Second, collecting coins by mintmark is a popular strategy among many numismatic buyers. Whether it is due to the part of the country in which they were born, historical appreciation or some other reason, some collectors and investors will choose to specialize in Barber Dimes struck in only one Mint.

**Important Varieties:** This book is not an attribution guide, although you will find a subsection devoted to important varieties near the beginning of each date and mintmark analysis. I have chosen to define the term "important" in this context as only those varieties that are recognized by the third-party grading services Professional Coin Grading Service (PCGS) and/or Numismatic Guaranty Corporation (NGC), carry a significant premium over regular examples of their respective issues and/ or are visually dramatic. If you are seeking a more comprehensive study of Barber Dime varieties, I highly recommend, among other books, *The Complete Guide to Barber Dimes* by David Lawrence, *Cherrypickers' Guide to Rare Die Varieties of United States Coins,* Fourth Edition, Volume II by Bill Fivaz and J.T. Stanton and *Walter Breen's Complete Encyclopedia of United States and Colonial Coins.*

**General Comments:** This brief introductory paragraph provides a summation of the issue's relative rarity in the Barber Dime series.

**Strike:** I have analyzed every proof and business strike Barber Dime in the area of striking quality. I consider my observations in this section as fact *for the majority of examples that I have examined for each issue in this series.* Many Barber Dime issues, particularly those from the Philadelphia Mint, were produced in fairly sizeable numbers, and there is sometimes considerable variation between coins struck from different die pairs, during different press runs from the same die pair or even during the same press run. Additionally, and although I have handled numerous Barber Dimes over the course of my career as a professional numismatist, no one researcher can ever hope to see every single example of a given issue. This is particularly true of common issues with hundreds, if not thousands of proof or Mint State examples known, of which there are several in the Barber Dime series. Please accept my observations as indicative of the striking characteristics for the *majority* of examples of a given issue that you are likely to encounter in the numismatic market.

**Luster (Finish for the Proof Issues):** The luster or finish of every issue in the Barber Dime series has also received detailed analysis. I consider my observations in this section as fact *for the majority of examples that I have examined for each issue in this series*. Many Barber Dime issues, particularly those from the Philadelphia Mint, were produced in fairly sizeable numbers, and there is sometimes considerable variation between coins struck from different die pairs, during different press runs from the same die pair or even during the same press run. Additionally, and although I have handled many Barber Dimes over the course of my career as a professional numismatist, no one researcher can ever hope to see every single example of a given issue. This is particularly true of common issues with hundreds, if not thousands of proof or Mint State examples known, of which there are several in the Barber Dime series. Please accept my observations as indicative of the luster quality or finish for the *majority* of examples of a given issue that you are likely to encounter in the numismatic market.

**Surfaces:** The level of surface preservation of a proof or Mint State coin is a critical factor in determining its specific numeric designation on the 70-point numismatic grading scale. As such, I have assigned this section to a discussion of the *average* level of surface preservation for each issue in the Barber Dime series. I consider my observations in this section as fact for the *majority of examples that I have examined for each issue in this series*. Many Barber Dime issues were widely distributed after leaving the Mint, the coins handled and stored in many different ways by both collectors and non-collectors. As such, there can be considerable variation between surface preservation for, say, two different Mint State examples of the 1916 Barber Dime. Additionally, and although I have handled many Barber Dimes over the course of my career as a professional numismatist, no one researcher can ever hope to see every single example of a given issue. This is particularly true of common issues with hundreds, if not thousands of proof or Mint State examples known, of which there are several in the Barber Dime series. Please accept my observations as indicative of the level of surface preservation for the *majority* of examples of a given issue that you are likely to encounter in the numismatic market.

**Toning:** This is the one of the most subjective criteria by which I have chosen to analyze each issue in the Barber Dime series. A particular type of toning that appeals to some collectors might be looked upon as unattractive by other buyers. Additionally, many numismatists find toning in any form to be a distracting feature and prefer to purchase only brilliant coins. With these thoughts in mind, you should consider my opinion of what constitutes attractive or unattractive qualities in a toned Barber Dime as just that: personal opinion. Additionally, it can be difficult even for professional numismatic researchers to determine whether a coin has been dipped at one time, and opinions often vary for individual examples. My comments regarding Barber Dimes that have been dipped also represent personal opinion.

I consider my observations in this section as indicative of the *majority of examples that I have examined for each issue in this series*. Many Barber Dime issues were widely distributed after leaving the Mint, the coins handled and stored in many different ways by both collectors and non-collectors. As such, there can be considerable variation in toning for, say, two different Mint State examples of the 1916 Barber Dime. And although I have handled many Barber Dimes over the course of my career as a professional numismatist, no one researcher can ever hope to see every single example of a given issue. This is particularly true of common issues with hundreds, if not thousands of proof or Mint State examples known, of which there are several in the Barber Dime series. Please accept my observations as indicative of the type, depth and/or distribution of toning that characterize the *majority* of examples of a given issue that you are likely to encounter in the numismatic market.

**Eye Appeal:** Like toning, this is a highly subjective criterion for assessing an issue in any U.S. coin series. Using a mix of striking quality, luster (or finish), surface preservation and toning, I have provided an overall eye appeal assessment for each issue in the Barber Dime series. Some collectors will weigh one criterion more highly than others, however, and there is also the fact that what constitutes attractive in the areas of luster type and/or toning often varies considerably among buyers. With these thoughts in mind, you should consider my opinion of what constitutes attractive or unattractive qualities in a Barber Dime as just that: personal opinion.

**Significant Examples:** Each date and mintmark analysis provides a list of significant examples. This list is *not* a Condition Census. I have not attempted a Condition Census for the Barber Dime series primarily because it is becoming increasingly difficult to keep track of individual examples in today's market. Coins are continually being upgraded due to changing grading standards, crossed from an NGC holder to a PCGS holder (or vice versa) at the same grade level, dipped to remove unsightly toning or submitted to Numismatic Conservation Service (NCS, a division of NGC) to remove spots or other harmful elements on the surfaces. These comments are not meant to disparage the practice of dipping or the excellent services that NCS provides—they are simply a statement of widely accepted practices that form the basis of how coins are conserved and traded in the U.S. rare coin market of the 21st century.

The sections on significant examples that I have provided for each issue, therefore, are merely a listing of some of the finest-known examples that have passed through auction during the final years of the 20th and, to a much greater extent, the early years of the 21st centuries. Every effort has been made to cross-reference auction records in order to determine multiple auction appearances for the same coin. I believe that I have largely succeeded in this endeavor, although some duplication of the same coin(s) may be present within an issue's significant examples list due to the aforementioned difficulties in tracing individual coins in today's market. Poor-quality photos in auction catalogs can also cause difficulties in this regard by obscuring small, yet important pedigree markers. Finally, some coins might be missing from an issue's significant examples list either because I was not aware of the coin's existence at the time this book went to print or because the coin has largely traded outside of auction. Direct sales between dealers and from dealers to collectors/investors are very difficult to track because they are often private and known only to the parties involved. The lists of significant examples, therefore, do not include dealer and collector intermediaries that might have owned the coin before and/or after their appearance at auction.

One final note is in order regarding the lists of significant examples within the issue-by-issue analysis, and it is a critical one. *I have listed each significant example according to the grade that it carried at the time of the most recent auction appearance.* The reader that personally verifies the auction pedigrees provided in this book will find that earlier appearances for many coins in the significant examples sections have the coin in the holder of a different third-party grading service, in a completely different grade and/or with a different appearance to the surfaces. This is illustrative of changing grading standards in the numismatic market, the widespread practice of numismatic conservation and other factors that I have discussed in the preceding paragraphs.

**Total Known and Value Breakdown by Grade:** I have provided estimates on the number of proof or Mint State coins that have survived for each issue in the Barber Dime series, as well as a breakdown of the estimate by grade. These estimates are based on figures listed in the PCGS Population Report and NCG Census, as well as my own experience handling Barber Dimes that have been consigned to major auctions during the 11-year period from 1999-2009. (The figures that I have gleaned from the *PCGS Population Report* and *NGC Census* are current as of November-December of 2008.) The population figures provided by PCGS and NGC are useful in determining *relative* rarity between issues in the Barber Dime series, but they should not be used to assess *absolute* rarity. Both the *PCGS Population Report* and *NGC Census* are skewed by resubmissions of the same coin(s) in an effort to obtain a higher grade. Although both services encourage the submitter to return old inserts, these small yet valuable pieces of paper are often discarded before PCGS and NGC have the opportunity to update their population figures.

Likewise, the values that I have provided for each issue in the Barber Dime series are estimates and should not be taken as a definitive price range in which you should be able to buy an example in a specific grade. Values for Barber Dimes fluctuate over time and, while the series is not as volatile as, say Walking Liberty Half Dollars, Morgan Dollars and Saint-Gaudens Double Eagles, you should still conduct your own research in order to determine the current market value of an individual coin. My value estimates are based largely on prices realized data published by leading auction firms as well as select knowledge of private treaty sales.

**Collecting and Investing Strategies:** The conclusions presented in this section are drawn in large part from the Investment Potential Ratios that are summarized in the appendices at the end of this book. These Investment Potential Ratios, in turn, are derived from a formula that I have developed for determining whether individual issues in the Barber Dime series are underrated or overrated, and to what degree. I have used this formula to analyze each proof and Mint State Barber Dime in the four popular and highly desirable grades from Proof-64/MS-64 to Proof-67/MS-67.

Using the MS-64 grade level to illustrate this formula, I first totaled up all Barber Dimes believed to exist in MS-64. By dividing this total by the number of issues in the entire Barber Dime series, I determined the average population for the series as a whole in MS-64. Within each issue, I then multiplied the number of MS-64s believed to exist by the average price that the issue commands in that grade to determine what I call the Total Value for that issue. By summing the Total Value for all Barber Dimes in MS-64 and dividing that number by the total number of MS-64s believed to exist for the entire series, I derived what I call the Optimum Value for a Barber Dime in MS-64. I then took the percentage of the value for each individual issue in the Barber Dime series compared to the Optimum Value, as well as the percentage of the population for each individual issue relative to the average population for the series as a whole. The difference between these two percentages is the Investment Potential Ratio for that issue. A difference of 0% would theoretically represent a coin that has the perfect balance between rarity and price in that grade. Negative percentages represent underrated issues, while positive percentages are indicative of overrated issues.

In this section you will also find useful tips and hints, as well as potential pitfalls to avoid concerning the various issues in the Barber Dime series. The goal of this section as a whole is to pass on the considerable knowledge about these coins that I have amassed during the years that I have served as a numismatic professional. It is my hope that the lessons that I have learned and observations that I have made will first help you focus on those issues and grades that offer the best potential for future price appreciation. Second, I hope that my tips and hints enable you to acquire the finest example of a given Barber Dime issue that your money can buy.

## A DISCLAIMER ON INVESTING IN RARE COINS

Bear in mind that I am offering my opinion about how and what to invest in or collect. Like any investment or collectible, there is no crystal ball listing future values for an entire numismatic collection or an individual coin. Gather enough numismatic experts in a room today and they will likely each hold different opinions about the current merits, attributes and even the actual value of a particular coin. In the end, the market dictates. With that said I do make every effort to point out coins that I believe are undervalued or have greater potential to appreciate in value, as well as those that are overvalued with correspondingly little potential for future growth. *It goes without saying, however, that ultimately the choice of what to buy and how much to pay is yours alone.* Armed with the right information, you will make better choices. Reading this book is certainly the most important step you will take in that direction as far as the Barber Dime series is concerned.

# CHAPTER ONE

# *Popular Collecting and Investing Strategies for Barber Dimes*

The Barber Dime series has not attained the same level of popularity, or won as many adherents in the collecting and investing communities, as many other series in U.S. numismatics. Compared to series such as the Walking Liberty Half Dollar, Morgan Dollar and Saint-Gaudens Double Eagle, there are few collectors and investors specializing in Barber Dimes. There are several reasons for this, one of which is the design of the coin. The Barber Dime has one of the more drab designs in U.S. coinage history, and it simply lacks the artistic merit or symbolism of such other classic coins as the Buffalo Nickel, Mercury Dime, Standing Liberty Quarter and Peace Dollar.

Many collectors and investors have overlooked the Barber Dime simply because they are not familiar with this coin. While Barber Dimes continued to circulate into the early 1960s, these coins were just not as numerous in commerce during the 1940s and 1950s as Buffalo Nickels, Mercury Dimes, Standing Liberty Quarters and Walking Liberty Half Dollars. As such, relatively few of the seasoned numismatists active in the market of the early 21st century grew up handling large numbers of Barber Dimes. This lack of familiarity at an early age has contributed to a lack of numismatic interest in maturity.

The Barber Dime series also suffers from the fact that so many issues are very scarce, if not downright rare in Mint State. This was a workhorse series, and relatively few examples were set aside for the sake of posterity—a fact that is particularly true of both early-date Philadelphia Mint issues struck before 1910 and most of those from the branch mints in Denver, New Orleans and San Francisco. Many Barber Dimes also have fairly limited mintages by 20th century U.S. Mint standards, and the issue is riddled with numerous coins that have low mintages by any standard. These facts also contribute to the relative dearth of Mint State Barber Dimes in today's numismatic market. By comparison, issues such as the Walking Liberty Half Dollar, Morgan Dollar and Saint-Gaudens Double Eagle are very common in Mint State with tens, if not hundreds of thousands of Uncirculated examples believed to exist. Translated into dollars and cents, you will need at least $450-$500 to acquire a common-date Barber Dime (1892 or 1916, for example) in MS-65. A similarly graded example of a common-date Walker will set you back just $100-$150, while a common-date Morgan in MS-65 can be had for about the same at $125-$140.

Not to be overlooked in this context is the negative affect that a relatively limited Mint State population has on the marketability and, hence, recognition of Barber Dimes. Series like Morgan Dollars and Saint-Gaudens Double Eagle readily lend themselves to mass-marketing programs conducted by telemarketing and other large numismatic firms. The fact that those coins are so easy to obtain in quantity means that they are perfectly suited for use as centerpieces in large marketing campaigns. A vault full of a few thousand Mint State Morgan Dollars, indeed, represents an opportunity for a nation-wide selling program that includes radio, newspaper and other forms of mainstream advertising. Such exposure, by extension, leads to greater recognition for the coins involved among the general public. Conversely, a numismatic marketer is not going to spend thousands of dollars in a national advertising campaign to sell four Mint State Barber Dimes. Such a decision, although a wise one from a business standpoint, limits the opportunities for these coins to gain in recognition among the non-collecting public.

There is one final reason underlying the relative lack of collecting and investing interest in Barber Dimes, and that is the dearth of information on this series in the numismatic literature. This gap in numismatic research has been addressed in detail in the Preface to this book, and it is my hope that this work will go a long way toward increasing understanding and appreciation for this overlooked series.

Although long overlooked by many collectors and investors, the Barber Dime is actually no less versatile than, say, the Waking Liberty Half Dollar or Morgan Dollar. There are actually many ways to form a meaningful collection or numismatic investment portfolio that includes one or more Barber Dimes. Let's take a closer look at some of the more important collecting and investing strategies for this series.

## Short Type Set

Assembling a short type set is a great way to get started with coin collecting or numismatic investing because it allows you to build a meaningful holding without having to acquire a large number of coins. Short type sets are usually assembled using coins that share one or more characteristics. Examples of some unifying themes for short type sets are denomination, historic era in which the coins were struck and coin designers. The possibilities are essentially limitless, however, and a short type set allows you considerable freedom to assemble a collection or portfolio using any criteria that you see fit.

Nevertheless, some strategies for assembling short type sets have proven particularly popular in the numismatic market. Some of the more widely adopted strategies that would have to include an example of the Barber Dime are:

• **United States Dime Types.** This set could be assembled with just eight coins or with as many as 14 coins depending on how many different types from the Capped Bust, Seated and Roosevelt series you want to include. The 14-piece set must include one example of each of the following types:

~ *Draped Bust, Small Eagle Reverse (1796-1797)*

~ *Draped Bust, Large Eagle Reverse (1798-1807)*

~ *Capped Bust, Large Size (1809-1828)*

~ *Capped Bust, Reduced Size (1828-1837)*

~ *Seated, No Stars (1837-1838)*

~ *Seated, Stars Obverse, No Drapery (1838-1840)*

~ *Seated, Stars Obverse, Drapery (1840-1853, 1856-1860)*

~ *Seated, Stars Obverse, Arrows at Date (1853-1855)*

~ *Seated, Legend Obverse (1860-1873, 1875-1891)*

~ *Seated, Legend Obverse, Arrows at Date (1873-1874)*

~ ***Barber (1892-1916)***

~ *Mercury (1916-1945)*

~ *Roosevelt, Silver (1946-1964)*

~ *Roosevelt, Copper-Nickel Clad (1965-Date)*

• **United States 20th Century Coin Types.** This is another versatile set that can be shortened or expanded depending on how many different types you want to represent for series such as the Lincoln Cent, Buffalo Nickel, Standing Liberty Quarter and Kennedy Half Dollar. You also have the option to include or exclude the gold coinage, although my experience has shown that most collectors that assemble 20th century type sets choose to represent only the minor and silver coinage. (Type sets of 20th century United States gold coins are also extremely popular, but they are usually assembled apart from the minor and silver coinage.) The most expansive 20th century type set that I can think of would be comprised of 47 coins and must include one example of each of the following types:

~ *Indian Cent, Bronze (1864-1909)*

~ *Lincoln Cent, Wheat Ears Reverse, V.D.B. (1909 only)*

~ *Lincoln Cent, Wheat Ears Reverse, Bronze (1909-1942, 1944-1958)*

~ *Lincoln Cent, Zinc-Coated Steel (1943 only)*

~ *Lincoln Cent, Memorial Reverse, Bronze (1959-1982)*

~ *Lincoln Cent, Copper-Plated Zinc (1982-Date)*

~ *Liberty Nickel, CENTS (1883-1912)*

~ *Buffalo Nickel, Type I (1913 only)*

~ *Buffalo Nickel, Type II (1913-1938)*

~ *Jefferson Nickel, Regular Composition, Mintmark Reverse (1938-1942, 1946-1967)*

~ *Jefferson Nickel, Wartime Alloy (1942-1945)*

~ *Jefferson Nickel, Regular Composition, Mintmark Obverse (1968-2003)*

~ ***Barber Dime (1892-1916)***

~ *Mercury Dime (1916-1945)*

~ *Roosevelt Dime, Silver (1946-1964)*

~ *Roosevelt Dime, Copper-Nickel Clad (1965-Date)*

~ *Barber Quarter (1892-1916)*

~ *Standing Liberty Quarter, Type I (1916-1917)*

~ *Standing Liberty Quarter, Type II, Pedestal Date (1917-1924)*

~ *Standing Liberty Quarter, Recessed Date (1925-1930)*

~ *Washington Quarter, Silver (1932-1964)*

~ *Washington Quarter, Copper-Nickel Clad, Eagle Reverse (1965-1974, 1977-1998)*

~ *Washington Quarter, Bicentennial Reverse (1976 only)*

~ *Statehood Quarter (1999 and 2000-dated issues only; 10 coins total)*

~ *Barber Half Dollar (1892-1915)*

~ *Walking Liberty Half Dollar (1916-1947)*

~ *Franklin Half Dollar (1948-1963)*

~ *Kennedy Half Dollar, Silver (1964 only)*

~ *Kennedy Half Dollar, Silver Clad (1965-1970)*

~ *Kennedy Half Dollar, Copper-Nickel Clad, Eagle Reverse (1971-1974, 1977-Date)*

~ *Kennedy Half Dollar, Bicentennial Reverse (1976 only)*

~ *Morgan Silver Dollar (1878-1921)*

~ *Peace Silver Dollar, High Relief (1921 only)*

~ *Peace Silver Dollar, Low Relief (1922-1935)*

~ *Eisenhower Dollar, Eagle Reverse (1971-1974, 1977-1978)*

~ *Eisenhower Dollar, Bicentennial Reverse (1976 only)*

~ *Susan B. Anthony Dollar (1979-1999)*

~ *Sacagawea Dollar (2000-Date)*

• **United States Coin Designs by Adolph A. Weinman.** An often overlooked strategy is one that focuses on the various designers that have contributed to the U.S. coinage family. The Barber Dime was designed by Chief Engraver Charles E. Barber, who also contributed four other coin types to the regular-issue U.S. Mint series:

> ~ *Liberty Nickel, No CENTS (1883 only)*
> ~ *Liberty Nickel, CENTS (1883-1912)*
> ~ ***Barber Dime (1892-1916)***
> ~ *Barber Quarter (1892-1916)*
> ~ *Barber Half Dollar (1892-1915)*

Regardless of what type of short type set they choose to assemble, many numismatists opt for an example of one of the more common issues in the various U.S. coin series. This is not always a wise choice, however, as sometimes the most common issue in a series, while the most affordable, is not the best positioned for future price appreciation. Consult the "Collecting and Investing Strategies" sections within the Date & Mintmark Analysis chapter in this book for my views on the best Barber Dimes to use for type purposes.

## Complete Type Set

A complete type set of United States coins comprises one example of each type of regular-issue, non-commemorative coin struck in the United States Mint. Whether you choose to build your set with minor, silver and gold coins or just minor and silver coins, you are going to have to acquire an example of the Barber Dime. Once again, consult the "Collecting and Investing Strategies" sections within the Date & Mintmark Analysis chapter in this book for my views on the best Barber Dimes to use for type purposes.

## Advanced Type Sets

There are several ways to modify a short or complete type set to increase your level of difficulty, financial requirement and, possibly, your upside potential when the time comes to sell. Two strategies that will affect how you approach the Barber Dime series come readily to mind.

**Rarer Issues:** This strategy requires that you obtain one of the more challenging and, hence, costly issues of each type that you are representing in your set. I have even met a few collectors that are assembling advanced type sets of key-date issues, although I do not recommend that particular strategy unless you have ample resources of time and money.

There are many issues in the Barber Dime series that would work well for advanced type purposes. Consult the Date & Mintmark Analysis chapter in this book, and specifically the "Collecting and Investing Strategies" sections at the end of each analysis, for better-date Barber Dimes that I believe offer the best prospects for future price appreciation in the MS-64 to MS-67 grade range.

**Issuing Mint:** Another strategy for expanding a short or basic type set is to include one example from each United States coinage facility in which a given type was struck. For the Barber Dime series, this strategy increases your requirement to four coins. Consult the Date & Mintmark Analysis chapter in this book, and specifically the "Collecting and Investing Strategies" sections at the end of each analysis, for Barber Dimes from the Philadelphia, Denver, New Orleans and San Francisco Mints that I believe offer the best prospects for future price appreciation in the MS-64 to MS-67 grade range.

# Proof Type Set

This is an underdeveloped form of type set building, a fact that is largely due to the fact that many U.S. coins are unknown or prohibitively rare in proof format. On the positive side, however, proof coins are almost always fully struck, and most possess a deeply mirrored finish that can be particularly attractive when viewed on either a brilliant or minimally toned coin. Additionally, proof coins are almost always more carefully produced and preserved than business strikes, which can make it easier to locate a pristine-looking example for inclusion in your type set.

Should you choose to apply this strategy to the completion of a type set of United States coinage, consult the "Collecting and Investing Strategies" sections within Date & Mintmark Analysis chapter in this book for my views on the best proof Barber Dimes to use for type purposes.

# Assembling a Complete Set

I have seen very few complete sets of Barber Dimes pass through auction or dealers' hands over the 11-year period from 1999-2009—a testament to the significant challenges of rarity and cost that this series represents in the numismatic market of the 21st century. Nevertheless, there are five types of complete sets that you could consider assembling for this series.

**Year Set:** To successfully complete this set for the Barber Dime series, you will need to acquire 25 coins. Each example must be from a different year in which the United States Mint struck Dimes of this type. The price will vary according to the grade level(s) that you select for building your set, as well as whether you select the most common issues from each year, better-date issues or a mix of both types of coins. A year set of Barber Dimes comprised of only the most common issues would require one example of each of the following 25 issues:

~ *1892*
~ *1893*
~ *1894*
~ *1895-S*

~ *1896*
~ *1897*
~ *1898*
~ *1899*
~ *1900*
~ *1901*
~ *1902*
~ *1903*
~ *1904*
~ *1905*
~ *1906*
~ *1907*
~ *1908*
~ *1909*
~ *1910*
~ *1911*
~ *1912*
~ *1913*
~ *1914*
~ *1915*
~ *1916*

**Complete Set by Issuing Mint:** This strategy can be assembled in one of four ways for the Barber Dime series, inasmuch as four different coinage facilities struck coins of this type. A complete set of Philadelphia Mint Barber Dimes requires 25 coins, that for the Denver Mint only eight coins while that for the New Orleans Mint needs 17 coins. The San Francisco Mint is tricky because the 1894-S, while obviously a product of that coinage facility, is a proof issue and not a business strike. Since the 1894-S is also a legendary rarity in U.S. numismatics with a consequently high cost, I advise leaving that issue out of your S-mint Barber Dime set and acquiring only one example of each of the 24 business strike issues from the San Francisco Mint. Total cost for each of these sets, of course, will vary depending upon the exact grade(s) that you choose for each issue when building your collection/portfolio.

**Date and Mint Set:** This strategy dictates that you obtain one example of each business strike issue in the Barber Dime series. The requirement is for 74 coins—a total that excludes both the branch mint proof 1894-S and major varieties such as the 1893/'2' and 1905-O Micro O. This is one of the most comprehensive ways to collect Barber Dimes, but it is by no means an inexpensive one if you choose to focus on the Mint State grades.

A complete set of Barber Dimes in MS-64 will require that you spend approximately $90,000. In MS-65, your financial requirement will double to approximately $180,000.

**Proof Set:** This is an easier and less costly strategy for the Barber Dime series than assembling a complete date and mint set. Discounting the branch mint 1894-S, there are only 24 issues in the proof Barber Dime series. In Proof-64, your financial burden for this strategy will be approximately $17,500, while you should expect to part with at least $32,000 for a set of Proof-65s.

**Registry Set:** These sets are essentially complete sets of one form or another, but they are assembled using the highest-graded coins listed at PCGS and/or NGC. While you could, for example, assemble a PCGS Registry Set of Barber Dimes that grades MS-62, in practice the concept behind these sets is to pit collectors and investors against one another with the goal being to assemble the highest-graded set possible. Both PCGS and NGC maintain Registry Set programs, but whereas PCGS allows only its own coins on the Set Registry, NGC will accept coins certified by both services.

As of November 2008, there are more than 170 Barber Dime sets registered at PCGS and NGC. These sets are grouped under several different categories, among which are year sets, date and mint sets and proof sets. I am particularly fond of the Registry Set concept because there is a strong motivating factor in numismatics when you can track your progress and rate your achievements against those of other collectors. This is true even if you are not competing for the top ranking on the PCGS or NGC Registry. For more information on Registry Sets, visit the PCGS and NGC websites at www.pcgs.com and www.ngccoin.com, respectively.

# CHAPTER TWO

## Considerations for Buying Barber Dimes

As the value of rare United States coins has steadily increased, so too has the number of sellers in the market. Most dealers are honest, reputable experts who thoroughly enjoy buying, selling and studying coins. Many of them even got their start in the industry as collectors, and almost all possess tremendous knowledge of rare coins and the market in which they trade. What's more, reputable dealers are usually very willing to share their expertise and offer sound advice that can prove invaluable when building a meaningful collection or investment portfolio. The benefits of a relationship with a recognized industry expert are numerous, and you should get to know as many reputable dealers as possible and enlist their aid in the attainment of your collecting and/or investing goals. This advice is particularly sound if you are planning on specializing in Barber Dimes. There are some dealers in the market that also specialize in Barber coinage, and their buying and selling activities often provide them with comprehensive, up-to-date information that may not be available in print.

There are many possible ways to find a reputable United States coin dealer. Chartered by Congress in 1891, the American Numismatic Association (ANA) is the leading hobby organization in U.S. numismatics. The association's website, www.money.org, maintains a searchable database of member dealers. Another excellent source is the Professional Numismatists Guild (PNG), an organization of rare coin and paper money experts whose members are held to high standards of integrity and professionalism. Members of the PNG can be found at the organization's website, www.pngdealers.com. Both the ANA and the PNG are non-profit organizations.

One of the most underutilized methods of finding a reputable numismatic dealer is simply to ask other collectors and investors for recommendations. Word-of-mouth can be a powerful tool. Honest, knowledgeable dealers will enjoy a good reputation among veteran buyers, while less-trustworthy individuals or companies are often treated accordingly in the collector and investor communities. A prerequisite for carrying out this kind of research might be to join a local, regional or national numismatic association. Not only can membership in an organization such as the ANA put you in touch with other collectors and investors, but it could provide access to research tools, current events and other useful technical and market information.

Many of the coins that trade in today's numismatic market pass through auctions instead of being bought and sold outright by dealers. Auction houses are also excellent places to buy Barber Dimes. The catalogs that these firms produce not only strive to provide detailed descriptions of a coin's physical attributes, but they often contain a wealth of historical and analytical information. The best sources for finding reputable auction houses are the ANA, PNG and by word-of-mouth.

Auctioneers offer another powerful, yet underutilized tool for the Barber Dime specialist: the lot viewing sessions that take place in the weeks or days leading up to an auction. Through these venues, you can view relatively large numbers of proof and Mint State Barber Dimes, as well as many circulated examples of key-date issues such as the 1895-O and 1901-S. And the more coins that you view, the more familiar you will become with third-party grading standards for this series and issue-specific characteristics such as strike, luster and toning. If schedules and budgets permit, I strongly suggest spending some time at auction lot viewing. Registration is required to participate, but it is almost always free. Furthermore, I have yet to encounter an auctioneer that has made it mandatory to bid after you register. In other words, you should be able to view lots even if you are not interested in bidding in that particular sale.

After finding a reputable dealer and/or auctioneer, what else should you consider before buying your first Barber Dime? Whether you are a veteran collector or a beginner, it is a good idea to acquire only those pieces that have been graded and encapsulated by Professional Coin Grading Service (PCGS) and Numismatic Guaranty Corporation (NGC). Founded in 1986 and 1987, respectively, these two firms revolutionized the numismatic industry. Coins submitted to these services are evaluated by teams of professional numismatic graders and authenticators. Pieces that are determined to be genuine, unaltered and problem free for their respective level of preservation are assigned a numeric grade on a 1-70 scale. The coins are then sonically sealed in tamper-evident plastic holders with a paper insert that lists the date, denomination, grade, variety (if applicable) and a unique barcode for identification purposes. Once certified by PCGS or NGC, a coin carries a grade that can help to determine the level at which it will trade in the market. PCGS and NGC-certified coins enjoy universal acceptance, and they also have a high level of liquidity due to the strong reputations that these firms enjoy. In short, PCGS and NGC are the standards for the rare coin industry of the 21st century. They provide a measure of confidence for both novice and veteran collectors when trading in a dynamic market.

It is important to consider that grading is subjective, particularly since both PCGS and NGC take into account a coin's eye appeal when assigning a grade. A characteristic that I consider attractive in a Barber Dime might be construed as a negative either in your eyes or in the eyes of the expert graders at PCGS and NGC. For example, I might prefer fully brilliant coins with frosty-white surfaces that are free of even the lightest toning. You, however, could be assembling a Barber Dime set with coins that possess richly original, multicolored toning on both sides. It is always a good idea to evaluate coins— even certified pieces—firsthand before buying. In-person inspection will allow you to get comfortable with a coin's assigned grade and determine whether or not the piece will make an attractive addition to your set.

The subjectivity of grading has been brought into even clearer focus with the launch of Certified Acceptance Corporation—(CAC)—in November of 2007. An independent, third-party numismatic authentication service, CAC evaluates coins that have already been certified by PCGS and NGC. Those coins that meet their strict grading criteria receive a green-label sticker on the insert, while those that exceed CAC's standards receive a gold-label sticker. The goal of CAC is to dente those coins that are solidly graded or above average for their assigned grade—the premium-quality, or PQ examples—and separate them from low-end pieces or coins that they feel have been just plain overgraded.

A relatively new service as of the writing of this book, the number of Barber Dimes that have already been submitted to CAC is fairly limited. Additionally, the market has yet to fully determine whether or not coins with CAC stickers should command a premium and, if so, how much of a premium. I do believe that CAC—or a derivative thereof—is here to stay, however, and I also believe that it is a potentially valuable service for the collector or investor. Buying a coin with a CAC sticker gives you that extra piece of mind that the coin is solidly graded, and the green or gold sticker is also likely to result in a stronger price when the time comes to sell. While you could still do very well buying Barber Dimes without a CAC sticker as long as you are selective about the coins you choose, the collector or investor who is less confident with their grading abilities might want to pursue only those coins that have already met CAC's standards. For more information about CAC, visit their website at www.caccoin.com.

One other aspect of third-party grading as it pertains to Barber Dimes is critically important in order to be successful at collecting and/or investing in this series. A perusal of the Significant Examples listings in this book will reveal that there is sometimes considerable variation between the prices that two different Barber Dimes of the same issue trade for even if they have been certified by PCGS and NGC at the same grade level. This difference can be particularly pronounced in the highest grades, where pressure from Registry Set collectors is greatest. PCGS and NGC sometimes apply slightly different grading standards when evaluating coins for encapsulation, standards that you should familiarize yourself with before you buy a high-grade Barber Dime. This book provides much of the information that you will need in this regard, but it may also be a good idea to enlist the aid of a reputable, trustworthy dealer when the time comes to buy. It would be even better if you had a personal relationship with one or more dealers that specialize in Barber coinage. Some numismatic professionals might even be willing to evaluate a coin that is being offered through auction and help you determine the optimum level at which to bid.

# CHAPTER THREE

## *A Brief History of the Barber Dime*

## The Design

By the 1890s, the only silver-coin designs that most contemporary Americans had ever seen or handled throughout their lives were examples of the various Seated Liberty series. The basic Seated Liberty design is credited to Christian Gobrecht, and its initial appearance in the regular-issue U.S. coin series came in late 1836 with the striking of the first Name on Base Gobrecht Dollars. When, in 1887, Mint Director James P. Kimball expressed his unhappiness with the Seated Liberty design, the stage was set for the introduction of the Barber Dime.

At Kimball's prodding, Congress passed the Act of September 26, 1890 that allowed the Mint to redesign all U.S. coins that had been in use for at least 25 years. For the Dime, Quarter and Half Dollar, the act specified that redesign could be initiated in 1892. Moving in this direction, the Treasury Department initially opted for a competition between 10 of the most renowned artists living in the United States at that time. Monetary problems and the lack of sufficient time for the artists to prepare their entries forced Treasury Department officials to throw the competition open to the public.

Tensions immediately arose between Augustus Saint-Gaudens and Chief Engraver of the Mint Charles Edward Barber, both of whom felt that they were best qualified to execute the new coinage designs. The two subsequently contributed to the elimination of all designs submitted through the public competition and, after Barber received the backing of the new mint director Edward O. Leech, he was able to proceed with redesigning the Dime, Quarter and Half Dollar.

Barber's final design for the Dime that bears his name exhibits a right-facing bust of Liberty on the obverse that is very similar to that used on several bronze and silver coins of the French Third Republic. On the Barber Dime, Liberty is wearing a soft cap ornamented with a simple wreath and a headband inscribed LIBERTY. The legend UNITED STATES OF AMERICA is around the border and the date is below the bust. Barber's initial B can be found on the truncation of the neck. For the reverse Barber retained James Longacre's (one of his predecessors as chief engraver) "cereal wreath" design that had been introduced in the Seated Dime series in 1860. The mintmark position is on the reverse below the knot of the ribbon that binds the wreath.

The basic design of the Barber Dime remained unchanged throughout its use in regular-issue production, although the Mint did introduce extremely minor refinements to the obverse in 1900 and the reverse in 1901. Much derided for its banality both in its time and after, the Barber Dime yielded to the more artistically accomplished Mercury Dime in 1916 after the mandatory 25-year time period had been achieved.

## Yearly Mintages and Distribution

The Philadelphia, New Orleans and San Francisco Mints all struck their first Barber Dimes in 1892. While production totals at all three facilities were initially quite large by the standards of the 19th century United States Mint, the Panic of 1893 soon forced a reduction in Dime production. Yearly mintages fell off markedly at all three coinage facilities beginning that year, and the San Francisco Mint did not produce business strike Dimes at all in 1894. Only in 1897—after the U.S. economy started to recover—did the Philadelphia Mint once again strike more than 10 million Barber Dimes. Production at that facility remained strong through the series' end in 1916.

The New Orleans and San Francisco Mints were more erratic with their Barber Dime deliveries beginning in 1897, with some years seeing an output of several million pieces from both facilities and others (like 1913 at the San Francisco Mint) accounting for only about a half-million coins struck.

The Denver Mint opened its doors as a coinage facility in 1906, and it contributed eight issues to the Barber Dime series from that year through 1914. D-mint Barber Dime production was quite plentiful throughout this period of time, and it was on a scale that was large enough to finally help convince the federal government to close the New Orleans Mint as a coinage facility. That event occurred in 1909 after, among other issues, a delivery of 2.2 million Barber Dimes that year.

Throughout the series 25-year run on the coinage presses, the Barber Dime was produced for a single purpose: to serve as a circulating medium of exchange within the United States. All issues in this series served that function to a greater or lesser degree, even to the point where well-worn Barber Dimes could still be found in circulation as late as the early 1960s. As a rule, the earlier, pre-1905 issues in this series were not saved to an appreciable extent by the contemporary public, thus explaining their greater rarity in Mint State. This is particularly true of O and S-mint issues for, while the publication of Augustus Heaton's treatise on mintmarks in the 1890s did begin to awaken the American public to the importance of branch mint coinage as numismatic collectibles, most collectors were still concentrated in the Northeast where Philadelphia mint coinage prevailed. In fact, throughout the entire Barber Dime series the branch mint issues from Denver, New Orleans and San Francisco received far less attention from contemporary collectors, dealers and others than their identically dated Philadelphia Mint counterparts.

Beginning circa 1905, however, larger quantities of Barber Dimes from all coinage facilities were kept from entering circulation and subsequently preserved in Mint State. How, why, when or by whom this was done is not clear in all instances, but I do believe that contemporary dealers played at least some part in this process. (If we accept the interpretation of how this happened in Walter Breen's 1988 *Encyclopedia*, "contemporary" in this context includes dealers that were active as late as the mid-1930s.) Banks were also probably unknowing participants in benefiting future generations of collectors, a greater output of coins from the Mints allowing more pieces to remain in bank vaults without experiencing the rigors of circulation.

Dealer stocks and bank reserves probably accounted for the lion's share of Barber Dimes that eventually found their way into coin albums in the 1940s and 1950s. By the latter decade, at least, most original rolls had been broken up by dealers and collectors. A not insignificant number of the individual coins must have spent at least some period of time in albums as evidenced by the existence of numerous low-grade Mint State Barber Dimes that display distracting slidemarks over and around the obverse portrait.

# CHAPTER FOUR

## *Date and Mintmark Analysis of Barber Dimes*

## SPECIFICATIONS

**Years Issued:** *1892-1916*
**Issuing Mints:** *Philadelphia, Denver, New Orleans, San Francisco*
**Designer:** *Charles Edward Barber, Sixth Chief Engraver of the United States Mint*
**Weight:** *2.50 grams*
**Composition:** *90% Silver, 10% Copper*
**Precious Metal Content:** *0.07234 ounces of pure silver*
**Diameter:** *17.9 millimeters*
**Edge:** *Reeded*

The information in this chapter is based on my experience studying thousands of Barber Dimes that were consigned to auction, bought and sold or otherwise distributed through the rare coin market during the 11-year period from 1999 to 2009.

This book contains the results of my endeavor to rank the proof and business strike issues in this series sequentially in terms of both overall rarity in Proof/ Mint State and rarity in high grades (Proof-65/MS-65 or finer). The proof issues are also ranked sequentially in terms of rarity with a Cameo and Deep/ Ultra Cameo finish, while the business strikes are also ranked sequentially in terms of rarity by issuing Mint. These results of these rankings are located at the beginning of each date and mintmark analysis, as well as in Appendices A-F at the end of this book.

After brief introductory paragraphs under the "Important Varieties" and "General Comments" headers, you will then find my observations concerning Strike, Luster (Finish for the proofs), Surfaces, Toning and Eye Appeal for the issue. I have also provided detailed pedigree information for some of the finest examples of each Barber Dime issue known to exist. This pedigree information can be found under the header of "Significant Examples." Each date and mintmark analysis concludes with my estimates on the number of proof and Mint State coins that have survived for each issue, vital pricing date and a section entitled "Collecting and Investing Strategies."

The "Collecting and Investing Strategies" sections include my recommendations on what to emphasize and what to avoid when searching for an example of each proof and business strike issue in the Barber Dime series. I have paid special attention to the investment potential of each Barber Dime issue, predominantly through the use of a specially-designed formula that calculates what I call the Investment Potential Ratio for each proof and business strike issue in the Barber Dime series. These Investment Potential Ratios are summarized in Appendices G and H at the end of this book. For a detailed analysis of the formula used to derive these Investment Potential Ratios, please refer to the Introduction of this book.

# Proof
# 1892
## MINTAGE
1,245

Courtesy of Bowers and Merena

## RARITY
## RANKINGS

*Overall, All Proof Grades: 23rd of 25*
*High Grade, Proof-65 or Finer: 21st of 25*
*Overall, Cameo Finish: 19th of 24*
*Overall, Deep/Ultra Cameo Finish: 5th of 12*

**Important Varieties:** None.

**General Comments:** The Philadelphia Mint struck 1,245 proof Barber Dimes in 1892, the largest yearly total for a proof of this type and the only issue with an original mintage of more than 1,000 coins. The high mintage of the proof 1892 Dime is attributable to the first year of the Barber series. Mint officials clearly anticipated that contemporary Americans would order large numbers of these coins as the first proof examples of their type. This seems to have been the case, and today this issue is one of the most plentiful proof Barber Dimes in terms of both total number of coins known and number of coins known to exist in high grades. The 1892 is also a relatively obtainable proof Barber Dime with a Cameo finish, although it is very rare in Deep/Ultra Cameo.

**Strike:** The proof 1892 almost always comes with full, razor-sharp striking detail to all elements of the design.

**Finish:** Examples run the gamut from all brilliant to deeply cameoed in finish. The typical proof 1892 has at least some degree of field-to-device contrast. This is even true of many coins that have not received a Cameo designation from PCGS or NGC. Such pieces often have sufficient field-to-device contrast on only one side of the coin (usually the reverse), or they are so extensively toned that the Cameo finish is not readily perceptible to the eye.

**Surfaces:** As an issue, the 1892 has a higher incidence of hairlines and other contact marks than most other proofs in the Barber Dime series. I believe that this fact is due to the widespread distribution of examples among non-collectors. Since general public interest in the new design waned after the first year or two of the series, later proof Barber Dime issues were of interest primarily to numismatists that had the desire and expertise to handle the coins with greater care over the years.

In an absolute sense, nevertheless, it is not all that difficult to locate a proof 1892 Barber Dime whose surfaces are free of singularly distracting contact marks. Enough Gem-quality examples have survived that pieces grading Proof-65, Proof-66 and even Proof-67 trade on a fairly regular basis during a typical year of numismatic activity.

**Toning:** I believe that most, if not all original proof 1892 Barber Dimes display moderate-to-deep toning. Such pieces can be either quite dull with darker colors such as russet and charcoal or highly attractive with vivid toning that can include blue, sea-green or red highlights.

There are also many proof 1892 Barber Dimes in the market whose surfaces are either completely brilliant or minimally toned in light patination. Most of those coins have been dipped to bring out the full vibrancy of the mint finish. Several of the more lightly toned pieces have either started to retone or possessed such deep toning that it could not be completely removed by the dipping solution without impairing the original mint finish.

**Eye Appeal:** This issue has only average eye appeal, an assessment that I attribute both to the fairly large percentage of lower-grade examples in the market and the prevalence of darkly and/or unevenly toned coins among the original examples. In grades of Proof-65 and finer, however, the proof 1892 has strong eye appeal, particularly if the coin in question possesses vivid colors to the toning and/or has bold field-to-device contrast. Untoned pieces in high grades are also highly attractive, although it is important to remember that most of those examples have been dipped and, as such, do not possess completely original surfaces.

**Significant Examples:**

   **1. PCGS Proof-68 Cameo.** *Ex: The Bruce Scher #1 All-Time PCGS Registry Set (Heritage, 2/2005), lot 4052, where it realized $12,650.*

   **2. NGC Proof-67 Ultra Cameo.** *Ex: CSNS Signature Coin Auction (Heritage, 5/2007), lot 2065, unsold; Summer FUN Signature Coin Auction (Heritage, 7/2007), lot 555, where it realized $5,175.*

**3. PCGS Proof-67 Deep Cameo.** *Ex: The Bruce Scher #1 All-Time PCGS Registry Set (Heritage, 2/2005), lot 4053, where it realized $10,925*

**Total Known:** 455-530 Coins

**Total Known and Value Breakdown by Grade:**

| BRILLIANT-FINISH COINS | | | |
|---|---|---|---|
| **Proof-60-62** | **Proof-63** | **Proof-64** | **Proof-65** |
| 55-65 Coins | 75-85 Coins | 95-110 Coins | 70-80 Coins |
| N/A | $450-$550 | $650-$750 | $1,200-$1,300 |
| **Proof-66-67** | **Proof-68** | **Proof-69** | **Proof 70** |
| 65-75 Coins | 25-30 Coins | 0 Coins | 0 Coins |
| $1,750-$2,200 | $2,250-$2,750 | -- | -- |

| CAMEO COINS | | | |
|---|---|---|---|
| **Proof-60-62 Cameo** | **Proof-63 Cameo** | **Proof-64 Cameo** | **Proof-65 Cameo** |
| 2-3 Coins | 8-10 Coins | 15-20 Coins | 20-25 Coins |
| N/A | $600-$700 | $750-$850 | $1,400-$1,800 |
| **Proof-66 Cameo** | **Proof-67 Cameo** | **Proof-68 Cameo** | **Proof-69-70 Cameo** |
| 8-10 Coins | 12-15 Coins | 1-2 Coins | 0 Coins |
| $2,250-$2,500 | $2,750-$3,750 | $12,500-$15,000 | -- |

| DEEP/ULTRA CAMEO | | | |
|---|---|---|---|
| **Proof-60-62 Deep/Ultra Cameo** | **Proof-63 Deep/Ultra Cameo** | **Proof-64 Deep/Ultra Cameo** | **Proof-65 Deep/Ultra Cameo** |
| 0 Coins | 0 Coins | 0 Coins | 0 Coins |
| -- | -- | -- | -- |
| **Proof-66 Deep/Ultra Cameo** | **Proof-67 Deep/Ultra Cameo** | **Proof-68 Deep/Ultra Cameo** | **Proof-69-70 Deep/Ultra Cameo** |
| 2-3 Coins | 1 Coin | 0 Coins | 0 Coins |
| $4,000-$6,000 | $7,500-$12,500 | -- | -- |

*Note:* The conclusions presented in the following "Collecting and Investing Strategies" section are drawn in large part from the Investment Potential Ratios that are summarized in Appendices G and H at the end of this book. For a detailed analysis of the formula used to derive these Investment Potential Ratios, please refer to the Introduction of this book.

**Collecting and Investing Strategies:** As the first proof issue of the type, the 1892 is one of the most popular Barber Dimes for specimen type purposes. Indeed, strong type collector pressure has driven the price of Proof-65s and Proof-66s up to the point where such coins are actually a bit overvalued in the market. As such, I would avoid the proof 1892 in these grades unless you insist on acquiring a rarer piece with a Cameo designation from PCGS or NGC. Deep/Ultra Cameo specimens are also desirable, but they are so rare as to trade only with the utmost infrequency.

The 1892 is somewhat underrated in Proof-64, however, but the issue can be challenging to locate with good eye appeal in that grade. The most desirable grade for this issue from the standpoint of investment potential seems to be Proof-67. The 1892 is an underrated proof Barber Dime at that grade level, and it is more undervalued as a Superb Gem than the lower-mintage 1893, 1906 and 1910. A Proof-67, if you can afford one and if the coin is accurately graded, also has the distinction of solid technical quality and (in most cases) strong eye appeal.

Regardless of whether you are looking for an all-brilliant or Cameo proof 1892 Barber Dime, I would definitely avoid coins that are darkly and/or unevenly toned. On the other hand, you could do well by acquiring an original example with only moderate toning that still allows ready appreciation of the mint finish. This is particularly sound advice for Cameo specimens, on which you should be able to see the field-to-device contrast without undue effort in order to justify the premium that you will have to pay for such a coin.

If your penchant is for untoned coins, there is also no reason to fear proof 1892 Barber Dimes that have been dipped by numismatic experts and subsequently graded by PCGS or NGC. Just make sure that the coin you are buying retains full vibrancy to the mint finish and is free of hazy overtones that are either remnants of the original toning or evidence of improper rinsing after the coin was removed from the dipping solution.

# 1892

**MINTAGE**
12,120,000

*Courtesy of Bowers and Merena*

**RARITY RANKINGS**

*Overall, Mint State: 74th of 74*
*High Grade, MS-65 or Finer: 74th of 74*

## PHILADELPHIA MINT ISSUES

*Overall, Mint State: 25th of 25*
*High Grade, MS-65 or Finer: 25th of 25*

**Important Varieties:** There are several Repunched Date varieties known for the 1892 Barber Dime, the two most popular of which carry the attributions FS-301/FS-008.3 and FS-302/FS-008.4/Lawrence-102.

**General Comments:** The 1892 edges out the 1916 and 1911, respectively, as the most common Barber Dime in all Mint State grades and the most common Barber Dime in high grades. While there are several issues in this series with greater mintages, the 1892 was saved in larger numbers than any other business strike Barber Dime due to its status as the first Philadelphia Mint issue of the type.

**Strike:** This is a well-produced issue, and all examples that I have seen possess a sharp-to-full strike.

**Luster:** The 1892 also has excellent luster that is usually frosty in texture.

**Surfaces:** Surface preservation for this issue varies widely, although the typically encountered example in today's market will possess at least a couple of noticeable abrasions.

**Toning:** This first-year Barber Dime issue is usually offered with some degree of toning. Most original examples are actually quite extensively patinated and vivid colors, when they are present at all, are usually hidden from view at all but the most direct light angles. There are exceptions, of course, and I have definitely seen some 1892 Barber Dimes with bright, vivid toning that dominates the outward appearance on one or both sides of the coin. Many of the brilliant pieces that I have handled have been dipped to remove the original toning.

**Eye Appeal:** With a relatively large number of Mint State survivors scattered quite widely throughout the Mint State grading scale, it should come as no surprise to read that the 1892 varies considerably in the eye appeal category. The typical coin that you will encounter has average eye appeal. The luster and strike are apt to be excellent, while a few scattered abrasions and, to a lesser extent, unsightly toning have the potential to inhibit the eye appeal. Coins that grade MS-65 or finer and possess either attractively original toning or brilliant, radiant surfaces are among the most aesthetically pleasing survivors from the entire business strike Barber Dime series.

**Significant Examples:**

**1. NGC MS-67.** *Ex: The Belle Glade Collection (Heritage, 8/2007), lot 564, where it realized $2,530; FUN Signature Coin Auction (Heritage, 1/2008), lot 1019, where it realized $2,415; Chicago Rarities Sale (Bowers and Merena, 4/2008), lot 252, where it realized $2,530.*

**2. NGC MS-67 ★.** *Ex: CSNS Signature Auction (Heritage, 5/2005), lot 6591, where it realized $2,990; San Francisco, CA ANA Signature Auction (Heritage, 7/2005), lot 5880, where it realized $2,530; ANA Charlotte National Show Auction (Heritage, 3/2007), lot 494, unsold; Baltimore Auction (Bowers and Merena, 6/2007), lot 672, where it realized $2,645.*

**3. NGC MS-67.** *Ex: The Benson Collection (Ira & Larry Goldberg, 2/2003), lot 338, where it realized $1,955; Denver, CO Signature & Platinum Night Auction (Heritage, 8/2006), lot 926, unsold; Dallas Signature Coin Auction (Heritage, 10/2006), lot 750, where it realized $2,875.*

**4. PCGS MS-67.** *Ex: The Albert E. Willis Collection (Heritage, 12/2005), lot 474, where it realized $2,300; Atlanta, GA ANA Signature Auction (Heritage, 4/2006), lot 428, where it realized $4,313.*

**5. PCGS MS-67.** *Ex: The Collection of Dr. Steven L. Duckor (Heritage, 1/2006), lot 969, where it realized $4,313.*

**6. NGC MS-67 ★.** *Ex: Long Beach Signature Auction (Heritage, 2/2005), lot 2416, where it realized $2,990.*

_Note_: The certified population for the 1892 Barber Dime tops out at the MS-67 grade level (December/2008). Due to the relatively large number of coins certified by PCGS and NGC at that level, this list of Significant Examples is merely a sampling of MS-67s that have appeared at auction during the early years of the 21st century.

**Total Known in Mint State:** 1,550-1,800 Coins

**Total Known and Value Breakdown by Grade:**

| MS-60-62 | MS-63 | MS-64 | MS-65 |
|---|---|---|---|
| 365-415 Coins | 390-440 Coins | 460-560 Coins | 190-230 Coins |
| N/A | $150-$200 | $250-$300 | $575-$675 |

| MS-66 | MS-67 | MS-68 | MS-69 to MS-70 |
|---|---|---|---|
| 110-135 Coins | 25-30 Coins | 0 Coins | 0 Coins |
| $700-$1,400 | $2,500-$5,000 | -- | -- |

_Note:_ The conclusions presented in the following "Collecting and Investing Strategies" section are drawn in large part from the Investment Potential Ratios that are summarized in Appendices G and H at the end of this book. For a detailed analysis of the formula used to derive these Investment Potential Ratios, please refer to the Introduction of this book.

**Collecting and Investing Strategies:** The first-year 1892 has long been numbered among the most popular Barber Dimes for high-grade type purposes. Indeed, the 1892 has the largest population of Mint State survivors in this series, and it is offered frequently enough that you should be confronted with several buying opportunities during any given year of numismatic trading. Another potentially desirable attribute for the 1892 as a type coin is that the issue is one of the most affordable Barber Dimes in all Mint State grades.

These facts notwithstanding, I would avoid the 1892 for type purposes. This issue is overrated in the popular grades of MS-64, MS-65, MS-66 and MS-67, such coins commanding too high of a price relative to the number of coins extant. From the standpoint of investment potential, there are many other issues in this series that are more favorably positioned than the 1892.

If you are assembling a complete set of Barber Dimes, or if you must acquire a Mint State 1892 for any other reason, a word of caution is in order as far as toned examples are concerned. Many such pieces are usually quite dark and/or possessed of splotchy coloration on one or both sides. Avoid those coins and select either a more evenly toned example (particularly one with at least some vivid colors present on the surfaces) or a brilliant coin.

# 1892-O

## MINTAGE
3,841,700

*Courtesy of David Lawrence*

## RARITY RANKINGS

*Overall, Mint State: 51st of 74*
*High Grade, MS-65 or Finer: 41st of 74 (Tie)*

## NEW ORLEANS MINT ISSUES

*Overall, Mint State: 17th of 17*
*High Grade, MS-65 or Finer: 13th of 17 (Tie)*

**Important Varieties:** There is a prominent, well-known Repunched Date variety for the 1892-O. The attributions FS-301, FS-008.5 and Lawrence-101 all refer to this RPD.

**General Comments:** The 1892-O is the most frequently encountered New Orleans Mint Barber Dime in Mint State, and I believe that a fair number of examples were set aside at the time of issue as the first O-mint coins of this type. The 1892-O, however, is not the most common New Orleans Mint Barber Dime in high grades. It is rarer than the 1905-O, 1906-O and 1908-O at and above the MS-65 grade level, and compares favorably with the 1907-O in this regard. The 1892-O is also similar in rarity to the 1908-D in Gem Mint State.

**Strike:** The 1892-O is a well-struck issue by the standards of the New Orleans Mint Barber Dime series, and most examples that I have handled are actually quite sharply impressed. When present at all, lack of detail for the issue is usually minor and confined to the haircurls over Liberty's brow, a few of the leaves in the laurel wreath on Liberty's head and/or the finer elements of the large leaf in the reverse wreath below the letter D in DIME.

**Luster:** This issue has only average luster, and it is not usually as vibrant as that seen on the typical 1892. The 1892-O usually displays slightly subdued luster with either a softly frosted or satin finish to the surfaces.

**Surfaces:** One of the more challenging early-date Barber Dimes to locate with smooth-looking surfaces, the 1892-O usually displays at least a few scattered abrasions. Fortunately, distractions are seldom large even in lower grades—a testament to the small size and relatively light weight of these coins.

**Toning:** Toned surfaces are the norm for this issue, the colors usually moderate-to-deep in shade. Coins with light, somewhat hazy toning or fully brilliant surfaces have probably been dipped at one time to remove original patina. This is especially true of coins with light toning only at the rims. Originally toned examples often have the deepest colors at the rims, and the deeper the patina the more difficult it is to remove entirely without impairing the coin's luster.

**Eye Appeal:** The 1892-O has below-average eye appeal. Scattered abrasions are almost always present, even if they are only few in number and small in size. Additionally, the luster is seldom vibrant, a problem that is often exacerbated by dark toning or dipping.

**Significant Examples:**

**1. NGC MS-67.** *Ex: The John C. Hugon Collection (Heritage, 1/2005), lot 4002, where it realized $4,888.*

**2. NGC MS-67.** *Ex: Long Beach Signature Sale (Heritage, 10/2001), lot 6079, unsold.*

**3. NGC MS-66.** *Ex: Long Beach, CA Signature U.S. Coin Auction (Heritage, 5/2007), lot 704, where it realized $1,495.*

**4. NGC MS-66.** *Ex: Atlanta, GA ANA Signature Auction (Heritage, 4/2006), lot 429, where it realized $1,495.*

**5. PCGS MS-66.** *Ex: The Collection of Dr. Steven L. Duckor (Heritage, 1/2006), lot 970, where it realized $5,463.*

**6. NGC MS-66.** *Ex: Long Beach Signature Sale (Heritage, 9/2002), lot 6275, where it realized $1,610.*

**7. PCGS MS-66.** *Ex: The Whitney P. Sunderland Collection (Bowers and Merena, 3/1994), lot 1507, where it realized $1,650.*

**8. NGC Specimen MS-64.** *Ex: Charlotte ANA National Money Sale (Heritage, 3/2003), lot 5559, where it realized $9,775.*

To the best of my knowledge, there is no mention of a branch mint proof or specimen striking of the 1892-O Barber Dime in any of the numismatic literature. In the 1977 book *Walter Breen's Encyclopedia of United States and Colonial Proof Coins: 1722-1977*, however, the author does mention the possible existence of a branch mint proof 1892-O Morgan Dollar. On the other hand, Wayne Miller (*The Morgan and Peace Dollar Textbook*) asserts that the 1892-O Dollar to which Breen refers is not a branch mint proof. Nevertheless, the possibility remains that a few proof silver coins were prepared at the New Orleans Mint that year to mark the end of the various Seated series and the introduction of the new Barber design in Dime, Quarter and Half Dollar format. I have not seen the example that NGC has certified as Specimen MS-64 and, thus, cannot offer an opinion regarding the validity of the Specimen designation on the insert.

**Total Known in Mint State:** 240-285 Coins

**Total Known and Value Breakdown by Grade:**

| MS-60 to MS-62 | MS-63 | MS-64 | MS-65 |
|---|---|---|---|
| 60-70 Coins | 55-65 Coins | 80-95 Coins | 35-40 Coins |
| N/A | $250-$300 | $350-$500 | $950-$1,100 |

| MS-66 | MS-67 | MS-68 | MS-69 to MS-70 |
|---|---|---|---|
| 10-12 Coins | 2-3 Coins | 0 Coins | 0 Coins |
| $1,500-$7,500 | $5,000-$15,000 | -- | -- |

*Note:* The conclusions presented in the following "Collecting and Investing Strategies" section are drawn in large part from the Investment Potential Ratios that are summarized in Appendices G and H at the end of this book. For a detailed analysis of the formula used to derive these Investment Potential Ratios, please refer to the Introduction of this book.

**Collecting and Investing Strategies**: Unlike the 1892, the 1892-O is an underrated Barber Dime in the popular Mint State grades from MS-64 through MS-67. This issue is most undervalued in MS-65 and MS-66, which are also highly desirable grades given the fact that many lower-grade examples of the 1892-O are plagued by excessive abrasions and/or muted luster.

Even as a Gem, the 1892-O will require some patience to procure a desirable example. Insist on acquiring a coin with attractive toning and uncommonly vibrant luster for the issue. I would also pay attention to the strike as the 1892-O can sometimes be a tad softly defined in isolated areas. Remember, though, that the 1892-O is scarce in MS-65 and rare in MS-66. Do not be too picky with this issue, therefore, or you might never make a purchase. Just strike a comfortable balance between eye appeal, technical quality and the amount of time that you are willing to devote to locating a suitable example and you should be able to acquire a Gem 1892-O that will serve as a highlight of your numismatic holdings.

# 1892-S

## MINTAGE
990,710

Courtesy of David Lawrence

## RARITY RANKINGS

***Overall, Mint State:*** *22nd of 74 (Tie)*
***High Grade, MS-65 or Finer:*** *7th of 74 (Tie)*

## SAN FRANCISCO MINT ISSUES

***Overall, Mint State:*** *11th of 24*
***High Grade, MS-65 or Finer:*** *3rd of 24 (Tie)*

**Important Varieties:** None.

**General Comments:** This San Francisco Mint issue boasts the lowest mintage of the three 1892-dated deliveries in the business strike Barber Dime series, and it is considerably rarer than the 1892 and 1892-O in all Mint State grades. The 1892-S vies with the 1898-S as the seventh-rarest Barber Dime in high grades (read: MS-65 or finer). Among San Francisco Mint issues in this series, only the 1895-S and 1907-S are more challenging to locate in Gem Mint State than the 1892-S.

**Strike:** The 1892-S is invariably sharp in strike with crisp delineation between even the finer elements of the design.

**Luster:** Like the 1892 but unlike the 1892-O, the 1892-S has very good-to-excellent luster. Most examples are either satiny or frosty in finish, although a few semi-prooflike pieces are known.

**Surfaces:** This issue is very similar to the 1892-O in terms of surface preservation insomuch as the typically offered Mint State example will exhibit at least a few scattered abrasions. Even coins that are overall smooth are very difficult to come by in the numismatic market.

**Toning:** The 1892-S is usually offered quite deeply toned with relatively dark patina. Vivid colors are seldom seen.

**Eye Appeal:** Eye appeal for this issue is only average. While strike and luster are definite strong suits, scattered abrasions and fairly dark toning often limit the desirability of Mint State examples.

**Significant Examples:**

**1. PCGS MS-66.** *Ex: The John C. Hugon Collection (Heritage, 1/2005), lot 4003, where it realized $25,300.*

**2. NGC MS-66.** *Ex: New York, NY Signature Sale (Heritage, 7/2002), lot 7600, where it realized $3,335.*

**Total Known in Mint State:** 105-135 Coins

**Total Known and Value Breakdown by Grade:**

| MS-60 to MS-62 | MS-63 | MS-64 | MS-65 |
|---|---|---|---|
| 30-35 Coins | 25-35 Coins | 35-45 Coins | 13-17 Coins |
| N/A | $575-$725 | $1,425-$1,575 | $3,250-$4,000 |

| MS-66 | MS-67 | MS-68 | MS-69 to MS-70 |
|---|---|---|---|
| 3-4 Coins | 0 Coins | 0 Coins | 0 Coins |
| $8,500-$27,500 | -- | -- | -- |

*Note:* The conclusions presented in the following "Collecting and Investing Strategies" section are drawn in large part from the Investment Potential Ratios that are summarized in Appendices G and H at the end of this book. For a detailed analysis of the formula used to derive these Investment Potential Ratios, please refer to the Introduction of this book.

**Collecting and Investing Strategies:** With a mintage of fewer than 1 million coins and status as the premier S-mint issue in the Barber Dime series, the 1892-S has long been high on collector "Want Lists." Market demand for this issue has been such that the 1892-S is actually overrated in MS-64, MS-65 and MS-66. As such, I do not recommend this issue for inclusion in a numismatic portfolio.

Date and mint collectors, of course, will have to contend with the 1892-S in order to complete a set of Barber Dimes. Since MS-65s are not as overvalued as MS-64s or MS-66s relative to their rarity, I would focus on that grade for inclusion in a high-grade set. Even in that grade, however, the 1892-S is an issue that will require some compromising. For starters, there are just not all that many MS-65s from which to choose in the market. Of even greater significance in this regard is the fact that many examples, while completely original, are unattractively toned in dark colors. Few Mint State survivors in all grades have been dipped, but if you can locate a brilliant example it will probably be preferable to a deeply toned piece. Be mindful, however, of coins that have been dipped to the point where the surfaces are now subdued with a washed out, almost lackluster appearance. Even more desirable than a dipped example, therefore, is a Gem 1892-S Dimes with lighter, albeit still 100% original surfaces that display either iridescent toning throughout or deeper patina that is confined to the rims.

# Proof
# 1893/'2'

## MINTAGE
Part of 792
(Includes Proof
1893)

Courtesy of David Lawrence

## RARITY
## RANKINGS
### *Not applicable*

**Important Varieties:** None.

**General Comments:** The status of this variety as a true overdate is in doubt. Both Walter Breen (*Walter Breen's Encyclopedia of United States and Colonial Proof Coins: 1722-1977, 1977,* and *Walter Breen's Complete Encyclopedia of U.S. and Colonial Coins,* 1988) and David Lawrence (*The Complete Guide to Barber Dimes, 1991*) state that the 1893/'2' does exist in proof format. This variety is also listed in the 62nd edition of the book *A Guide Book of United States Coins* by R.S. Yeoman. On the other hand, the proof 1893/'2' is not listed in the fourth edition (2006) of the book *Cherrypickers' Guide to Rare Die Varieties of United States Coins* by Bill Fivaz and J.T. Stanton.

For an unknown period of time prior to 2008, NGC acknowledged the existence of this overdate in proof format and certified a small number of examples with the "1893/2" attribution on the insert. When I contacted NGC during preparation of this book, however, Research Director David Lange informed me that NGC no longer recognizes the proof 1893/'2' and has removed the variety from its Census.

While preparing the manuscript for this book, I also took the opportunity to speak with PCGS Co-Founder John Dannreuther regarding his firm's view of the 1893/'2' and was told that PCGS does not recognize this overdate in proof format. PCGS's conclusion regarding this variety came after John conducted extensive research on an example of the proof 1893/'2' and concluded unequivocally that this variety is really an 1893/3 repunched date. It is John's belief (and mine, as well) that PCGS has never certified a proof 1893/'2' Barber Dime.

I agree with the professionals at both PCGS and NGC that the proof 1893/'2' is not a true overdate. This conclusion explains my decision to place the digit 2 in quotation marks when referring to this variety, as well as to remove it from the rarity rankings that I have conducted for the rest of the proof Barber Dime series. Nevertheless, I have decided to discuss the proof 1893/'2' in considerable detail in this book. As recently as 2008/2009, the indispensible reference *A Guide Book of United States Coins* (a.k.a. The Red Book) by R.S. Yeoman still provides a listing for the proof 1893/'2' as well as a value for the variety in Proof-63. The proof 1893/'2' still commands a premium in the market—the added value attached to these coins making it critical that the buyer understand every nuance of this variety before deciding whether or not to make a purchase. Finally, I am aware of a small number of specimens that NGC has certified as overdates in the past, so it is entirely possible that the buyer might encounter one of these coins in the market at some point in time.

**Strike:** The few examples known to exist are fully struck throughout. A loupe will reveal remnants of another 3 beneath the primary digit 3 in the date.

**Finish:** All known examples have deeply mirrored fields but only light-to-moderate frosting over the major devices.

**Surfaces:** The few specimens known to me run the gamut from heavily hairlined to virtually pristine.

**Toning:** I have only personally examined two proof 1893/'2' Barber Dimes, one of which is deeply toned and the other of which is lightly patinated in iridescent shades.

**Eye Appeal:** With only a few examples known that are widely scattered across the grading scale, it is difficult to assign a general eye appeal rating to this variety. The Proof-61s are assumed to have limited eye appeal due to heavy hairlining or other impairments, while the Proof-67 is a simply beautiful coin. The NGC Proof-64 has only average eye appeal because, while the strike is typically full for the variety and there are only a few stray handling marks, the toning is fairly deep and it does obscure the reflectivity in the fields at several angles.

**Significant Examples:**

**1. NGC Proof-67.** *Ex: The Dr. Juan XII Suros Collection (Superior, 2/1999), lot 122, where it realized $4,830. The overdate attribution was not included on the NGC insert at the time of sale.*

**2. NGC Proof-66.** *Ex: The Bradley Bloch Collection (Ira & Larry Goldberg, 9/1999), lot 1194, where it realized $3,200.*

**3. NGC Proof-64.** *Ex: The Irving Goodman Collection (Superior, 5/1996), lot 723, unsold; The William H. LaBelle, Sr. Collection (American Numismatic Rarities, 7/2005), lot 1008, where it realized $23,000; Dallas Signature Auction (Heritage, 12/2005), lot 514, unsold; Atlanta, GA ANA Signature Auction (Heritage, 4/2006), lot 445, unsold; The Lake Michigan & Springdale Collections (American Numismatic Rarities, 6/2006), lot 1268, unsold; Denver, CO Signature & Platinum Night Auction (Heritage, 8/2006), lot 958, unsold; Milwaukee Rarities Sale (Bowers and Merena, 8/2007), lot 550, where it realized $17,250.*

**4. NGC Proof-61.** *Ex: The Richmond Collection (David Lawrence, 3/2005), lot 1364, where it realized $17,250.*

**Total Known:** 5 Coins (approximate)

**Total Known and Value Breakdown by Grade:**

| Brilliant-Finish Coins | | | |
|---|---|---|---|
| **Proof-60-62** | **Proof-63** | **Proof-64** | **Proof-65** |
| 2 Coins | 0 Coins | 1 Coin | 0 Coins |
| N/A | -- | $20,000-$25,000 | -- |
| **Proof-66** | **Proof-67** | **Proof-68** | **Proof-69-70** |
| 1 Coin | 1 Coin | 0 Coins | 0 Coins |
| $35,000-$40,000 | $40,000-$60,000+ | -- | -- |

| Cameo Coins | | | |
|---|---|---|---|
| **Proof-60-62 Cameo** | **Proof-63 Cameo** | **Proof-64 Cameo** | **Proof-65 Cameo** |
| 0 Coins | 0 Coins | 0 Coins | 0 Coins |
| -- | -- | -- | -- |
| **Proof-66 Cameo** | **Proof-67 Cameo** | **Proof-68 Cameo** | **Proof-69-70 Cameo** |
| 0 Coins | 0 Coins | 0 Coins | 0 Coins |
| -- | -- | -- | -- |

| Deep/Ultra Cameo Coins | | | |
|---|---|---|---|
| Proof-60-62 Deep/ Ultra Cameo | Proof-63 Deep/ Ultra Cameo | Proof-64 Deep/ Ultra Cameo | Proof-65 Deep/ Ultra Cameo |
| 0 Coins | 0 Coins | 0 Coins | 0 Coins |
| -- | -- | -- | -- |
| Proof-66 Deep/ Ultra Cameo | Proof-67 Deep/ Ultra Cameo | Proof-68 Deep/ Ultra Cameo | Proof-69-70 Deep/ Ultra Cameo |
| 0 Coins | 0 Coins | 0 Coins | 0 Coins |
| -- | -- | -- | -- |

**Collecting and Investing Strategies:** I do not recommend acquiring any proof 1893/'2' Barber Dime. While there are still different opinions regarding this variety in numismatic circles, neither of the two major certification services credit the 1893/'2' as a true overdate. Even so, examples of the proof 1893/'2' still command a premium in the numismatic market over what you would expect to pay for a normal date proof 1893 Barber Dime. Nothing would be worse for a numismatic collector or investor to pay a premium for a coin based on a debatable variety only to find out later that the market no longer attaches a significant premium to that variety. With this possibility in mind, I would avoid the proof 1893/'2' under all circumstances.

# Proof
# 1893

## MINTAGE
Part of 792
(Includes Proof
1893/'2')

Courtesy of David Lawrence

## RARITY RANKINGS

*Overall, All Proof Grades: 18th of 25*
*High Grade, Proof-65 or Finer: 22nd of 25*
*Overall, Cameo Finish: 24th of 24*
*Overall, Deep/Ultra Cameo Finish: 8th of 12*

**Important Varieties:** There is a so-called 1893/'2' overdate, and it is discussed in the preceding section.

**General Comments:** The normal date 1893 accounts for the vast majority of proof Barber Dimes struck in the Philadelphia Mint that year. This issue is among the more common in its series, but it is actually the rarest proof Dime struck during the 1890s after only the branch mint proof 1894-S. An original mintage of 792 pieces represents a significant reduction from the 1,245-piece mintage that the Mint achieved for the proof 1892. This fact probably helps to explain the relative rarity of the proof 1893 in today's market. Additionally, the contemporary public probably ordered far fewer examples of the proof 1893. Most buyers looking for a proof striking of the new Dime type would certainly have satiated their desire by buying an example of the first-year 1892.

The proof 1893 is not ranked as high when we consider only coins that grade Proof-65 or finer. In high grades, nonetheless, this issue is still rarer than the proof 1894, 1895 and 1898. Interestingly, the 1893 is the most plentiful proof Barber Dime with a Cameo finish.

**Strike:** This is an expertly produced issue, and all examples that I have seen possess full striking detail and broad, squared-off rims.

**Finish:** The proof 1893 usually displays at least some degree of field-to-device contrast, but it is often confined to only one side of the coin or is partially obscured by deep toning. The fields are always deeply mirrored in finish.

**Surfaces:** The typical proof 1893 Barber Dime is a well-preserved coin with few, if any wispy hairlines. This issue tends to come better preserved than the proof 1892, indicating that many of the original buyers were numismatists who subsequently handled the coins with great care.

**Toning:** Lightly toned and brilliant examples of the proof 1893 exist in greater numbers than they do for the proof 1892. There are also many deeply toned specimens extant, some of which are lighter on the obverse than they are on the reverse. Toned examples of the proof 1893 tend to be more attractive than similarly patinated examples of the proof 1892.

**Eye Appeal:** As an issue, the proof 1893 has strong eye appeal. The typical example is fully struck with at least some degree of field-to-device contrast, and hairlines tend to be few in number or virtually nonexistent. Additionally, the proof 1893 is usually offered with either attractive toning or bright, untoned surfaces.

**Significant Examples:**

**1. NGC Proof-68.** *Ex: The John C. Hugon Collection (Heritage, 1/2005), lot 4077, where it realized $5,463.*

**2. NGC Proof-68.** *Ex: The Benson Collection (Ira & Larry Goldberg, 2/2003), lot 340, where it realized $5,463; CSNS Signature Sale (Heritage, 5/2004), lot 6690, where it realized $6,325; Mandalay Bay Rarities Sale (Bowers and Merena, 10/2004), lot 281, where it realized $5,750.*

**3. NGC Proof-68.** *Ex: Baltimore ANA Auction (Bowers and Merena, 7/2003), lot 1003, where it realized $5,520; Long Beach Signature Sale (Heritage, 6/2004), lot 6047, unsold; Pittsburgh, PA ANA Signature Sale (Heritage, 8/2004), lot 5715, unsold.*

**4. PCGS Proof-68.** *Ex: Atlanta, GA Signature Sale (Heritage, 8/2001), lot 5740, where it realized $8,050; The Trane Collection (Heritage, 5/2003), lot 5799, unsold; CSNS Signature Sale (Heritage, 5/2004), lot 6689, where it realized $8,625.*

**5. NGC Proof-68.** *Ex: Long Beach Signature Sale (Heritage, 9/2002), lot 6302, where it realized $6,095.*

**6. NGC Proof-68 ★ Cameo.** *Ex: Dallas, TX Coin Signature Auction (Heritage, 7/2006), lot 683, where it realized $6,038; The Southwest Collection (Heritage, 2/2008), lot 218, where it realized $8,625.*

**7. NGC Proof-68 Cameo.** *Ex: The William H. LaBelle, Sr. Collection (American Numismatic Rarities, 7/2005), lot 1009, where it realized $6,900.*

**8. NGC Proof-68 Cameo.** *Ex: The J.B. Worthington Collection (American Numismatic Rarities, 5/2005), lot 170, where it realized $6,900.*

**9. NGC Proof-68 Cameo.** *Ex: Pittsburgh, PA Signature Sale (Heritage, 8/2004), lot 5716, unsold.*

**10. PCGS Proof-67 Deep Cameo.** *Ex: The Bruce Scher #1 All-Time PCGS Registry Set (Heritage, 2/2005), lot 4053, where it realized $10,925.*

**Total Known:** 365-440 Coins

**Total Known and Value Breakdown by Grade:**

| Brilliant-Finish Coins | | | |
|---|---|---|---|
| **Proof-60-62** | **Proof-63** | **Proof-64** | **Proof-65** |
| 20-25 Coins | 35-45 Coins | 75-85 Coins | 60-70 Coins |
| N/A | $450-$550 | $750-$850 | $1,200-$1,300 |
| **Proof-66** | **Proof-67** | **Proof-68** | **Proof-69-70** |
| 55-65 Coins | 25-30 Coins | 5-7 Coins | 1 Coin |
| $1,500-$2000 | $2,250-$2,750 | $6,000-$10,000 | N/A |

| Cameo Coins | | | |
|---|---|---|---|
| **Proof-60-62 Cameo** | **Proof-63 Cameo** | **Proof-64 Cameo** | **Proof-65 Cameo** |
| 3-4 Coins | 6-8 Coins | 13-17 Coins | 15-20 Coins |
| N/A | $600-$700 | $850-$950 | $1,250-$1,500 |
| **Proof-66 Cameo** | **Proof-67 Cameo** | **Proof-68 Cameo** | **Proof-69-70 Cameo** |
| 25-30 Coins | 15-20 Coins | 5-7 Coins | 0 Coins |
| $1,750-$2,250 | $2,500-$3,000 | $8,500-$9,500 | -- |

| DeepUltra Cameo Coins | | | |
|---|---|---|---|
| **Proof-60-62 Deep/ Ultra Cameo** | **Proof-63 Deep/ Ultra Cameo** | **Proof-64 Deep/ Ultra Cameo** | **Proof-65 Deep/ Ultra Cameo** |
| 0 Coins | 0 Coins | 0 Coins | 2-3 Coins |
| -- | -- | -- | $2,000-$3,000 |

| Deep/Ultra Cameo Coins (cont.) | | | |
|---|---|---|---|
| Proof-66 Deep/ Ultra Cameo | Proof-67 Deep/ Ultra Cameo | Proof-68 Deep/ Ultra Cameo | Proof-69-70 Deep/ Ultra Cameo |
| 2-3 Coins | 2-3 Coins | 0 Coins | 0 Coins |
| $3,500-$4,500 | $6,000-$12,000 | -- | -- |

*Note:* The conclusions presented in the following "Collecting and Investing Strategies" section are drawn in large part from the Investment Potential Ratios that are summarized in Appendices G and H at the end of this book. For a detailed analysis of the formula used to derive these Investment Potential Ratios, please refer to the Introduction of this book.

**Collecting and Investing Strategies:** If you are searching for a better-date proof type coin from the early Barber Dime series, I would focus on the second-year 1893. Proof-65s and Proof-66s offer fairly solid value at reported price levels, and this issue is actually underrated in both Proof-64 and Proof-67. As a near-Gem, in fact, the 1893 is the most undervalued proof Barber Dime after only the 1905, 1914, 1897 and 1898. What's more, the proof 1893 tends to come nice in all grades. The untoned examples allow full appreciation of at least appreciable Cameo contrast while the originally toned pieces are seldom as dark or unsightly as similarly toned examples of the proof 1892.

# 1893/'2'

## MINTAGE
Part of 3,339,940
(Includes 1893)

Courtesy of David Lawrence

## RARITY RANKINGS
*Not Applicable*

**Important Varieties:** None.

**General Comments:** Like its identically dated proof counterpart, the 1893/'2' is a curious variety the exact attribution for which has not been agreed upon by numismatic professionals. Walter Breen (1988) and David Lawrence (1991) accept this variety as a true overdate. This variety is also listed in the 62nd edition of the book *A Guide Book of United States Coins* by R.S. Yeoman, but it is not listed in the fourth edition (2006) of the book *Cherrypickers' Guide to Rare Die Varieties of United States Coins* by Bill Fivaz and J.T. Stanton.

According to NGC Research Director David Lange, NGC used to certify the business strike 1893/'2' in the past but no longer recognizes the variety as an overdate. As with the proof 1893/'2,' the business strike 1893/'2' has been delisted on the NGC Census.

In conversation with PCGS Co-Founder John Dannreuther, I learned that his firm still recognizes the 1893/'2' in business strike format. On the other hand, John's conclusion that the proof 1893/'2' is really an 1893/3 repunched date casts doubt on the status of the business strike 1893/'2' as a true overdate. If it is determined that the business strike 1893/'2' is also a repunched date, PCGS will likely change their attribution for this variety to 1893/3.

It is my belief that the business strike 1893/'2' is also an 1893/3 repunched date like its proof counterpart. Due to the ongoing debate surrounding this variety's true classification, however, I have decided to place the digit 2 in quotation marks when referring to this variety. I have also removed it from the rarity rankings that I have conducted for most of the rest of the Barber Dime series. Even so, I have decided to discuss the 1893/'2' in considerable detail in this book. As recently as 2008/2009, the indispensible reference *A Guide Book of United States Coins* (a.k.a. The Red Book) by R.S. Yeoman still provides a listing for the proof 1893/'2' as well as values for the variety in all grades from Good-4 through MS-63. I am also aware of approximately 25-30 Mint State examples that PCGS and NGC have certified as overdates, and these coins continue to command a premium when they trade in the market.

**Strike:** The few examples known are sharp-to-full in strike. As with the proof 1893/'2,' the business strike 1893/'2' reveals remnants of another digit beneath the primary digit 3 in the date. The underdigit is probably another 3.

**Luster:** The 1893/'2' has excellent luster of either the satin or frosty type.

**Surfaces:** Mint State examples are fairly evenly spread throughout the MS-62 to MS-66 grade range, which means that their surface preservation varies from noticeably abraded to virtually pristine.

**Toning:** Most of the survivors are brilliant or lightly toned, predominantly from having been dipped at one time. Pieces that are of undeniable originality tend to be richly toned, the colors ranging from dark to somewhat vivid.

**Eye Appeal:** As a whole, this variety has above-average eye appeal. Even though lower-end Mint State examples are quite baggy, and a few pieces are darkly toned, the sharpness of strike and vibrancy of luster for which the 1893/'2' is known provide a pleasing appearance at most levels of Mint State preservation.

**Significant Examples:**

**1. PCGS MS-66.** *Ex: The Richmond Collection (David Lawrence, 3/2005), lot 1289, where it realized $7,763; The Collection of Dr. Steven L. Duckor (Heritage, 1/2006), lot 972, where it realized $11,500.*

**2. PCGS MS-66.** *Ex: FUN Signature Sale (Heritage, 1/2004), lot 5660, where it realized $6,825.*

**3. PCGS MS-66.** *Ex: Long Beach Signature Sale (Heritage, 6/2000), lot 7123, where it realized $5,290.*

**4. PCGS MS-65.** *Ex: The Dr. Juan XII Suros Collection (Superior, 2/1999), lot 123, where it realized $2,760.*

**Total Known in Mint State:** 25-30 Coins

### Total Known and Value Breakdown by Grade:

| MS-60 to MS-62 | MS-63 | MS-64 | MS-65 |
|---|---|---|---|
| 4-5 Coins | 5-7 Coins | 8-10 Coins | 3-4 Coins |
| N/A | $1,300-$1,600 | $2,500-$3,000 | $3,750-$4,250 |

| MS-66 | MS-67 | MS-68 | MS-69 to MS-70 |
|---|---|---|---|
| 5-6 Coins | 0 Coins | 0 Coins | 0 Coins |
| $8,500-$12,500 | -- | -- | -- |

**Collecting and Investing Strategies:** Since NGC no longer recognizes this variety as an overdate and PCGS is leaning in that direction, I do not recommend acquiring an example of the 1893/'2' for inclusion in your collection or portfolio. The few coins certified do carry premiums over the prices paid for the normal date 1893. It would be unwise to pay these premiums, however, only to find out later that the market as a whole no longer recognizes this variety as a true overdate.

# 1893

## MINTAGE
Part of 3,339,940
(Includes 1893/'2')

Courtesy of David Lawrence

## RARITY RANKINGS

*Overall, Mint State: 56th of 74*
*High Grade, MS-65 or Finer: 62nd of 74 (Tie)*

## PHILADELPHIA MINT ISSUES

*Overall, Mint State: 9th of 25*
*High Grade, MS-65 or Finer: 15th of 25 (Tie)*

**Important Varieties:** There is a so-called 1893/'2' overdate, and it is discussed in the preceding section.

**General Comments:** The 1893 is considerably rarer than the 1892 in all grades, a fact that I attribute both to a much lower mintage and less-widespread hoarding among the contemporary public. This issue is actually the ninth-rarest Philadelphia Mint Barber Dime in terms of total number of Mint State coins known to exist. When viewed in the wider context of this series, nevertheless, the 1893 is still one of the more readily obtainable Barber Dimes in Mint State, particularly in MS-65 and MS-66. Superb Gems in MS-67 are very rare, however, and the issue is unknown any finer.

**Strike:** The 1893 almost always comes with sharp-to-full striking detail.

**Luster:** Most examples possess richly frosted luster. Satiny and semi-prooflike pieces are also seen on occasion, but they are in the minority among survivors. Regardless of exactly which type of finish the coin in question displays, the 1893 has very good, if not excellent luster quality.

**Surfaces:** Examples range from noticeably abraded to virtually pristine, although the typically encountered 1893 Barber Dime is well preserved with no more than a few small, well-scattered distractions.

**Toning:** Most fully original examples of the 1893 are moderately-to-deeply toned, often with very pretty color that is more vibrant than that seen on the typical 1892. Dipped pieces are becoming more prevalent, however, and these usually display bright, fully untoned surfaces or light toning that tends to be present only at and near the rims.

**Eye Appeal:** As a whole, the 1893 has above-average, if not strong eye appeal—a statement that applies equally to originally toned pieces and brilliant examples.

### Significant Examples:

**1. NGC MS-67.** *Ex: The Benson Collection (Ira & Larry Goldberg, 2/2002), lot 565, where it realized $2,645; The John F. Rindge and Alan J. Harlan Collections (Bowers and Merena, 12/2003), lot 1104, unsold; Long Beach Signature Sale (Heritage, 2/2005), lot 6278, unsold.*

**2. NGC MS-67.** *Ex: The John C. Hugon Collection (Heritage, 1/2005), lot 4004, where it realized $3,738.*

**3. NGC MS-67 ★.** *Ex: Pittsburgh, PA Signature Sale (Heritage, 8/2004), lot 5698, where it realized $7,475.*

**4. NGC MS-67.** *Ex: Pre-Long Beach Sale (Superior, 2/2000), lot 189, where it realized $2,300.*

**5. PCGS MS-67.** *Ex: James Macallister (1944); The Benson Collection (Ira & Larry Goldberg, 2/2002), lot 564, unsold.*

**Total Known in Mint State:** 335-400 Coins

**Total Known and Value Breakdown by Grade:**

| MS-60 to MS-62 | MS-63 | MS-64 | MS-65 |
|---|---|---|---|
| 80-95 Coins | 80-95 Coins | 80-95 Coins | 60-70 Coins |
| N/A | $150-$200 | $250-$350 | $800-$900 |

| MS-66 | MS-67 | MS-68 | MS-69 to MS-70 |
|---|---|---|---|
| 30-35 Coins | 5-7 Coins | 0 Coins | 0 Coins |
| $1,250-$2,750 | $5,000-$10,000 | -- | -- |

*Note:* The conclusions presented in the following "Collecting and Investing Strategies" section are drawn in large part from the Investment Potential Ratios that are summarized in Appendices G and H at the end of this book. For a detailed analysis of the formula used to derive these Investment Potential Ratios, please refer to the Introduction of this book.

**Collecting and Investing Strategies:** The 1893 is the most underrated P-mint Barber Dime in MS-64 after only the 1896, 1902, 1903 and 1905. This issue also offers solid value in MS-65 and MS-66, but it is overrated in MS-67 and should be avoided in that grade.

The 1893 tends to come nice with good luster and striking detail. Your choice between a brilliant or toned coin should be based on personal preference as well as the other coins in your collection or investment portfolio. If you do opt for a toned 1893, make sure it possesses vibrant colors and is free of dark and/or splotchy patina. There are quite a few colorfully and attractively toned 1893 Dimes in numismatic circles, and some of the nicest pieces that I have handled exhibit halos of pretty blue color at the rim on one or both sides.

# 1893-O

**MINTAGE**
1,760,000

*Courtesy of David Lawrence*

## RARITY RANKINGS

***Overall, Mint State:*** *35th of 74 (Tie)*
***High Grade, MS-65 or Finer:*** *18th of 74*

## NEW ORLEANS MINT ISSUES

***Overall, Mint State:*** *13th of 17*
***High Grade, MS-65 or Finer:*** *8th of 17*

**Important Varieties:** None.

**General Comments:** Beginning with this issue and continuing through 1897, the New Orleans Mint produced relatively few Barber Dimes. Indeed, all O-mint issues produced from 1893 to 1897 are semi-key and key-date issues in this series. That being said, the 1893-O is more plentiful than the 1894-O, 1895-O and 1896-O in all Mint State grades. While the 1893-O is not as rare as the low-mintage 1897-O in an absolute sense, it is the rarer of the two issues in high grades. The 1893-O is also similar in rarity to the 1896 in terms of total number of Mint State coins believed to exist, and it is actually rarer (if only marginally) in high grades than the low-mintage 1895, 1896-S, 1902-S, 1903-S, 1913-S and 1915-S. Perhaps surprisingly for such a conditionally challenging issue, there are a couple of beautiful Superb Gems in MS-67 and MS-68 known for the 1893-O, but this issue is clearly a major rarity in those grades.

**Strike:** The 1893-O is not as well struck as the 1892-O, and the typical example is apt to display softness of detail on the obverse over the haircurls above Liberty's forehead and on the reverse over the lower-left portion of the wreath. Several pieces are quite well defined on the obverse above Liberty's forehead, but even such coins are still apt to display incompleteness of detail in the reverse wreath.

**Luster:** Most 1893-O Barber Dimes possess inferior luster that is either softly frosted or satiny in texture, almost always with a considerably subdued appearance.

**Surfaces:** The vast majority of Mint State examples exhibit a small-to-moderate number of abrasions scattered about on the obverse and/or reverse. Coins with even overall smooth surfaces are very challenging to find, while pieces that approach perfection are very rare.

**Toning:** Toned coins are in the majority among extant 1893-O Dimes, and these can possess either attractive, relatively vivid colors or unsightly patina in dark and/or mottled shades. Most of the brilliant or minimally toned pieces that I have seen were dipped at one time.

**Eye Appeal:** Overall eye appeal for this issue is only average at best. Scattered abrasions are almost always present, as is incompleteness of strike (if only on the reverse). Subdued luster is also a problem for this issue, and toning can be if it is dark and/or mottled in appearance. There is, however, a small number of highly attractive 1893-O Dimes known to exist. Those coins possess above-average luster and striking quality for the issue, as well as either attractively toned or bright, brilliant surfaces.

**Significant Examples:**

1. **NGC MS-67.** *Ex: The Collection of Dr. Steven L. Duckor (Heritage, 1/2006), lot 974, where it realized $4,888; Dallas Signature Coin Auction (Heritage, 11/2006), lot 535, unsold; Baltimore Auction (Bowers and Merena, 6/2007), lot 673, where it realized $8,338; FUN Signature Coin Auction (Heritage, 1/2008), lot 1024, where it realized $8,913.*

2. **PCGS MS-67.** *Ex: William M. Friesner Sale (6/1894); J.M. Clapp; Clapp estate (1942); The Louis E. Eliasberg, Sr. Collection (Bowers and Merena, 5/1996), lot 1246, where it realized $3,960; Portland Rarities Sale (Bowers and Merena, 8/1998), lot 118,where it realized $6,670.*

3. **PCGS MS-66.** *Ex: Long Beach, CA Signature Coin Auction (Heritage, 5/2008), lot 119, where it realized $4,600.*

4. **NGC MS-66.** *Ex: Long Beach Signature Sale (Heritage, 9/2004), lot 6184, where it realized $3,105; Dallas Signature Coin Auction (Heritage, 10/2006), lot 752, where it realized $2,990; The Southwest Collection (Heritage, 2/2008), lot 143, where it realized $3,220.*

**5. NGC MS-66★.** *Ex: Orlando Rarities Sale (Bowers and Merena, 1/2008), lot 122, where it realized $3,278.*

**6. PCGS MS-66.** *Ex: FUN Signature Sale (Heritage, 1/2001), lot 6774, unsold; Long Beach Signature Sale (Heritage, 2/2001), lot 5687, where it realized $2,200; The Belle Glade Collection (Heritage, 8/2006), lot 929, where it realized $4,025.*

**7. PCGS MS-66.** *Ex: The John C. Hugon Collection (Heritage, 1/2005), lot 4005, where it realized $5,175.*

**8. PCGS MS-66.** *Ex: The Frog Run Farm Collection (American Numismatic Rarities, 11/2004), lot 646, where it realized $4,140.*

**9. NGC MS-66.** *Ex: Long Beach Signature Sale (Heritage, 2/2003), lot 6332, unsold.*

**10. NGC MS-66.** *Ex: Portland ANA Signature Sale (Heritage, 8/1998), lot 6367, where it realized $2,530.*

**Total Known in Mint State:** 150-190 Coins

**Total Known and Value Breakdown by Grade:**

| MS-60 to MS-62 | MS-63 | MS-64 | MS-65 |
|---|---|---|---|
| 35-45 Coins | 40-50 Coins | 50-60 Coins | 13-17 Coins |
| N/A | $450-$600 | $950-$1,200 | $2,250-$3,000 |

| MS-66 | MS-67 | MS-68 | MS-69 to MS-70 |
|---|---|---|---|
| 10-12 Coins | 3-4 Coins | 1 Coin | 0 Coins |
| $3,500-$5,500 | $8,000-$12,000 | $25,000-$50,000 | -- |

*Note:* The conclusions presented in the following "Collecting and Investing Strategies" section are drawn in large part from the Investment Potential Ratios that are summarized in Appendices G and H at the end of this book. For a detailed analysis of the formula used to derive these Investment Potential Ratios, please refer to the Introduction of this book.

**Collecting and Investing Strategies:** The 1893-O is an overrated issue in MS-64, a fact that I attribute to the rarity of higher-grade examples in numismatic circles. (The difficulty and cost associated with acquiring an 1893-O that grades MS-65 or finer has resulted in uncommonly strong demand—and consequently inflated pieces—for MS-64s.) Interestingly, this issue is underrated in MS-65 and MS-66 at the price levels given in this book, although the handful of MS-67s known to exist are overvalued in light of their true rarity.

Obviously, I would focus on the MS-65 and MS-66 grade levels when pursuing the 1893-O Barber Dime. I also recommend cherrypicking for strike, luster, surface preservation and eye appeal when it comes to this issue. Look for bold-to-sharp definition over the haircurls above Liberty's brow, vibrant luster that is either satiny or frosty in texture and colorfully toned or brilliant surfaces. Avoid examples that are unattractively toned or are so deeply toned that the luster has become impaired. Expect to spend a significant amount of time searching for a Gem-quality 1893-O that meets all of these criteria, perhaps even upward of two or three years, but your efforts will be rewarded with an example that is among the most desirable and potentially lucrative survivors of this challenging O-mint issue.

# 1893-S

## MINTAGE
2,491,401

Courtesy of David Lawrence

## RARITY RANKINGS

**Overall, Mint State:** *30th of 74*
**High Grade, MS-65 or Finer:** *19th of 74 (Tie)*

### *SAN FRANCISCO MINT ISSUES*

**Overall, Mint State:** *15th of 24*
**High Grade, MS-65 or Finer:** *10th of 24 (Tie)*

**Important Varieties:** Several Repunched Mintmark varieties are known for the 1893-S, the most significant of which exhibits bold remnants of the first S to the right of the primary mintmark. That particular variety is known by the attributions FS-501, FS-009, Lawrence-101 and Breen-3484.

**General Comments:** Dime production at the San Francisco Mint increased markedly in 1893 over the total reported for 1892. This fact, however, can be misleading when determining the absolute and relative rarity of the 1893-S. This issue circulated widely, and it is rarer in all Mint State grades that the low-mintage 1913-S and 1915-S. In terms of high-grade rarity, the 1893-S compares favorably to the low-mintage 1896-S, 1897-O, 1902-S and 1903-S, as well as the 1901-O. The 1893-S is scarce in the MS-60 to MS-64 grade range, rare as a Gem and all but unobtainable as a Superb Gem.

**Strike:** The 1893-S always displays a sharp strike to the devices on both the obverse and the reverse.

**Luster:** Luster is also a strong suit for this issue, and the typical example exhibits either a satin or semi-prooflike sheen to the surfaces.

**Surfaces:** The 1893-S usually exhibits at least a few scattered abrasions, and many lower-grade Mint State pieces are quite baggy. This is one of the more challenging S-mint Barber Dimes to locate with overall smooth-to-pristine surfaces.

**Toning:** Most examples are extensively toned, and the colors are quite dark and relatively unattractive on several pieces. The more moderately toned coins are usually quite desirable, but even then the toning is seldom vivid except perhaps at and near the rims. Lightly toned and fully brilliant pieces are not seen all that often, and those that I have handled have been dipped at one time to remove deeper toning.

**Eye Appeal:** The 1893-S has average to slightly above-average eye appeal. Scattered abrasions are a problem, as is an abundance of toned coins whose surfaces are not especially vivid. On the other hand, this is a well-struck issue with excellent luster quality.

### Significant Examples:

**1. PCGS MS-67.** *Ex: The Palakika Collection (Heritage, 5/2007), lot 2074, where it realized $63,250.*

**2. PCGS MS-66.** *Ex: CSNS Signature Coin Auction (Heritage, 4/2008), lot 610, where it realized $8,050.*

**3. NGC MS-66.** *Ex: Superior's sale of 2/1999, lot 630, where it realized $2,990; The Belle Glade Collection (Heritage, 8/2007), lot 567, where it realized $4,025.*

**4. PCGS MS-66.** *Ex: The Collection of Dr. Steven L. Duckor (Heritage, 1/2006), lot 975, where it realized $9,200.*

**5. PCGS MS-66.** *Ex: CSNS Signature Auction (Heritage, 5/2005), lot 6601, where it realized $9,775.*

**6. PCGS MS-66.** *Ex: Long Beach Signature Sale (Heritage, 6/2002), lot 5618, where it realized $3,680.*

**Total Known in Mint State:** 130-160 Coins

**Total Known and Value Breakdown by Grade:**

| MS-60 to MS-62 | MS-63 | MS-64 | MS-65 |
|---|---|---|---|
| 35-45 Coins | 35-40 Coins | 35-40 Coins | 20-25 Coins |
| N/A | $500-$700 | $1,250-$1,500 | $2,500-$3,250 |

| MS-66 | MS-67 | MS-68 | MS-69 to MS-70 |
|---|---|---|---|
| 5-6 Coins | 1 Coin | 0 Coins | 0 Coins |
| $5,000-$15,000 | $50,000-$75,000 | -- | -- |

*Note:* The conclusions presented in the following "Collecting and Investing Strategies" section are drawn in large part from the Investment Potential Ratios that are summarized in Appendices G and H at the end of this book. For a detailed analysis of the formula used to derive these Investment Potential Ratios, please refer to the Introduction of this book.

**Collecting and Investing Strategies:** I do not recommend this issue in any grade below MS-66. While MS-64s do offer solid value at the price levels given in this book, such coins tend to have at least a few noticeable abrasions, and they are often quite darkly toned with some impairment of the luster. (The same can be said for lower-grade pieces in the MS-60 to MS-63 range.) Gems in MS-65 are overrated, and the 1893-S is actually the most overrated Barber Dime in MS-67. The single MS-67 known to PCGS sold for an inflated premium in 2007 due to pressure from Registry Set collectors. Unless you are also assembling a top-ranked Barber Dime set on the PCGS Registry, I would avoid that MS-67 if and when it is offered for sale in the future.

The handful of MS-66s known for the 1893-S offer solid value in light of their rarity, and this is the grade level on which I would focus when pursuing this issue. Toning, however, can be a problem for this issue in MS-66. Even if it is not too deep to obscure the luster, the toning that many 1893-S Dimes display tends to be comprised of darker, less vibrant colors. On the other hand, I am also not a fan of dipped coins as far as the 1893-S is concerned. Most pieces that have been conserved in that way reveal splotchy remnants of the original toning and/or no longer retain full vibrancy to the mint luster.

Your best bet for locating a desirable 1893-S Barber Dime, therefore, is to wait until one of the more attractively toned MS-66s becomes available for purchase. These coins will still tend to be extensively toned, but a few do include more vivid colors on one or both sides, particularly at and near the rims.

# Proof
# 1894

## MINTAGE
972

Courtesy of David Lawrence

## RARITY RANKINGS

***Overall, All Proof Grades:*** *25th of 25*
***High Grade, Proof-65 or Finer:*** *25th of 25*
***Overall, Cameo Finish:*** *22nd of 24 (Tie)*
***Overall, Deep/Ultra Cameo Finish:*** *1st of 12 (Tie)*

**Important Varieties:** None.

**General Comments:** At 972 pieces produced, the 1894 has the second-highest mintage in the proof Barber Dime series after the 1892. The 1894 is actually the most common proof Barber Dime both in terms of total number of coins known to exist and number of coins extant in high grades. On the other hand, the proof 1894 is not as easy to obtain with a Cameo finish as the proof 1893. Even more interesting, however, is the fact that the proof 1894 is tied with the proof 1906, proof 1910 and proof 1911 as the rarest collectible proof Barber Dime with a Deep/Ultra Cameo finish.

**Strike:** Virtually all examples that I have seen are fully struck on both the obverse and the reverse. There are a few examples on which the haircurls immediately above Liberty's forehead are not 100% full, but the lack of detail is trivial and such pieces still present as overall sharply defined.

**Finish:** The proof 1894 is always deeply mirrored in the fields. The devices are usually frosty, but the texture is often quite shallow and it is easily obscured by toning. Pieces with one or both of those characteristics will not receive a Cameo designation from PCGS or NGC.

**Surfaces:** This is generally a well-preserved issue, and most examples are either minimally hairlined or free of distracting blemishes. The 1894 is also one of the easiest proof Barber Dimes to locate with virtually pristine surfaces.

**Toning:** There is about a 75-25 mix of toned and brilliant examples in the market. When present on a proof 1894 Barber Dime, toning tends to be quite deep, although the colors are often relatively pleasing, if not beautiful. Most brilliant examples have been dipped, probably to allow better appreciation of field-to-device contrast and ensure that the coin would receive either a Cameo or Deep/Ultra Cameo designation when submitted to PCGS or NGC. The dipped pieces that I have seen have largely been well treated, meaning that the surfaces are radiant and free of bothersome haziness.

**Eye Appeal:** The proof 1894 has strong eye appeal. Strike, finish and surface preservation are almost always excellent. There are also plenty of attractive examples to choose from regardless of whether your preference is for originally toned or brilliant coins.

### Significant Examples:

**1. NGC Proof-68 ★.** *CAC. Ex: Dallas Signature Coin Auction (Heritage, 11/2006), lot 549, unsold; Dallas, TX U.S. Coin Signature Auction (Heritage, 11/2007), lot 442, unsold; CSNS Signature Coin Auction (Heritage, 4/2008), lot 639, where it realized $6,900.*

**2. NGC Proof-68.** *Ex: FUN Signature Sale (Heritage, 1/2004), lot 5696, where it realized $5,290; Pre-Long Beach Rarities Sale (Bowers and Merena, 2/2007), lot 236, where it realized $6,613.*

**3. NGC Proof-68 ★.** *Ex: San Francisco Rarities Sale (Bowers and Merena, 7/2005), lot 403, where it realized $6,613.*

**4. NGC Proof-68 Cameo.** *Ex: The J.B. Worthington Collection (American Numismatic Rarities, 5/2005), lot 171, where it realized $5,520.*

**5. PCGS Proof-67 Cameo.** *CAC. Ex: Baltimore Rarities Sale (Bowers and Merena, 7/2007), lot 465, where it realized $6,038.*

**6. PCGS Proof-67 Cameo.** *Ex: Dallas Signature Auction (Heritage, 12/2005), lot 496, where it realized $4,313.*

**7. NGC Proof-67 Cameo.** *Ex: CSNS Signature Auction (Heritage, 5/2005), lot 6698, unsold; Long Beach Signature Auction (Heritage, 9/2005), lot 2461, where it realized $2,760.*

**8. PCGS Proof-67 Cameo.** *Ex: Beverly Hills Rarities Sale (Bowers and Merena, 9/2003), lot 74, where it realized $5,463.*

**9. NGC Proof-67 Cameo.** Ex: Central States Sale (Heritage, 5/2000), lot 7238, where it realized $2,760.

**Total Known:** 500-600 Coins

## Total Known and Value Breakdown by Grade:

| Brilliant-Finish Coins | | | |
|---|---|---|---|
| Proof-60-62 | Proof-63 | Proof-64 | Proof-65 |
| 40-50 Coins | 55-65 Coins | 135-160 Coins | 95-110 Coins |
| N/A | $450-$550 | $650-$750 | $1,200-$1,400 |
| Proof-66 | Proof-67 | Proof-68 | Proof-69-70 |
| 60-70 Coins | 35-45 Coins | 7-9 Coins | 0 Coins |
| $1,500-$1,750 | $2,500-$5,000 | $7,000-$9,000 | -- |

| Cameo Coins | | | |
|---|---|---|---|
| Proof-60-62 Cameo | Proof-63 Cameo | Proof-64 Cameo | Proof-65 Cameo |
| 0 Coins | 2-3 Coins | 20-25 Coins | 20-25 Coins |
| N/A | $600-$700 | $750-$950 | $1,100-$1,500 |
| Proof-66 Cameo | Proof-67 Cameo | Proof-68 Cameo | Proof-69-70 Cameo |
| 23-28 Coins | 10-12 Coins | 1-2 Coins | 0 Coins |
| $2,000-$2,750 | $3,000-$5,000 | $8,000-$10,000 | -- |

| Deep/Ultra Cameo Coins | | | |
|---|---|---|---|
| Proof-60-62 Deep/ Ultra Cameo | Proof-63 Deep/ Ultra Cameo | Proof-64 Deep/ Ultra Cameo | Proof-65 Deep/ Ultra Cameo |
| 0 Coins | 0 Coins | 1 Coin | 0 Coins |
| -- | -- | $5,000-$10,000 | -- |
| Proof-66 Deep/ Ultra Cameo | Proof-67 Deep/ Ultra Cameo | Proof-68 Deep/ Ultra Cameo | Proof-69-70 Deep/ Ultra Cameo |
| 0 Coins | 0 Coins | 0 Coins | 0 Coins |
| -- | -- | -- | -- |

*Note:* The conclusions presented in the following "Collecting and Investing Strategies" section are drawn in large part from the Investment Potential Ratios that are summarized in Appendices G and H at the end of this book. For a detailed analysis of the formula used to derive these Investment Potential Ratios, please refer to the Introduction of this book.

**Collecting and Investing Strategies:** The 1894 does not offer good value or solid investment potential in most grades, as it is overrated in Proof-64, Proof-65 and Proof-67. I would also be wary of Cameo designations that PCGS and NGC have assigned to many proof 1894 Dimes. The mint frost on the devices is quite thin on many examples, and I have seen some pieces certified as Cameo by the leading grading services that are only marginally better than examples that have not received that designation. Always be sure to view Cameo-designated pieces in person prior to making a purchase to ensure that you really are getting what is being marketed on the insert. If you are unfamiliar with proof coinage from the 1890s, it is also probably a good idea to seek the advice of a trusted dealer or other numismatic professional who is willing to look at the coin for you and provide an expert opinion.

The only grade in which I would consider acquiring an example of this issue is Proof-66. Such pieces do offer solid value, and many are lovely examples with beautiful, fully original toning. On the other hand, some of the toned pieces that I have seen are really quite dark. Those coins also tend to display mottled colors that can further limit the eye appeal. Avoid those examples at all costs so that you do not end up purchasing a coin that may be difficult to sell in the future.

# 1894

## MINTAGE
1,330,000

*Courtesy of Bowers and Merena*

## RARITY RANKINGS

***Overall, Mint State:*** *42nd of 74*
***High Grade, MS-65 or Finer:*** *44th of 74 (Tie)*

## PHILADELPHIA MINT ISSUES

***Overall, Mint State:*** *4th of 25*
***High Grade, MS-65 or Finer:*** *6th of 25*

**Important Varieties:** None.

**General Comments:** Despite having been produced to the extent of just 1.3 million pieces, the 1894 is a coin that circulated widely beginning in the year of issue and continuing well into the 20th century. Most examples are well worn, and even low-end Mint State coins are far scarcer than many numismatists realize. In terms of total number of Mint State coins believed to exist, in fact, the 1894 is the fourth-rarest Philadelphia Mint Barber Dime after the 1895, 1896 and 1903. The 1894 is also rarer in Mint State than the branch mint 1905-S, 1906-O, 1907-O, 1912-S and 1914-S, to say nothing of the 1892-O, 1914-D and 1916-S. When we consider only those survivors than grade MS-65 or finer, the 1894 emerges as similar in rarity to the 1905-O, and it is actually more elusive than the low-mintage 1913-S in those grades.

**Strike:** The 1894 is almost always offered with more-or-less sharp striking detail.

**Luster:** The full range of luster types is available on Barber Dimes of this issue, although frosty examples are seen much more frequently than either satiny or semi-proof-like pieces.

**Surfaces:** Despite its status as a Philadelphia Mint issue, the 1894 is anything but common with overall smooth surfaces. The typical survivor possesses at least a few wispy abrasions, and many Mint State pieces are actually quite baggy.

**Toning:** There are nearly as many brilliant 1894 Dimes in numismatic circles as there are toned pieces. The toned pieces tend to be more-or-less dark, but many do include relatively vibrant colors such as blue and lavender. Brilliant examples are largely the result of dipping, although such pieces tend to be more attractive than the toned coins.

**Eye Appeal:** Overall eye appeal for the 1894 is decidedly below average. The primary culprit here is the paucity of overall smooth, to say nothing of virtually pristine examples in the market. Many of the originally toned pieces are even less appealing, such is the depth of color that such coins often possess.

**Significant Examples:**

**1. NGC MS-66.** *Ex: The Arnold & Harriet Collection (Heritage, 9/2007), lot 1019, where it realized $1,725.*

**2. PCGS MS-66.** *Ex: The Haig A. Koshkarian Collection (American Numismatic Rarities, 3/2004), lot 507, where it realized $1,955; The Collection of Dr. Steven L. Duckor (Heritage, 1/2006), lot 976, where it realized $2,300.*

**3. PCGS MS-66.** *Ex: FUN Signature Auction (Heritage, 1/2006), lot 1812, where it realized $2,530.*

**4. PCGS MS-66.** *Ex: CSNS Signature Sale (Heritage, 5/2005), lot 6602, where it realized $2,200.*

**5. NGC MS-66.** *Ex: CSNS Signature Sale (Heritage, 5/2004), lot 6639, where it realized $1,840.*

**Total Known in Mint State:** 175-220 Coins

**Total Known and Value Breakdown by Grade:**

| MS-60-62 | MS-63 | MS-64 | MS-65 |
|---|---|---|---|
| 40-50 Coins | 35-45 Coins | 50-60 Coins | 35-45 Coins |
| N/A | $400-$600 | $700-$850 | $1,250-$1,500 |

| MS-66 | MS-67 | MS-68 | MS-69-70 |
|---|---|---|---|
| 11-14 Coins | 3-4 Coins | 0 Coins | 0 Coins |
| $2,000-$3,500 | $5,000-$10,000 | -- | -- |

*Note:* The conclusions presented in the following "Collecting and Investing Strategies" section are drawn in large part from the Investment Potential

Ratios that are summarized in Appendices G and H at the end of this book. For a detailed analysis of the formula used to derive these Investment Potential Ratios, please refer to the Introduction of this book.

**Collecting and Investing Strategies:** This issue offers sold value for the money at the MS-65 and MS-67 grade levels, and it is actually an underrated P-mint Barber Dime in MS-64 and MS-66. These facts suggest that a high-grade 1894 could prove to be a valuable asset to a numismatic portfolio.

On the other hand, the time and patience required to locate an attractive, high-grade 1894 Barber Dime might surprise you. With that in mind, there are a few things you should consider before you begin your search for a suitable 1894 Barber Dime to add to your holdings. First, be sure to check current auction prices realized records before buying an example in order to determine what you will really need to pay for a PCGS or NGC-certified coin. I have found that some price guides (including the Coin Dealer Newsletter—CDN, commonly referred to as The Greysheet) can be grossly underpriced for this issue in grades such as MS-65.

Second, be prepared to pass over many unattractively toned coins. This is definitely one issue in the Barber Dime series for which I recommend purchasing an example that has been dipped by a numismatic expert and subsequently certified by PCGS or NGC. Coins that have been treated in that manner are much more desirable than the typically encountered toned piece with dark and/or splotchy colors on the surfaces. In fact, most dipped MS-65s and MS-66s that I have seen are highly desirable with radiant surfaces that allow ready appreciation of strong luster and sharp striking detail.

Third, steel yourself for a long search and do not give into frustration. Just keep searching and remind yourself that an attractive, high-grade example of this issue will eventually become available.

Finally, it is probably a good idea to set aside sufficient funds to purchase an 1894 when the right piece appears in the market. There is nothing worse for the collector than spending their precious monetary resources on more plentiful coins only to be caught with empty pockets when that scarcer, highly desirable piece suddenly becomes available.

# 1894-O

## MINTAGE
720,000

Courtesy of David Lawrence

## RARITY RANKINGS

**Overall, Mint State:** *2nd of 74*
**High Grade, MS-65 or Finer:** *1st of 74*

### NEW ORLEANS MINT ISSUES

**Overall, Mint State:** *2nd of 17*
**High Grade, MS-65 or Finer:** *1st of 17*

**Important Varieties:** None.

**General Comments:** An undisputed key-date issue in the Barber Dime series, the 1894-O is the rarest business strike Barber Dime in Mint State after only the 1895-O. It is actually rarer than the 1895-O in high grades, and the 1894-O is actually the rarest business strike Barber Dime at and above the MS-65 grade level. The mintage for the 1894-O is a scant 720,000 pieces, and the contemporary public obviously prevented very few of those coins from entering circulation. Gems in MS-65 and MS-66 are particularly elusive, and the issue is all but unknown as a Superb Gem.

**Strike:** The 1894-O has a similar quality of strike to the 1892-O, which means that it is better produced than the 1893-O. Most examples are sharply impressed and, if present at all, lack of detail is usually trivial and confined to the finer elements of the haircurls over Liberty's brow and/or the lower-left portion of the reverse wreath.

**Luster:** Luster is not a strong suit for this issue, and the typical example is somewhat subdued with either a satin or softly frosted texture to the surfaces.

Coins that are vibrantly lustrous are distinctly in the minority among Mint State 1894-O Dimes.

**Surfaces:** The 1894-O is almost always offered with a least one or two noticeable abrasions. This fact even applies to most of the MS-65s and MS-66s that have been certified by PCGS and NGC.

**Toning:** Many Mint State examples have been dipped, and it is becoming increasingly difficult to locate an 1894-O Dime with fully original surfaces. On the positive side, the toned coins that I have seen tend to be fairly attractive. Such pieces, while usually fairly dark, often include more vivid colors, if only around the peripheries. Additionally, the toning that is typically encountered for this issue is seldom as splotchy as that seen, say, on most Mint State examples of the 1894-P.

**Eye Appeal:** The 1894-O has below-average eye appeal, a rating that I attribute predominantly to inferior luster and the difficulty of locating a truly distraction-free example.

### Significant Examples:

**1. NGC MS-67.** *Ex: CSNS Signature Auction (Heritage, 5/2005), lot 6604, where it realized $31,050.*

**2. PCGS MS-66.** *Ex: The Collections of Phillip Flanagan, Dr. Robert I. Hinkley, Dr. John C. Wong and Tree Many Feathers (Bowers and Merena, 11/2001), lot 6164, where it realized $8,625; The Frog Run Farm Collection (American Numismatic Rarities, 11/2004), lot 650, where it realized $16,100; The Collection of Dr. Steven L. Duckor (Heritage, 1/2006), lot 977, where it realized $17,250.*

**3. PCGS MS-66.** *Ex: The Robert W. Miller, Sr. Collection (Bowers and Merena, 11/1992), lot 1280, where it realized $6,600; Long Beach Signature Sale (Heritage, 6/2000), lot 7128, where it realized $10,063; The John C. Hugon Collection (Heritage, 1/2005), lot 4008, where it realized $20,700.*

**4. NGC MS-65.** *Ex: San Francisco, CA ANA Signature Auction (Heritage, 7/2005), lot 101059, where it realized $10,925; The Southwest Collection (Heritage, 2/2008), lot 147, where it realized $13,800.*

**5. PCGS MS-65.** *Ex: Palm Beach, FL Signature Auction (Heritage, 3/2006), lot 474, where it realized $14,950.*

**6. NGC MS-65.** *Ex: Portland ANA Signature Sale (Heritage, 8/1998), lot 6368, where it realized $9,200.*

**Total Known in Mint State:** 40-55 Coins

### Total Known and Value Breakdown by Grade:

| MS-60-62 | MS-63 | MS-64 | MS-65 |
|---|---|---|---|
| 11-14 Coins | 13-17 Coins | 11-14 Coins | 3 Coins |
| N/A | $2,000-$3,000 | $5,000-$7,500 | $12,500-$15,000 |

| MS-66 | MS-67 | MS-68 | MS-69-70 |
|---|---|---|---|
| 4-6 Coins | 1 Coin | 0 Coins | 0 Coins |
| $20,000-$35,000 | $40,000-$50,000 | -- | -- |

*Note:* The conclusions presented in the following "Collecting and Investing Strategies" section are drawn in large part from the Investment Potential Ratios that are summarized in Appendices G and H at the end of this book. For a detailed analysis of the formula used to derive these Investment Potential Ratios, please refer to the Introduction of this book.

**Collecting and Investing Strategies:** As a leading rarity in the Barber Dime series, the 1894-O has long enjoyed strong numismatic demand in both circulated and Mint State grades. I do not believe that the 1894-O is a good buy in MS-64, MS-66 or MS-67, however, as my research indicates that the issue is overvalued in those grades. Only in MS-65 do I recommend this issue for inclusion in a numismatic portfolio. In that grade the 1894-O is actually the most underrated Barber Dime after only the 1903-S and 1907-S.

With so few MS-65s from which to choose, I do not advise being overly selective when it comes to the 1894-O. Even the leading third-party grading services have relaxed their standards for this issue, as evidenced by the presence of noticeable abrasions on several of the MS-65s and MS-66s that I have seen in PCGS and NGC holders. Just try to find a coin that is not overly abraded for the assigned grade, and make sure there is at least some "flash" to the luster. Neither strike nor toning should pose significant impediments to locating an attractive piece.

# Proof
# 1894-S

## MINTAGE
## 24

Courtesy of David Lawrence

## RARITY
## RANKINGS

*Overall, All Proof Grades:* 1st of 25
*High Grade, Proof-65 or Finer:* 1st of 25
*Cameo Finish:* Unknown
*Deep/Ultra Cameo Finish:* Unknown

**Important Varieties:** None.

**General Comments:** With an original mintage of just 24 coins and a surviving population of only nine positively confirmed specimens, the 1894-S is the single-rarest issue in the entire Barber Dime series of 1892-1916. It is also one of the most famous and eagerly sought rarities in all of numismatics, being ranked sixth in the 2005 book *100 Greatest U.S. Coins* by Jeff Garrett and Ron Guth. The 1894-S enjoys a reputation that is equal to or nearly on par with those of other classic U.S. coin rarities such as the 1913 Liberty Nickel, 1876-CC Twenty-Cent piece, 1804 Silver Dollar, 1884 and 1885 Trade Dollars and the 1822 Half Eagle.

Unlike several of the other numismatic luminaries on the aforementioned list, the 1894-S is an official Mint issue that was listed in the Mint Director's report for that year. Even so, the "why" of the 1894-S has long been debated by numismatic scholars. Indeed, there are very few hard facts surrounding the 1894-S Barber Dime, and much of what has been written about these coins over the years is assumption based on rumor, hearsay or what professional numismatists call "traditional numismatic wisdom." All we know about the 1894-S Barber Dime from records and documents that have survived to the present day is that 24 examples were struck in the San Francisco Mint on June

9, 1894 and that five of those coins were reserved for assay purposes. Those five coins are presumed to have been destroyed as part of the assay process, leaving a net mintage after melting of no more than 19 pieces.

The surviving coins themselves also tell us that, despite what many numismatists have come to accept as fact, the 1894-S Dimes are not true proofs. The examples that I have seen lack the depth of mirrors in the fields that is customary for contemporary proof coins struck in the Philadelphia Mint. Most also lack 100% full striking definition, even if only at the denticles on one or both sides of the coin. In my opinion, the 1894-S Barber Dimes are semi-to-fully prooflike business strikes, the limited press run imparting more-or-less superior workmanship to most (but not all!) of the known examples. Although some numismatic scholars have chosen to describe the 1894-S Barber Dime as a "presentation" or "specimen" striking, I hesitate to assign such a classification to this issue without hard evidence confirming that these coins were indeed made for presentation purposes.

On the other hand, numismatic tradition has it that the 1894-S is one of a select group of branch mint proof coins attributable to the San Francisco Mint. In deference to that tradition—which is also honored by PCGS and NGC, both services of which certify unimpaired 1894-S Dimes as proofs—and because the term has become sort of an honorary title for this issue, I have chosen to refer to the 1894-S Barber Dime as a branch mint proof throughout this book.

It is beyond the scope of this study to provide detailed analyses and critical commentary on the various theories that have been put forth to explain both the existence and extreme rarity of this issue. I will say, however, that the 1894-S Barber Dime was probably struck in such limited numbers for one of two reasons. These specimens could have been made to round out the total dollar value of silver coins struck in the San Francisco Mint during fiscal-year 1894. (Archival evidence put forth by Kevin Flynn in the 2005 book *The 1894-S Dime: A Mystery Unraveled* seems to support this theory.) Employees at the San Francisco Mint undoubtedly believed that they would be called upon to strike additional 1894-S Dimes during the latter half of that year, thereby precluding this issue from developing into a low-mintage rarity. When the anticipated orders did not arrive, however, the 24 coins struck turned out to be the entire mintage for this issue.

It is also possible, although less likely, that the 1894-S Barber Dimes were struck for presentation purposes at the request of former Superintendent of the San Francisco Mint John Daggett. As previously stated, however, there is no evidence that any of the 1894-S Barber Dimes were prepared for presentation purposes. The fact that two of the known examples are heavily circulated suggests that at least some of these coins were paid out through the cashier at the San Francisco Mint—an unlikely scenario had this issue been prepared for presentation or other special purposes.

In all likelihood, the full story of the 1894-S Barber Dime will never be known. This is hardly a detriment to the issue, however, as its extreme rarity and instant recognition even among more casual collectors guarantees that the 1894-S Barber Dime will remain as one of the most eagerly sought coins in all of U.S history.

**Strike:** Most high-grade examples present as sharply struck to the unaided eye, although close examination often reveals some minor lack of detail over either the highest elements of the obverse portrait or in isolated peripheral areas on one or both sides. The Norweb Specimen (see below) is very softly struck over the top of Liberty's brow on the obverse and, more significantly, on the reverse over the left half of the wreath.

**Finish:** The 1894-S usually exhibits some reflective tendencies to the surfaces, although the finish is not as deeply mirrored as you should expect to see in a proof Barber Dime struck in the Philadelphia Mint.

**Surfaces:** The nine examples known range from heavily worn to virtually pristine.

**Toning:** Most of the known examples display some degree of toning, and several are quite deeply patinated. At least one example has reportedly been dipped several times.

**Eye Appeal:** Assigning an eye appeal rating to an issue with only nine specimens known is a moot point since the rarity of these coins ensures that each example enjoys extremely strong demand in numismatic circles. I will say, however, that most of the high-grade pieces are genuinely attractive coins relatively sharp striking detail, original toning and no notable blemishes.

**Significant Examples:** Due to the extreme rarity and importance of the 1894-S, I have decided to depart from my normal standard of listing auction appearances for a handful of the finest-known examples. Instead, what follows are complete pedigrees for all nine examples that are positively confirmed to exist. (Additional "examples" that have appeared in numismatic literature over the years but are either unverified or confirmed as non-genuine are listed in the following section.) The foundation of this Census listing is credited to Heritage Auction Galleries' FUN Signature Sale of January 2005, lot 30164, David Lawrence's sale of the Richmond Collection, March 2005, lot 1295 and Stack's 72nd Anniversary Sale of October 2007, lot 4921. I have made additions, deletions and corrections to the rosters provided in those three catalogs in order to provide a single roster that is as up-to-date and accurate as possible as of the printing of this book.

**1. PCGS Proof-66.** *The James Stack Specimen. Ex: J.M. Clapp (acquired circa 1900); John H. Clapp; Clapp estate; Stack's (1942); Louis E. Eliasberg, Sr.; The H.R. Lee Collection Sale (Stack's, 10/1947), lot 348, where it realized $2,150; The James A. Stack, Sr. Collection Sale (Stack's, 1/1990), lot 206, where it realized $275,000; Jay Parrino; David Lawrence Rare Coins (12/1998), sold to the following for $825,000; Bradley Hirst; The Richmond Collection (David Lawrence, 3/2005), lot 1295, where it realized $1,322,500; Dan Rosenthal, owner of the "Just Having Fun Collection;" private investor (7/2007), via a private treaty sale for $1,900,000 brokered by Mitchell Spivack and David Lawrence Rare Coins. This is the plate coin on page 19 of the 2005 book* 100 Greatest U.S. Coins *by Jeff Garrett and Ron Guth, as well as on the website www.CoinFacts.com.*

*Pedigree Marker(s): A contact mark or planchet flaw is present in the right-obverse field below the letters ME in AMERICA.*

For many years, this coin was listed as two different specimens in the roster of known 1894-S Barber Dimes. (See, for example, the pedigree listings in the 1977 book *Walter Breen's Encyclopedia of United States and Colonial Proof Coins: 1722-1977*, where this coin is listed as both the #3 and #4 specimens.) I believe that the confusion surrounding this coin's pedigree first arose in Stack's cataloging of the 1947 H.R. Lee Collection Sale, which included duplicates from the collection of Louis E. Eliasberg, Sr. This catalog strongly implies that the coin in the H.R. Lee Collection Sale is different from the two specimens from the Clapp Collection that had since been acquired by Louis E. Eliasberg, Sr.

In their cataloging for the 1957 Empire Collection sale Stack's also asserts that the H.R. Lee specimen is different from the Clapp/Eliasberg duplicate that eventually went to James A. Stack. Sr. In their 1990 sale of the James A. Stack, Sr. Collection, however, Stack's corrected this error and stated unequivocally that the buyer of the Eliasberg duplicate out of the H.R. Lee Collection sale was indeed James A. Stack. Plate matching between the H.R. Lee specimen and the James A. Stack specimen confirms that they are indeed the same coin.

**2. PCGS Proof-65.** *The Daggett-Lawrence Specimen. Ex: John Daggett; Hallie Daggett; Earl Parker; James Johnson; Abner Kreisberg; World-Wide Coin Co.; Rare Coin Review No. 21 (Bowers and Ruddy, 9-10/1974), at $97,500; John Deland; Orlando Sale (Superior, 8/1992), lot 104, where it realized $165,000; Spectrum Numismatics; David Lawrence Rare Coins and David Schweitz Coins (10/2002), at which* *time it was renamed the Daggett-Lawrence Specimen in memory of David Lawrence Feigenbaum; FUN Signature Sale (Heritage, 1/2005), lot 30164, where it realized $1,035,000. This is the plate coin on page 237 of the 1977 book* Walter Breen's Encyclopedia of United States and Colonial Proof Coins: 1722-1977 *and on page 323 of the 1988 book* Walter Breen's Complete Encyclopedia of U.S. and Colonial Coins.

*Pedigree Marker(s): There is a prominent planchet flaw is present in the obverse field between the letter D in UNITED and the back of Liberty's head, and another planchet flaw is evident at the lower-reverse rim below the left side of the S mintmark.*

*While there is also a prominent lintmark in the obverse field above Liberty's portrait, that feature cannot be used for pedigree purposes because the Gillespie Specimen (see below) also exhibits a prominent lintmark in the same area.*

The pedigree for this coin has long been agreed upon by most numismatic researchers.

**3. Proof-65.** *The Eliasberg Specimen. Ex: J.M. Clapp (acquired circa 1900); John H. Clapp; Clapp estate; Stack's (1942); The Louis E. Eliasberg, Sr. Collection (Bowers and Merena, 5/1996), lot 1250, where it realized $451,000; Harvey Stack; private collector.*

*Pedigree Marker(s): A lintmark is present in the obverse field between Liberty's chin and neck.*

The pedigree for this coin has long been agreed upon by most numismatic researchers.

**4. PCGS Proof-64.** *The Gillespie Specimen. Ex: The Dr. Samuel Joseph Gillespie Sale/Long Beach Auction (Art Kagin, 10/1984), lot 4176; Kagin's; private collector (1985); 72nd Anniversary Sale (Stack's, 10/2007), lot 4921, where it realized $1,552,500.*

*Pedigree Marker(s): A tiny carbon spot is present in the obverse field at the bottom rear of Liberty's neck and what appears to be either a planchet flaw or a toning spot protrudes into the obverse field from the left side of the I in UNITED just below the midpoint of that letter.*

When this coin was offered as part of Kagin's 1984 Dr. Samuel Joseph Gillespie Sale, it was erroneously pedigreed as the Daggett-Lawrence specimen. I believe that the cataloger made this mistake because both coins share a few similar as-struck pedigree markers, most noticeably a lintmark in the obverse field above Liberty's portrait. Plate matching of other pedigree markers shows that the two coins are different examples, however, but the lintmark does suggest that the two pieces were produced during the same press run. A small piece of lint probably adhered to the die and imparted the same lintmark to at least two examples of the 1894-S Barber Dime.

The pedigree of this coin prior to its appearance in the Dr. Samuel Joseph Gillespie Sale is unknown. It could be the Chicago Specimen listed below, although there are a number of problems with linking these two pedigrees apart from the fact that there is no solid evidence for doing so. A more detailed analysis of the Chicago Specimen and the problems associated with linking these two pedigrees can be found below under my discussion of that piece.

**5. NGC Proof-62.** *The Norweb Specimen. Ex: Dr. Charles Cass; The Empire Collection (Stack's, 1957), lot 881, where it realized $4,750; Empire Coin Company (1958); Mrs. R. Henry Norweb; The Norweb Collection (Bowers and Merena, 10/1987), lot 584, where it realized $77,000; Allen F. Lovejoy; The Allen F. Lovejoy Reference Collection of United States Dimes: 1792-1945 (Stack's, 10/1990), lot 504, where it realized $93,500; RARCOA (1991); Charles Litman of Coin Exchange in Pittsburgh, Pennsylvania.*

*Pedigree Marker(s): There is a horizontal scratch across Liberty's cheek and the large leaf in the lower-left reverse wreath is bluntly struck.*

The pedigree for this coin has long been agreed upon by most numismatic researchers.

**6. Proof-60.** *The Newcomer Specimen. Ex: Waldo C. Newcomer; B. Max Mehl (1933); F.C.C. Boyd; The World's Greatest Collection (Numismatic Gallery, 5/1945), lot 756, where it realized $2,350; The Will W. Neil Collection (B. Max Mehl, 6/1947), lot 1433, where it realized $2,325; The Edwin M. Hydeman Collection (Abe Kosoff, 3/1961), lot 387, where it realized $13,000; Empire Coin Company; Hazen Hinman; The Century Collection (Paramount, 4/1965), lot 724, where it realized $12,250; Leo A. Young; Auction '80 (RARCOA's session, 7/1980), lot 1578, where it realized $145,000; Gary L. Young; Ron Gillio; Pacific Coast Auctions' sale of 9/1986, lot 110, where it realized $91,300; private collector.*

*Pedigree Marker(s): What appear to be planchet flaws, toning streaks or lintmarks are present at the reverse at the rim between the tops of the wreath, as well as near the lower-left side of the letter O in ONE. The image of this coin in the Auction '80 catalog also shows a prominent obverse spot at the rear of Liberty's jaw, but this feature is not present in the images used in the World's Greatest Collection and*

*Will W. Neil Collection catalogs.*

*It is also important to note that the image in the Edwin M. Hydeman Collection catalog cannot be used for confirming the pedigree of this piece. The image that Abe Kosoff used in that catalog is the same that he used earlier in the catalog for the 1950 Adolphe Menjou Collection, even though he clearly states in his cataloging that the two coins are different examples.*

The pedigree for this coin has long been agreed upon by most numismatic researchers.

**7. Proof, Impaired.** *The Dr. Jerry Buss Specimen. Ex: John Daggett; Hallie Daggett; Earl Parker; James Kelly; Malcolm Chell-Frost; The F.S. Guggenheimer Collection (Stack's, 1/1953), lot 772, where it realized $2,100; 1973 MANA Sale/Sale of the '70s (Kagin's, 11/1973), lot 1114, where it realized $52,000; Superior Galleries (1978); The Dr. Jerry Buss Collection (Superior; 1/1985), lot 617, where it realized $50,600; Michelle Johnson, purchased for Robert Beaumont; The H.W. Blevins Estate and George Bodway Collections Sale (Superior, 6/1988), lot 4510, where it realized $70,400.*

*Pedigree Marker(s): A reverse planchet flaw obscures the lower-right side of the S mintmark and there are several scratches along the lower-reverse rim to the right of the mintmark.*

This coin is missing from some of the earliest-known pedigree listings of 1894-S Dimes, most significantly that compiled by James Johnson in 1972-1973 and reprinted in Bowers and Ruddy's Rare Coin Review No. 21 (9-10/1974).

**8. Good-4.** *The So-Called "Ice Cream" Specimen. Ex: Robert Friedberg (Gimbels Department Store, New York, 1957); Art Kagin; New Netherlands Coin Co.'s 51st Sale (6/1958), lot 581, where it realized $3,200; Art Kagin; Harmer Rooke's sale of 11/1969, where it realized $7,400; James G. Johnson; 1980 ANA Sale (Steve Ivy), lot 1804, where it realized $31,000; The William R. Sieck Collection (Bowers and Ruddy, 7-8/1981), lot 2921, where it realized $25,500; Four Landmark Collections (Bowers and Merena, 3/1989), lot 191, where it realized $33,000; private collector.*

*Pedigree Marker(s): There is a scratch on the reverse above and through the denomination ONE DIME.*

This is the example that, according to popular numismatic legend, Hallie Daggett used to buy ice cream. That story is neither positively confirmed nor definitively linked to this piece. Furthermore, and, as related below in my discussion of the Chicago Specimen, it is entirely possible that Hallie Daggett never actually spent one of her 1894-S Barber Dimes to buy ice cream but, instead, sold all three examples to California dealer Earl Parker in the late 1940s/early 1950s. Although this particular 1894-S could very well have been placed into circulation by someone else under entirely different circumstances, numismatic scholars continue to refer to this coin as Hallie Daggett's "Ice Cream" Specimen.

**9. NGC AG-3.** *The Romito Specimen. Ex: Romito (acquired 1911); Montesano; Stack's sale in 1942, withdrawn; unknown intermediaries; John Hipps; Laura Sperber (1990); private collector.*

*Pedigree Marker(s): A circular cut is present in the center of the obverse.*

The pedigree for this coin has long been agreed upon by most numismatic researchers.

**Unverified Examples:** A few additional 1894-S Barber Dimes have been reported over the years. Those "coins" are either non-genuine examples or they represent earlier pedigrees of one or more of the nine specimens that have been positively confirmed to exist as of the late 20th/early 21st centuries. These include:

**1.** *The Chicago Specimen. Ex: John Daggett; Hallie Daggett; Earl Parker; Dan Brown; Stack's; Chicago private collector.*

This coin may be the Gillespie Specimen listed above, although there are a number of problems with linking the two pedigrees apart from the fact that there is no solid evidence for doing so. If this earlier pedigree is also linked to the Gillespie Specimen, then the Chicago Specimen would be the third of three 1894-S Barber Dimes that Mint Superintendent John Daggett gave to his daughter Hallie. In order to credit this statement as fact, we must assume that Hallie Daggett DID NOT spend one of her 1894-S Dimes to buy ice cream, as popular numismatic legend has it, and that she later sold ALL THREE coins (and not just two examples) to California dealer Earl Parker. Unfortunately, the pedigree of the Gillespie Specimen prior to its appearance in the October 1984 Kagin's sale is unknown, there is no way to positively confirm the ice cream story and Hallie Daggett supposedly sold only two 1894-S Dimes to Earl Parker. Until such time that the Chicago Specimen can be either positively linked to one of the nine specimens listed above or is confirmed as a distinct coin, it must remain as an unverified or non-genuine example of the 1894-S Barber Dime.

**2. The Rappaport Specimen.** *Ex: Rappaport; Art Kagin; Reuter; Abner Kreisberg; Empire Coin Company, mentioned in an article in "Empire Topics," 1958, Issue No. 2; Pennsylvania estate.*

This coin is untraced as of the late 1950s. Even so, it has continued to appear in some pedigree listings at least as late as 2007, thereby explaining the mistaken belief in certain numismatic circles that there are 10 1894-S known to exist. Until such time that it is positively confirmed either as a different 1894-S Barber Dime or one of the nine specimens positively confirmed to exist, however, this pedigree must be considered as referring to an unverified example.

Several pedigree listings for 1894-S Barber Dimes state that this piece was offered in a 1958 Bowers and Ruddy Fixed Price List at $6,000. I believe that listing to be an erroneous entry that, instead, should refer to the aforementioned article in the 1958 issue of "Empire Topics."

Interestingly, the same "Empire Topics" article asserts that this coin was, "...originally sold to James Stack from the collection of John Clapp." That statement is false since James Stack acquired his 1894-S Dime from Stack's 1947 sale of the H.R. Lee Collection. The coin subsequently remained in his collection and, later, his estate until it was sold through auction in 1990.

**3. The Menjou Specimen.** *Ex: The Adolphe Menjou Collection (Numismatic Gallery, 1950), lot 311, where it sold for $1,850.*

This pedigree is often omitted from Census listings of 1894-S Barber Dimes. The reason for this seems to be the inability of numismatic researchers to determine exactly where this piece fits among the roster of known 1894-S Barber Dimes. The catalog description in the Menjou Sale does not provide any pedigree information, and the image in the catalog is of such poor quality that it is impossible to match this coin to any of the other known specimens. Further muddying the waters is the fact that Abe Kosoff recycled the image of the 1894-S Dime from the 1950 Menjou Sale catalog for use in his sale of the Edwin M. Hydeman Collection in March of 1961, this despite the fact that Kosoff himself knew that the two coins were different examples.

In his cataloging for the Menjou Collection, Kosoff states that this coin is not the same coin that Will W. Neil purchased from the World's Greatest Collection sale, meaning that it is not the Newcomer Specimen. This coin also cannot be the James Stack Specimen or the Eliasberg Specimen since both of those pieces were already part of tightly held collection at the time of the 1950 Menjou Sale. It is also probably not the Dr. Jerry Buss Specimen since the earlier appearance of that coin in the

F.S. Guggenheimer Collection was accompanied by a detailed pedigree of the piece through 1953. That pedigree does not include mention of the Menjou Collection sale. And of course, the Menjou Specimen cannot be either the "Ice Cream" or Romito specimens, both of which are heavily worn.

On the other hand, the 1894-S Dime in the Menjou Collection sale could represent an earlier appearance of the Daggett-Lawrence Specimen, the Gillespie Specimen or the Norweb Specimen. It could also be the Chicago Specimen or the Rappaport Specimen, both of which are unconfirmed as of the writing of this book. Finally, I cannot rule out the possibility that the Menjou Specimen may be a completely different example of the 1894-S Dime that has been untraced since the 1950s.

**Non-Genuine Example:** This pedigree has been positively confirmed as erroneous and does not represent another 1894-S Dime.

**1.** ***The Mitchelson Specimen.*** *Ex: J.C. Mitchelson; Connecticut State Library.*

This listing is erroneous, and it is based on a report in the June 1900 edition of The Numismatist in which George Heath states that Mitchelson supposedly located an 1894-S Barber Dime in San Francisco around that time. Walter Breen erroneously pedigreed this coin as going to the Connecticut State Library along with the rest of the Mitchelson Collection. According to Heritage's January 2005 FUN Signature Sale catalog, however, numismatic researcher Phil Carrigan has confirmed that the Connecticut State Library does not own an example of the 1894-S Barber Dime.

**Total Known:** 9 Coins

**Total Known and Value Breakdown by Grade:**

| Brilliant-Finish Coins | | | |
|---|---|---|---|
| **Proof-60-62** | **Proof-63** | **Proof-64** | **Proof-65** |
| 3 Coins | 0 Coins | 1 Coin | 2 Coins |
| N/A | -- | $1,500,000-$2,000,000 | $2,000,000-$2,500,000 |
| **Proof-66** | **Proof-67** | **Proof-68** | **Proof-69-70** |
| 1 Coin | 0 Coins | 0 Coins | 0 Coins |
| $2,000,000-$2,500,000 | -- | -- | -- |

| Cameo Coins | | | |
|---|---|---|---|
| **Proof-60-62 Cameo** | **Proof-63 Cameo** | **Proof-64 Cameo** | **Proof-65 Cameo** |
| 0 Coins | 0 Coins | 0 Coins | 0 Coins |
| -- | -- | -- | -- |
| **Proof-66 Cameo** | **Proof-67 Cameo** | **Proof-68 Cameo** | **Proof-69-70 Cameo** |
| 0 Coins | 0 Coins | 0 Coins | 0 Coins |
| -- | -- | -- | -- |

| | | | |
|---|---|---|---|
| **Proof-60-62 Deep/ Ultra Cameo** | **Proof-63 Deep/ Ultra Cameo** | **Proof-64 Deep/ Ultra Cameo** | **Proof-65 Deep/ Ultra Cameo** |
| 0 Coins | 0 Coins | 0 Coins | 0 Coins |
| -- | -- | -- | -- |
| **Proof-66 Deep/ Ultra Cameo** | **Proof-67 Deep/ Ultra Cameo** | **Proof-68 Deep/ Ultra Cameo** | **Proof-69-70 Deep/ Ultra Cameo** |
| 0 Coins | 0 Coins | 0 Coins | 0 Coins |
| -- | -- | -- | -- |

**Collecting and Investing Strategies:** The 1894-S is a classic rarity in U.S. numismatics, and all specimens are extremely important coins that would serve as centerpieces in the finest collection or investment portfolio. The only advice I can offer regarding this issue concerns those pieces that have not been certified by PCGS or NGC. As the roster given above indicates, quite a few of the known specimens are Uncertified because they are currently untraced, impaired or because the current owner does not wish to have the pieces certified. Should you ever come across a buying opportunity for an Uncertified 1894-S Dime, therefore, make sure that the coin is being offered by a reputable dealer or auctioneer that guarantees the authenticity of the piece. It also cannot hurt to solicit the opinion of other numismatic professionals before acquiring such a piece, particularly if the coin is being offered for outright purchase (i.e., not through auction).

# Proof
# 1895

## MINTAGE
880

*Courtesy of David Lawrence*

## RARITY
## RANKINGS

***Overall, All Proof Grades:*** *24th of 25*
***High Grade, Proof-65 or Finer:*** *24th of 25*
***Overall, Cameo Finish:*** *18th of 24*
***Overall, Deep/Ultra Cameo Finish:*** *6th of 12 (Tie)*

**Important Varieties:** None.

**General Comments:** After only the 1894, the 1895 is the most plentiful issue in the proof Barber Dime series. Even so, the proof 1895 commands a premium in all grades because the business strike 1895 is a low-mintage issue with just 690,000 pieces produced. With a Cameo finish the proof 1895 is also among the more common issues of its type, although it is actually the second-rarest proof Barber Dime from the 1890s with that finish after the proof 1899 (discounting, of course, the proof 1894-S). Deep/Ultra Cameo examples are extremely rare and on par with those of the proof 1897.

**Strike:** As with the proof 1894, the proof 1895 almost always displays 100% full striking detail on both sides. Every once in a while, however, I encounter an example with slight softness of detail to the haircurls immediately above Liberty's brow on the obverse. Such lack of detail, when present at all, is minimal and anything but distracting to the eye.

**Finish:** The typical proof 1895 displays an all-brilliant finish with minimal, if any contrast between the fields and devices. Even many Cameo-designated pieces in PCGS and NGC holders that I have seen display only light, shallow mint frost to the devices. There are exceptions, of course, but very rare indeed is the proof 1894 with sharp enough contrast to qualify for a Deep/Ultra Cameo designation.

**Surfaces:** Most proof 1895 Dimes are well preserved with no more than a few wispy hairlines. Many examples are overall smooth, if not virtually pristine in outward appearance.

**Toning:** The majority of examples are toned, most quite deeply with dark, sometimes splotchy colors on one or both sides. The same coins, however, often exhibit vivid, more vibrant undertones that are best appreciated with the aid of a strong light source. Untoned pieces are generally the result of dipping, and they are usually quite attractive with bright surfaces and little to no haziness.

**Eye Appeal:** This issue has above-average eye appeal, although it is not as strong in this regard as the proof 1894. Dark, unsightly toning can be a problem for the proof 1895, but pieces that are free of that feature tend to be highly attractive with full striking detail and well-preserved surfaces.

### Significant Examples:

**1. NGC Proof-68.** *Ex: New York ANA Sale (Superior, 8/2002), lot 756, unsold; Pre-Long Beach Elite Coin Auction (Superior, 5/2004), lot 1260, where it realized $10,925; Dallas, TX Signature Auction (Heritage, 11/2005), lot 1050, unsold; FUN Signature Auction (Heritage, 1/2006), lot 1845, where it realized $9,775.*

**2. NGC Proof-68.** *Ex: Walter H. Childs, who is believed to have acquired the coin directly from the Philadelphia Mint in 1895; The Walter H. Childs Collection (Bowers and Merena, 8/1999), lot 214, where it realized $4,600; The John C. Hugon Collection (Heritage, 1/2005), lot 4079, where it realized $5,463.*

**3. NGC Proof-68 Cameo.** *Ex: The William H. LaBelle, Sr. Collection (American Numismatic Rarities, 7/2005), lot 101, where it realized $8,338.*

**4. NGC Proof-68 Cameo.** *Ex: The John F. Rindge and Alan J. Harlan Collections (Bowers and Merena, 12/2003), lot 1006, where it realized $6,613; Long Beach Signature Sale (Heritage, 6/2004), lot 6048, where it realized $6,613; New York, NY Signature Auction (Heritage, 6/2005), lot 5411, where it realized $5,463.*

**5. PCGS Proof-67 Cameo.** *Ex: Dallas Signature Coin Auction (Heritage, 10/2006), lot 772, where it realized $4,313; Long Beach, CA Signature Auction (Heritage, 5/2008), lot 149, where it realized $4,888.*

**6. NGC Proof-67 Cameo.** *Ex: The Greenhill Collection (Ira & Larry Goldberg, 9/2006), lot 1499, where it realized $2,703.*

**7. PCGS Proof-67 Cameo.** *Ex: Ft. Lauderdale Rarities Sale (Bowers and Merena, 1/2005), lot 1404, unsold; Baltimore Auction (Bowers and Merena, 2/2008), lot 2385, where it realized $4,600. The coin did not* *sell in the first-listed auction. It was then consigned to the February 2008 Baltimore Auction as part of a complete six-piece 1895 Proof Set. The coins were sold individually, however, thus dispersing the set.*

**8. NGC Proof-67 ★ Cameo.** *Ex: Baltimore Auction (Bowers and Merena, 11/2007), lot 821, where it realized $3,680.*

**9. NGC Proof-67 Cameo.** *Ex: Long Beach, CA Signature U.S. Coin Auction (Heritage, 5/2007), lot 739, where it realized $2,301.*

**10. NGC Proof-67 Ultra Cameo.** *Ex: The J.B. Worthington Collection (American Numismatic Rarities, 5/2005), lot 172, where it realized $2,760; CSNS Signature Coin Auction (Heritage, 4/2008), lot 643, where it realized $6,325.*

**Total Known:** 455-550 Coins

**Total Known and Value Breakdown by Grade:**

| Brilliant-Finish Coins | | | |
|---|---|---|---|
| **Proof-60-62** | **Proof-63** | **Proof-64** | **Proof-65** |
| 30-35 Coins | 60-70 Coins | 115-140 Coins | 85-100 Coins |
| N/A | $475-$575 | $800-$1,000 | $1,400-$1,600 |
| **Proof-66** | **Proof-67** | **Proof-68** | **Proof-69-70** |
| 60-70 Coins | 35-45 Coins | 4-6 Coins | 0 Coins |
| $1,600-$3,000 | $3,750-$5,000 | $7,500-$10,000 | -- |

| Cameo Coins | | | |
|---|---|---|---|
| **Proof-60-62 Cameo** | **Proof-63 Cameo** | **Proof-64 Cameo** | **Proof-65 Cameo** |
| 1 Coin | 1-2 Coins | 10-12 Coins | 15-20 Coins |
| N/A | $800-$1,000 | $1,200-$1,400 | $1,500-$1,750 |
| **Proof-66 Cameo** | **Proof-67 Cameo** | **Proof-68 Cameo** | **Proof-69-70 Cameo** |
| 20-25 Coins | 12-15 Coins | 3-4 Coins | 0 Coins |
| $2,000-$3,000 | $3,750-$5,000 | $8,000-$10,000 | -- |

| Deep/Ultra Cameo Coins | | | |
|---|---|---|---|
| **Proof-60-62 Deep/ Ultra Cameo** | **Proof-63 Deep/ Ultra Cameo** | **Proof-64 Deep/ Ultra Cameo** | **Proof-65 Deep/ Ultra Cameo** |
| 0 Coins | 0 Coins | 0 Coins | 0 Coins |
| -- | -- | -- | -- |
| **Proof-66 Deep/ Ultra Cameo** | **Proof-67 Deep/ Ultra Cameo** | **Proof-68 Deep/ Ultra Cameo** | **Proof-69-70 Deep/ Ultra Cameo** |
| 1-2 Coins | 2-3 Coins | 0 Coins | 0 Coins |
| $4,000-$6,000 | $6,000-$8,000 | -- | -- |

*Note:* The conclusions presented in the following "Collecting and Investing Strategies" section are drawn in large part from the Investment Potential Ratios that are summarized in Appendices G and H at the end of this book. For a detailed analysis of the formula used to derive these Investment Potential Ratios, please refer to the Introduction of this book.

**Collecting and Investing Strategies:** The 1895 is a poor choice for inclusion in either a proof type set or a numismatic investment portfolio comprised of a wide variety of coins. It is the most overrated proof Barber Dime in Proof-64, Proof-65 and Proof-66, and even Proof-67s are overvalued at the price levels reported in this book. The added premium that this issue carries is due to the low-mintage, key-date status of the business strike 1895. As such, I do not advise paying the premium for this issue unless you are assembling a date set of Barber Dimes and prefer proof coins to business strikes. Of course, collectors building complete set of proof Barber Dimes will also have to acquire an example of the 1895.

If you must or still choose to acquire a proof 1895 Barber Dime, beware of color photos in auction catalogs and on numismatic websites that display an example of this issue with vividly toned surfaces. While such pictures are almost always true to life, they often represent how the coin looks only when viewed under a strong light source. The same coin usually presents as much darker when the surfaces are turned away from a light. I suggest viewing any toned proof 1895 Barber Dime in person prior to making a purchase to be sure that you are comfortable with how the coin looks at all angles. In the same vein, I also suggest taking full advantage of any buying opportunity involving a proof 1895 Barber Dime with truly vivid toning. Such pieces are quite rare, and they are far more likely to draw the attention of future buyers than either a darkly toned coin or one that has been dipped to brilliance.

# 1895

## MINTAGE
690,000

Courtesy of David Lawrence

## RARITY RANKINGS

*Overall, Mint State: 29th of 74*
*High Grade, MS-65 or Finer: 25th of 74 (Tie)*

## PHILADELPHIA MINT ISSUES

*Overall, Mint State: 1st of 25*
*High Grade, MS-65 or Finer: 1st of 25*

**Important Varieties:** None.

**General Comments:** The 1895 is the lowest-mintage Barber Dime struck in the Philadelphia Mint, and the only one with a mintage of fewer than 1 million coins. This issue is the rarest P-mint Barber Dime in all Mint State grades, and it is also rarer than such mintmarked issues in this series as the 1893-S, 1906-D, 1906-S, 1908-O, and 1915-S, as well as the lower-mintage 1913-S.

**Strike:** This issue usually possesses full striking detail, and examples with less than sharp definition are rarely encountered in numismatic circles.

**Luster:** The 1895 almost always displays either a satiny or frosty finish from the dies. Both luster types are equally vibrant when offered in an example of this issue.

**Surfaces:** Like the 1894, the 1895 is a conditionally challenging issue that is remarkably challenging to locate with overall smooth, to say nothing of pristine-looking surfaces. The typical piece encountered in today's market is apt to display at least a few noticeable distractions. Fortunately, such abrasions tend to be small in size. Low-end Mint State coins are usually limited in grade by impaired luster, although I have seen quite a few BU-quality examples in MS-61 and MS-62 with scuffy surfaces.

**Toning:** The typical 1895 Barber Dime is toned to one degree or another. Toning for this issue ranges from mottled to even, vivid to quite dark. It is usually relatively pleasing, if not outright attractive. The handful of completely brilliant pieces that I have handled are dipped.

**Eye Appeal:** Eye appeal for the 1895 varies much more extensively than it does for, say, the 1894. Most low-end Mint State pieces that I have seen are unattractive, with subdued luster, splotchy toning and/or heavily abraded surfaces. Eye appeal tends to improve with grade, although dark, mottled toning can still be a problem even at the highest levels of Mint State preservation. Minimally abraded coins that grade MS-64 or finer are usually pleasing to the eye, especially if they are brilliant or possessed of attractive toning.

### Significant Examples:

**1. NGC MS-68.** *Ex: The John C. Hugon Collection (Heritage, 1/2005), lot 4009, where it realized $46,000; CSNS Signature Auction (Heritage, 5/2005), lot 6607, unsold; Dallas, TX Signature Auction (Heritage, 11/2005), lot 2074, unsold; Denver ANA Auction (Bowers and Merena, 8/2006), lot 751, unsold; FUN Signature Coin Auction (Heritage, 1/2007), lot 879, where it realized $37,375.*

**2. NGC MS-67.** *CAC. Ex: Denver, CO Signature & Platinum Night Auction (Heritage, 8/2006), lot 933, where it realized $16,100; Dallas Signature Coin Auction (Heritage, 10/2006), lot 753, unsold; Long Beach, CA Signature U.S. Coin Auction (Heritage, 5/2007), lot 705, unsold; Dallas, TX U.S. Coin Signature Auction (Heritage, 11/2007), lot 420, unsold; Phoenix, AZ ANA Signature Auction (Heritage, 3/2008), lot 417, where it realized $16,100.*

**3. PCGS MS-66.** *Ex: CSNS Signature Coin Auction (Heritage, 4/2008), lot 2268, where it realized $11,500.*

**4. PCGS MS-66.** *Ex: The Collection of Dr. Steven L. Duckor (Heritage, 1/2006), lot 978, where it realized $4,600.*

**5. PCGS MS-66.** *Ex: New York, NY Signature Sale (Heritage, 7/2004), lot 5811, unsold; Palm Beach, FL Signature Sale (Heritage, 11/2004), lot 6271, where it realized $4,025.*

**Total Known in Mint State:** 120-150 Coins

## Total Known and Value Breakdown by Grade:

| MS-60-62 | MS-63 | MS-64 | MS-65 |
|---|---|---|---|
| 25-30 Coins | 25-30 Coins | 45-55 Coins | 15-20 Coins |
| N/A | $800-$1,000 | $1,150-$1,350 | $2,000-$2,750 |

| MS-66 | MS-67 | MS-68 | MS-69-70 |
|---|---|---|---|
| 8-10 Coins | 3-4 Coins | 1 Coin | 0 Coins |
| $8,500-$15,000 | $15,000-$40,000 | $35,000-$45,000 | -- |

*Note:* The conclusions presented in the following "Collecting and Investing Strategies" section are drawn in large part from the Investment Potential Ratios that are summarized in Appendices G and H at the end of this book. For a detailed analysis of the formula used to derive these Investment Potential Ratios, please refer to the Introduction of this book.

**Collecting and Investing Strategies:** Among the finer Mint State grades, the only one that I recommend for the 1895 is MS-65. This issue is the most overrated Philadelphia Mint Barber Dime in MS-64, MS-66 and MS-67. MS-65s, on the other hand, are actually underrated relative to their true rarity, although even in that grade I would be very critical of any 1895 that you are contemplating adding to your collection or portfolio.

Avoid any Gem 1895 Barber Dime with dark and/or mottled toning because such coins are almost always difficult to sell and often trade at a discount. Also pay close attention to surface preservation as the difficulty of locating a truly high-quality 1895 means that "gradeflation" has become quite rampant for this issue at the higher levels of Mint State preservation. Make sure that the coin you are acquiring is accurately graded, which basically means to avoid any example that displays too many noticeable abrasions or is too subdued in the luster category for the grade assigned by PCGS or NGC.

# 1895-O

## MINTAGE
440,000

Courtesy of Bowers and Merena

## RARITY RANKINGS

*Overall, Mint State: 1st of 74*
*High Grade, MS-65 or Finer: 5th of 74*

## NEW ORLEANS MINT ISSUES

*Overall, Mint State: 1st of 17*
*High Grade, MS-65 or Finer: 3rd of 17*

**Important Varieties:** None.

**General Comments:** The 1895-O is the prime rarity in the Barber Dime series in Mint State. The vast majority of coins that have been submitted to PCGS and NGC for third-party certification are circulated, and even a BU-quality example in MS-60 or MS-61 represents an important buying opportunity in today's market. On the other hand, the 1895-O is not the rarest Barber Dime at or above the MS-65 grade level. In high grades, in fact, the 1894-O, 1895-S, 1902-O and 1907-S are all rarer than the 1895-O. When viewed in the wider context of the numismatic market, of course, a Gem 1895-O Barber Dime in MS-65 and MS-66 is still a very rare coin. Superb Gems are unknown.

**Strike:** The 1895-O Dime is remarkably well produced for a New Orleans Mint Barber coin, and it is superior to the 1892-O and 1894-O (to say nothing of the 1893-O) in this regard. Most examples are actually quite sharp, although the reverse is sometimes a bit unevenly impressed with minor lack of detail confined to the lower-left or upper-right portion of the wreath. Trivial lack of detail to the haircurls over Liberty's brow on the obverse is not seen all that often.

**Luster:** This issue is slightly better off than the 1894-O in the area of luster quality. Mint State coins that grade MS-64 or finer tend to be fairly vibrant with either a satin or softly frosted texture to the surfaces.

**Surfaces:** Excessive abrasions are seldom a problem for this issue, and most Mint State survivors are actually overall smooth. Subdued or lackluster surfaces, rather than numerous and/or large-size abrasions, are usually the culprits for an Uncirculated example grading lower than MS-63 when submitted to PCGS or NGC.

**Toning:** Dipped examples with brilliant or minimally patinated surfaces are nearly as prevalent as coins that retain fully original toning to both sides. Most coins that have survived with completely original surfaces are richly toned throughout, the colors tending more toward deeper, less vibrant shades. Vivid colors are rarely, if ever seen on originally toned 1895-O Dimes.

**Eye Appeal:** For an O-mint Barber Dime that is so rare in Mint State, the 1895-O has surprisingly strong eye appeal. Most Uncirculated survivors are quite well preserved, and the luster tends to be relatively vibrant by the standards of the issuing Mint. Toning, while seldom vivid, is usually more-or-less even and often provides a handsome, antique appearance to the surfaces.

**Significant Examples:**

**1. PCGS MS-66.** *Ex: Denver, CO Signature & Platinum Night Auction (Heritage, 8/2006), lot 5146, where it realized $52,900.*

**2. PCGS MS-66.** *Ex: The Kennywood Collection (American Numismatic Rarities, 1/2005), lot 389, where it realized $41,400.*

**3. PCGS MS-65.** *Ex: The Official Auction of the ANA Las Vegas Coin Show (Bowers and Merena, 10/2005), lot 5417, where it realized $33,350; Long Beach Signature Auction (Heritage, 2/2006), lot 784, unsold.*

**4. PCGS MS-65.** *Ex: The Collection of Dr. Steven L. Duckor (Heritage, 1/2006), lot 979, where it realized $20,700.*

**5. PCGS MS-65.** *Ex: Dallas, TX Signature Auction (Heritage, 11/2005), lot 2075, where it realized $27,600.*

**6. PCGS MS-65.** *Ex: The William H. LaBelle, Sr. Collection (American Numismatic Rarities, 7/2005), lot 1013, where it realized $26,450.*

**7. PCGS MS-65.** *Ex: The John C. Hugon Collection (Heritage, 1/2005), lot 4010, where it realized $29,900.*

**8. NGC MS-65.** *Ex: The Charles S. Mamiye Collection (Bowers and Merena, 3/1998), lot 574, where it realized $7,040; FUN Signature Sale (Heritage, 1/1999), lot 6457, where it realized $10,350.*

**9. PCGS MS-65.** *Auction '89 (RARCOA's session, 7/1989), lot 115 where it realized $7,150.*

**Total Known in Mint State:** 40-50 Coins

**Total Known and Value Breakdown by Grade:**

| MS-60-62 | MS-63 | MS-64 | MS-65 |
|---|---|---|---|
| 10-12 Coins | 8-10 Coins | 10-12 Coins | 11-14 Coins |
| N/A | $6,000-$8,000 | $10,000-$15,000 | $20,000-$35,000 |

| MS-66 | MS-67 | MS-68 | MS-69-70 |
|---|---|---|---|
| 2-3 Coins | 0 Coins | 0 Coins | 0 Coins |
| $40,000-$75,000 | -- | -- | -- |

*Note:* The conclusions presented in the following "Collecting and Investing Strategies" section are drawn in large part from the Investment Potential Ratios that are summarized in Appendices G and H at the end of this book. For a detailed analysis of the formula used to derive these Investment Potential Ratios, please refer to the Introduction of this book.

**Collecting and Investing Strategies:** The 1895-O is the most overrated and, hence, overvalued Barber Dime in all Mint State grades from MS-64 through MS-66. This is perhaps understandable since the overall rarity of the issue even in circulated grades ensures that high-quality survivors command a strong premium in the market. Even so, I would not acquire a Mint State example of the 1895-O unless you are assembling a complete set of Barber Dimes. The prices that Choice and Gem-quality pieces demand from buyers are just too high in relation to the issue's actual rarity in those grades.

There is good news, however, for those collectors that either must purchase a Mint State 1895-O or choose to do so for any reason. This issue is generally well produced, and most examples are nicely preserved with a relative lack of overly distracting abrasions. Regardless of exactly which Mint State grade you choose to pursue, the first or second buying opportunity that comes your way will probably be for a more-or-less attractive coin. And if you are assembling a complete set of Barber Dimes, I would definitely not pass up more than one or two examples of the 1895-O before making a purchase. The rarity and key-date status of this issue is well known even among less specialized collectors, and Mint State examples seldom remain on the open market for long.

# 1895-S

**MINTAGE**
1,120,000

Courtesy of David Lawrence

## RARITY RANKINGS

*Overall, Mint State: 26th of 74*
*High Grade, MS-65 or Finer: 2nd of 74*

### SAN FRANCISCO MINT ISSUES

*Overall, Mint State: 13th of 24*
*High Grade, MS-65 or Finer: 1st of 24*

**Important Varieties:** There is a Repunched Date variety for the 1895-S, and it is attributed alternately as FS-301, FS-009.2, Lawrence-101 and Breen-3495.

**General Comments:** The 1895-S is one of the most interesting Barber Dimes in terms of overall and high-grade rarity rankings. An original mintage of 1.1 million pieces, while certainly limited in the context of this series, was sufficient enough to ensure the survival of a fair number of Mint State coins. This is also despite the fact that the lack of a business strike 1894-S issue should have resulted in strong demand for the 1895-S in commerce. Nevertheless, the 1895-S is only a median rarity in the S-mint Barber Dime series in terms of total number of Mint State coins believed to exist. It is rarer in Mint State than the low-mintage 1913-S and 1915-S, however, as well as the more heavily circulated 1893-S and 1899-S.

In high grades (read: MS-65 or finer), the relative ranking of the 1895-S changes dramatically. The 1895-S is actually the rarest San Francisco Mint Barber Dime in Gem Mint State, and it is also the rarest coin of this type in high grades after only the 1894-O. This issue is unknown any finer than MS-66.

**Strike:** The 1895-S is a well-struck issue that almost always displays sharp-to-full definition throughout.

**Luster:** As with the other S-mint Barber Dimes from the 1890s, the 1895-S has excellent luster quality. Most examples that I have seen possess a vibrant mint finish that is either satiny or semi-prooflike in sheen.

**Surfaces:** This issue almost always displays at least a few scattered abrasions. Even with overall smooth-looking surfaces, the 1895-S is much more similar in rarity to the 1893-O, 1894-O and even the key-date 1895-O than it is to the 1892-S or 1893-S.

**Toning:** This early-date Barber Dime is almost always offered with at least some degree of toning, and most examples actually display moderate-to-deep patination. Relatively few pieces that I have seen are dipped, and even such coins tend to retain at least faint remnants of the original toning.

**Eye Appeal:** The 1895-S is a generally attractive issue, although some of the toned pieces possess dark and/or mottled patina. Strike and luster are definitely strong suits for this issue, while scattered abrasions, although almost always present, tend to be small in size and singularly inconspicuous, if only on coins that grade MS-64 or finer.

### Significant Examples:

**1. PCGS MS-66.** *Ex: The Lindesmith Collection (Bowers and Merena, 3/2000), lot 398, where it realized $6,325; The Collection of Dr. Steven L. Duckor (Heritage, 1/2006), lot 980, where it realized $14,950.*

**2. NGC MS-65.** *Ex: Long Beach, CA Signature Coin Auction (Heritage, 2/2008), lot 149, where it realized $5,750.*

**3. PCGS MS-65.** *Ex: FUN Signature Coin Auction (Heritage, 1/2008), lot 1027, where it realized $5,750.*

**4. PCGS MS-65.** *Ex: The John C. Hugon Collection (Heritage, 1/2005), lot 4011, where it realized $6,325.*

**5. NGC MS-65.** *Ex: New York ANA Sale (Superior, 8/2002), lot 757, unsold.*

**6. NGC MS-65.** *Ex: Denver ANA Signature Sale (Heritage, 8/1996), lot 6981, unsold.*

**Total Known in Mint State:** 110-140 Coins

**Total Known and Value Breakdown by Grade:**

| MS-60-62 | MS-63 | MS-64 | MS-65 |
|---|---|---|---|
| 35-45 Coins | 30-35 Coins | 35-45 Coins | 6-8 Coins |
| N/A | $800-$1,000 | $2,000-$2,750 | $5,750-$7,750 |

**Total Known and Value Breakdown by Grade:**

| MS-66 | MS-67 | MS-68 | MS-69-70 |
|---|---|---|---|
| 3-4 Coins | 0 Coins | 0 Coins | 0 Coins |
| $10,000-$20,000 | -- | -- | -- |

*Note*: The conclusions presented in the following "Collecting and Investing Strategies" section are drawn in large part from the Investment Potential Ratios that are summarized in Appendices G and H at the end of this book. For a detailed analysis of the formula used to derive these Investment Potential Ratios, please refer to the Introduction of this book.

**Collecting and Investing Strategies:** The 1895-S offers the best value for the money only at the MS-65 and MS-66 grade levels. MS-64s are overrated. MS-65s are actually underrated, however, and MS-66s are fairly well priced at reported levels in light of their actual rarity. Since this issue is also among the more aesthetically pleasing, early-date issues in the San Francisco Mint Barber Dime series, a Gem 1895-S would make an attractive and desirable addition to any numismatic holding. Just be sure to cherrypick for attractive toning or vibrant, brilliant surfaces. Absolutely avoid any MS-65 or MS-66 with singularly conspicuous abrasions.

# Proof
# 1896

## MINTAGE
762

Courtesy of David Lawrence

## RARITY
## RANKINGS

*Overall, All Proof Grades: 21st of 25*
*High Grade, Proof-65 or Finer: 19th of 25*
*Overall, Cameo Finish: 20th of 24*
*Overall, Deep/Ultra Cameo Finish: 10th of 12*

**Important Varieties:** None.

**General Comments:** The 1896 is clearly one of the most common issues in the proof Barber Dime series, although it is still rarer than the 1892, 1894, 1895 and 1898. The 1896 is also a relatively obtainable issue with a Cameo finish, and it is has a greater population of coins in Deep/Ultra Cameo than any other proof Barber Dime with the exception of only the 1898 and 1899.

**Strike:** As with virtually all other proofs in the Barber Dimes series, the 1896 typically displays full striking detail on both the obverse and the reverse.

**Finish:** The level of workmanship that the Philadelphia Mint applied to this issue is superior to that used to strike the proof 1892, proof 1893, proof 1894 and proof 1895. The typical proof 1896, in fact, displays at least some degree of field-to-device contrast. Many examples actually have a bold Cameo finish, and Deep/Ultra Cameo examples exist in greater numbers than they do for most other proof issues of this type.

**Surfaces:** The proof 1896 is an overall well-preserved issue, and the typical example offered in today's market will display no more than a few wispy hairlines and/or tiny contact marks. Many pieces are quite smooth, if not virtually pristine.

**Toning:** The coins that I have handled over the years run the gamut from fully brilliant to deeply toned. Most examples are either lightly or moderately toned, yet rarely with vivid colors and sometimes even with overly dark or splotchy patina.

**Eye Appeal:** Eye appeal varies quite markedly among survivors of this issue, and the desirability of an individual specimen usually rests in large measure on the toning. Brilliant or lightly toned coins that allow ready appreciation of bold field-to-device contrast are almost always highly attractive pieces. Colorfully toned examples, while rare, also possess strong eye appeal. On the other hand, those pieces with dark, splotchy toning that obscures the original mint finish are decidedly below average in the eye appeal category.

**Significant Examples:**

**1. NGC Proof-67 ★ Cameo.** *Ex: Long Beach, CA Signature Coin Auction (Heritage, 9/2007), lot 1045, unsold.*

**2. NGC Proof-67 Cameo.** *Ex: Long Beach Signature Sale (Heritage, 2/2005), lot 6312, unsold; CSNS Signature Auction (Heritage, 5/2005), lot 6702, unsold; Pre-Long Beach Auction (Ira & Larry Goldberg, 5/2006), lot 1706, where it realized $3,220.*

**3. NGC Proof-67 Cameo.** *Ex: Palm Beach, FL Signature Sale (Heritage, 3/2005), lot 5490, where it realized $2,933.*

**4. NGC Proof-67 Cameo.** *Ex: The J.B. Worthington Collection (American Numismatic Rarities, 5/2005), lot 173, where it realized $2,760.*

**5. PCGS Proof-67 Cameo.** *Ex: The Bruce Scher #1 All-Time PCGS Registry Set (Heritage, 2/2005), lot 4056, where it realized $4,002.*

**6. PCGS Proof-67 Cameo.** *Ex: Dallas Signature Sale (Heritage, 12/2004), lot 5787, where it realized $4,313.*

**7. PCGS Proof-67 Cameo.** *Ex: Palm Beach, FL Signature Sale (Heritage, 11/2004), lot 6305, where it realized $4,255.*

**8. NGC Proof-67 Cameo.** *Ex: Baltimore, MD Signature Sale (Heritage, 7/2003), lot 6635, where it realized $3,450.*

**9. PCGS Proof-67 Cameo.** *Ex: The Wayne S. Rich Collection (Bowers and Merena, 3/2002), lot 2079, where it realized $3,910.*

**10. NGC Proof-67 ★ Ultra Cameo. CAC.** *Ex: ANA Signature Auction (Heritage, 3/2008), lot 425, where it realized $6,900.*

**11. PCGS Proof-67 Deep Cameo.** *Ex: Milwaukee, WI ANA Signature Coin Auction (Heritage, 8/2007), lot 593, where it realized $8,050.*

**Total Known:** 395-485 Coins

**Total Known and Value Breakdown by Grade:**

| Brilliant-Finish Coins | | | |
|---|---|---|---|
| **Proof-60-62** | **Proof-63** | **Proof-64** | **Proof-65** |
| 30-40 Coins | 50-60 Coins | 95-120 Coins | 60-70 Coins |
| N/A | $400-$500 | $600-$750 | $1,100-$1,400 |
| **Proof-66** | **Proof-67** | **Proof-68** | **Proof-69-70** |
| 65-75 Coins | 15-18 Coins | 1 Coin | 0 Coins |
| $1,750-$2,500 | $3,000-$4,000 | $6,500-$8,500 | -- |

| Cameo Coins | | | |
|---|---|---|---|
| **Proof-60-62 Cameo** | **Proof-63 Cameo** | **Proof-64 Cameo** | **Proof-65 Cameo** |
| 0 Coins | 2-3 Coins | 15-20 Coins | 18-23 Coins |
| -- | $600-$700 | $1,000-$1,300 | $1,400-$1,750 |
| **Proof-66 Cameo** | **Proof-67 Cameo** | **Proof-68 Cameo** | **Proof-69-70 Cameo** |
| 20-25 Coins | 12-15 Coins | 1-2 Coins | 0 Coins |
| $1,500-$2,500 | $4,000-$6,000 | $$7,000-$9,500 | -- |

| Deep/Ultra Cameo Coins | | | |
|---|---|---|---|
| **Proof-60-62 Deep/ Ultra Cameo** | **Proof-63 Deep/ Ultra Cameo** | **Proof-64 Deep/ Ultra Cameo** | **Proof-65 Deep/ Ultra Cameo** |
| 0 Coins | 1 Coin | 2-3 Coins | 1 Coin |
| -- | $850-$1,000 | $1,300-$1,500 | $2,000-$4,000 |
| **Proof-66 Deep/ Ultra Cameo** | **Proof-67 Deep/ Ultra Cameo** | **Proof-68 Deep/ Ultra Cameo** | **Proof-69-70 Deep/ Ultra Cameo** |
| 3-4 Coins | 2-3 Coins | 0 Coins | 0 Coins |
| $2,250-$5,500 | $7,000-$9,000 | -- | -- |

*Note*: The conclusions presented in the following "Collecting and Investing Strategies" section are drawn in large part from the Investment Potential Ratios that are summarized in Appendices G and H at the end of this book. For a detailed analysis of the formula used to derive these Investment Potential Ratios, please refer to the Introduction of this book.

**Collecting and Investing Strategies:** The proof 1896 is relatively well priced for its rarity in Proof-64 and Proof-65, and the issue is actually underrated in Proof-67. Only in Proof-66 is the 1894 really an overrated coin, and I would definitely refrain from acquiring an example in that grade.

Given the beauty of this issue with Cameo-finish surfaces, as well as the relative availability of such coins when viewed in the wider context of the proof

Barber Dime series, I really like the 1894 in Proof-64, Proof-65 and Proof-67 with a Cameo designation as part of the grade. (Deep/Ultra Cameo examples are even more visually dramatic, but they are quite elusive and are seen in the market much less often than Cameo pieces.) In order to best appreciate the bold field-to-device contrast that is a prerequisite for receiving this designation, I suggest obtaining a specimen with either untoned or minimally toned surfaces. Many proof 1896 Barber Dimes are also well preserved with minimal handling marks, so a high-grade Cameo specimen is sure to be a coin that will delight its owner time and again.

# 1896

**MINTAGE**
2,000,000

Courtesy of David Lawrence

**RARITY RANKINGS**

*Overall, Mint State: 35th of 74 (Tie)*
*High Grade, MS-65 or Finer: 35th of 74 (Tie)*

## PHILADELPHIA MINT ISSUES

*Overall, Mint State: 2nd of 25*
*High Grade, MS-65 or Finer: 3rd of 25*

**Important Varieties:** There is an impressive Repunched Date variety known for the 1896, and it carries the attributions FS-301, FS-009.3 and Breen-3497.

**General Comments:** The 1896 is the second-rarest Philadelphia Mint Barber Dime in Mint State after the 1895, although in high grades the 1904 is also more challenging to locate. In an absolute sense the 1896 compares favorably to the lower-mintage 1893-O, and it is rarer than such other mintmarked issues in this series as the 1900-S, 1905-O, 1908-D and 1915-S.

At and above the MS--65 grade level, the 1896 is equally as rare as the low-mintage 1909-D. High-grade examples are rarer than those of the low-mintage 1913-S, as well as numerous other mintmarked issues of this type including the 1892-O, 1900-S, 1906-S, 1907-O, 1908-D and 1914-S.

**Strike:** When it comes to the 1896, sharp striking detail is the order of the day. This issue is universally well produced, and I would be hard pressed to recall handling more than five or six Mint State examples that displayed even trivial lack of detail in one or two isolated areas.

**Luster:** Luster is also a praiseworthy attribute for this issue. Most examples display either satiny, semi or fully prooflike luster. Coins with a frosty finish are in the minority among Mint State survivors.

**Surfaces:** Abrasions are seldom a problem for this issue, as even lower-grade coins in the MS-60 to MS-63 grade range rarely possess numerous and/or large-size handling marks. The typical Mint State example offered in today's market, nonetheless, will display a few wispy abrasions. The 1896 is nearly as challenging to locate with overall smooth-looking surfaces as the 1895, and it is rarer when virtually pristine.

**Toning:** Original examples with toned surfaces are still in the majority among Mint State 1896 Barber Dimes, although dipped pieces are becoming more plentiful. The toned pieces exhibit the full range of colors found on originally preserved silver coins, and these can be either vivid or quite dark. Most examples, however, are relatively pleasing in the area of toning, the more vibrant colors sometimes being confined to the peripheries on one or both sides.

**Eye Appeal:** The 1896 has above-average, if not strong eye appeal. Luster quality is among the more impressive in this series, and abrasions are seldom either excessive in number or large in size. A sharp strike and relatively appealing toning are also significant attributes.

**Significant Examples:**

**1. PCGS MS-67.** *Ex: Long Beach Signature Sale (Heritage, 2/2003), lot 6336, where it realized $1,840; The Collection of Dr. Steven L. Duckor (Heritage, 1/2006), lot 981, where it realized $14,950.*

**2. NGC MS-66.** *Ex: New York, NY Signature Sale (Heritage, 7/2002), lot 7603, where it realized $1,208; Long Beach, CA Signature U.S. Coin Auction (Heritage, 5/2007), lot 707, where it realized $978; Dallas, TX U.S. Coin Signature Auction (Heritage, 11/2007), lot 421, where it realized $1,380.*

**3. PCGS MS-66.** *Ex: CSNS Signature Auction (Heritage, 5/2005), lot 6610, unsold.*

**4. PCGS MS-66.** *Ex: Long Beach Signature Sale (Heritage, 2/2005), lot 6281, where it realized $1,840.*

**5. PCGS MS-66.** *Ex: Orlando Rarities Sale (Bowers and Merena, 1/2001), lot 147, where it realized $2,415.*

**Total Known in Mint State:** 150-190 Coins

## Total Known and Value Breakdown by Grade:

| MS-60-62 | MS-63 | MS-64 | MS-65 |
|----------|-------|-------|-------|
| 40-50 Coins | 35-40 Coins | 40-50 Coins | 25-30 Coins |
| N/A | $300-$400 | $475-$575 | $1,100-$1,400 |

| MS-66 | MS-67 | MS-68 | MS-69 to MS-70 |
|-------|-------|-------|----------------|
| 12-15 Coins | 1 Coin | 0 Coins | 0 Coins |
| $1,750-$5,000 | $12,500-$17,500 | -- | -- |

*Note:* The conclusions presented in the following "Collecting and Investing Strategies" section are drawn in large part from the Investment Potential Ratios that are summarized in Appendices G and H at the end of this book. For a detailed analysis of the formula used to derive these Investment Potential Ratios, please refer to the Introduction of this book.

**Collecting and Investing Strategies:** The 1896 is definitely a key-date issue in this series, although it is not widely recognized as such. I have seen many auction catalogers provide only two or three sentences even for examples that grade MS-65 and MS-66—a description length that is usually reserved for the more common and, hence, less important offerings in a sale. In reality, the 1896 is one of the more underrated P-mint Barber Dimes in the finer Mint State grades. This fact, when taken in conjunction with the status of the 1896 as an overlooked issue, argues strongly in favor of your acquiring an example in the MS-64 to MS-67 grade range before the true rarity of this issue in Mint State becomes known in numismatic circles. MS-64s are particularly undervalued, ranking behind only similarly graded examples of the 1898-O, 1898-S, 1902-S, 1903, 1910-D and 1910-S in this regard.

If you are assembling a complete set of Barber Dimes, I strongly suggest including the 1896 among your earlier acquisitions. It is always sound advice to get the key-date issues out of the way first so that the demands on your time and financial resources become more manageable with time. If your interest in numismatics is more general, or if your primary concern is to maximize return on a numismatic investment, you could also do well by purchasing a high-grade 1896.

When purchasing an 1896 for any purpose, you can usually relax your standards for quality since this issue tends to come nice. I would, however, avoid the occasional darkly toned piece in favor of a coin with either brilliant surfaces or more vibrant, if not vivid patina.

# 1896-O

## MINTAGE
610,000

Courtesy of David Lawrence

## RARITY RANKINGS

*Overall, Mint State: 3rd of 74*
*High Grade, MS-65 or Finer: 11th of 74*

## NEW ORLEANS MINT ISSUES

*Overall, Mint State: 3rd of 17*
*High Grade, MS-65 or Finer: 5th of 17*

**Important Varieties:** None.

**General Comments:** The 1896-O is the third and penultimate issue in the quartet of rare, key-date New Orleans Mint Barber Dimes struck from 1894-1897. This issue is not quite as challenging to locate as the 1894-O or 1895-O, but it is rarer in Mint State than all other New Orleans Mint Dimes of this type. The 1896-O is not ranked as high when we consider only grades of MS-65 and finer, as the 1902-O and 1903-O are also rarer in those grades. This is because the surviving population of the 1896-O in Mint State is fairly evenly distributed throughout the MS-60 to MS-66 grade range. There are even one or two coins known that grade MS-67. A high-grade 1896-O Barber Dime, nevertheless, is still a rare coin when viewed in the wider context of the numismatic market.

**Strike:** Many numismatic catalogers and other professionals classify the 1896-O as an important strike rarity in this series. I do not believe that this is technically correct, since many of the Mint State coins that I have handled are actually quite well defined. The overall striking detail for this issue is usually bold, if not sharp, and a decent number of the Mint State survivors are actually free of excessive lack of detail. Softness of strike, when it is present on an example of this issue, is almost always confined to the reverse wreath either over the large leaf at the lower left or next to the right (facing) bow of the ribbon knot.

**Luster:** The 1896-O usually displays satiny luster that, like the 1894-O, tends to be somewhat subdued and not particularly vibrant. A few frosty examples are known, however, and these tend to be more appealing in the area of luster quality.

**Surfaces:** This is not a heavily abraded issue. Impaired luster, rather than an excessive number of handling marks, is usually what results in a grade in the MS-60 to MS-63 range for many of the lower-end Mint State survivors.

**Toning:** I cannot recall having seen more than one or two 1896-O Barber Dimes with completely brilliant surfaces on both sides. Even the widespread practice of dipping and other forms of numismatic conservation in today's market have yet to effect this issue to an appreciable degree. Virtually all Mint State survivors are extensively toned, most so deeply that attempts to remove the toning would almost certainly result in noticeable impairment to the luster. I have seen a couple of examples that were definitely dipped at one time, their surfaces now displaying remnants of the original toning over dull, nearly lifeless luster.

**Eye Appeal:** This is a very challenging issue to locate with strong eye appeal, and virtually all-known Mint State examples are below average in this regard. Primary culprits here are inferior luster and the prevalence of dark toning among the survivors.

**Significant Examples:**

**1. NGC MS-67.** *Ex: FUN Signature Coin Auction (Heritage, 1/2007), lot 881, unsold.*

**2. PCGS MS-66.** *Ex: Long Beach Signature Sale (Heritage, 6/2004), lot 6046, where it realized $10,638; The Collection of Dr. Steven L. Duckor (Heritage, 1/2006), lot 982, where it realized $13,800.*

**3. NGC MS-66.** *Ex: Long Beach Signature Auction (Heritage, 9/2005), lot 2422, where it realized $9,488.*

**4. PCGS MS-66.** *Ex: CSNS Signature Sale (Heritage, 4/2002), lot 5489, where it realized $8,625.*

**5. PCGS MS-66.** *Ex: Long Beach Signature Sale (Heritage, 2/1999), lot 5846, where it realized $7,475; Orlando Rarities Sale (Bowers and Merena, 1/2002), lot 374, where it realized $7,188.*

**Total Known in Mint State:** 50-60 Coins

## Total Known and Value Breakdown by Grade:

| MS-60-62 | MS-63 | MS-64 | MS-65 |
|---|---|---|---|
| 5-6 Coins | 7-9 Coins | 18-22 Coins | 8-10 Coins |
| N/A | $1,750-$2,250 | $3,750-$4,750 | $7,000-$8,000 |

| MS-66 | MS-67 | MS-68 | MS-69 to MS-70 |
|---|---|---|---|
| 8-10 Coins | 1-2 Coins | 0 Coins | 0 Coins |
| $12,500-$17,500 | $20,000-$30,000 | -- | -- |

*Note:* The conclusions presented in the following "Collecting and Investing Strategies" section are drawn in large part from the Investment Potential Ratios that are summarized in Appendices G and H at the end of this book. For a detailed analysis of the formula used to derive these Investment Potential Ratios, please refer to the Introduction of this book.

**Collecting and Investing Strategies:** Although not as overrated as the 1894-O or 1895-O in most grades, the 1896-O is still one of the most overvalued Barber Dimes in MS-64, MS-65, MS-66 and MS-67. The reason for this fact is the same as with the 1894-O and 1895-O—the paucity of circulated examples has driven the value of Mint State coins to a level that is not commensurate with their actual rarity. This is another issue, therefore, that I do not recommend acquiring unless you are assembling a complete date and mint set of Barber Dimes.

If you must purchase a high-grade 1896-O Dime, or choose to do so for any other reason, absolutely avoid those coins that were too darkly toned before being dipped. Such coins are easy to spot. Look for hazy silver and/or gold toning that is deepest near the rims and dull, muted surfaces with impaired luster. Also stay away from coins that, while still original, are so darkly toned that they are unappealing to the eye.

On the other hand, it will be difficult to acquire an 1896-O Barber Dime that does not display at least some degree of toning. Try to find a coin that still retains some vibrancy to the luster, which is easier to do if you select one of the few frosty examples over a satiny piece. Finally, look for a coin with overall sharp striking detail. Quite a few of the nicer Mint State examples that I have seen possess this attribute, so there might not be a reason for you to settle for a coin with noticeable softness of strike in a few isolated areas.

# 1896-S

## MINTAGE
575,056

*Courtesy of David Lawrence*

## RARITY RANKINGS

**Overall, Mint State:** *12th of 74 (Tie)*
**High Grade, MS-65 or Finer:** *19th of 74 (Tie)*

## SAN FRANCISCO MINT ISSUES

**Overall, Mint State:** *5th of 24 (Tie)*
**High Grade, MS-65 or Finer:** *10th of 24 (Tie)*

**Important Varieties:** None.

**General Comments:** After only the 1913-S, the 1896-S has the lowest mintage among business strike Barber Dimes from the San Francisco Mint. The 1896-S was saved in far fewer numbers than the 1913-S, however, and it is also rarer than the low-mintage 1914-S and 1915-S in terms of total number of Mint State coins believed extant. The 1896-S compares favorably to the 1909-S in terms of overall rarity, and it is akin to the 1893-S, 1902-S and 1903-S in high-grade rarity. This issue is unknown any finer than MS-66.

**Strike:** Striking quality for the 1896-S is almost always beyond reproach, and most examples that you encounter in the market will display sharp-to-full definition on both sides.

**Luster:** The 1896-S has excellent luster that is usually of a satin or softly frosted texture. A few examples are also known with semi, if not fully prooflike luster.

**Surfaces:** The extant population of the 1896-S in Mint State is fairly evenly distributed throughout the MS-60 to MS-66 grade range, with the result that you are just as likely to encounter a noticeably abraded example as an overall smooth-looking piece. Most coins in the former category display only small, wispy abrasions, although some of the BU-quality examples have more detracting slidemarks on Liberty's portrait.

**Toning:** This issue is easier to locate with brilliant surfaces than the 1896-O, although the vast majority of Mint State survivors display at least some degree of toning. Colors range from light to deep, dull to quite vivid.

**Eye Appeal:** This is a generally attractive issue that, when available in Mint State at all, tends to come with more-or-less strong eye appeal.

### Significant Examples:

**1. NGC MS-66 Prooflike.** *Ex: St. Louis Rarities Sale (Bowers and Merena, 5/2007), lot 48, where it realized $9,775.*

**2. NGC MS-66.** *Ex: The Belle Glade Collection (Heritage, 8/2007), lot 569, where it realized $4,313.*

**3. PCGS MS-66.** *Ex: The Collection of Dr. Steven L. Duckor (Heritage, 1/2006), lot 983, where it realized $7,475.*

**4. PCGS MS-66.** *Ex: Long Beach Signature Auction (Heritage, 6/2005), lot 5825, where it realized $9,775.*

**5. PCGS MS-66.** *Ex: FUN Signature Sale (Heritage, 1/2003) lot 6469, where it realized $19,550.*

**6. NGC MS-66.** *Ex: Long Beach Signature Sale (Heritage, 6/2002), lot 5619, where it realized $3,680.*

**7. NGC MS-66.** *Ex: FUN Signature Sale (Heritage, 1/1999), lot 6458, where it realized $3,105.*

**8. NGC MS-66.** *Ex: Orlando Rarities Sale (Bowers and Merena, 1/1997), lot 95, unsold.*

**Total Known in Mint State:** 80-95 Coins

**Total Known and Value Breakdown by Grade:**

| MS-60-62 | MS-63 | MS-64 | MS-65 |
|---|---|---|---|
| 18-22 Coins | 8-10 Coins | 30-35 Coins | 12-15 Coins |
| N/A | $1,150-$1,250 | $2,500-$3,000 | $3,500-$5,000 |

| MS-66 | MS-67 | MS-68 | MS-69-70 |
|---|---|---|---|
| 12-14 Coins | 0 Coins | 0 Coins | 0 Coins |
| $5,000-$12,500 | -- | -- | -- |

*Note:* The conclusions presented in the following "Collecting and Investing Strategies" section are drawn in large part from the Investment Potential Ratios that are summarized in Appendices G and H at the end of this book. For a detailed analysis of the formula used to derive these Investment Potential Ratios, please refer to the Introduction of this book.

**Collecting and Investing Strategies:** Like the 1896-O, the 1896-S is an overrated issue that is not a good buy in any grade from MS-64 to MS-66. Conversely, most Mint State survivors of this issue possess relatively strong eye appeal in the context of the assigned grade. The latter fact is good news for date and mint collectors, although any other category of numismatic buyer should avoid this issue in the finer Mint State grades because such coins are overvalued relative to their actual rarity.

Cherrypicking for either brilliant or attractively toned surfaces is recommended for this issue. Additionally, and if your numismatic budget precludes acquiring an 1896-S that grades finer than MS-63, try to avoid coins with slidemarks on Liberty's portrait. Some '96-S Dimes are confined to lower Mint State grades because of impaired luster, and those coins may be preferable to pieces with large, singularly conspicuous abrasions on one or both sides.

# Proof
# 1897

## MINTAGE
731

*Courtesy of David Lawrence*

## RARITY
## RANKINGS

***Overall, All Proof Grades:*** *19th of 25*
***High Grade, Proof-65 or Finer:*** *20th of 25*
***Overall, Cameo Finish:*** *21st of 24*
***Overall, Deep/Ultra Cameo Finish:*** *6th of 12 (Tie)*

**Important Varieties:** None.

**General Comments:** The poof 1897 has an original mintage that is very similar to that of the proof 1896, although it is a slightly rarer issue in today's market in terms of total number of coins believed to exist. In an absolute sense, the 1897 is actually rarer than all other proof Barber Dimes struck during the 1890s with the exception of the 1893 and the branch mint 1894-S. On the other hand, the proof 1897 is a relatively obtainable issue with a Cameo finish, and it is nearly identical to the proof 1894, proof 1896 and proof 1898 in this regard. Seldom offered as a Deep/Ultra Cameo, the proof 1897 is similar to the proof 1895 in terms of rarity with that finish.

**Strike:** All proof 1897 Barber Dimes that I have seen possess full striking detail that even extends to the most intricate elements of the design.

**Finish:** As with the proof 1896 and proof 1898, the proof 1897 is usually encountered with at least some degree of Cameo contrast. Many examples exhibit particularly heavy frost over the devices. In fact, my experience suggests that many (but certainly not all!) examples that have not received either a Cameo or Deep/Ultra Cameo designation from PCGS or NGC are too deeply toned to allow full appreciation of field-to-device contrast.

**Surfaces:** Most proof 1897 Barber Dimes are well preserved with no more than a few wispy hairlines or other trivial contact marks.

**Toning:** There is about a 40-60 mix of originally toned and fully brilliant specimens in the numismatic market. Examples in the former category are usually quite dark, but the surfaces often reveal brighter, more vibrant undertones when viewed under a good light source. The brilliant specimens are largely the result of dipping.

**Eye Appeal:** This is a very attractive issue, indeed, one of the most consistently attractive in the entire proof Barber Dime series of 1892-1915. The proof 1897 is a well-preserved coin, and most survivors have been handled with great care since leaving the Mint.

**Significant Examples:**

1. **NGC Proof-68.** *Ex: Long Beach, CA Signature Auction (Heritage, 9/2006), lot 1361, where it realized $5,319.*

2. **PCGS Proof-68.** *Ex: The Charles River Collection (Stack's/American Numismatic Rarities, 6/2004), lot 2655, where it realized $10,350.*

3. **NGC Proof-68 Cameo.** *Ex: New York, NY Signature Sale (Heritage, 7/2002), lot 7633, unsold; The J.B. Worthington Collection (American Numismatic Rarities, 5/2005), lot 174, where it realized $5,290; San Francisco Rarities Sale (Bowers and Merena, 7/2005), lot 405, unsold; Dallas, TX Signature Auction (Heritage, 11/2005), lot 1052, unsold; Beverly Hills Rarities Sale (Bowers and Merena, 2/2006), lot 197, where it realized $5,175.*

4. **NGC Proof-68 Cameo.** *Ex: Pre-Long Beach Auction (Ira & Larry Goldberg, 2/2006), lot 667, where it realized $4,715.*

5. **NGC Proof-68 ★ Cameo.** *Ex: Pittsburgh, PA Signature Sale (Heritage, 8/2004), lot 57819, unsold; FUN Signature Sale (Heritage, 1/2005), lot 30163, unsold; San Francisco, CA ANA Signature Auction (Heritage, 7/2005), lot 5919, unsold; Dallas, TX Signature Auction (Heritage, 11/2005), lot 1051, unsold; FUN Signature Auction (Heritage, 1/2006), lot 1850, where it realized $6,670.*

6. **NGC Proof-68 ★ Cameo.** *Ex: FUN Signature Sale (Heritage, 1/1999), lot 6468, unsold; The John C. Hugon Collection (Heritage, 1/2005), lot 4081, where it realized $6,038.*

7. **PCGS Proof-68 Cameo.** *Ex: Baltimore, MD Signature Sale (Heritage, 7/2003), lot 6637, where it realized $8,625.*

**Total Known**: 365-445 Coins

## Total Known and Value Breakdown by Grade:

| Brilliant-Finish Coins | | | |
|---|---|---|---|
| **Proof-60-62** | **Proof-63** | **Proof-64** | **Proof-65** |
| 30-40 Coins | 45-55 Coins | 75-85 Coins | 60-70 Coins |
| N/A | $400-$525 | $600-$750 | $1,100-$1,400 |
| **Proof-66** | **Proof-67** | **Proof-68** | **Proof-69-70** |
| 45-55 Coins | 25-30 Coins | 5-7 Coins | 0 Coins |
| $1,500-$2,000 | $3,000-$4,000 | $6,000-$12,000 | -- |

| Cameo Coins | | | |
|---|---|---|---|
| **Proof-60-62 Cameo** | **Proof-63 Cameo** | **Proof-64 Cameo** | **Proof-65 Cameo** |
| 2-3 Coins | 1 Coin | 12-15 Coins | 12-15 Coins |
| N/A | $600-$700 | $1,000-$1,300 | $1,400-$1,600 |
| **Proof-66 Cameo** | **Proof-67 Cameo** | **Proof-68 Cameo** | **Proof-69-70 Cameo** |
| 25-30 Coins | 20-25 Coins | 5 Coins | 0 Coins |
| $1,500-$2,000 | $3,000-$5,000 | $7,500-$15,000 | -- |

| Deep/Ultra Cameo Coins | | | |
|---|---|---|---|
| **Proof-60-62 Deep/ Ultra Cameo** | **Proof-63 Deep/ Ultra Cameo** | **Proof-64 Deep/ Ultra Cameo** | **Proof-65 Deep/ Ultra Cameo** |
| 0 Coins | 0 Coins | 0 Coins | 1-2 Coins |
| -- | -- | -- | $2,000-$4,000 |
| **Proof-66 Deep/ Ultra Cameo** | **Proof-67 Deep/ Ultra Cameo** | **Proof-68 Deep/ Ultra Cameo** | **Proof-69-70 Deep/ Ultra Cameo** |
| 2-3 Coins | 0 Coins | 1 Coin | 0 Coins |
| $4,000-$7,000 | -- | $8,000-$10,000 | -- |

*Note:* The conclusions presented in the following "Collecting and Investing Strategies" section are drawn in large part from the Investment Potential Ratios that are summarized in Appendices G and H at the end of this book. For a detailed analysis of the formula used to derive these Investment Potential Ratios, please refer to the Introduction of this book.

**Collecting and Investing Strategies:** More so than any other issue in the proof Barber Dime series, the 1897 comes highly recommended for inclusion in a specimen type set. This issue is very well produced and, as a rule, well preserved with most examples possessing strong eye appeal. Additionally, and of great importance to the collector/investor or pure numismatic investor, the 1897 has a sound relationship between price and rarity in the Proof-64 to Proof-67 grade range. In Proof-64, in fact, the 1897 is actually the most underrated proof Barber Dime.

Since this issue is usually characterized by bold field-to-device contrast, and since such pieces are relatively obtainable in numismatic circles, a proof 1897 with a Cameo designation as part of the grade is probably more desirable than a piece with an all-brilliant finish. The coin that you select can be either brilliant or toned depending upon your personal preference, but I would make sure that a toned example is not so dark as to prevent ready appreciation of the Cameo finish.

# 1897

**MINTAGE**
10,868,533

*Courtesy of David Lawrence*

## RARITY RANKINGS

*Overall, Mint State: 65th of 74*
*High Grade, MS-65 or Finer: 66th of 74*

## PHILADELPHIA MINT ISSUES

*Overall, Mint State: 17th of 25*
*High Grade, MS-65 or Finer: 17th of 25*

**Important Varieties:** There are two significant Repunched Date varieties known for the 1897. FS-301/Lawrence-101 is quite dramatic, while FS-302/FS-009.51 is less so and can be difficult to discern.

**General Comments:** After only the 1892 and 1898, the 1897 is the most common P-mint Barber Dime from the 1890s. This is actually one of the most plentiful of all Barber Dimes, although the 1897 is rarer in Mint State than the later-date 1910, 1911, 1912, 1913, 1914 and 1916. Superb Gems in MS-67 are nothing short of rare from a condition standpoint.

**Strike:** This is an overall sharply struck issue, and the typical example is actually fully defined in most, if not all areas. Interestingly, I have seen a couple of coins with soft definition over the denticles in a few isolated rim areas. That feature, however, is not all that detracting to the overall appearance.

**Luster:** The 1897 has above-average, if not strong luster that is usually of a frosty type. Satiny pieces also exist, but they are seen much less frequently than coins with a frosty texture to the surfaces.

**Surfaces:** Despite the relative availability of Mint State survivors in today's market, the 1897 can be a challenging issue to locate with overall smooth surfaces. The majority of pieces that I have seen possess at least a few noticeable abrasions, although these tend to be small in size and singularly inconspicuous. There are surprisingly few survivors with virtually pristine surfaces for a P-mint issue with such a sizeable original mintage.

**Toning:** This early-date Barber Dime is usually offered with moderately-to-deeply toned surfaces. Most pieces with lighter patination or fully brilliant surfaces have been dipped.

**Eye Appeal:** With such a large number of coins struck and a generous population of Mint State survivors, it should come as no surprise to read that eye appeal varies widely for this issue. Most 1897 Barber Dimes, nonetheless, possess at least above-average eye appeal, while coins that grade finer than MS-65 are usually very attractive coins.

**Significant Examples:**

    **1. NGC MS-67.** *Ex: The J.B. Worthington Collection (American Numismatic Rarities, 5/2005), lot 175, where it realized $2,415; CSNS Signature Coin Auction (Heritage, 5/2007), lot 363, unsold; Long Beach, CA Signature Coin Auction (Heritage, 9/2007), lot 1021, where it realized $3,450.*

    **2. PCGS MS-67.** *Ex: The Collection of Dr. Steven L. Duckor (Heritage, 1/2006), lot 984, where it realized $5,463.*

    **3. NGC MS-67 ★.** *Ex: California Sale (Ira & Larry Goldberg, 10/2000), lot 1641, where it realized $2,530; San Francisco, CA ANA Signature Auction (Heritage, 7/2005), lot 5886, where it realized $3,450.*

    **4. NGC MS-67.** *Ex: Long Beach Signature Auction (Heritage, 6/2005), lot 5826, unsold.*

    **5. PCGS MS-67.** *Ex: Santa Clara Signature Sale (Heritage, 11/2000), lot 6837, where it realized $6,440.*

    **6. NGC MS-67.** *Ex: FUN Signature Sale (Heritage, 1/1998), lot 6685, where it realized $1,783.*

**Total Known in Mint State:** 500-605 Coins

**Total Known and Value Breakdown by Grade:**

| MS-60 to MS-62 | MS-63 | MS-64 | MS-65 |
|---|---|---|---|
| 110-135 Coins | 110-135 Coins | 155-180 Coins | 70-85 Coins |
| N/A | $125-$175 | $250-$300 | $475-$600 |

### Total Known and Value Breakdown by Grade:

| MS-66 | MS-67 | MS-68 | MS-69 to MS-70 |
|---|---|---|---|
| 50-60 Coins | 7-9 Coins | 0 Coins | 0 Coins |
| $1,100-$2,000 | $3,500-$5,750 | -- | -- |

*Note:* The conclusions presented in the following "Collecting and Investing Strategies" section are drawn in large part from the Investment Potential Ratios that are summarized in Appendices G and H at the end of this book. For a detailed analysis of the formula used to derive these Investment Potential Ratios, please refer to the Introduction of this book.

**Collecting and Investing Strategies:** This issue is neither appreciably overrated nor significantly underrated in any grade from MS-64 through MS-67. As such, the 1897 offers good value relative to its rarity in the finer Mint State grades. That being said, however, I particularly like MS-66s in this regard as they are a bit more underrated than examples in MS-64, MS-65 and MS-67.

A premium Gem 1897 Barber Dime will also allow you to best appreciate the sharp striking detail and strong luster quality for which the 1897 is known. You could even do very well acquiring a richly toned example in MS-66 as many original 1897 Dimes possess handsome patination to the surfaces. There are even some vividly toned coins from which to choose, although you should expect to pay at least a slight premium for these pieces since they enjoy heightened demand among toning enthusiasts.

# 1897-O

**MINTAGE**
666,000

Courtesy of David Lawrence

**RARITY**
**RANKINGS**

*Overall, Mint State: 18th of 74*
*High Grade, MS-65 or Finer: 19th of 74 (Tie)*

## NEW ORLEANS MINT ISSUES

*Overall, Mint State: 9th of 17*
*High Grade, MS-65 or Finer: 9th of 17 (Tie)*

**Important Varieties:** None.

**General Comments:** The 1897-O is the most obtainable of the four rare, key-date New Orleans Mint Barber Dimes struck from 1894-1897. In fact, the 1897-O is only a median rarity in the O-mint Barber Dime series, and it is not as rare in Mint State as the 1898-O, 1899-O, 1900-O, 1901-O or 1902-O. The 1897-O does compare favorably with the 1901-O in terms of high-grade rarity, and it is actually one of the more elusive New Orleans Mint Barber Dimes at and above the MS-65 grade level. Superb Gems are not unknown, but they are so elusive as to be encountered only once in a very long while.

**Strike:** Striking detail for the 1897-O ranges from overall sharp to a bit blunt in isolated areas. As a whole, though, the 1897-O is a bit more challenging to locate with overall sharp definition than the 1896-O and (definitely) the 1895-O. Lack of detail, when present on an example of this issue, is usually confined to the obverse over the leaves immediately above the ribbon inscribed LIBERTY, the lower-left reverse wreath, the upper-right reverse wreath and/or the right (facing) bow of the ribbon knot. A number of 1897-O Dimes were struck from a reverse die that was rotated several degrees counterclockwise in the press.

**Luster:** The 1897-O has superior luster quality to that seen in the typical 1894-O or 1896-O. The finish tends to be relatively vibrant with either a satin or softly frosted texture.

**Surfaces:** Perhaps surprisingly for an issue that can be so elusive in Mint State, the 1897-O is seldom plagued by excessive abrasions. Most Mint State survivors are actually quite smooth, and there are seldom more than a few small, singularly inconspicuous abrasions to report.

**Toning:** Toning is the rule for this issue, and most Mint State examples exhibit richly original patina on one or both sides. The colors tend to be either quite deep with a handsome, "antique" appearance or relatively vibrant to include shades of sea-green, cobalt-blue and reddish-russet. Minimally toned and brilliant pieces are encountered much less often in the market, and most of those coins have been dipped to remove deeper patination.

**Eye Appeal:** Despite its key-date status among Barber Dimes, the 1897-O is not really all that challenging to locate with above-average eye appeal. The luster tends to be more-or-less vibrant, and the surfaces are usually relatively well preserved. Noteworthy detractions for this issue include slight unevenness of strike and, to a lesser extent, dark toning. Neither of those attributes, however, are all that significant for a New Orleans Mint Barber Dime that dates to the 1890s.

### Significant Examples:

**1. PCGS MS-67.** *Ex: Long Beach, CA Signature Coin Auction (Heritage, 2/2007), lot 2941, unsold; CSNS Signature Coin Auction (Heritage, 5/2007), lot 2075, unsold.*

**2. PCGS MS-67.** *Ex: Pittsburgh, PA Signature Sale (Heritage, 8/2004), lot 5700, where it realized $7,475; Dallas Signature Sale (Heritage, 12/2004), lot 5765, where it realized $18,400.*

**3. PCGS MS-67.** *Ex: Long Beach Signature Sale (Heritage, 9/2003), lot 6446, where it realized $28,750.*

**4. PCGS MS-66.** *Ex: The Turkus Sale (Superior, 6/1981), lot 390; The Jascha Heifetz Collection (Superior, 10/1989), lot 3586, where it realized $6,050; The Collection of Dr. Steven L. Duckor (Heritage, 1/2006), lot 985, where it realized $6,325.*

**5. PCGS MS-66.** *Ex: The John C. Hugon Collection (Heritage, 1/2005), lot 4016, where it realized $5,175.*

**6. NGC MS-66.** *Ex: CSNS Signature Sale (Heritage, 5/2004), lot 6644, where it realized $4,600.*

**7. PCGS MS-66.** *Ex: Dr. Steven L. Duckor; The Dr. Robert W. Swan and*

*Rod Sweet Collections (Bowers and Merena, 3/2004), lot 1200, where it realized $7,475.*

**8. NGC MS-66.** *Ex: The Dr. Robert W. Swan and Rod Sweet Collections (Bowers and Merena, 3/2004), lot 1201, where it realized $4,255; Baltimore Auction (Bowers and Merena, 12/2004), lot 755, where it realized $3,795.*

**9. PCGS MS-66.** *Ex: Philadelphia 2000 Signature Sale (Heritage, 8/2000), lot 6963, unsold.*

**Total Known in Mint State:** 85-105 Coins

**Total Known and Value Breakdown by Grade:**

| MS-60 to MS-62 | MS-63 | MS-64 | MS-65 |
|---|---|---|---|
| 18-22 Coins | 17-21 Coins | 25-30 Coins | 12-15 Coins |
| N/A | $1,200-$1,500 | $2,250-$2,750 | $3,500-$7,500 |

| MS-66 | MS-67 | MS-68 | MS-69 to MS-70 |
|---|---|---|---|
| 8-10 Coins | 4-5 Coins | 0 Coins | 0 Coins |
| $5,000-$12,500 | $20,000-$25,000 | -- | -- |

*Note:* The conclusions presented in the following "Collecting and Investing Strategies" section are drawn in large part from the Investment Potential Ratios that are summarized in Appendices G and H at the end of this book. For a detailed analysis of the formula used to derive these Investment Potential Ratios, please refer to the Introduction of this book.

**Collecting and Investing Strategies:** The 1897-O is one of the most overrated Barber Dimes in the finer Mint State grades, and I do not recommend this issue for any purposes other than inclusion in a complete set of this series. Absolutely avoid MS-65s and MS-67s, for the 1897-O is the third most overvalued Barber Dime in both of those grades.

In addition to value, the market also tends to overstate the difficulty of locating an attractive 1897-O. The latter falsehood, in particular, has received particularly widespread exposure in numismatic catalogs and other literature. In truth, the 1897-O tends to come much nicer than the 1894-O and 1896-O, and you can afford to be somewhat selective when it comes to adding a Mint State example of this issue to a Barber Dime set. While you will probably have to accept some isolated softness of detail on one or both sides, insist on acquiring a coin with pleasing luster and freedom from individually conspicuous abrasions. Most of the dipped pieces that I have seen are more-or-less attractive, and you could also do well by selecting one of the richly toned examples for inclusion in your collection. For coins in the latter category, insist on colors that are relatively vibrant and then make sure that the underlying luster remains sufficiently vibrant in the context of the assigned grade.

# 1897-S

## MINTAGE
1,342,844

*Courtesy of Bowers and Merena*

## RARITY RANKINGS

*Overall, Mint State: 16th of 74*
*High Grade, MS-65 or Finer: 9th of 74*

## SAN FRANCISCO MINT ISSUES

*Overall, Mint State: 7th of 24*
*High Grade, MS-65 or Finer: 5th of 24*

**Important Varieties:** None.

**General Comments:** Despite a mintage that is more than twice as large, the 1897-S is not much easier to obtain in Mint State than the 1896-S. The 1897-S is actually rarer than the lower-mintage 1904-S, 1913-S and 1915-S, to name just three other issues in the S-mint Barber Dime series. This issue also has an impressive ranking in high grades, and it is rarer at and above the MS-65 grade level than all other San Francisco Mint Barber Dimes with the exception of the 1892-S, 1895-S, 1898-S and 1907-S.

The 1897-S holds up equally as well when compared to Barber Dime issues from other Mints. It is rarer in Mint State than all P-mint issues of the type (including the low-mintage 1895), all Denver Mint issues save for the 1907-D (which is also more common than the 1897-S in high grades) and all but a handful of O-mint issues such as the 1894-O, 1895-O and 1896-O.

**Strike:** In keeping with the standards set by the San Francisco Mint at the outset of the Barber Dime series, the 1897-S is almost always encountered with a sharp-to-full strike.

**Luster:** Unlike the preceding S-mint issues in this series, the 1897-S has below-average luster. Most examples exhibit either a satin or semi-prooflike finish, the surfaces seldom vibrant and usually possessed of a flat, subdued appearance. Dipping tends to exaggerate this feature.

**Surfaces:** A conditionally rare issue beginning at the MS-65 grade level, the 1897-S is almost always encountered with distracting abrasions. Marks also tend to be larger for this issue than for most other Barber Dimes from the 1890s, which suggests that the 1897-S was roughly handled by Mint employees.

**Toning:** Original examples usually display moderate-to-deep toning. A fair number of Mint State pieces have been dipped, and these typically display either brilliant surfaces or light gold or silver overtones.

**Eye Appeal:** The 1897-S is an extremely challenging issue to locate with strong eye appeal, and most Mint State survivors are decidedly below average in this category. The luster is seldom vibrant, and you will probably experience considerable difficulty locating a coin that is free of distracting abrasions.

**Significant Examples:**

**1. PCGS MS-66.** *Ex: CSNS Signature Sale (Heritage, 5/2004), lot 6605, where it realized $5,750; Palm Beach, FL Signature Sale (Heritage, 11/2004), lot 6275, where it realized $6,900; The Collection of Dr. Steven L. Duckor (Heritage, 1/2006), lot 986, where it realized $7,475.*

**2. PCGS MS-66.** *Ex: The John C. Hugon Collection (Heritage, 1/2005), lot 4017, where it realized $8,050.*

**Total Known in Mint State:** 80-105 Coins

**Total Known and Value Breakdown by Grade:**

| MS-60 to MS-62 | MS-63 | MS-64 | MS-65 |
|---|---|---|---|
| 13-17 Coins | 18-22 Coins | 35-45 Coins | 10-12 Coins |
| N/A | $750-$900 | $1,750-$2,500 | $3,250-$4,000 |

| MS-66 | MS-67 | MS-68 | MS-69 to MS-70 |
|---|---|---|---|
| 4-6 Coins | 1-2 Coins | 0 Coins | 0 Coins |
| $7,500-$10,000 | $12,500-$20,000 | -- | -- |

*Note:* The conclusions presented in the following "Collecting and Investing Strategies" section are drawn in large part from the Investment Potential Ratios that are summarized in Appendices G and H at the end of this book. For a detailed analysis of the formula used to derive these Investment Potential Ratios, please refer to the Introduction of this book.

**Collecting and Investing Strategies:** I particularly like the 1897-S in MS-65 and MS-66 for inclusion in a numismatic investment portfolio as this issue is decidedly underrated in those grades. MS-67s are also a good buy as they are priced fairly accurately in light of their rarity, but MS-64s are overvalued and should be avoided if at all possible.

When buying a high-grade 1897-S, try to avoid a coin that has been dipped as the solution tends to further subdue the already muted luster for which this issue is known. I would even suggest obtaining a coin with original toning as the color can provide the vibrancy to the surfaces that is often lacking in the luster. Additionally, make sure that the coin you are buying meets the technical criteria for the grade assigned by PCGS or NGC. Given the rarity of this issue in high grades, a few premium-quality MS-64s have found their way into Gem-quality holders over the years. Look for sizeable or otherwise individually distracting abrasions on coins that grade MS-65 or MS-66 as these can be an indication of a piece that has been overgraded.

# Proof
# 1898

## MINTAGE
### 735

Courtesy of David Lawrence

## RARITY
## RANKINGS

***Overall, All Proof Grades:** 22nd of 25*
***High Grade, Proof-65 or Finer:** 23rd of 25*
***Overall, Cameo Finish:** 22nd of 24 (Tie)*
***Overall, Deep/Ultra Cameo Finish:** 12th of 12*

**Important Varieties:** None.

**General Comments:** One of the most common issues in the proof Barber Dime series, the 1898 is easier to obtain in all grades than all other proofs of this type save for the 1894, 1895 and, in an absolute sense only, the first-year 1892. Only the proof 1893 is more plentiful than the proof 1898 with a Cameo finish, and no other issue in this series has a greater population of Deep/Ultra Cameo specimens.

**Strike:** This issue rarely possesses less than full striking detail.

**Finish:** In my opinion, the 1898 is the best-produced issue in the entire Barber Dime series. Even more so than the proof 1896 and proof 1897, this issue is characterized by appreciable Cameo contrast between frosty devices and mirror-finish fields. Many examples possess extremely bold field-to-device contrast that is unsurpassable in a proof Dime of this type.

**Surfaces:** There are some truly breathtaking proof 1898 Barber Dimes extant and, as a whole, the issue has been carefully preserved over the years.

**Toning:** Untoned examples are becoming more prevalent in the numismatic market of the 21st century. The strength of field-to-device contrast with which most proof 1898 Barber Dimes were struck means that this issue is very susceptible to dipping. Dealers and collectors will often dip classic U.S. proof coinage to ensure that they receive a Cameo or Deep/Ultra Cameo designation when the coin is submitted for certification. Brilliant examples also tend to sell better because they allow full appreciation of bold contrast between heavily frosted devices and watery, mirror-finish fields.

For the proponent of originality, I must say that there are also many proof 1898 Barber Dimes with handsome, richly original toning to their surfaces. These pieces are dwindling in number as more and more examples are dipped to bring out the strength of Cameo contrast to the surfaces.

**Eye Appeal:** This is an extremely attractive issue that I believe is the most consistently appealing in the entire Barber Dime series.

**Significant Examples:**

**1. PCGS Proof-68.** *Ex: Milwaukee, WI ANA Signature Coin Auction (Heritage, 8/2007), lot 1635, where it realized $10,925.*

**2. NGC Proof-68.** *Ex: J. M. Clapp, who purchased the coin directly from the Philadelphia Mint in 1898; Clapp estate; The Louis E. Eliasberg, Sr. Collection (Bowers and Merena, 5/1996), lot 1260, where it realized $4,400; The John C. Hugon Collection (Heritage, 1/2005), lot 4082, where it realized $6,325; The William H. LaBelle, Sr. Collection (American Numismatic Rarities, 7/2005), lot 1016, where it realized $6,325; FUN Signature Auction (Heritage, 1/2006), lot 1851, where it realized $6,326; Denver ANA Auction (Bowers and Merena, 8/2006), lot 755, unsold.*

**3. NGC Proof-68.** *Ex: The Andre Dawson Collection of All-American Coins (Heritage, 9/1998), lot 6626, where it realized $5,520.*

This coin displays such awesome field-to-device contrast that is must surely have been placed into a Cameo, if not Deep or Ultra Cameo holder by now.

**4. NGC Proof-68 Cameo.** *Ex: Dallas, TX U.S. Coin Signature Auction (Heritage, 11/2007), lot 445, where it realized $6,325.*

**5. NGC Proof-68 Cameo.** *Ex: Long Beach, CA Signature Coin Auction (Heritage, 2/2007), lot 2962, where it realized $7,274.*

**6. NGC Proof-68 Cameo.** *Ex: New York, NY Signature Sale (Heritage, 7/2004), lot 5835, where it realized $36,800.*

**7. NGC Proof-68 Ultra Cameo.** *Ex: Baltimore Auction (Bowers and Merena, 2/2008), lot 429, where it realized $12,650.*

**8. NGC Proof-68 Ultra Cameo.** *Ex: The Frog Rum Farm Collection (American Numismatic Rarities, 11/2004), lot 660, unsold; Drew St.*

*John Sale (American Numismatic Rarities, 6/2005), lot 453, where it realized $8,050; Long Beach Signature Auction (Heritage, 2/2006), lot 814, unsold; Atlanta, GA ANA Signature Sale (Heritage, 4/2006), lot 448, where it realized $8,338.*

**9. NGC Proof-68 Ultra Cameo.** *Ex: The J.B. Worthington Collection (American Numismatic Rarities, 5/2005), lot 176, where it realized $6,900.*

**10. PCGS Proof-68 Deep Cameo.** *Ex: The Bruce Scher #1 All-Time PCGS Registry Set (Heritage, 2/2005), lot 4058, where it realized $19,550.*

**Total Known:** 410-480 Coins

**Total Known and Value Breakdown by Grade:**

| Brilliant-Finish Coins | | | |
|---|---|---|---|
| **Proof-60-62** | **Proof-63** | **Proof-64** | **Proof-65** |
| 30-35 Coins | 55-65 Coins | 85-95 Coins | 55-65 Coins |
| N/A | $400-$525 | $600-$750 | $1,100-$1,400 |
| **Proof-66** | **Proof-67** | **Proof-68** | **Proof-69-70** |
| 55-65 Coins | 30-35 Coins | 7-9 Coins | 0 Coins |
| $1,750-$2,500 | $3,000-$8,000 | $8,500-$12,500 | -- |

| Cameo Coins | | | |
|---|---|---|---|
| **Proof-60-62 Cameo** | **Proof-63 Cameo** | **Proof-64 Cameo** | **Proof-65 Cameo** |
| 1-2 Coins | 3-4 Coins | 8-10 Coins | 15-18 Coins |
| N/A | $700-$900 | $1,100-$1,350 | $1,400-$1,600 |
| **Proof-66 Cameo** | **Proof-67 Cameo** | **Proof-68 Cameo** | **Proof-69-70 Cameo** |
| 25-30 Coins | 20-25 Coins | 4-5 Coins | 0 Coins |
| $2,000-$3,000 | $3,000-$8,000 | $7,500-$15,000 | -- |

| Deep/Ultra Cameo Coins | | | |
|---|---|---|---|
| **Proof-60 Deep/ Ultra Cameo** | **Proof-63 Deep/ Ultra Cameo** | **Proof-64 Deep/ Ultra Cameo** | **Proof-65 Deep/ Ultra Cameo** |
| 0 Coins | 1-2 Coins | 1 Coin | 2-3 Coins |
| -- | $1,000-$1,100 | $1,250-$1,750 | $2,500-$5,000 |
| **Proof-66 Deep/ Ultra Cameo** | **Proof-67 Deep/ Ultra Cameo** | **Proof-68 Deep/ Ultra Cameo** | **Proof-69 Deep/ Ultra Cameo** |
| 4-5 Coins | 3-4 Coins | 4-5 Coins | 0 Coins |
| $5,000-$7,000 | $7,500-$10,000 | $10,000-$25,000 | -- |

<u>Note:</u> The conclusions presented in the following "Collecting and Investing Strategies" section are drawn in large part from the Investment Potential Ratios that are summarized in Appendices G and H at the end of this book. For a detailed analysis of the formula used to derive these Investment Potential Ratios, please refer to the Introduction of this book.

**Collecting and Investing Strategies:** The 1898 vies with the 1896 and 1897 as the most consistently attractive issue in the proof Barber Dime series. Even so, I am only fond of the 1898 for type purposes in Proof-64 and Proof-65. Brilliant-finish coins that grade higher are overrated relative to their actual rarity.

Since this issue is usually characterized by bold field-to-device contrast, and since such pieces are relatively obtainable in numismatic circles, I suggest acquiring a proof 1898 with either a Cameo or Deep/Ultra Cameo designation as part of the grade. In order to best appreciate these highly desirable finishes in a proof 1898 Dime, look for a coin with bright, untoned surfaces. Chances are good that the coin will have been dipped, but such pieces have generally been well handled and do not show any ill effects from the conservation.

# 1898

**MINTAGE**
16,320,000

Courtesy of David Lawrence

**RARITY
RANKINGS**

*Overall, Mint State: 68th of 74*
*High Grade, MS-65 or Finer: 68th of 74*

## PHILADELPHIA MINT ISSUES

*Overall, Mint State: 19th of 25*
*High Grade, MS-65 or Finer: 19th of 25*

**Important Varieties:** None.

**General Comments:** The 1898 has the second-highest mintage of any Barber Dime struck during the 1890s, and it is the most plentiful issue from the decade after only the really common 1892. In Mint State, however, the population of the 1898 is also smaller than those of the 1913 and 1914, and it is much smaller than those of the 1911, 1912 and 1916. The 1898, of course, is still a readily obtainable issue in all grades up to and including MS-65. Even MS-66s, while scarce, can still be had with patience. Superb Gems, however, are very rare and are only available once in a long while.

**Strike:** The 1898 is a well-struck issue, and most Mint State survivors are sharply impressed.

**Luster:** Luster quality for this issue is also excellent, and I have seen both satin and frosty textured examples. The frosty pieces tend to be a bit more vibrant, but both luster types are usually very appealing when offered in an 1898 Barber Dime. An occasional semi-to-fully prooflike example does surface, but the issue is quite rare with that finish.

**Surfaces:** Surface preservation for the 1898 varies from noticeably abraded to virtually pristine. Most examples possess at least a few scattered abrasions, although this issue is anything but rare with overall smooth surfaces.

**Toning:** The Mint State coins that I have seen run the gamut from brilliant to deeply toned. Most examples have at least some degree of patination to the surfaces, and even many dipped pieces still retain some color from the original toning.

**Eye Appeal:** Eye appeal for this issue varies considerably with grade, given the fact that the surviving population is relatively large and widely scattered throughout the Mint State grading scale. Generally speaking, however, the 1898 has above-average-to-strong eye appeal.

**Significant Examples:**

1. **NGC MS-68.** *Ex: Drew St. John Sale (American Numismatic Rarities, 6/2005), lot 1455, where it realized $9,775; Long Beach Signature Auction (Heritage, 5/2006), lot 1104, unsold; Dallas Signature Coin Auction (Heritage, 11/2006), lot 538, unsold.*

2. **NGC MS-67 ★.** *Ex: The William H. LaBelle, Sr. Collection (American Numismatic Rarities, 7/2005), lot 1017, unsold; The Official Auction of the ANA Las Vegas Coin Show (Bowers and Merena, 10/2005), lot 5418, unsold.*

3. **NGC MS-67.** *Ex: Charlotte ANA National Money Show Auction (Heritage, 3/2003), lot 5565, where it realized $2,128.*

**Total Known in Mint State:** 580-715 Coins

**Total Known and Value Breakdown by Grade:**

| MS-60 to MS-62 | MS-63 | MS-64 | MS-65 |
|---|---|---|---|
| 125-150 Coins | 160-185 Coins | 150-200 Coins | 100-125 Coins |
| N/A | $125-$175 | $225-$300 | $500-$650 |

| MS-66 | MS-67 | MS-68 | MS-69 to MS-70 |
|---|---|---|---|
| 35-45 Coins | 8-10 Coins | 1 Coin | 0 Coins |
| $1,000-$1,750 | $2,500-$5,000 | $7,500-$10,000 | -- |

*Note:* The conclusions presented in the following "Collecting and Investing Strategies" section are drawn in large part from the Investment Potential Ratios that are summarized in Appendices G and H at the end of this book. For a detailed analysis of the formula used to derive these Investment Potential Ratios, please refer to the Introduction of this book.

**Collecting and Investing Strategies:** The 1898 is a respectable, middle-of-the-road Barber Dime that is neither overrated nor underrated to a significant degree in the finer Mint State grades. While the issue does not have the investment potential of many other issues in this series, it is also not a poor buy in any grade from MS-64 to MS-67. As such, the 1898 is probably more appropriate for inclusion in a type or date set as opposed to a numismatic investment portfolio.

Take your time when searching for a Mint State 1898 Dime and make sure that the coin you choose meets with all of your criteria for technical quality and eye appeal. Principal among these should be the coin's ability to fit into your existing collection. If you like toned coins, buy an 1898 with richly original toning. If you prefer brilliant coins, buy an untoned example. And make sure that the coin you are purchasing is sharply struck with vibrant luster and no abrasions or other distractions that are out of context with the assigned grade.

# 1898-O

**MINTAGE**
2,130,000

Courtesy of David Lawrence

## RARITY RANKINGS

*Overall, Mint State: 5th of 74*
*High Grade, MS-65 or Finer: 12th of 74 (Tie)*

### NEW ORLEANS MINT ISSUES

*Overall, Mint State: 4th of 17*
*High Grade, MS-65 or Finer: 6th of 17 (Tie)*

**Important Varieties:** None.

**General Comments:** After producing far fewer than 1 million coins per year from 1894 through 1897, the New Orleans Mint struck more than 2 million Barber Dimes in 1898. Such a respectable mintage belies this issue's true rarity in Mint State. The 1898-O is actually more challenging to locate in Mint State than the lower-mintage 1897-O, and it trails only the 1894-O, 1895-O and 1896-O as the rarest New Orleans Mint Barber Dime in Mint State. The 1898-O is also rarer in all Mint State grades than the 1903-S, 1904-S, 1913-S and 1915-S—all of which are (much) lower-mintage issues that are often touted as "major rarities" by casual or less well-informed numismatists.

Beginning at the MS-65 grade level, the 1898-O is not ranked quite as high, although it is still more elusive as a Gem than the 1903-S, 1907-D, 1913-S and 1915-S. The 1898-O compares favorably with the 1899-O, 1899-S, 1901-S, 1909-S and 1910-D in high-grade rarity.

**Strike:** The 1898-O is one of the most poorly struck issues in the Barber Dime series. It is extremely challenging, if not impossible to locate a coin that is free of even minor lack of detail in one or more areas, and many examples are noticeably blunt. Softness of strike for the 1898-O is usually seen at the top of Liberty's portrait over and around the word LIBERTY, the upper-right portion of the reverse wreath, the lower-left portion of the reverse wreath and/or the right (facing) bow of the ribbon knot and the adjoining section of the reverse wreath.

**Luster:** This issue typically comes with better luster quality than the 1894-O and 1896-O. Most Mint State examples are satiny in texture, although a few are noticeably semi-prooflike with some "flash" to the fields.

**Surfaces:** The 1898-O is not a heavily abraded issue, and incompleteness of strike and/or impaired luster usually serve to limit the grade for low-end Mint State pieces.

**Toning:** Many examples have been dipped, and it is becoming increasingly more difficult to locate an 1898-O with fully original toning. The toned pieces usually exhibit only light-to-moderate overtones, but there are a few pieces with deep, rich color to the surfaces.

**Eye Appeal:** Due primarily to inadequacies with the strike, the 1898-O has below-average eye appeal. Subdued luster can also sometimes be a problem, especially in grades below MS-64.

### Significant Examples:

**1. PCGS MS-67.** *Ex: The John C. Hugon Collection (Heritage, 1/2005), lot 4019, where it realized $36,800.*

**2. PCGS MS-66.** *Ex: The Dr. Carl A. Minning, Jr. Collection (Bowers and Merena, 8/1999), lot 1332, where it realized $3,220.*

**3. NGC MS-66.** *Ex: J.M. Clapp, who acquired the coin directly from the New Orleans Mint in 1898; Clapp estate; The Louis E. Eliasberg, Sr. Collection (Bowers and Merena, 5/1996), lot 1261, where it realized $5,720; FUN Signature Sale (Heritage, 1/1999), lot 6460, where it realized $4,025.*

**Total Known in Mint State:** 65-80 Coins

**Total Known and Value Breakdown by Grade:**

| MS-60 to MS-62 | MS-63 | MS-64 | MS-65 |
|---|---|---|---|
| 12-15 Coins | 20-25 Coins | 12-15 Coins | 12-15 Coins |
| N/A | $1,000-$1,500 | $2,000-$2,500 | $2,500-$5,000 |

| MS-66 | MS-67 | MS-68 | MS-69 to MS-70 |
|---|---|---|---|
| 5-7 Coins | 1 Coin | 1 Coin | 0 Coins |
| $10,000-$25,000 | $35,000-$40,000 | $40,000-$50,000 | -- |

*Note:* The conclusions presented in the following "Collecting and Investing Strategies" section are drawn in large part from the Investment Potential Ratios that are summarized in Appendices G and H at the end of this book. For a detailed analysis of the formula used to derive these Investment Potential Ratios, please refer to the Introduction of this book.

**Collecting and Investing Strategies:** The optimum grade for the 1898-O is MS-64, at which level this issue is the most underrated Barber Dime. Gems in MS-65 offer solid value at the price levels given in this book, but I would absolutely avoid examples in MS-66 and MS-67 as the 1898-O is overrated at those levels.

Regardless of what grade you choose to acquire for the 1898-O, make sure that the coin you are buying has a full LIBERTY on the obverse headband. You should also be able to locate an example with at least emerging definition over the upper-right and lower portions of the reverse wreath. I would also be mindful of toning when pursuing this issue, as there are quite a few low-end Mint State coins with surfaces that are so dark as to be almost devoid of luster. This is less of a problem in higher grades, but avoid coins that grade MS-64 or finer with hazy surfaces and/or noticeable muting of the luster. Several deeply toned coins have been dipped, the solution failing to remove all of the color but still being sufficient to subdue the luster.

# 1898-S

**MINTAGE**
1,702,507

Courtesy of David Lawrence

## RARITY RANKINGS

*Overall, Mint State: 4th of 74*
*High Grade, MS-65 or Finer: 7th of 74 (Tie)*

### SAN FRANCISCO MINT ISSUES

*Overall, Mint State: 1st of 24*
*High Grade, MS-65 or Finer: 3rd of 24 (Tie)*

**Important Varieties:** None.

**General Comments:** Like the 1898-O, the 1898-S is a heavily circulated issue that is much more challenging to locate in all Mint State grades than the original mintage might imply. The 1898-S actually edges out the 1901-S and 1903-S as the rarest San Francisco Mint Barber Dime in Mint State, and it is actually the rarest issue in the series as a whole after only the triumvirate of O-mint issues produced from 1894-1896.

The 1898-S is not ranked as high when we consider only those grades at or above the MS-65 level, where it vies with the 1892-S as the third-rarest San Francisco Mint Barber Dime. It is still a leading condition rarity in the Barber Dime series as a whole, and a Gem 1898-S is even rarer than a similarly graded example of the key-date 1896-O.

**Strike:** The 1898-S is a well-struck issue that usually displays overall sharp definition to both sides. The lower-left portion of the reverse wreath near the ribbon bow is often a tad softly impressed, although this feature is anything but distracting to the eye.

**Luster:** I am definitely a fan of the 1898-S in the area of luster quality. The finish is usually quite vibrant with either a satin or softly frosted texture.

**Surfaces:** As with the 1897-S, the 1898-S is an issue that does not appear to have been handled with much care in the Mint prior to the coins' release into circulation. The vast majority of Mint State survivors possess scattered abrasions, and these tend to be a bit larger in size than those seen for most other issues in the Barber Dime series. Even Gem 1898-S Barber Dimes in MS-65 and MS-66 are apt to display one or two outwardly distracting abrasions, and these are usually seen on the obverse over Liberty's portrait and/or in the reverse field around the denomination ONE DIME.

**Toning:** Richly toned coins are in the majority among Mint State survivors. The colors are usually quite deep, but they often include more vivid overtones at and near the rims. I have not handled too many brilliant pieces, and the ones that I have seen are dipped pieces that usually retain faint, mottled remnants of the original toning.

**Eye Appeal:** The 1898-S is an interesting issue from the standpoint of eye appeal. There is no denying the fact that strike, luster and even toning are strong suits for this issue. On the other hand, the prevalence of distracting abrasions even in the finer Mint State grades serves to limit the final eye appeal rating for this issue. As a whole, therefore, I would rate the 1898-S as only slightly above average in this regard.

**Significant Examples:**

**1. PCGS MS-67.** *Ex: The John C. Hugon Collection (Heritage, 1/2005), lot 4020, where it realized $25,300.*

**2. NGC MS-66.** *Ex: The Belle Glade Collection (Heritage, 8/2007), lot 1632, where it realized $6,900.*

**3. NGC MS-66.** *Ex: Long Beach, CA Signature Coin Auction (Heritage, 2/2007), lot 2942, unsold; CSNS Signature Coin Auction (Heritage, 5/2007), lot 365, where it realized $14,950.*

**4. PCGS MS-66.** *Ex: The Bay Area Collection (Heritage, 3/2003), lot 5566, where it realized $14,950; The Collection of Dr. Steven L. Duckor (Heritage, 1/2006), lot 989, where it realized $12,650.*

**5. PCGS MS-66.** *Ex: J.M. Clapp, who purchased the coin directly from the San Francisco Mint in November of 1898; Clapp estate (1942); The Louis E. Eliasberg, Sr. Collection (Bowers and Merena, 5/1996), lot 1262, where it realized $4,840; The Richmond Collection (David Lawrence, 3/2005), lot 1307, where it realized $7,475; San Francisco, CA ANA Signature Auction (Heritage, 7/2005), lot 10160, where it realized $10,925.*

**Total Known in Mint State:** 60-75 Coins

**Total Known and Value Breakdown by Grade:**

| MS-60 to MS-62 | MS-63 | MS-64 | MS-65 |
|---|---|---|---|
| 20-25 Coins | 7-9 Coins | 15-20 Coins | 8-10 Coins |
| N/A | $900-$1,100 | $1,750-$2,500 | $2,750-$3,500 |

| MS-66 | MS-67 | MS-68 | MS-69 to MS-70 |
|---|---|---|---|
| 7-9 Coins | 1 Coin | 0 Coins | 0 Coins |
| $7,500-$17,500 | $25,000-$35,000 | -- | -- |

*Note:* The conclusions presented in the following "Collecting and Investing Strategies" section are drawn in large part from the Investment Potential Ratios that are summarized in Appendices G and H at the end of this book. For a detailed analysis of the formula used to derive these Investment Potential Ratios, please refer to the Introduction of this book.

**Collecting and Investing Strategies:** Another very rare mintmarked issue from the 1890s, the 1898-S represents an important buying opportunity in most Mint State grades. MS-64s and MS-65s are grossly underrated at the price levels provided in this book, and even at the MS-67 level the 1898-S is an undervalued coin. Among the finer Mint State grades, in fact, MS-66 is the only level at which I believe the 1898-S to be an overrated Barber Dime.

Before you rush out and buy the first 1898-S in MS-64 or MS-65 that comes your way, remember that this issue is extremely challenging to locate with overall smooth-looking surfaces. For this reason, I would be mindful of overgraded coins and avoid any example with too many distracting abrasions in the context of the assigned grade.

# Proof
# 1899

## MINTAGE
846

Courtesy of David Lawrence

## RARITY RANKINGS

*Overall, All Proof Grades: 20th of 25*
*High Grade, Proof-65 or Finer: 17th of 25*
*Overall, Cameo Finish: 14th of 24*
**Overall, Deep/Ultra Cameo Finish:** *11th of 12*

**Important Varieties:** None.

**General Comments:** The 1899 is one of the more common issues in the proof Barber Dime series, although it is rarer than all other proofs of this type from the 1890s with the exception of only the 1893, 1894-S and 1897. In high grades (Proof-65 or finer), the 1899 is actually the rarest proof Barber Dime from the 1890s after only the branch mint 1894-S. This issue is a median rarity in the series with a Cameo finish and, although very rare in Deep/Ultra Cameo, the 1899 is actually the most common proof Barber Dime with that finish after only the 1898.

**Strike:** As with virtually all proof Barber Dimes, the 1899 is an expertly produced issue that almost always exhibits sharp-to-full striking detail.

**Finish:** The proof 1899 has a similar finish to the pre-1896 issues in this series. Although most examples possess some degree of field-to-device contrast, the Cameo effect is seldom as profound for this issue as it is for the proof 1896, proof 1897 and proof 1898.

**Surfaces:** Most examples are at least well preserved, and many are nearly pristine with a noteworthy lack of bothersome hairlines, contact marks and other blemishes.

**Toning:** There is a nearly 50-50 split between deeply toned examples and coins with either untoned or lightly patinated surfaces. Toning for many proof 1899 Barber Dimes is best appreciated at direct angles, where you can often see pretty multicolored undertones that assume much deeper, less vibrant colors when the coin turns away from a light.

**Eye Appeal:** A well-produced and overall carefully preserved issue, the proof 1899 has above-average-to-strong eye appeal.

**Significant Examples:**

**1. NGC Proof-68.** *Ex: The John C. Hugon Collection (Heritage, 1/2005), lot 4083, where it realized $5,463.*

**2. PCGS Proof-68.** *Ex: J.M. Clapp, who acquired the coin directly from the Philadelphia Mint in 1899; Clapp estate (1942); The Louis E. Eliasberg, Sr. Collection (Bowers and Merena, 5/1996), lot 1263, where it realized $6,160; The Collections of Craig N. Smith and George William Youngman (Bowers and Merena, 3/2003), lot 1311, where it realized $5,175.*

**3. NGC Proof-68 ★ Cameo.** *Ex: Santa Clara Elite Sale (Superior, 11/2004), lot 1362, where it realized $6,440.*

**4. NGC Proof-67 Cameo.** *Ex: Long Beach Signature Auction (Heritage, 6/2006), lot 1130, where it realized $2,990.*

**5. PCGS Proof-67 Cameo.** *Ex: Baltimore, MD Signature Sale (Heritage, 7/2003), lot 6640, where it realized $2,990; Long Beach Signature Auction (Heritage, 6/2006), lot 1131, where it realized $4,888.*

**6. NGC Proof-67 Cameo.** *Ex: FUN Signature Sale (Heritage, 1/2004), lot 5703, unsold; CSNS Signature Sale (Heritage, 5/2004), lot 6696, where it realized $2,990.*

**7. PCGS Proof-67 Deep Cameo.** *Ex: The J.B. Worthington Collection (American Numismatic Rarities, 5/2005), lot 177, where it realized $4,600.*

**8. PCGS Proof-67 Deep Cameo.** *Ex: The Bruce Scher #1 All-Time PCGS Registry Set (Heritage, 2/2005), lot 4059, where it realized $4,888.*

**9. PCGS Proof-67 Deep Cameo.** *Ex: The Indiana Collection (Heritage, 7/2002), lot 7635, where it realized $4,140; The Allison Park Collection (American Numismatic Rarities, 8/2004), lot 319, where it realized $5,290.*

**10. PCGS Proof-67 Deep Cameo.** *Ex: New York, NY Signature Sale (Heritage, 7/2002), lot 7634, where it realized $4,025.*

**Total Known:** 375-460 Coins

**Total Known and Value Breakdown by Grade:**

| Brilliant-Finish Coins | | | |
|---|---|---|---|
| **Proof-60-62** | **Proof-63** | **Proof-64** | **Proof-65** |
| 45-55 Coins | 50-60 Coins | 85-100 Coins | 55-65 Coins |
| N/A | $425-$525 | $725-$850 | $1,300-$1,500 |
| **Proof-66** | **Proof-67** | **Proof-68** | **Proof-69-70** |
| 50-60 Coins | 30-40 Coins | 2-3 Coins | 0 Coins |
| $1,600-$2,250 | $3,000-$8,000 | $7,500-$15,000 | -- |

| Cameo Coins | | | |
|---|---|---|---|
| **Proof-60-62 Cameo** | **Proof-63 Cameo** | **Proof-64 Cameo** | **Proof-65 Cameo** |
| 1-2 Coins | 3-4 Coins | 12-15 Coins | 8-10 Coins |
| N/A | $750-$950 | $1,250-$1,450 | $1,500-$1,700 |
| **Proof-66 Cameo** | **Proof-67 Cameo** | **Proof-68 Cameo** | **Proof-69-70 Cameo** |
| 14-18 Coins | 4-6 Coins | 1 Coin | 0 Coins |
| $2,500-$3,000 | $3,000-$5,000 | $7,500-$10,000 | -- |

| Deep/Ultra Cameo Coins | | | |
|---|---|---|---|
| **Proof-60-62 Deep/ Ultra Cameo** | **Proof-63 Deep/ Ultra Cameo** | **Proof-64 Deep/ Ultra Cameo** | **Proof-65 Deep/ Ultra Cameo** |
| 0 Coins | 0 Coins | 1-2 Coins | 2-3 Coins |
| -- | -- | $1,300-$1,500 | $2,500-$5,000 |
| **Proof-66 Deep/ Ultra Cameo** | **Proof-67 Deep/ Ultra Cameo** | **Proof-68 Deep/ Ultra Cameo** | **Proof-69-70 Deep/ Ultra Cameo** |
| 1 Coin | 6-8 Coins | 0 Coins | 0 Coins |
| $4,000-$6,000 | $7,500-$10,000 | -- | -- |

*Note:* The conclusions presented in the following "Collecting and Investing Strategies" section are drawn in large part from the Investment Potential Ratios that are summarized in Appendices G and H at the end of this book. For a detailed analysis of the formula used to derive these Investment Potential Ratios, please refer to the Introduction of this book.

**Collecting and Investing Strategies:** At the Proof-64, Proof-65 and Proof-66 grade levels, the 1899 offers a relatively good mix of rarity and value at the price levels given in this book. In fact, I would only avoid this issue in Proof-67, for at that level it is actually the most overrated proof Barber Dime.

Due to their relatively availability in the context of this series, I would try to acquire a proof 1899 with either a Cameo or Deep/Ultra Cameo finish as designated by PCGS or NGC. This is particularly sound advice since the 1899 is one of the last issues of the type that the Mint produced using Cameo proofing techniques. In order to best appreciate field-to-device contrast, I suggest obtaining a proof 1899 with either untoned or lightly toned surfaces.

# 1899

### MINTAGE
### 19,580,000

Courtesy of Bowers and Merena

### RARITY
### RANKINGS

*Overall, Mint State: 61st of 74*
*High Grade, MS-65 or Finer: 58th of 74*

## PHILADELPHIA MINT ISSUES

**Overall, Mint State:** *13th of 25*
**High Grade, MS-65 or Finer:** *12th of 25*

**Important Varieties:** None.

**General Comments:** The 1899 is the highest-mintage Barber Dime from the 1890s. The relative rankings of this issue may come as a surprise, however, and the 1899 is actually a median rarity in Mint State among Philadelphia Mint Barber Dimes. The 1899 is rarer in Mint State than the similar-mintage 1906, as well as the lower-mintage 1897, 1898, 1908 and 1910. This issue is much rarer than the truly common coins of the type such as the 1892, 1911 and 1916. In an absolute sense, however, the 1899 is still an easy coin to locate in grades through MS-64. MS-65s are moderately scarce, MS-66s are quite rare and Superb Gems in MS-67 are very rare.

**Strike:** The typical '99-P is well struck with bold-to-sharp definition on both sides. Only a few examples are a bit bluntly struck on the reverse over the lower-left portion of the wreath, particularly the large leaf below the letter D in DIME. Soft, partially indistinct denticulation is also sometimes a problem for the 1899.

**Luster:** The 1899 has fairly good luster, but it is not quite as vibrant as either the 1897 or 1898. Luster types for this issue are usually confined to satin and softly frosted, but a few exceptional pieces are known that possess a richly frosted texture to the surfaces. NGC has even certified a single example as MS-65 Prooflike (December/2008).

**Surfaces:** Expect most Mint State survivors to reveal at least a few scattered abrasions. Many examples are actually quite scuffy with numerous distracting marks, and you will probably experience more than a little bit of difficulty locating an example with surfaces that are smooth enough to grade finer than MS-64.

**Toning:** Most Mint State pieces are toned, and many exhibit fairly deep patination to one or both sides. On the other hand, toned examples often include more-or-less vivid colors such as cobalt-blue, sea-green and orange-red. Colors such as these are sometimes only appreciable with the aid of a direct light, or sometimes only at and near the rims. The few brilliant coins that I have handled have been dipped.

**Eye Appeal:** As with the 1898, eye appeal for the 1899 varies considerably among survivors. It is seldom less than average, however, as even low-end survivors usually possess some redeeming attributes to offset distracting abrasions and/or impaired luster. High-grade examples almost always possess above-average or strong eye appeal, those with particularly vibrant mint frost and/or vivid toning definitely falling into the latter category.

**Significant Examples:**

**1. PCGS MS-67.** *Ex: Denver ANA Auction (Bowers and Merena, 8/2006), lot 756, where it realized $11,500.*

**2. NGC MS-67.** *Ex: Long Beach Signature Sale (Heritage, 6/2000), lot 7145, where it realized $1,898.*

**Total Known in Mint State:** 400-485 Coins

**Total Known and Value Breakdown by Grade:**

| MS-60 to MS-62 | MS-63 | MS-64 | MS-65 |
|---|---|---|---|
| 90-110 Coins | 100-125 Coins | 135-160 Coins | 55-65 Coins |
| N/A | $125-$175 | $250-$325 | $500-$650 |

| MS-66 | MS-67 | MS-68 | MS-69 to MS-70 |
|---|---|---|---|
| 15-20 Coins | 4-5 Coins | 0 Coins | 0 Coins |
| $1,250-$2,500 | $5,000-$12,500 | -- | -- |

*Note:* The conclusions presented in the following "Collecting and Investing Strategies" section are drawn in large part from the Investment Potential Ratios that are summarized in Appendices G and H at the end of this book. For

a detailed analysis of the formula used to derive these Investment Potential Ratios, please refer to the Introduction of this book.

**Collecting and Investing Strategies:** A good buy in the MS-64 to MS-66 grade range, the 1899 is either accurately priced or undervalued at those levels of preservation. On the other hand, I do not prefer the 1899 in MS-67 because the issue is actually somewhat overrated as a Superb Gem.

I have seen a number of Mint State 1899 Barber Dimes with a soft strike either at the denticles or over the lower-left reverse wreath. Avoid those coins in favor of an example with overall sharp definition. My personal favorites for this issue from an aesthetic standpoint are the handful of coins with thick mint frost to both sides. Most of those coins are concentrated at the MS-65 and MS-66 levels—good news in light of the fact that the issue is underrated in those grades—and they also typically come with richly original toning. Even on those pieces, however, I would be mindful of the striking detail since PCGS and NGC do not always take strike into consideration when grading this issue.

# 1899-O

## MINTAGE
2,650,000

Courtesy of David Lawrence

## RARITY RANKINGS

**Overall, Mint State:** *6th of 74 (Tie)*
**High Grade, MS-65 or Finer:** *12th of 74 (Tie)*

### NEW ORLEANS MINT ISSUES

**Overall, Mint State:** *5th of 17*
**High Grade, MS-65 or Finer:** *6th of 17 (Tie)*

**Important Varieties:** There are two important varieties for this issue. The first is a Repunched Date with the attributions FS-301 and FS-009.83. The second is a Repunched Mintmark that is attributed as FS-501, FS-009.8 and Lawrence-103.

**General Comments:** Dime production at the New Orleans Mint continued to increase in 1899. This issue is actually the highest-mintage New Orleans Mint Barber Dime from the 1890s after only the first-year 1892-O. Do not let this fact fool you; the 1899-O is actually a very rare issue in Mint State that is comparable to the 1898-O both from absolute and high-grade standpoints. In terms of total number of Mint State coins believed to exist, the 1899-O is also similar in rarity to the much lower-mintage 1901-S and 1903-S.

High-grade rarity for the 1899-O is also akin to that of the 1901-S, as well as the 1899-S, 1909-S and 1910-D—all of which are lower-mintage issues except for the 1910-D. The best that the market can usually muster in an 1899-O Barber Dime is an MS-64. Gems in MS-65 and MS-66 are rare, and there are no more than two MS-67s known to exist.

**Strike:** The 1899-O is much easier to locate with overall bold striking detail than the 1898-O. Many examples are actually quite sharp with no areas of particularly troublesome lack of detail. Other pieces are softly impressed here and there, usually over the lower-left reverse wreath, upper-left reverse wreath and/or on the obverse at the top of Liberty's portrait.

**Luster:** Luster quality is below average for this issue, the typical piece displaying a satiny texture that is often a bit subdued even in higher Mint State grades.

**Surfaces:** Excessive abrasions are seldom a problem for the 1899-O. Rather, it is often lackluster surfaces that confine many examples to lower Mint State grades through MS-63. MS-64s and MS-65s do tend to display a few abrasions, however, but in those grades such distractions are usually small in size and singularly inconspicuous.

**Toning:** Original surfaces for a Mint State example of this issue are defined by rich toning that can be either relatively vivid or quite dark. Dipped pieces are becoming more prevalent, and these typically display brilliant surfaces or light, iridescent toning in pale-gold or similar shades.

**Eye Appeal:** The 1899-O is stronger in the eye appeal category than the 1898-O, although the issue is still not much better than average in this regard. The primary culprit here is the luster, which is seldom vibrant. Dipped coins tend to be even more lackluster, although such treatment—if executed properly—can still be beneficial for a coin with unsightly toning.

**Significant Examples:**

**1. NGC MS-66 Prooflike.** *Ex: The Southwest Collection (Heritage, 2/2008), lot 159, where it realized $7,475.*

**2. PCGS MS-66.** *Ex: The John C. Hugon Collection (Heritage, 1/2005), lot 4022, where it realized $6,038; The Collection of Dr. Steven L. Duckor (Heritage, 1/2005), lot 991, where it realized $8,050.*

**3. NGC MS-66.** *Ex: Atlanta, GA Signature Sale (Heritage, 8/2001), lot 5722, where it realized $2,760; Elite Sale (Superior, 1/2002), lot 1114, where it realized $1,725.*

**4. NGC MS-66.** *Ex: The Dr. Fred Firestone Collection (Heritage, 8/2001), lot 5721, where it realized $5,060.*

**Total Known in Mint State:** 65-85 Coins

**Total Known and Value Breakdown by Grade:**

| MS-60 to MS-62 | MS-63 | MS-64 | MS-65 |
|---|---|---|---|
| 20-25 Coins | 13-17 Coins | 15-20 Coins | 10-12 Coins |
| N/A | $8,000-$1,200 | $2,000-$2,500 | $3,000-$6,000 |

## Total Known and Value Breakdown by Grade (cont.):

| MS-66 | MS-67 | MS-68 | MS-69 to MS-70 |
|---|---|---|---|
| 8-10 Coins | 1-2 Coins | 0 Coins | 0 Coins |
| $7,000-$10,000 | $15,000-$25,000 | -- | -- |

*Note:* The conclusions presented in the following "Collecting and Investing Strategies" section are drawn in large part from the Investment Potential Ratios that are summarized in Appendices G and H at the end of this book. For a detailed analysis of the formula used to derive these Investment Potential Ratios, please refer to the Introduction of this book.

**Collecting and Investing Strategies:** The optimum grade for the 1899-O from the standpoint of investment potential is MS-64, for the issue is decidedly undervalued at that level of preservation. MS-65s are also underrated, if less so, but you should definitely avoid the 1899-O is MS-66 and MS-67 as such pieces are overpriced in relation to their actual rarity.

Your search for a pleasing 1899-O in MS-64 or MS-65 is sure to be a difficult one, as almost every example that I have handled is characterized by inferior luster. This being the case, I would ignore this criterion and instead focus on characteristics that are more varied from coin-to-coin. Look for an 1899-O with overall sharp striking detail in favor of a coin with isolated softness of detail on one or both sides. Additionally, I would stay away from darkly toned examples with colors that further subdue the surfaces. The same should also be said for coins that have been dipped to the point where the luster is adversely affected. Dipped examples can be attractive, but for this issue in particular make sure that the coin still retains some vibrancy to the luster. And as for originally toned examples, you would be well served to acquire a piece with even toning and at least some vividness to the color(s).

# 1899-S

### MINTAGE
1,867,493

Courtesy of David Lawrence

### RARITY RANKINGS

*Overall, Mint State: 27th of 74*
*High Grade, MS-65 or Finer: 12th of 74 (Tie)*

### SAN FRANCISCO MINT ISSUES

*Overall, Mint State: 14th of 24*
*High Grade, MS-65 or Finer: 7th of 24 (Tie)*

**Important Varieties:** None.

**General Comments:** In terms of total number of Mint State coins extant, the 1899-S is the most readily obtainable San Francisco Mint Barber Dime from the 1890s after only the 1893-S. This issue is still a median rarity in the S-mint Barber Dime series as a whole, and it is more elusive in Mint State than such other issues as the 1900-S, 1905-S and 1906-S, as well as the low-mintage 1913-S and 1915-S.

The 1899-S is even more favorably ranked when we consider only coins that grades MS-65 or finer. At an above that level, the 1899-S compares favorably with the low-mintage 1901-S and 1909-S, as well as the conditionally challenging 1898-O, 1899-O and 1910-D. Very scarce even in lower grades through MS-63, the 1899-S is rare as a near-Gem and very rare any finer.

**Strike:** This is a sharply struck issue that seldom displays even trivial lack of detail on either the obverse or the reverse.

**Luster:** The 1899-S has very good, if not excellent luster that is usually either satiny or softly frosted in texture. A few semi-prooflike and fully prooflike examples are known, but the 1899-S is quite rare with that type of finish.

**Surfaces:** This issue is similar to the 1897-S and 1898-S in terms of surface preservation, and distracting abrasions are almost always present on one or both sides. Abrasions tend to be fairly sizeable, and they can even be outwardly distracting on examples that PCGS and NGC have graded as high as MS-65.

**Toning:** I have seen some really beautifully toned 1899-S Dimes, and such pieces are usually characterized by soft-to-moderate colors that include more vivid shades such as reddish-orange, gold and blue. Deeply toned coins are not seen all that often, but dipped pieces with either lightly patinated or completely untoned surfaces are fairly plentiful.

**Eye Appeal:** Overall eye appeal for this issue is above average, this despite the difficulty of locating an example that is free of bothersome abrasions. Strike, luster and toning are almost always positive attributes, and the combination of these features has produced some really attractive examples of the 1899-S.

**Significant Examples:**

**1. NGC MS-67.** *Ex: The Wes Rasmussen Collection Sale (Superior, 2/1998), lot 1864, where it realized $3,300; Cleveland, OH ANA National Money Sale (Heritage, 3/1997), lot 5924, where it realized $2,990.*

**2. PCGS MS-67.** *Ex: The Irving Goodman Collection (Superior, 5/1996), lot 727, unsold; Orlando Rarities Sale (Bowers and Merena, 1/1997), lot 97, unsold.*

**3. PCGS MS-66.** *Ex: FUN Signature Sale (Heritage, 1/1998), lot 6688, unsold; Long Beach Signature Sale (Heritage, 6/2000), lot 7147, where it realized $3,335; The Collection of Dr. Steven L. Duckor (Heritage, 1/2006), lot 992, where it realized $4,600.*

**4. NGC MS-66 Prooflike.** *Ex: FUN Signature Sale (Heritage, 1/2006), lot 1815, where it realized $3,738.*

**5. PCGS MS-66.** *Ex: The John C. Hugon Collection (Heritage, 1/2005), lot 4023, where it realized $8,050.*

**6. NGC MS-66.** *Ex: Pre-Long Beach Elite Coin Auction (Superior, 9/2003), lot 1500, where it realized $4,370.*

**7. NGC MS-66.** *Ex: The Stetson University Collection (Bowers and Merena, 5/1993), lot 198, unsold; The Kenneth C. Long Estate Collection (Bowers and Merena, 5/1995), lot 1082, unsold.*

**Total Known in Mint State:** 115-140 Coins

**Total Known and Value Breakdown by Grade:**

| MS-60 to MS-62 | MS-63 | MS-64 | MS-65 |
|---|---|---|---|
| 35-40 Coins | 25-30 Coins | 35-45 Coins | 8-10 Coins |
| N/A | $400-$600 | $1,450-$1,650 | $2,750-$3,500 |

| MS-66 | MS-67 | MS-68 | MS-69 to MS-70 |
|---|---|---|---|
| 10-12 Coins | 3-4 Coins | 0 Coins | 0 Coins |
| $4,000-$7,500 | $8,000-$12,500 | -- | -- |

*Note:* The conclusions presented in the following "Collecting and Investing Strategies" section are drawn in large part from the Investment Potential Ratios that are summarized in Appendices G and H at the end of this book. For a detailed analysis of the formula used to derive these Investment Potential Ratios, please refer to the Introduction of this book.

**Collecting and Investing Strategies:** Unless you opt for a coin in MS-65, I would avoid the 1899-S in the finer Mint State grades. MS-64s, MS-66s and MS-67s are all overrated to one degree or another, and only in MS-65 is the 1899-S an underrated coin. In fact, this issue is the most undervalued Barber Dime in MS-65 after only the 1894-O, 1898-S, 1903-S, 1907-S and 1910-D.

Among the more heavily abraded San Francisco Mint issues, the 1899-S, like the 1897-S and 1898-S, is subject to overgrading. This seems to be an especially significant problem in MS-65, at which level I have seen a few certified coins with sizeable abrasions. These tend to be concentrated on the obverse over and around Liberty's portrait. Avoid these coins at all costs since they will probably be difficult to sell in the future. Even if you can sell such a coin, your chances are not good for registering a strong return on your initial investment. Excessive abrasions aside, the 1899-S tends to come nice, and properly graded Gems are usually beautiful coins.

# Proof

# 1900

## MINTAGE
912

Courtesy of David Lawrence

## RARITY
## RANKINGS

*Overall, All Proof Grades: 13th of 25*
*High Grade, Proof-65 or Finer: 13th of 25*
*Overall, Cameo Finish: 17th of 24*
*Overall, Deep/Ultra Cameo Finish: 9th of 12*

**Important Varieties:** None.

**General Comments:** The 1900 has the highest mintage of any proof Barber Dime produced from 1895 through the series' end in 1915. The reason for the relatively large production that year is the Mint's belief that there would be an increase in public demand for proof coins to mark the turn of the 20th century. Either the anticipated demand did not materialize, or many specimens were sold to non-collectors among the contemporary public who subsequently mishandled and/or lost a sizeable number of examples. Today, the 1900 is a median rarity in the proof Barber Dime series both in terms of total number of coins known and number of coins extant in high grades. It is rarer in an absolute sense than such lower-mintage issues in this series as the 1904 and 1909, as well as all proof Barber Dimes from the 1890s with the sole exception of the 1894-S.

In high grades, the proof 1900 is ranked ahead of the lower-mintage proof 1901, proof 1905, proof 1909 and proof 1911. Cameo-finish specimens are more elusive than those of the proof 1901 and proof 1911, as well as most 1890s issues in this series. The proof 1900 is very rare in Deep/Ultra Cameo, although not unknown, and such pieces are seen more often than those of other issues in this series such as the proof 1906, proof 1910 and proof 1911.

**Strike:** Striking detail for this issue is usually full, and it is seldom less than sharp.

**Finish:** The typical proof 1900 displays at least some degree of field-to-device contrast, and many examples are strong enough in this area to secure a Cameo or Deep/Ultra Cameo designation from the leading certification services. Even so, the incidence of Cameo-finish coins for the proof 1900 is less than it is for the proof 1896-1898 issues.

**Surfaces:** Among those coins that have survived, the proof 1900 is a well-preserved issue. Surfaces are usually free of outwardly distracting blemishes, if not virtually pristine, and even lower-grade examples through Proof-64 seldom display more than a few wispy hairlines and/or other tiny contact marks.

**Toning:** As with the proof 1899, the proof 1900 is an issue that is just as easy to locate with brilliant surfaces as it is with original toning. Most of the brilliant examples have been dipped but, since this has largely been done by numismatic experts, the coins' surfaces tend to be radiant with no detracting haziness. Many toned pieces are quite dark, while only a small percentage of coins that I have handled exhibit light or vivid patination.

**Eye Appeal:** Discounting examples with excessively dark toning, the proof 1900 has very strong eye appeal. The issue was well made, and most of those coins that were fortunate enough to survive to the present day did so while retaining vibrant, more-or-less mark-free surfaces.

**Significant Examples:**

**1. NGC Proof-68.** *Ex: John M. Clapp, who acquired the coin directly from the Philadelphia Mint in 1900; Clapp estate (1942); The Louis E. Eliasberg, Sr. Collection (Bowers and Merena, 5/1996), lot 1266, where it realized $2,970; The Wes Rasmussen Collection Sale (Superior, 2/1998), lot 1865, where it realized $4,125; ANA Sale of the Millennium (Bowers and Merena, 8/2000), lot 1156, where it realized $5,290; Atlanta, GA Signature Sale (Heritage, 8/2001), lot 5746, unsold.*

**2. PCGS Proof-68 Cameo.** *Ex: Long Beach Signature Auction (Heritage, 6/2006), lot 1135, where it realized $9,200.*

**3. NGC Proof-68 Cameo.** *Ex: The J.B. Worthington Collection (American Numismatic Rarities, 5/2005), lot 178, where it realized $5,520.*

**4. PCGS Proof-67 Cameo.** CAC. *Ex: Phoenix, AZ ANA Signature Auction (Heritage, 3/2008), lot 427, where it realized $4,313.*

**5. NGC Proof-67 Cameo.** *Ex: The James Paul Collection (Heritage, 1/2007), lot 2679, where it realized $2,760.*

**6. PCGS Proof-67 Cameo.** *Ex: Dallas Signature Auction (Heritage, 12/2005), lot 501, where it realized $4,313; Long Beach Signature Auction (Heritage, 6/2006), lot 1134, unsold; Long Beach, CA Signature Auction (Heritage, 9/2006), lot 1364, unsold.*

**7. NGC Proof-67 Cameo.** *Ex: Long Beach Signature Auction (Heritage, 6/2006), lot 1133, where it realized $5,463.*

**8. NGC Proof-67 Cameo.** *Ex: CSNS Signature Auction (Heritage, 4/2006), lot 1337, where it realized $3,738.*

**9. PCGS Proof-67 Cameo.** *Ex: FUN Signature Sale (Heritage, 1/2004), lot 5706, where it realized $7,188; The Bruce Scher #1 All-Time PCGS Registry Set (Heritage, 2/2005), lot 4060, where it realized $6,038.*

**10. PCGS Proof-67 Cameo.** *Ex: November Signature Sale (Heritage, 11/2003), lot 6041, where it realized $7,475.*

**11. NGC Proof-67 Cameo.** *Ex: Pre-Long Beach Sale (Ira & Larry Goldberg, 6/2002), lot 2173, where it realized $2,645.*

**12. NGC Proof-67 Cameo.** *Ex: Long Beach Signature Sale (Heritage, 5/2001), lot 8046, where it realized $3,163.*

**13. PCGS Proof-67 Deep Cameo.** *Ex: Milwaukee, WI ANA Signature Coin Auction (Heritage, 8/2007), lot 596, where it realized $8,625.*

**Total Known:** 340-410 Coins

**Total Known and Value Breakdown by Grade:**

| Brilliant-Finish Coins | | | |
|---|---|---|---|
| **Proof-60-62** | **Proof-63** | **Proof-64** | **Proof-65** |
| 35-45 Coins | 50-60 Coins | 80-90 Coins | 35-45 Coins |
| N/A | $425-$525 | $725-$850 | $1,350-$1,600 |
| **Proof-66** | **Proof-67** | **Proof-68** | **Proof-69-70** |
| 40-50 Coins | 23-28 Coins | 5-7 Coins | 0 Coins |
| $1,750-$2,500 | $3,000-$4,000 | $7,000-$10,000 | -- |

| Cameo Coins | | | |
|---|---|---|---|
| **Proof-60-62 Cameo** | **Proof-63 Cameo** | **Proof-64 Cameo** | **Proof-65 Cameo** |
| 1 Coin | 3-4 Coins | 18-22 Coins | 12-15 Coins |
| N/A | $750-$850 | $9,00-$1,250 | $1,650-$2,000 |
| **Proof-66 Cameo** | **Proof-67 Cameo** | **Proof-68 Cameo** | **Proof-69-70 Cameo** |
| 12-15 Coins | 12-15 Coins | 4-5 Coins | 0 Coins |
| $2,250-$3,250 | $3,500-$7,500 | $8,500-$15,000 | -- |

| Deep/Ultra Cameo | | | |
|---|---|---|---|
| **Proof-60-62 Deep/ Ultra Cameo** | **Proof-63 Deep/ Ultra Cameo** | **Proof-64 Deep/ Ultra Cameo** | **Proof-65 Deep/ Ultra Cameo** |
| 0 Coins | 0 Coins | 0 Coins | 1 Coin |
| -- | -- | -- | $4,000-$6,000 |
| **Proof-66 Deep/ Ultra Cameo** | **Proof-67 Deep/ Ultra Cameo** | **Proof-68 Deep/ Ultra Cameo** | **Proof-69-70 Deep/ Ultra Cameo** |
| 2-3 Coins | 4-5 Coins | 0 Coins | 0 Coins |

*Note:* The conclusions presented in the following "Collecting and Investing Strategies" section are drawn in large part from the Investment Potential Ratios that are summarized in Appendices G and H at the end of this book. For a detailed analysis of the formula used to derive these Investment Potential Ratios, please refer to the Introduction of this book.

**Collecting and Investing Strategies:** As a turn-of-the-century issue, the 1900 is among the most popular type candidates in the proof Barber Dime series. While Proof-66s and Proof-67s offer fairly solid value in light of their rarity, I prefer examples in Proof-64 and Proof-65. The 1900 is actually the third most underrated Barber Dime in Proof-65 after the 1908 and 1915, and such pieces are much rarer than market values indicate.

The 1900 is not as easy to locate with strong eye appeal as the proof Barber Dimes struck in 1896, 1897 and 1898. Still, there are some really attractive examples of the proof 1900 in numismatic circles, and these pieces do trade from time-to-time. Insist on full striking detail and enough field-to-device contrast to secure at least a Cameo designation from PCGS or NGC. The brilliant specimens that I have seen are really pleasing to the eye.

If you insist on acquiring a toned proof 1900, you are probably going to have to pass over the offerings in several major auctions before the right coin becomes available. Not only are originally toned specimens diminishing in number as dipping becomes more widespread, but most toned examples of the proof 1900 are rather dark. Insist on acquiring one of the more vividly toned specimens, and then again make sure that the colors are not too deep as to obscure the Mint-made reflectivity in the fields and, if applicable, the field-to-device contrast. The Bruce Scher Specimen on the above list of Significant Examples is an excellent example of a Cameo-finish proof 1900 Barber Dime with vivid toning and vibrant surfaces.

# 1900

## MINTAGE
### 17,600,000

Courtesy of David Lawrence

## RARITY RANKINGS

**Overall, Mint State:** *52nd of 74*
**High Grade, MS-65 or Finer:** *49th of 74*

### PHILADELPHIA MINT ISSUES

**Overall, Mint State:** *8th of 25*
**High Grade, MS-65 or Finer:** *8th of 25*

**Important Varieties:** None.

**General Comments:** The 1900 is a much scarcer issue than a sizeable mintage of 17.6 million pieces might suggest. It is the eighth-rarest Philadelphia Mint Barber Dime after the 1894, 1895, 1896, 1902, 1903, 1904 and 1905—a statement that applies to both total number of Mint State survivors and total number of coins extant in high grades. When viewed in the wider context of the Barber Dime series, however, the 1900 emerges as one of the more readily obtainable issues of the type, at least in grades through MS-64. Coins that grade MS-65 or finer are scarce-to-rare, however, and the 1900 is actually more challenging to locate in high grades than such mintmarked issues in this series as the 1906-O, 1906-S, 1908-O and even the low-mintage 1913-S.

I believe that a small group of perhaps six-to-eight, high-grade 1900 Barber Dimes entered the market in early 2002. These coins all display richly original, multicolored toning, and most were certified as MS-66 or MS-67 before being offered through auction. This group comprises approximately one third of the extant population for this issue in grades above MS-65.

**Strike:** This issue typically displays sharp-to-full striking definition. Only rarely have I seen a Mint State example with a touch of striking softness to the haircurls over Liberty's brow on the obverse and/or over the right ribbon (facing) bow on the reverse. Even on such pieces, however, the lack of full definition is not readily evident after a more cursory glance, and even under close examination of the surfaces this feature is not overly distracting to the eye.

**Luster:** The 1900 comes with very good, if not excellent luster that is almost always of either the satin or softly frosted type.

**Surfaces:** Scattered abrasions are the norm for this issue, and most Mint State survivors that I have seen are marred by at least a few wispy blemishes. It is anything but easy to locate a 1900 Barber Dime with overall smooth-looking surfaces.

**Toning:** Many examples have been dipped, their surfaces now either fully brilliant or retaining only minimal remnants of light toning. Based on the toning that I have seen on most Mint State survivors, it is probably best that so many 1900 Barber Dimes have been dipped. Original toning for this issue is usually quite dark and, for lower-grade examples through MS-64, the patination can be so deep as to obscure the luster. There are exceptions, however, and those coins are usually confined to the higher Mint State grades beginning in MS-65. The toned coins that I have seen at those levels of preservation retain strong luster and include at least some vividness to the patination.

**Eye Appeal:** This issue can be challenging to locate with strong eye appeal, and most Mint State examples are decidedly below average in this regard. Grade-limiting abrasions and/or dark toning are quite prevalent, especially in the MS-60 to MS-64 grade range where most coins are concentrated. On the other hand, the relatively few Gems and Superb Gems that have survived tend to be highly attractive coins with excellent striking quality and carefully preserved surfaces.

**Significant Examples:**

**1. PCGS MS-67.** *Ex: The Collection of Dr. Steven L. Duckor (Heritage, 1/2006), lot 993, where it realized $8,625.*

**2. NGC MS-67.** *Ex: FUN Signature Sale (Heritage, 1/2002), lot 5927, where it realized $3,680; The John C. Hugon Collection (Heritage, 1/2005), lot 4024, where it realized $5,750.*

**3. NGC MS-67.** *Ex: The Burke & Clemente Collections (Bowers and Merena, 5/1994), lot 1227, where it realized $2,860.*

**4. PCGS MS-66.** *Ex: FUN Signature Coin Auction (Heritage, 1/2008), lot 1028, where it realized $2,415.*

**5. PCGS MS-66.** *Ex: The Wayne S. Rich Collection (Heritage, 3/2002), lot 2089, where it realized $1,265.*

**6. NGC MS-66.** *Ex: FUN Signature Sale (Heritage, 1/2002), lot 5922, unsold.*

**7. NGC MS-66.** *Ex: FUN Signature Sale (Heritage, 1/2002), lot 5923, unsold.*

**8. NGC MS-66.** *Ex: FUN Signature Sale (Heritage, 1/2002), lot 5924, unsold.*

**9. NGC MS-66.** *Ex: FUN Signature Sale (Heritage, 1/2002), lot 5925, where it realized $891.*

**10. NGC MS-66.** *Ex: FUN Signature Sale (Heritage, 1/2002), lot 5926, where it realized $891.*

**Total Known in Mint State:** 275-340 Coins

**Total Known and Value Breakdown by Grade:**

| MS-60 to MS-62 | MS-63 | MS-64 | MS-65 |
|---|---|---|---|
| 75-95 Coins | 65-80 Coins | 80-100 Coins | 35-45 Coins |
| N/A | $135-$185 | $250-$350 | $550-$700 |

| MS-66 | MS-67 | MS-68 | MS-69 to MS-70 |
|---|---|---|---|
| 12-14 Coins | 6-8 Coins | 0 Coins | 0 Coins |
| $1,100-$2,500 | $6,250-$10,000 | -- | -- |

*Note:* The conclusions presented in the following "Collecting and Investing Strategies" section are drawn in large part from the Investment Potential Ratios that are summarized in Appendices G and H at the end of this book. For a detailed analysis of the formula used to derive these Investment Potential Ratios, please refer to the Introduction of this book.

**Collecting and Investing Strategies:** You are going to have to focus on grades in the MS-64 to MS-66 range in order to maximize your investment potential in a 1900 Barber Dime. In those grades, the 1900 is consistently among the most underrated Philadelphia Mint issues in this series. MS-67s, on the other hand, are overrated coins that should only be acquired if you are assembling a top-ranked Barber Dime set on the PCGS or NGC registries.

You should not have too much difficulty locating a 1900 Barber Dime in the MS-64 to MS-66 grade range that is overall smooth with excellent luster and either attractive toning or fully brilliant surfaces. The strike is apt to be sharp, if not full, but keep your eyes open for even the occasional Gem with a touch of softness to the detail in one or two isolated areas.

# 1900-O

## MINTAGE
2,010,000

Courtesy of David Lawrence

## RARITY RANKINGS

*Overall, Mint State: 9th of 74*
*High Grade, MS-65 or Finer: 25th of 74 (Tie)*

### NEW ORLEANS MINT ISSUES

*Overall, Mint State: 6th of 17*
*High Grade, MS-65 or Finer: 11th of 17*

**Important Varieties:** None.

**General Comments:** The 1900-O falls in behind the triumvirate of key-date issues from 1894-1896, as well as the underrated 1898-O and 1899-O, as the sixth-rarest New Orleans Mint Barber Dime. In terms of total number of Mint State coins known, the 1900-O is also rarer than the low-mintage 1895, 1896-S, 1904-S, 1909-S, 1913-S and 1915-S.

This issue is not quite as impressively ranked when we consider only high-grade examples at and above the MS-65 level, but the 1900-O still bests the 1892-O, 1905-O, 1907-O, 1906-O, 1908-O and 1909-O in this category. From the other Mints that struck Barber Dimes, the 1895 and 1907-D are similar in high-grade rarity to the 1900-O. This issue is very scarce in the MS-60 to MS-64 grade range, rare in MS-65 and very rare any finer. Superb Gems in MS-67 are all but unknown in numismatic circles.

**Strike:** This is a surprisingly well-struck issue for a Barber coin from the New Orleans Mint. Virtually all Mint State examples have a similar quality of strike that is otherwise sharp with only trivial softness of detail on the reverse at the top of both sides of the wreath.

**Luster:** The typical 1900-O has satiny mint luster that is superior to that often seen for New Orleans Mint issues in this series.

**Surfaces:** Perhaps surprisingly for such a rare issue in all Mint State grades, the 1900-O usually does not have too many problems with overly abraded surfaces. If you are fortunate enough to locate a Mint State coin in today's market, chances are pretty good that it will be a minimally abraded example in MS-64 or MS-65. Even at lower reaches of Mint State subdued luster rather than excessive abrasions tends to be the grade-limiting factor for most 1900-O Dimes.

**Toning:** Originally toned examples still outnumber dipped, all-brilliant coins in the market. The depth of toning that usually characterizes this issue is not conducive to dipping, and the originally preserved examples often display more-or-less deep patination that is either confined to the peripheries or blankets the entire surface area on one or both sides. Some of the dipped examples still retain remnants of original toning in the form of light hazy-gold tinting.

**Eye Appeal:** Despite the paucity of Mint State survivors, eye appeal for the 1900-O is above average by New Orleans Mint standards. An overall sharp strike is a noteworthy attribute, and distracting abrasions are seldom a significant stumbling block to locating a pleasing example. Fully lustrous, minimally marked examples in MS-64 and higher grades, therefore, tend to be fairly nice, as long as the toning is not too dark.

**Significant Examples:**

**1. NGC MS-66.** *Ex: CSNS Signature Auction (Heritage, 5/2005), lot 6629, where it realized $3,738; Dallas Signature Auction (Heritage, 12/2005), lot 482, where it realized $4,600; FUN Signature Coin Auction (Heritage, 1/2008), lot 1029, unsold.*

**2. PCGS MS-66.** *Ex: The Richmond Collection (David Lawrence, 3/2005), lot 1312, where it realized $8,338; San Francisco, CA ANA Signature Auction (Heritage, 7/2005), lot 10161, where it realized $10,925.*

**3. PCGS MS-66.** *Ex: J.M. Clapp, who acquired the coin directly from the New Orleans Mint in 1900; Clapp estate (1942); The Louis E. Eliasberg, Sr. Collection (Bowers and Merena, 5/1996), lot 1267, where it realized $7,920; The John C. Hugon Collection (Heritage, 1/2005), lot 4025, where it realized $12,650.*

**4. NGC MS-66.** *Ex: Baltimore ANA Auction (Bowers and Merena, 7/2003), lot 1019, where it realized $6,728.*

**5. NGC MS-66.** *Ex: FUN Signature Sale (Heritage, 1/1999), lot 6461, unsold.*

**Total Known in Mint State:** 70-90 Coins

**Total Known and Value Breakdown by Grade:**

| MS-60 to MS-62 | MS-63 | MS-64 | MS-65 |
|---|---|---|---|
| 12-15 Coins | 12-15 Coins | 20-25 Coins | 18-22 Coins |
| N/A | $750-$1,000 | $1,850-$2,250 | $4,250-$5,250 |

| MS-66 | MS-67 | MS-68 | MS-69 to MS-70 |
|---|---|---|---|
| 8-10 Coins | 1 Coin | 0 Coins | 0 Coins |
| $5,500-$12,500 | $10,000-$15,000 | -- | -- |

*Note:* The conclusions presented in the following "Collecting and Investing Strategies" section are drawn in large part from the Investment Potential Ratios that are summarized in Appendices G and H at the end of this book. For a detailed analysis of the formula used to derive these Investment Potential Ratios, please refer to the Introduction of this book.

**Collecting and Investing Strategies:** Avoid this issue in MS-65 and MS-66 as such pieces are overrated and, hence, overpriced. MS-64s offer far better prospects for the numismatic investor, and the single MS-67 known to the major certification services is also an underrated coin.

The 1900-O is usually a relatively pleasing coin in the finer Mint State grades. An MS-64 should have minimal impairment to the luster. Even in that grade, however, be mindful of darkly and/or irregularly toned examples. Although such pieces can be quite colorful, the depth or distribution of the toning can be a detriment when the time comes to sell. Deep toning can also make it difficult to appreciate the luster even on a high-grade Mint State coin.

# 1900-S

**MINTAGE**
5,168,270

Courtesy of David Lawrence

**RARITY RANKINGS**

*Overall, Mint State: 38th of 74*
*High Grade, MS-65 or Finer: 37th of 74 (Tie)*

## SAN FRANCISCO MINT ISSUES

*Overall, Mint State: 19th of 24*
*High Grade, MS-65 or Finer: 18th of 24 (Tie)*

**Important Varieties:** None.

**General Comments:** The 1900-S is more plentiful in Mint State than any other San Francisco Mint Barber Dime produced up until that point in time. It is rarer than the later-date 1905-S, 1911-S, 1912-S, 1914-S and 1916-S, however, as well as the 1905-O, 1908-D, 1906-O, 1907-O, 1911-D, 1912-D and 1914-D among Barber Dime issues from other coinage facilities.

In high grades (MS-65 or finer), the 1900-S is similar in rarity to the 1914-S and rarer than the 1906-S, 1911-S, 1912-S, 1913-S and 1916-S. Compared to most other mintmarked issues in this series, however, you should not experience too much difficulty locating a 1900-S in the MS-60 to MS-64 grade range. MS-65s are genuinely rare, while MS-66s are very rare and seldom encountered in the market. Superb Gems are virtually unknown.

**Strike:** The 1900-S is another sharply struck Barber Dime from the San Francisco Mint. Most Mint State survivors are actually fully defined, and I cannot recall ever handling an example of this issue with bothersome lack of detail that was attributable to a poor quality of strike.

**Luster:** Satiny mint luster is the rule for the 1900-S, and it is typically quite vibrant, sometimes even with some "flash" in the fields.

**Surfaces:** While most Mint State examples are limited in grade by scattered abrasions, these tend to be small in number and not overly conspicuous to the unaided eye. Truly smooth-looking examples, on the other hand, can be difficult to acquire.

**Toning:** Mint State examples run the gamut from fully brilliant to deeply toned. The typical example will display some degree of light or moderate patination, the deeper colors usually confined to the peripheries and, as a rule, not all that vivid.

**Eye Appeal:** This is an attractive issue and, so long as you can avoid the few darkly toned pieces, there should be no difficulty locating a pleasing example in the context of the assigned grade.

**Significant Examples:**

**1. PCGS MS-66.** *Ex: The Collection of Dr. Steven L. Duckor (Heritage, 1/2006), lot 995, where it realized $4,888.*

**2. PCGS MS-66.** *Ex: New York ANA Signature Sale (Heritage, 8/1997), lot 6176, where it realized $1,725.*

**3. NGC MS-66.** *Ex: Cleveland, Ohio ANA National Money Show Signature Sale (Heritage, 3/1997), lot 5925, unsold.*

**Total Known in Mint State:** 160-200 Coins

**Total Known and Value Breakdown by Grade:**

| MS-60 to MS-62 | MS-63 | MS-64 | MS-65 |
|---|---|---|---|
| 45-55 Coins | 30-40 Coins | 45-55 Coins | 30-35 Coins |
| N/A | $300-$400 | $525-$750 | $1,250-$2,000 |

| MS-66 | MS-67 | MS-68 | MS-69 to MS-70 |
|---|---|---|---|
| 10-12 Coins | 1 Coin | 0 Coins | 0 Coins |
| $5,000-$7,000 | $15,000-$20,000 | -- | -- |

*Note:* The conclusions presented in the following "Collecting and Investing Strategies" section are drawn in large part from the Investment Potential Ratios that are summarized in Appendices G and H at the end of this book. For a detailed analysis of the formula used to derive these Investment Potential Ratios, please refer to the Introduction of this book.

**Collecting and Investing Strategies:** The 1900-S is either fairly accurately priced or underrated in all of the finer Mint State grades except for MS-66. This issue is most underrated in MS-67 but, since there is only a single coin graded as such by PCGS and NGC combined, it is probably not realistic for you to expect to acquire that piece. Instead, focus on this issue in MS-64.

This issue tends to come nice, and grade is usually determined by the number or lack of wispy abrasions rather than any deficiencies with the strike and/or luster. Since dark or splotchy toning is also not seen all that often among Mint State survivors, you should be able to locate an attractive example even at the near-Gem grade level.

# Proof
# 1901

## MINTAGE
813

Courtesy of Bowers and Merena

## RARITY RANKINGS

***Overall, All Proof Grades:*** *14th of 25*
***High Grade, Proof-65 or Finer:*** *14th of 25 (Tie)*
***Overall, Cameo Finish:*** *15th of 24*
***Deep/Ultra Cameo Finish:*** *Unknown*

**Important Varieties:** None.

**General Comments:** After an unusually high mintage of coins in 1900, proof Barber Dime production in 1901 returned to a level that is more commensurate with those of most other issues from the 1890s and early years of the 20th century. The 1901 is a median rarity in the proof Barber Dime series, although it is actually easier to obtain than the higher-mintage 1900 in all grades. A few more proof 1901 Dimes may have been distributed to contemporary collectors than to the general public, the former of who were much more likely to preserve the coins for future generations of numismatists. (This may not have been the case, however, as indicated below in my discussion of the overall surface preservation for this issue.) The 1901 is rarer in all grades than most proof Barber Dimes from the 1890s, as well as the 1905 and 1909. This issue is also rarer than the proof 1904 is an absolute sense, and it compares favorably with the proof 1911 in terms of high-grade rarity.

The proof 1901 is a median rarity among Barber Dimes with a Cameo finish, surpassing such other issues as the proof 1892, proof 1900 and proof 1911 in this regard. The issue is unknown with a Deep/Ultra Cameo finish.

**Strike:** The proof 1901 is rarely, if ever offered with anything less than full striking detail.

**Finish:** This issue is the last in the proof Barber Dime series that the Mint produced using Cameo proofing techniques. Even so, the typical proof 1901 will display much less contrast between the fields and devices than, say, a proof 1897, proof 1898 or even a proof 1900.

**Surfaces:** More so than most other issues in this series, the 1901 is a challenging proof Dime to locate with minimally marked surfaces. The vast majority of survivors exhibit at least a few wispy hairlines, and I have even seen a couple of coins with deep, detracting cuts on the surfaces. How or why this issue was so roughly handled is a mystery, especially since the proof 1900 was much more likely to be distributed to non-collectors at the time of delivery due to its status as a turn-of-the-century issue.

**Toning:** Despite the prevalence of dipping and other forms of numismatic conservation in the market of the early 21st century, brilliant examples of the proof 1901 remain in the minority among survivors. Most pieces that I have handled are extensively toned, sometimes even with fairly dark color to one or both sides. The more attractively original specimens—and there are many—possess vivid patina with a more iridescent quality that does not inhibit the underlying Mint finish. Toning for such pieces is sometimes a bit mottled in distribution, or confined solely to the peripheries on one or both sides.

**Eye Appeal:** The proof 1901 is a surprisingly difficult issue to locate with strong eye appeal, and most examples are either below average or only average in this regard. Grade-limiting contact marks and unsightly toning bear much of the blame for this curious phenomenon although, as usually the case with numismatics, there are some notable exceptions. When carefully preserved with either beautiful toning or brilliant surfaces, the proof 1901 is an exquisite coin to behold.

### Significant Examples:

**1. NGC Proof-67 Cameo.** *Ex: Dallas, TX Signature Auction (Heritage, 2/2005), lot 1056, unsold; Houston, TX U.S. Coin Signature Auction (Heritage, 11/2007), lot 60450, where it realized $3,220.*

**2. PCGS Proof-67 Cameo.** *Ex: CSNS Signature Auction (Heritage, 5/2005), lot 6711, unsold; San Francisco, CA ANA Signature Auction (Heritage, 7/2005), lot 5921, where it realized $4,600.*

**3. NGC Proof-67 Cameo.** *Ex: The John C. Hugon Collection (Heritage, 1/2005), lot 4085, where it realized $5,750.*

**Total Known:** 360-435 Coins

## Total Known and Value Breakdown by Grade:

| Brilliant-Finish Coins | | | |
|---|---|---|---|
| **Proof-60-62** | **Proof-63** | **Proof-64** | **Proof-65** |
| 40-50 Coins | 40-50 Coins | 95-115 Coins | 65-75 Coins |
| N/A | $425-$500 | $700-$800 | $1,250-$1,600 |
| **Proof-66** | **Proof-67** | **Proof-68** | **Proof-69-70** |
| 55-65 Coins | 15-20 Coins | 1-2 Coins | 0 Coins |
| $1,750-$2,500 | $3,000-$4,500 | $7,500-$9,000 | -- |

| Cameo Coins | | | |
|---|---|---|---|
| **Proof-60-62 Cameo** | **Proof-63 Cameo** | **Proof-64 Cameo** | **Proof-65 Cameo** |
| 1-2 Coins | 2-3 Coins | 15-20 Coins | 8-10 Coins |
| N/A | $800-$900 | $1,000-$1,300 | $1,500-$2,500 |
| **Proof-66 Cameo** | **Proof-67 Cameo** | **Proof-68 Cameo** | **Proof-69-70 Cameo** |
| 12-15 Coins | 8-10 Coins | 0 Coins | 0 Coins |
| $1,750-$3,250 | $3,500-$7,500 | -- | -- |

| Deep/Ultra Cameo | | | |
|---|---|---|---|
| **Proof-60-62 Deep/ Ultra Cameo** | **Proof-63 Deep/ Ultra Cameo** | **Proof-64 Deep/ Ultra Cameo** | **Proof-65 Deep/ Ultra Cameo** |
| 0 Coins | 0 Coins | 0 Coins | 0 Coins |
| -- | -- | -- | -- |
| **Proof-66 Deep/ Ultra Cameo** | **Proof-67 Deep/ Ultra Cameo** | **Proof-68 Deep/ Ultra Cameo** | **Proof-69-70 Deep/ Ultra Cameo** |
| 0 Coins | 0 Coins | 0 Coins | 0 Coins |
| -- | -- | -- | -- |

*Note:* The conclusions presented in the following "Collecting and Investing Strategies" section are drawn in large part from the Investment Potential Ratios that are summarized in Appendices G and H at the end of this book. For a detailed analysis of the formula used to derive these Investment Potential Ratios, please refer to the Introduction of this book.

**Collecting and Investing Strategies:** The 1901 is a slightly overrated issue in the Proof-64 to Proof-66 grade range, and I would pass on such pieces for inclusion in a proof type set or a more generalized numismatic portfolio. Proof-67s are underrated, however, which is of further importance to potential buyers since lower-grade examples of this issue tend to be noticeably hairlined. A few Proof-65s that I have seen have even been flat out overgraded.

Another consideration for purchasing a desirable proof 1901 that has the potential to appreciate in value has to be the toning that the coin possesses. Absolutely avoid those originally toned examples that are overly dark and/or possesses of splotchy patination on one or both sides. Richly toned examples are fine, but make sure that the toning is not so deep that it obscures the underlying reflectivity. Even better in this regard are those untoned pieces that have been dipped. These have generally been well conserved, and the original mint finish usually remains vibrant and free of distracting haziness.

# 1901

Courtesy of David Lawrence

### MINTAGE
18,859,665

### RARITY RANKINGS

*Overall, Mint State:* 59th of 74
*High Grade, MS-65 or Finer:* 53rd of 74 (Tie)

## PHILADELPHIA MINT ISSUES

*Overall, Mint State:* 11th of 25
*High Grade, MS-65 or Finer:* 9th of 25 (Tie)

**Important Varieties:** None.

**General Comments:** For a P-mint Barber Dime from the 1900s with a sizeable mintage of nearly 19 million coins, the 1901 is surprisingly elusive in Mint State. This issue is much, much rarer than truly common Barber Dimes such as the 1892, 1911 and 1916, and it is also more challenging to collect than the lower-mintage 1897, 1898 and 1910, to name just a few other P-mint coins in this series.

The 1901 compares favorably to the 1909 and 1915 in terms of rarity at and above the MS-65 grade level, and it is also rarer than the 1914-D in high grades. Even so, the 1901 is still a readily obtainable issue in all grades through MS-64. Even MS-65s can only really be described as moderately scarce. In MS-66 and MS-67, however, the 1901 is a decidedly rare issue.

**Strike:** New obverse and reverse hubs were introduced to the Barber Dime series with the 1901, although they did not affect the striking quality of the type either in a positive or negative manner. The 1901 is almost always offered with an excellent quality of strike that is characterized by sharp-to-full definition.

**Luster:** Luster quality for the 1901 is also pleasing, and I have seen Mint State examples with both satin and frosty textures.

**Surfaces:** Abrasions for this issue tend to be small in size, relatively few in number and not overly conspicuous to the naked eye. Nevertheless, the 1901 is a very challenging issue to locate with surfaces that are free of even one or two wispy abrasions.

**Toning:** Original surfaces for 1901 Barber Dimes are usually characterized by some degree of toning. Many Mint State examples are extensively patinated with rich-to-dark color blanketing both sides. Others are only rim toned, or possess more vibrant toning at the denticles, and these tend to be more vivid in appearance. Fully brilliant examples are in the minority among Mint State survivors, and these are mostly the result of dipping. I have, however, seen a couple of untoned coins that have not been so treated and still possess a fully original "skin" to the surfaces.

**Eye Appeal:** With sharp-to-full striking detail, excellent luster quality and not overly abraded surfaces, the depth and color of toning is the factor that will usually sway the eye appeal of a 1901 Barber Dime one way or the other. In my experience, the peripherally toned coins tend to be highly attractive within the context of the assigned grade. Examples with fully toned surfaces vary from below average to above average in the eye appeal category depending upon whether the toning is dark or relatively vivid.

**Significant Examples:**

**1. NGC MS-67.** *Ex: The John C. Hugon Collection (Heritage, 1/2005), lot 4027, where it realized $3,450; The Phelan Collection (Bowers and Merena, 7/2008), lot 470, where it realized $3,220.*

**Total Known in Mint State:** 390-475 Coins

**Total Known and Value Breakdown by Grade:**

| MS-60 to MS-62 | MS-63 | MS-64 | MS-65 |
|---|---|---|---|
| 90-110 Coins | 110-135 Coins | 125-150 Coins | 45-55 Coins |
| N/A | $125-$175 | $250-$350 | $525-$650 |

| MS-66 | MS-67 | MS-68 | MS-69 to MS-70 |
|---|---|---|---|
| 15-18 Coins | 4-5 Coins | 0 Coins | 0 Coins |
| $1,400-$1,750 | $3,500-$10,000 | -- | -- |

*Note:* The conclusions presented in the following "Collecting and Investing Strategies" section are drawn in large part from the Investment Potential Ratios that are summarized in Appendices G and H at the end of this book. For a detailed analysis of the formula used to derive these Investment Potential Ratios, please refer to the Introduction of this book.

**Collecting and Investing Strategies:** Although far from the most underrated issue in the Barber Dime series, the 1901 is undervalued in the MS-64 to MS-66 grade range. MS-67s are not underrated, but nor are they significantly overrated. In sum, the 1901 is not likely to be a strong performer as part of a numismatic investment portfolio, but examples in the finer Mint State grades are also not overpriced at the levels reported in this book.

# 1901-O

**MINTAGE**
5,620,000

Courtesy of David Lawrence

## RARITY RANKINGS

*Overall, Mint State: 14th of 74 (Tie)*
*High Grade, MS-65 or Finer: 19th of 74 (Tie)*

## NEW ORLEANS MINT ISSUES

*Overall, Mint State: 8th of 17*
*High Grade, MS-65 or Finer: 9th of 17 (Tie)*

**Important Varieties:** There is an important Repunched Mintmark variety of the 1901-O that is usually referred to as an O/Horizontal O. Attributions for this RPM include FS-010, FS-501, Lawrence-103 and Breen-3529.

**General Comments:** The 1901-O falls close to the middle of the rarity scale among O-mint Barber Dimes both in all Mint State grades and in high grades at and above the MS-65 level. Expect to have a more difficult time locating a Mint State 1901-O than a similarly graded example of the 1905-O, 1906-O, 1907-O, 1908-O and 1909-O. This issue is also rarer than the 1893-O, 1897-O and 1903-O in an absolute sense, although it is similar in high-grade rarity to the 1897-O.

The 1901-O can be elusive even in the lowest Mint State grades. Gems in MS-65 and MS-66 are very rare, while there is only a single MS-67 known to PCGS and NGC (December/2008).

**Strike:** The 1901-O is not among the most poorly struck New Orleans Mint Barber Dimes, but it is still hardly ever encountered with 100% full definition. The typical example is more-or-less softly impressed on the reverse at the top of the wreath as well as over the lower-right portion of the wreath at and near the right (facing) bow of the ribbon knot. A few of the letters in the denomination ONE DIME are also sometimes affected by inadequate striking pressure. The obverse is usually the better struck of the two sides, but even on that side of the coin there is a tendency for softness of detail to creep in at the top of Liberty's portrait.

**Luster:** Luster quality for this issue is seldom better than average, and many examples are decidedly below average in this regard. Mint State coins are typically satiny in texture and sometimes a bit subdued even if the surfaces are not deeply toned or impaired due to cleaning or other mishandling.

**Surfaces:** As with many other O-mint issues in this series, the 1901-O is seldom encountered with noticeably abraded surfaces. A few wispy abrasions are often seen, nonetheless, but it is problems with the luster that usually account for lower Mint Sate grades from the major certification services for examples of this issue.

**Toning:** The 1901-O is almost always offered with some degree of toning to the surfaces. Completely originally examples tend to be richly toned throughout, the colors often fairly deep and sometimes mottled in distribution. Most brilliant-looking coins that I have seen have been dipped, and these often retain some portion of the original toning in the form of either a dull silver or gold sheen and/or scattered speckles of charcoal-russet color.

**Eye Appeal:** The 1901-O has below-average eye appeal due to inadequacies with the strike and luster, as well as the prevalence of dark or otherwise unsightly toning among Mint State survivors.

**Significant Examples:**

1. **PCGS MS-66.** *Ex: Palm Beach, FL Signature Sale (Heritage, 11/2004), lot 6276, unsold; CSNS Signature Auction (Heritage, 5/2005), lot 6634, where it realized $5,175; The Southwest Collection (Heritage, 2/2008), lot 164, where it realized $4,888.*

2. **PCGS MS-66.** *Ex: Long Beach, CA Signature Coin Auction (Heritage, 2/2007), lot 2945, where it realized $5,750.*

3. **NGC MS-66.** *Ex: FUN Signature Sale (Heritage, 1/1998), lot 6689, where it realized $2,415; FUN Signature Sale (Heritage, 1/1999), lot 6463, unsold; The Collections of Russell J. Logan & Gilbert G. Steinberg (Bowers and Merena, 11/2002), lot 1257, unsold; The Benson Collection (Ira & Larry Goldberg, 2/2003), lot 343, where it realized $2,530; The Medio and Da Costa Gomez Collections (Stack's/American Numismatic Rarities, 6/2004), lot 4235, where it realized $2,875; Long Beach Signature Auction (Heritage, 2/2006), lot 789, unsold.*

**4. PCGS MS-66.** *Ex: The Collection of Dr. Steven L. Duckor (Heritage, 1/2006), lot 997, where it realized $6,325.*

**5. PCGS MS-66.** *Ex: The Law Collection; The John C. Hugon Collection (Heritage, 1/2005), lot 4028, where it realized $5,463.*

**6. NGC MS-66.** *Ex: The John F. Rindge and Alan J. Harlan Collections (Bowers and Merena, 12/2003), lot 1013, unsold; The Dr. Robert W. Swan and Rod Sweet Collections (Bowers and Merena, 3/2004), lot 1204, where it realized $2,875.*

**7. PCGS MS-66.** *Ex: CSNS Signature Auction (Heritage, 5/2003), lot 5946, where it realized $5,290.*

This coin is an example of the O/Horizontal O (FS-101, FS-501, Lawrence-103, Breen-3529) variety.

**8. PCGS MS-66.** *Ex: Cleveland, OH ANA National Money Sale (Heritage, 3/1997), lot 5926, unsold; FUN Signature Sale (Heritage, 1/1999), lot 6462, where it realized $4,313.*

**Total Known in Mint State:** 80-100 Coins

**Total Known and Value Breakdown by Grade:**

| MS-60 to MS-62 | MS-63 | MS-64 | MS-65 |
|---|---|---|---|
| 18-22 Coins | 20-25 Coins | 15-20 Coins | 12-15 Coins |
| N/A | $700-$950 | $2,000-$2,500 | $2,750-$3,500 |

| MS-66 | MS-67 | MS-68 | MS-69 to MS-70 |
|---|---|---|---|
| 12-15 Coins | 1 Coin | 0 Coins | 0 Coins |
| $4,500-$7,500 | $10,000-$15,000 | -- | -- |

*Note:* The conclusions presented in the following "Collecting and Investing Strategies" section are drawn in large part from the Investment Potential Ratios that are summarized in Appendices G and H at the end of this book. For a detailed analysis of the formula used to derive these Investment Potential Ratios, please refer to the Introduction of this book.

**Collecting and Investing Strategies:** This is an underrated issue in all of the finer Mint State grades save for MS-66. MS-64s are particularly undervalued, and the 1901-O is similar to the 1899-O in this regard.

The 1901-O is one of numerous New Orleans Mint Barber Dimes that is going to require perseverance in order to acquire an attractive Mint State example. This issue is poorly produced with inferior luster and striking qualities that often limit the eye appeal. I would not even try to find an example with 100% full definition as I do not believe that the 1901-O comes with that kind of strike. On the other hand, you can still cherrypick for strike by selecting a coin with an overall sharp impression on the obverse and minimal lack of detail over the upper and lower-right portions of the reverse wreath.

As far as luster is concerned, try to select an example with above-average vibrancy to the surfaces. In this vein, I would stay away from dipped coins as most 1901-O Dimes that have been so treated are even more subdued in the luster category. Some dipped pieces even retain speckles of original toning that can be distracting to the eye. As long as you stay away from the overly dark and/or mottled pieces, an originally toned Gem is likely to be preferable to a dipped coin as far as this challenging issue is concerned.

# 1901-S

## MINTAGE
593,022

Courtesy of David Lawrence

## RARITY RANKINGS

**Overall, Mint State:** *6th of 74 (Tie)*
**High Grade, MS-65 or Finer:** *12th of 74 (Tie)*

## SAN FRANCISCO MINT ISSUES

**Overall, Mint State:** *2nd of 24 (Tie)*
**High Grade, MS-65 or Finer:** *7th of 24 (Tie)*

**Important Varieties:** None.

**General Comments:** With so few coins struck, it should come as no surprise to read that the 1901-S is tied with the 1903-S (another low-mintage issue) as the second-rarest San Francisco Mint Barber Dime after the conditionally challenging 1898-S. The low-mintage status of the 1901-S was recognized fairly early, however, and the issue vies with the 1899-S and 1909-S as only the seventh-rarest San Francisco Mint issue in this series in high grades. At and above the MS-65 level, however, the 1901-S is still a rare coin when viewed in the wider context of the numismatic market. It is even rarer in high grades than the 1903-S, 1913-S and 1915-S, as well as such other issues as the 1895, 1897-O and 1907-D. There are a few truly exceptional Superb Gems known in MS-67 and even MS-68, although the 1901-S is clearly a major condition rarity in the finest Mint State grades.

**Strike:** Strike for the 1901-S is usually sharp-to-full, although I have seen a couple of examples with slight softness of detail here and there at the denticles.

**Luster:** The typical Mint State example is highly lustrous with a vibrant, satiny texture to the surfaces.

**Surfaces:** Mint State survivors run the gamut from lightly abraded to virtually pristine, and examples at both ends of the spectrum appear in the market with nearly the same degree of frequency.

**Toning:** With only a few exceptions, the 1901-S always displays some degree of patination on one or both sides. Most examples are actually quite extensively toned, often with more vivid colors intermingled at and near the rims.

**Eye Appeal:** If you are fortunate enough to locate a Mint State 1901-S Barber Dime, chances are that it will be an attractive coin. This is a well-produced issue, and those few coins that have escaped circulation usually also display ample evidence of having been more-or-less carefully preserved over the years.

**Significant Examples:**

1. **NGC MS-68.** *Ex: The Russell B. Patterson Collection (Bowers and Merena, 3/1985), lot 697, where it realized $4,070; Long Beach Signature Sale (Heritage, 6/2001), lot 8031, where it realized $9,660; The John C. Hugon Collection (Heritage, 1/2005), lot 4029, where it realized $23,000.*

2. **PCGS MS-67.** *Ex: The Emery and Nichols Collections (Bowers and Merena, 11/1984), lot 399, where it realized $3,190; The Collection of Dr. Steven L. Duckor (Heritage, 1/2006), lot 998, where it realized $23,000.*

3. **PCGS MS-67.** *Ex: Palm Beach, FL Signature Sale (Heritage, 11/2004), lot 6269, where it realized $9,775.*

4. **PCGS MS-67.** *Ex: Long Beach Signature Sale (Heritage, 5/2001), lot 8032, where it realized $7,590. Along with a 1901-S Barber Quarter, Barber Half Dollar and Morgan Dollar, this coin was obtained by an ancestor of the consignor during a visit to the San Francisco Mint in 1901. These four coins were kept in the same family until consigned to Heritage's Long Beach Signature Sale of May, 2001.*

5. **PCGS MS-66.** *Ex: Baltimore Auction (Bowers and Merena, 7/2004), lot 463, unsold; Palm Beach, FL Signature Sale (Heritage, 11/2004), lot 6278, unsold; Baltimore Auction (Bowers and Merena, 3/2005), lot 449, unsold; CSNS Signature Coin Auction (Heritage, 4/2008), lot 616, where it realized $6,900.*

6. **PCGS MS-66.** *Ex: New York, NY Signature Auction (Heritage, 6/2005), lot 5400, unsold; Long Beach Signature Auction (Heritage, 9/2005), lot*

2430, unsold; Dallas Signature Auction (Heritage, 12/2005), lot 484, unsold; Pre-Long Beach Auction (Ira & Larry Goldberg, 9/2006), lot 1503, where it realized $7,360.

**7. PCGS MS-66.** *Ex: Long Beach Signature Auction (Heritage, 2/2006), lot 792, where it realized $5,750; CSNS Signature Auction (Heritage, 4/2006), lot 1297, unsold; Baltimore Auction (Bowers and Merena, 7/2006), lot 1021, where it realized $6,613.*

**8. PCGS MS-66.** *Ex: J.M. Clapp, who acquired this coin directly from the San Francisco Mint in 1901; Clapp estate (1942); The Louis E. Eliasberg, Sr. Collection (Bowers and Merena, 5/1996), lot 1271, where it realized $3,520; New York Rarities Sale (Bowers and Merena, 7/1997), unsold.*

**9. NGC MS-66.** *Ex: The Irving Goodman Collection (Superior, 5/1996), lot 729, where it realized $4,180.*

**Total Known in Mint State:** 65-85 Coins

**Total Known and Value Breakdown by Grade:**

| MS-60 to MS-62 | MS-63 | MS-64 | MS-65 |
|---|---|---|---|
| 12-15 Coins | 12-15 Coins | 20-25 Coins | 10-12 Coins |
| N/A | $1,250-$1,500 | $1,700-$1,900 | $4,250-$5,000 |

| MS-66 | MS-67 | MS-68 | MS-69 to MS-70 |
|---|---|---|---|
| 8-10 Coins | 3-4 Coins | 1 Coin | 0 Coins |
| $6,000-$8,500 | $15,000-$30,000 | $25,000-$30,000 | -- |

*Note:* The conclusions presented in the following "Collecting and Investing Strategies" section are drawn in large part from the Investment Potential Ratios that are summarized in Appendices G and H at the end of this book. For a detailed analysis of the formula used to derive these Investment Potential Ratios, please refer to the Introduction of this book.

**Collecting and Investing Strategies:** The 1901-S should only be considered for investment purposes at the MS-64 and MS-65 grade levels. In MS-66 and MS-67, the low-mintage, key-date status of this issue has driven prices to levels that are out of touch with the actual rarity of such coins. That the market is starting to awaken to this reality is evident by looking at the above Significant Examples list, where you will see that several MS-66s failed to sell in multiple auction appearances. While overgrading and/or poor eye appeal may have played a part, there is no escaping the fact that those coins were just reserved too high in light of what the market was willing to pay at that time.

I believe that an attractive 1901-S Barber Dime in MS-64 or MS-65 would make an important acquisition to not only a complete Barber Dime set, but also a more diverse numismatic holding. This issue has the fourth-lowest mintage in the series (discounting the proof-only 1894-S), and it is instantly recognizable as a key-date coin. The 1901-S also has the distinction of having been struck during the same year and in the same Mint as the 1901-S Barber Quarter and 1901-S Morgan Dollar—two issues that also enjoy semi or key-date status in their respective series. When we consider that the 1901-S Barber Half Dollar is also a low-mintage coin with fewer than 1 million pieces struck, 1901-S emerges as a "magic date" in the U.S. silver-coin family. As such, numismatic demand for all silver coins with the 1901-S date and mintmark combination is likely to remain strong in the coming decades. When we consider that MS-64s and MS-65s are also more affordable than higher-graded examples, chances are very good that you will find multiple buyers for a 1901-S Dime in those grades when the time comes to sell.

As long as you don't mind richly original toning, there should only be two impediments to acquiring an attractive 1901-S Barber Dime in MS-64 or MS-65: your ability to locate a coin that is for sale and, once you do so, your ability to pay for it. This is a well-produced issue, and even lower-end Mint State coins through MS-64 are usually very attractive in the context of the assigned grade.

# Proof
# 1902
## MINTAGE
777

Courtesy of Bowers and Merena

## RARITY
## RANKINGS

*Overall, All Proof Grades:* 8th of 25
*High Grade, Proof-65 or Finer:* 3rd of 25
*Overall, Cameo Finish:* 1st of 24
*Deep/Ultra Cameo Finish:* Unknown

**Important Varieties:** None.

**General Comments:** The 1902 is among the ten-rarest issues in the proof Barber Dime series, and it is actually the rarest coin of this type in high grades after only the legendary 1894-S and the low-mintage 1915. The proof 1902 is even rarer than the lower-mintage proof 1903, proof 1906, proof 1911 and proof 1913 in terms of total number of coins believed extant. It is the rarest collectible proof Barber Dime with a Cameo finish, and is unknown in Deep/Ultra Cameo.

**Strike:** Full striking definition is the rule for this issue, and I cannot recall ever having handled an example that was not at least sharply detailed.

**Finish:** Unlike the preceding issues since the inception of the proof Barber Dime series in 1892, the proof 1902 almost always comes with a uniformly brilliant finish in the fields and over the devices. A few pieces do have modest Cameo contrast on the reverse, but the obverse of even those coins is invariably overall brilliant in finish. Although PCGS has certified two specimens as Cameo (December/2008), any field-to-device contrast evident on a proof 1902 will never be as pronounced as it would be on a proof Barber Dime from the 1890s.

**Surfaces:** Most proof 1902 Barber Dimes display at least a few scattered hairlines that preclude a grade above the Proof-64 level. Distractions such as these can be quite numerous in Proof-62 and Proof-63, but they are seldom large in size or otherwise singularly inconspicuous.

**Toning:** The majority of examples that I have handled are originally toned. Lower-grade examples through Proof-64 seldom possess vivid patination, and some of these coins are so darkly toned that the original mint finish is obscured on one or both sides. Hazy surfaces can also be a problem in lower grades through Proof-64. Gem and Superb-quality proof 1902 Dimes often display very vibrant toning, the most vivid colors sometimes confined to the peripheries and/or only one side of the coin.

**Eye Appeal:** This issue has two markedly different eye appeal ratings depending upon which grade range we are discussing. For coins that grade Proof-60 to Proof-64, eye appeal is usually below average due to noticeable hairlining and/or subdued (if not outright dark) toning. The lack of bold field-to-device contrast also diminishes the appeal of lower-quality specimen. High-grade pieces at or above the Proof-65 level, however, are almost always very attractive with radiant mint brilliance and, many times, vivid toning.

**Significant Examples:**

**1. NGC Proof-67.** *Ex: The James Paul Collection (Heritage, 1/2007), lot 2682, where it realized $2,300.*

**2. NGC Proof-67.** *Ex: Atlanta, GA ANA Signature Auction (Heritage, 4/2006), lot 449, where it realized $3,105.*

**3. PCGS Proof-67.** *Ex: The Richard C. Jewell Collection (American Numismatic Rarities, 3/2005), lot 1619, unsold.*

**4. NGC Proof-67.** *Ex: The John C. Hugon Collection (Heritage, 1/2005), lot 4086, where it realized $2,990.*

**5. NGC Proof-67.** *Ex: FUN Signature Sale (Heritage, 1/2004), lot 5708, unsold; CSNS Signature Sale (Heritage, 5/2004), lot 6699, unsold.*

**6. NGC Proof-67.** *Ex: FUN Signature Sale (Heritage, 1/2003), lot 6491, where it realized $2,401.*

**7. PCGS Proof-65 Cameo.** *Ex: Dallas Signature Auction (Heritage, 12/2005), lot 503, where it realized $2,760.*

**Total Known:** 300-370 Coins

## Total Known and Value Breakdown by Grade:

| Brilliant-Finish Coins | | | |
|---|---|---|---|
| **Proof-60-62** | **Proof-63** | **Proof-64** | **Proof-65** |
| 45-55 Coins | 70-80 Coins | 105-130 Coins | 40-50 Coins |
| N/A | $425-$500 | $650-$775 | $1,350-$1,700 |
| **Proof-66** | **Proof-67** | **Proof-68** | **Proof-69-70** |
| 25-35 Coins | 12-15 Coins | 1 Coin | 0 Coins |
| $1,750-$2,500 | $2,750-$3,750 | $7,500-$9,000 | -- |

| Cameo Coins | | | |
|---|---|---|---|
| **Proof-60-62 Cameo** | **Proof-63 Cameo** | **Proof-64 Cameo** | **Proof-65 Cameo** |
| 1 Coin | 0 Coins | 0 Coins | 1 Coin |
| N/A | -- | -- | $3,000-$5,000 |
| **Proof-66 Cameo** | **Proof-67 Cameo** | **Proof-68 Cameo** | **Proof-69-70 Cameo** |
| 0 Coins | 0 Coins | 0 Coins | 0 Coins |
| -- | -- | -- | -- |

| Deep/Ultra Cameo | | | |
|---|---|---|---|
| **Proof-60-62 Deep/ Ultra Cameo** | **Proof-63 Deep/ Ultra Cameo** | **Proof-64 Deep/ Ultra Cameo** | **Proof-65 Deep/ Ultra Cameo** |
| 0 Coins | 0 Coins | 0 Coins | 0 Coins |
| -- | -- | -- | -- |
| **Proof-66 Deep/ Ultra Cameo** | **Proof-67 Deep/ Ultra Cameo** | **Proof-68 Deep/ Ultra Cameo** | **Proof-69-70 Deep/ Ultra Cameo** |
| 0 Coins | 0 Coins | 0 Coins | 0 Coins |
| -- | -- | -- | -- |

*Note:* The conclusions presented in the following "Collecting and Investing Strategies" section are drawn in large part from the Investment Potential Ratios that are summarized in Appendices G and H at the end of this book. For a detailed analysis of the formula used to derive these Investment Potential Ratios, please refer to the Introduction of this book.

**Collecting and Investing Strategies:** I do not recommend this issue in any grade below Proof-65. For starters, Proof-64s are overrated coins. Additionally, lower-quality proof 1902 Barber Dimes are often plagued by excessive hairlining, dark toning and/or hazy surfaces. Gems and Superb Gems, on the other hand, should display vibrant, reflective-finish features and, if present, more-or-less vibrant toning. Proof-65s and Proof-66s are also underrated coins, and in Proof-67 the 1902 is actually the most undervalued proof Barber Dime after only the 1912.

While this is not a prerequisite to finding a desirable example that has the potential to increase in value, you could hold out until a high-grade 1902 with some degree of field-to-device contrast is made available for purchase. Many such coins will only display significant contrast on the reverse, but given the extreme rarity of this issue with a Cameo finish, such a coin may be appealing to a greater number of future buyers than the typical all-brilliant specimen.

# 1902

**MINTAGE**
21,380,000

Courtesy of David Lawrence

## RARITY RANKINGS

*Overall, Mint State: 48th of 74*
*High Grade, MS-65 or Finer: 47th of 74 (Tie)*

## PHILADELPHIA MINT ISSUES

*Overall, Mint State: 5th of 25*
*High Grade, MS-65 or Finer: 7th of 25*

**Important Varieties:** None.

**General Comments:** The 1902 is surpassed by only the 1894, 1895, 1896 and 1903 as the rarest P-mint Barber Dime in Mint State. An issue that undoubtedly saw extensive commercial use, the 1902 is much more challenging to obtain even in lower Mint State grades than a large mintage of 21.3 million pieces might imply. This issue is particularly elusive above the MS-64 grade level. It is similar in high-grade rarity to the 1912-D and rarer in high grades than such lower-mintage issues as the 1893, 1908, 1911-S, 1913-S and 1915. The 1902 is unknown any finer than MS-67.

**Strike:** As a high-mintage issue with a relatively large number of Mint State examples known, it should come as no surprise to read that striking quality varies somewhat for the 1902. Most coins are overall sharply defined, nonetheless, but I have seen a few coins with isolated incompleteness of detail on the reverse at the top of the wreath and over the lower-right portion of the same device. Softness of strike even for those pieces is anything but distracting.

**Luster:** The 1902 has above-average luster that is usually of a softly frosted or, less often, satin type.

**Surfaces:** The typical Mint State example will have at least a couple of scattered ticks, and this is even true of many Gems in MS-65 and MS-66. Fortunately, abrasions for this issue tend to be small in size and not overly conspicuous to the unaided eye.

**Toning:** Most 1902 Dimes have come down to us with richly toned surfaces. Some of these coins are peripherally toned, while others exhibit rich patination throughout. The colors are seldom vivid, but rather they usually have an "antique look" that gives the coins a very handsome appearance.

**Eye Appeal:** Overall eye appeal for this issue is decidedly above average, this despite the paucity of survivors in the finest Mint State grades.

**Significant Examples:**

**1. PCGS MS-67.** *Ex: The Bristol Sale (Kingswood, 3/2001), lot 139, where it realized $5,031.*

**2. PCGS MS-66. CAC.** *Ex: The Southwest Collection (Heritage, 2/2008), lot 165, where it realized $4,025.*

**3. NGC MS-66.** *Ex: Dallas, TX Signature Coin Auction (Heritage, 4/2007), lot 555, unsold; FUN Signature Coin Auction (Heritage, 1/2008), lot 1032, where it realized $920.*

**4. PCGS MS-66.** *Ex: The Collection of Dr. Steven L. Duckor (Heritage, 1/2006), lot 999, where it realized $2,070; Denver, CO Signature & Platinum Night Auction (Heritage, 8/2006), lot 938, where it realized $2,070.*

**5. NGC MS-66.** *Ex: The John C. Hugon Collection (Heritage, 1/2005), lot 4030, where it realized $978.*

**6. PCGS MS-66.** *Ex: FUN Signature Sale (Heritage, 1/2004), lot 5666, where it realized $863.*

**Total Known in Mint State:** 215-260 Coins

**Total Known and Value Breakdown by Grade:**

| MS-60 to MS-62 | MS-63 | MS-64 | MS-65 |
|---|---|---|---|
| 55-65 Coins | 45-55 Coins | 65-75 Coins | 30-40 Coins |
| N/A | $125-$175 | $250-$350 | $525-$650 |

| MS-66 | MS-67 | MS-68 | MS-69 to MS-70 |
|---|---|---|---|
| 20-25 Coins | 1 Coin | 0 Coins | 0 Coins |
| $1,000-$5,000 | $8,000-$10,000 | -- | -- |

<u>Note:</u> The conclusions presented in the following "Collecting and Investing Strategies" section are drawn in large part from the Investment Potential Ratios that are summarized in Appendices G and H at the end of this book. For a detailed analysis of the formula used to derive these Investment Potential Ratios, please refer to the Introduction of this book.

**Collecting and Investing Strategies:** The 1902 is one of the most underrated Philadelphia Mint Barber Dimes in MS-64, MS-65 and MS-67. An example in any one of those grades, therefore, should be seriously considered for inclusion in either a complete Barber Dime set or a more diverse numismatic holding. In MS-66 the 1902 is overrated and should be avoided unless you are assembling a specialized collection of high-grade Barber Dimes. MS-66s are also potentially undesirable because of the significant difference in price between examples graded by PCGS and NGC. NGC examples are worth anywhere from two-to-four times less than PCGS coins, all other things being equal, although less reputable dealers are often disinclined to share this information with clients.

There are some really pretty 1902 Barber Dimes available in the market, and most of those are concentrated in the MS-65 to MS-67 grade range where distracting abrasions are less of a problem. Look for a coin with vibrant luster and attractive toning, and try to avoid the occasional piece that is a bit softly struck here and there on the reverse.

# 1902-O

## MINTAGE
4,500,000

Courtesy of David Lawrence

## RARITY RANKINGS

*Overall, Mint State: 10th of 74*
*High Grade, MS-65 or Finer: 4th of 74*

## NEW ORLEANS MINT ISSUES

*Overall, Mint State: 7th of 17*
*High Grade, MS-65 or Finer: 2nd of 17*

**Important Varieties:** None.

**General Comments:** The 1902-O is the rarest New Orleans Mint Barber Dime struck during the 20th century, and it is also more elusive in Mint State than the 1892-O, 1893-O and 1897-O. In high grades, the 1902-O is actually the rarest O-mint Barber Dime after only the 1894-O, and it even surpasses the fabled 1895-O in this regard. In fact, only the 1895-S and 1897-S from other coinage facilities join the 1894-O as being rarer than the 1902-O in grades at and above the MS-65 level.

**Strike:** The typical 1902-O has a similar quality of strike than such other O-mint Barber Dimes as the 1899-O, 1900-O and 1901-O. While I have seen some examples that are overall sharply impressed, most Mint State coins still display a touch of softness on the reverse at the top of the wreath, over and around the ribbon knot at the base of the wreath, over the lower-right side of the wreath and/or over the lower-left side of the wreath.

**Luster:** The 1902-O has stronger luster quality than most of the preceding New Orleans Mint issues in the Barber Dime series. Most examples are quite vibrant in finish with either a satin or softly frosted texture.

**Surfaces:** Scattered abrasions are more of a problem for the 1902-O than they are for the 1900-O and 1901-O, to name just a few earlier-date Barber Dimes from the New Orleans Mint. Expect to see at least a few distractions on the surfaces of the typical Mint State survivor, although these are often small in size and not overly distracting even in lower grades through MS-63.

**Toning:** Unlike most other mintmarked Barber Dimes from the 1890s and early years of the 20th century, the 1902-O is seldom encountered with richly toned surfaces. Such pieces definitely exist, but more common among Mint State survivors are those with either brilliant surfaces or light patination in gold and silver shades.

**Eye Appeal:** Eye appeal for the 1902-O is surprisingly strong given the conditionally challenging nature of this issue. With uncommonly vibrant luster by the standards of the issuing Mint and more-or-less sharp striking detail, even most lower-grade examples through MS-64 are relatively pleasing coins.

### Significant Examples:

**1. NGC MS-67.** *Ex: The John Jay Pittman Collection (David W. Akers, 10/1997), lot 702, where it realized $5225; The Belle Glade Collection (Heritage, 8/2007), lot 1633, where it realized $12,650.*

**2. PCGS MS-66.** *Ex: The Collection of Dr. Steven L. Duckor (Heritage, 1/2006), lot 1000, where it realized $10,925.*

**3. NGC MS-66.** *Ex: The John C. Hugon Collection (Heritage, 1/2005), lot 4031, where it realized $4,313.*

**4. NGC MS-65.** *Ex: FUN Signature Sale (Heritage, 1/2004), lot 5667, where it realized $2,070; The Southwest Collection (Heritage, 2/2008), lot 166, where it realized $3,220.*

**5. PCGS MS-65.** *Ex: Dallas, TX U.S. Coin Signature Auction (Heritage, 11/2007), lot 425, where it realized $3,738.*

**6. NGC MS-65.** *Ex: San Francisco, CA ANA Signature Coin Auction (Heritage, 7/2005), lot 5890, unsold.*

**7. PCGS MS-65.** *Ex: Atlanta, GA ANA Signature Sale (Heritage, 8/2001), lot 5726, where it realized $3,220.*

**8. NGC MS-65.** *Ex: Atlanta, GA ANA Signature Sale (Heritage, 8/2001), lot 5727, where it realized $2,530.*

**9. NGC MS-65.** *Ex: Cleveland, OH ANA National Money Sale (Heritage, 3/1997), lot 5927, where it realized $2,070; Long Beach Signature Sale (Heritage, 6/2000), lot 7155, where it realized $2,070.*

**10. PCGS MS-65.** *Ex: Long Beach Signature Sale (Heritage, 2/1999), lot 5855, where it realized $3,795.*

**11. NGC MS-65.** *Ex: FUN Signature Sale (Heritage, 1/1996), lot 5328, unsold.*

**Total Known in Mint State:** 70-95 Coins

**Total Known and Value Breakdown by Grade:**

| MS-60 to MS-62 | MS-63 | MS-64 | MS-65 |
|---|---|---|---|
| 20-25 Coins | 15-18 Coins | 25-35 Coins | 8-10 Coins |
| N/A | $700-$900 | $1,500-$2,250 | $3,250-$4,000 |

| MS-66 | MS-67 | MS-68 | MS-69 to MS-70 |
|---|---|---|---|
| 4-5 Coins | 1 Coin | 0 Coins | 0 Coins |
| $6,000-$12,500 | $12,500-$15,000 | -- | -- |

*Note:* The conclusions presented in the following "Collecting and Investing Strategies" section are drawn in large part from the Investment Potential Ratios that are summarized in Appendices G and H at the end of this book. For a detailed analysis of the formula used to derive these Investment Potential Ratios, please refer to the Introduction of this book.

**Collecting and Investing Strategies:** While such coins are decidedly rare and quite pricey, I would only acquire a 1902-O that grades MS-65, MS-66 or MS-67. This issue is underrated in all of those grades, while MS-64s are actually overvalued coins.

Luster quality is good enough for this issue that you should have no difficulty with this characteristic even at the MS-65 grade level. By selecting a high-grade example with an overall sharp strike and either brilliant surfaces or attractively original toning, you will have a good chance of realizing a strong return on your investment in the 1902-O Barber Dime.

# 1902-S

## MINTAGE
2,070,000

*Courtesy of Bowers and Merena*

## RARITY RANKINGS

*Overall, Mint State: 11th of 74*
*High Grade, MS-65 or Finer: 19th of 74 (Tie)*

## SAN FRANCISCO MINT ISSUES

*Overall, Mint State: 4th of 24*
*High Grade, MS-65 or Finer: 10th of 24 (Tie)*

**Important Varieties:** None.

**General Comments:** The 1902-S has the highest mintage of the three S-mint Barber Dimes struck from 1901-1903. While it is not as rare as the 1901-S, 1903-S or, for that matter, the 1898-S, the 1902-S is more elusive in Mint State than all other San Francisco Mint issues in this series. It handily outdistances even the lower-mintage 1904-S, 1909-S, 1913-S and 1915-S, as well as the 1895, 1896, 1897-O, 1907-D and 1909-D.

The 1902-S is also in the top ten among San Francisco Mint Barber Dimes in high grades, and it shares its ranking in this category with the 1893-S, 1896-S and 1903-S. The typical 1902-S encountered in one of today's leading rare coin auctions grades MS-63 to MS-65, although I stress that even such pieces can be elusive in the market. MS-66s are very rare, and Superb Gems in MS-67 are all but unknown.

**Strike:** Expect the typical 1902-S to possess very sharp striking detail. In fact, those pieces that are not fully impressed will usually exhibit only a touch of softness to the detail over the top of Liberty's portrait on the obverse and on the reverse over the upper and/or lower-right portion of the wreath. I have never seen a Mint State example of this issue where softness of strike was even the slightest bit distracting to the coin's overall appearance.

**Luster:** Luster quality for the 1902-S is not quite as impressive as it is for, say, the 1899-S, 1900-S or 1901-S. Nevertheless, the typical 1902-S is more than adequate in this category with either satin or softly frosted luster.

**Surfaces:** Abrasions for this issue and usually small in size and singularly inconspicuous, but they can be fairly numerous in lower Mint State grades through MS-63. A decent percentage of Mint State survivors, however, are either overall smooth or virtually pristine.

**Toning:** Most examples display some degree of toning, and the patination is often quite deep in color and usually more-or-less mottled in distribution. A few Mint State coins that I have seen possess exceptionally vivid colors to the toning, and there are also a fair number of completely brilliant examples in numismatic circles.

**Eye Appeal:** Eye appeal for the 1902-S is generally well above average, and even lower-end Mint State survivors are apt to be very pleasing in the context of their assigned grade. The only possible exception to this rule is for those pieces that exhibit dark and/or mottled toning, although even those coins are usually at least average in terms of overall eye appeal.

**Significant Examples:**

**1. PCGS MS-66. CAC.** *Ex: Baltimore Rarities Sale (Bowers and Merena, 7/2008), lot 471, where it realized $7,475.*

**2. PCGS MS-66.** *Ex: Long Beach, CA Signature Auction (Heritage, 5/2008), lot 131, where it realized $7,475.*

**3. PCGS MS-66.** *Ex: J.M. Clapp, who purchased the coin directly from the San Francisco Mint in October of 1902; Clapp estate (1942); The Louis E. Eliasberg, Sr. Collection (Bowers and Merena, 5/1996), lot 1274, where it realized $5,940; The Richmond Collection (David Lawrence, 3/2005), lot 1319, where it realized $7,763; Dallas, TX Signature Auction (Heritage, 11/2005), lot 1025, where it realized $7,475; The Collection of Dr. Steven L. Duckor (Heritage, 1/2006), lot 1001, where it realized $6,038.*

**4. NGC MS-66.** *Ex: Portland, OR Signature Sale (Heritage, 3/2004), lot 5537, where it realized $2,875.*

**5. NGC MS-66.** *Ex: Long Beach Signature Sale (Heritage, 6/2000), lot 7156, where it realized $3,335.*

**Total Known in Mint State:** 75-95 Coins

## Total Known and Value Breakdown by Grade:

| MS-60 to MS-62 | MS-63 | MS-64 | MS-65 |
|---|---|---|---|
| 15-20 Coins | 20-25 Coins | 18-22 Coins | 12-15 Coins |
| N/A | $650-$850 | $1,250-$1,750 | $2,750-$3,750 |

| MS-66 | MS-67 | MS-68 | MS-69 to MS-70 |
|---|---|---|---|
| 10-12 Coins | 1-2 Coins | 0 Coins | 0 Coins |
| $4,000-$8,000 | $8,000-$12,500 | -- | -- |

*Note:* The conclusions presented in the following "Collecting and Investing Strategies" section are drawn in large part from the Investment Potential Ratios that are summarized in Appendices G and H at the end of this book. For a detailed analysis of the formula used to derive these Investment Potential Ratios, please refer to the Introduction of this book.

**Collecting and Investing Strategies:** A relatively high mintage of 2 million coins has masked the true rarity of the 1902-S in the finer Mint State grades. The result is that this issue is the second most underrated Barber Dime in MS-64, and it is also an undervalued coin in MS-65 and MS-67. MS-66s, however, are overrated and should be avoided if possible.

Provided that you can find a Mint State example of this conditionally challenging issue that fits into your numismatic budget, you should have little difficulty purchasing an attractive 1902-S Barber Dime. Nonetheless, I would avoid the handful of darkly or otherwise unattractively toned examples that make their appearance in the market on occasion. You could also insist on acquiring a fully defined coin, but I do not believe that this is necessary since the 1902-S rarely (if ever) possesses less than a sharply executed strike.

# Proof
# 1903

## MINTAGE
755

Courtesy of Bowers and Merena

## RARITY RANKINGS

*Overall, All Proof Grades: 10th of 25 (Tie)*
*High Grade, Proof-65 or Finer: 6th of 25 (Tie)*
*Overall, Cameo Finish: 2nd of 24*
*Deep/Ultra Cameo Finish: Unknown*

**Important Varieties:** None.

**General Comments:** Similar in overall rarity to the 1913, the 1903 is among the more elusive proofs of this type. It is rarer than all proof Barber Dimes from the 1890s with the sole exception of the 1894-S, and it is also ranked ahead of the proof 1900, proof 1901, proof 1904, proof 1905 and proof 1911.

The proof 1903 is even more highly regarded when we consider only those coins that grade Proof-65 or finer. It is actually tied with the 1912 as the rarest proof Barber Dime in high grades after only the proof 1894-S, proof 1902, proof 1913, proof 1914 and proof 1915.

In an absolute sense, however, the proof 1903 is easy enough to obtain in all grades through the Proof-65 level. Premium-quality Gems in Proof-66 are very scarce, and Superb Gems are rare. The proof 1903 is the rarest collectible Barber Dime with a Cameo finish after only the proof 1902. The issue is unknown with a Deep/Ultra Cameo finish.

**Strike:** The proof 1903 typically comes with a razor-sharp, if not full strike.

**Finish:** In keeping with the all-brilliant proofing techniques that the Mint introduced to the Barber Dime series in 1902, the proof 1903 almost always displays uniform reflectivity in the fields and over the devices. Several pieces do display a modest Cameo finish on the reverse, but even most of those coins do not possess the required field-to-device contrast on the obverse to secure a Cameo designation from PCGS or NGC. Nevertheless, a small number of proof 1903 Dimes have been so designated by the major certification services. You should not expect those coins to have the same degree of contrast as a Cameo-finish proof Barber Dime from the 1890s.

**Surfaces:** The typical example is apt to display at least a few wispy hairlines, although I must stress that dark toning which inhibits the original finish also serves to limit the grade for many proof 1903 Dimes.

**Toning:** Originality is a hallmark of most examples, but the toning that is usually seen on examples of this issue is quite dark. A much smaller number of specimens possess brighter, sometimes even multicolored iridescence. Examples with both toning schemes tend to display at least some mottling of the color(s) on one or both sides of the coin.

**Eye Appeal:** Eye appeal for the proof 1903 is only average, an assessment that I attribute to the prevalence of darkly or otherwise unattractively toned coins among the surviving examples.

**Significant Examples:**

**1. PCGS Proof-67.** *Ex: Long Beach Signature Sale (Heritage, 6/2004), lot 8096, where it realized $2,818; Long Beach Signature Auction (Heritage, 5/2006), lot 1141, where it realized $3,220.*

**2. NGC Proof-67.** *Ex: The Sanctuary Sale (Bowers and Merena, 6/2003), lot 396, where it realized $2,645*

**3. NGC Proof-67 Cameo.** *Ex: The J.B. Worthington Collection (American Numismatic Rarities, 5/2005), lot 181, where it realized $2,645.*

**4. NGC Proof-66 Cameo.** *Ex: Milwaukee, WI ANA Signature Coin Auction (Heritage, 8/2007), lot 598, where it realized $2,530.*

**5. NGC Proof-66 Cameo.** *Ex: Pittsburgh, PA Signature Sale (Heritage, 8/2004), lot 5720, where it realized $1,852.*

**Total Known:** 320-395 Coins

## Total Known and Value Breakdown by Grade:

| Brilliant-Finish Coins | | | |
|---|---|---|---|
| **Proof-60-62** | **Proof-63** | **Proof-64** | **Proof-65** |
| 45-55 Coins | 60-70 Coins | 100-125 Coins | 60-70 Coins |
| N/A | $425-$500 | $600-$775 | $1,350-$1,700 |
| **Proof-66** | **Proof-67** | **Proof-68** | **Proof-69-70** |
| 40-50 Coins | 12-15 Coins | 0 Coins | 0 Coins |
| $1,750-$2,500 | $3,000-$4,000 | -- | -- |

| Cameo Coins | | | |
|---|---|---|---|
| **Proof-60-62 Cameo** | **Proof-63 Cameo** | **Proof-64 Cameo** | **Proof-65 Cameo** |
| 0 Coins | 0 Coins | 2-3 Coins | 1 Coin |
| -- | -- | $750-$1,000 | $1,500-$2,500 |
| **Proof-66 Cameo** | **Proof-67 Cameo** | **Proof-68 Cameo** | **Proof-69-70 Cameo** |
| 1-2 Coins | 1 Coin | 0 Coins | 0 Coins |
| $3,000-$4,000 | $5,000-$7,000 | -- | -- |

| Deep/Ultra Cameo | | | |
|---|---|---|---|
| **Proof-60-62 Deep/ Ultra Cameo** | **Proof-63 Deep/ Ultra Cameo** | **Proof-64 Deep/ Ultra Cameo** | **Proof-65 Deep/ Ultra Cameo** |
| 0 Coins | 0 Coins | 0 Coins | 0 Coins |
| -- | -- | -- | -- |
| **Proof-66 Deep/ Ultra Cameo** | **Proof-67 Deep/ Ultra Cameo** | **Proof-68 Deep/ Ultra Cameo** | **Proof-69-70 Deep/ Ultra Cameo** |
| 0 Coins | 0 Coins | 0 Coins | 0 Coins |
| -- | -- | -- | -- |

*Note:* The conclusions presented in the following "Collecting and Investing Strategies" section are drawn in large part from the Investment Potential Ratios that are summarized in Appendices G and H at the end of this book. For a detailed analysis of the formula used to derive these Investment Potential Ratios, please refer to the Introduction of this book.

**Collecting and Investing Strategies:** The 1903 offers solid value in Proof-64 and Proof-66, but the issue is the most overrated Barber Dime in Proof-66 after only the 1894 and 1895. In Proof-67, on the other hand, the 1903 is the most underrated proof Barber Dime behind just the 1902 and 1912. For that reason, I would focus on the Superb Gem grade level when pursuing this issue.

This issue is much more challenging to find "nice" than most buyers realize, and you are going to need a discerning eye and a good deal of patience in order to procure an attractive example of the 1903 even in Proof-67. The main impediment to locating a high-grade and high-quality example is toning. So many survivors are darkly toned, and even many of the more brightly colored specimens tend to display at least some mottling to the patina that can be distracting to the eye. The depth of toning has largely discouraged dipping for this issue, so I would not cling to the idea of being able to find an untoned example. While a few such pieces do exist, a more realistic strategy for this issue would be to acquire a toned coin with enough of an iridescent quality that the underlying Mint finish is still more-or-less vibrant. Fortunately, the more attractively toned pieces that I have seen tend to be concentrated in higher grades. I would still expect some mottling of the color on one or both sides, but this attribute can be mitigated somewhat by selecting a coin that also includes some more vivid overtones to the surfaces. And as always, avoid any Superb Gem with a sizeable or otherwise singularly conspicuous distraction, even if it is as struck (e.g., a planchet flaw or grease streak).

# 1903

## MINTAGE
19,500,000

Courtesy of Bowers and Merena

## RARITY RANKINGS

*Overall, Mint State: 39th of 74 (Tie)*
*High Grade, MS-65 or Finer: 37th of 74 (Tie)*

## PHILADELPHIA MINT ISSUES

*Overall, Mint State: 3rd of 25*
*High Grade, MS-65 or Finer: 4th of 25 (Tie)*

**Important Varieties:** There is a Repunched Date variety known that carries the attributions FS-025 and FS-301.

**General Comments:** The 1903 is the rarest Barber Dime in Mint State among Philadelphia Mint issues struck in during the 20th century. It is actually the third-rarest Philadelphia Mint issue of the type after the 1895 and 1896, although the 1904 is also rarer than the 1903 in high grades. The 1903 compares favorably to the 1905-O in terms of total number of Mint State coins believed to exist, and it is much more challenging to locate than a sizeable mintage of 19.5 million pieces might imply. This is particularly true in high grades, where the 1903 is rarer than even lower-mintage issues such as the 1894, 1905-O and 1913-S, to name just a few other Barber Dimes.

In an absolute sense, of course, the 1903 is still a relatively easy coin to locate in grades through MS-64. Gems in MS-65 are very scarce, however, and examples that grade any finer are genuinely rare.

**Strike:** The 1903 almost always comes with a sharp strike on both the obverse and the reverse. Those coins that fall short of this mark are apt to display only the slightest lack of detail on the reverse over the upper-right portion of the wreath or over and near the right (facing) loop of the ribbon bow.

**Luster:** Luster quality for the 1903 is overall strong, and the typical example displays a pleasing, frosty texture to the Mint finish.

**Surfaces:** If you are looking for a virtually pristine 1903 you had better steel yourself for a long search. Mint State survivors are almost always marred by at least a few scattered abrasions, and even relatively smooth MS-64s and MS-65s can be difficult to find.

**Toning:** I have handled very few 1903 Barber Dimes that were completely devoid of toning. Most Mint State examples are actually quite extensively toned, and even those that are not are still apt to display at least some patination around the peripheries.

**Eye Appeal:** Eye appeal for this issue is going to fluctuate widely with grade, the typical lower-end Mint State coin in MS-62 and MS-63 being below average in this regard. Pieces that grade higher are often attractive, an overall lack of distracting abrasions allowing full appreciation of impressive attributes in the areas of strike and luster quality.

### Significant Examples:

**1. PCGS MS-67.** *Ex: The Boyd E. Hayward, M.D. Collection (Bowers and Merena, 9/1997), lot 605, where it realized $3,300.*

**2. PCGS MS-66.** *Ex: CSNS Signature Coin Auction (Heritage, 4/2008), lot 618, unsold.*

**3. NGC MS-66.** *Ex: Long Beach Signature Auction (Heritage, 5/2006), lot 1109, where it realized $978; Dallas, TX Signature Coin Auction (Heritage, 4/2007), lot 556, unsold; Dallas, TX U.S. Coin Signature Auction (Heritage, 11/20007, lot 427), where it realized $1,610.*

**4. PCGS MS-66.** *Ex: Atlanta, GA ANA Signature Auction (Heritage, 4/2006), lot 435, where it realized $2,300.*

**5. PCGS MS-66.** *Ex: The Collection of Dr. Steven L. Duckor (Heritage, 1/2006), lot 1002, where it realized $2,530.*

**6. PCGS MS-66.** *Ex: Long Beach Signature Auction (Heritage, 9/2005), lot 2431, where it realized $2,300.*

**7. PCGS MS-66.** *Ex: Long Beach Signature Auction (Heritage, 9/2005), lot 2432, unsold.*

**8. NGC MS-66.** *Ex: CSNS Signature Auction (Heritage, 5/2005), lot 6644, where it realized $1,610.*

**Total Known in Mint State:** 165-205 Coins

**Total Known and Value Breakdown by Grade:**

| MS-60 to MS-62 | MS-63 | MS-64 | MS-65 |
|---|---|---|---|
| 40-50 Coins | 40-50 Coins | 45-55 Coins | 25-30 Coins |
| N/A | $135-$175 | $275-$375 | $800-$1,000 |

| MS-66 | MS-67 | MS-68 | MS-69 to MS-70 |
|---|---|---|---|
| 15-18 Coins | 1 Coin | 0 Coins | 0 Coins |
| $1,750-$2,500 | $7,500-$10,000 | -- | -- |

*Note:* The conclusions presented in the following "Collecting and Investing Strategies" section are drawn in large part from the Investment Potential Ratios that are summarized in Appendices G and H at the end of this book. For a detailed analysis of the formula used to derive these Investment Potential Ratios, please refer to the Introduction of this book.

**Collecting and Investing Strategies:** The 1903 is the most underrated P-mint Barber Dime in MS-64 and MS-65. MS-66s are also undervalued coins, and the 1903 is the second most underrated Barber Dime in MS-67 after the 1907.

Obviously, the 1903 comes highly recommended for inclusion in any numismatic holding, although I would be wary of examples in MS-65 holders with outwardly distracting abrasions. Coins of this denomination are relatively small in size, and a Gem should not possess any abrasions that are singularly conspicuous to the unaided eye. Nevertheless, I have seen a few examples of the 1903 in PCGS and NGC MS-65 holders in which this is clearly not the case. My thought is that the difficulty of locating examples that are accurately graded as MS-65 has prompted the third-party certification services to bump up a few PQ MS-64s. This is an example of a phenomenon that I like to call "relative grading," whereby the services apply different grading standards to different issues depending on their relative commonness or rarity at the higher levels of Mint State. To avoid this problem for the 1903, be highly selective with MS-65s before you make a purchase. Alternatively, you could select an MS-66 to virtually guarantee that you will be acquiring a Gem-quality coin.

# 1903-O

**MINTAGE**
8,180,000

Courtesy of David Lawrence

## RARITY RANKINGS

*Overall, Mint State: 24th of 74 (Tie)*
*High Grade, MS-65 or Finer: 6th of 74*

### NEW ORLEANS MINT ISSUES

*Overall, Mint State: 10th of 17*
*High Grade, MS-65 or Finer: 4th of 17*

**Important Varieties:** There is a minor Repunched Date variety with the attributions FS-301 and Breen-3536. Although sometimes referred to as a 1903/2-O, this variety is definitely an RPD and not an overdate.

**General Comments:** The 1903-O is in the bottom half of the New Orleans Mint Barber Dime series in terms of total number of Mint State coins believed extant. It is not a major rarity in an absolute sense, but the issue is still more challenging to locate than such other O-mint Barber Dimes as the 1893-O, 1908-O and 1909-O. The relative ranking of the 1903-O does, however, advance considerably when we consider only high grades beginning in MS-65. At those levels, the 1903-O is actually the rarest O-mint Barber Dime after only the 1894-O, 1895-O and 1902-O. The 1903-O even surpasses the 1898-S, 1896-O, 1901-S, 1904-S and 1909-S in high-grade rarity, all of which have significantly lower mintages.

The typical example of this issue that is offered either through auction or for outright purchase grades no finer than MS-64. MS-65s are rare, MS-66s are very rare and there is only a single MS-67 known to PCGS and NGC (December/2008).

**Strike:** This issue has a better quality of strike than the most poorly impressed New Orleans Mint Barber Dimes from the mid-1890s, and it is similar to the 1899-O, 1900-O, 1901-O and 1902-O in this regard. A fair number of pieces present as overall sharp in detail, but even on such coins close examination will reveal slight lack of detail to the olive leaves at the top of Liberty's portrait, the haircurls just below the ribbon upon which the word LIBERTY is inscribed and/or over the lower-right portion of the reverse wreath. I have seen a smaller number of coins (including the Eliasberg/Duckor specimen) that are softly impressed over the olive leaves above and behind Liberty's ear in the center of the obverse.

**Luster:** Luster is not a strong suit for the 1903-O, and even Gems in MS-65 and MS-66 are apt to appear a bit subdued. The typical example exhibits either satin or softly frosted luster that is not particularly vibrant.

**Surfaces:** Sizeable abrasions are seldom a problem for this issue. Even low-end Mint State examples are apt to be limited in grade more through luster deficiencies than an excessive number of marks.

**Toning:** As an issue, the 1903-O is not among the more extensively toned Barber Dimes. While there are certainly some deeply toned examples known, the typical Mint State survivor is only lightly-to-moderately patinated. Prevalent colors are silver-gray and golden-apricot shades, with russet and olive overtones being seen much less frequently. Some of the more extensively toned pieces are a bit mottled in appearance, while many of the golden-toned pieces are lightly dipped examples that still retain faint remnants of the original toning.

**Eye Appeal:** Deficiencies with the luster notwithstanding, the 1903-O has above-average eye appeal.

**Significant Examples:**

**1. NGC MS-65.** *Ex: The Richmond Collection (David Lawrence, 3/2005), lot 1321, where it realized $3,450; The Southwest Collection (Heritage, 2/2008), lot 169, where it realized $3,594.*

**2. PCGS MS-65.** *Ex: Baltimore, MD Signature Sale (Heritage, 7/2003), lot 6614, where it realized $3,910; Long Beach, CA Signature Coin Auction (Heritage, 2/2008), lot 170, where it realized $3,565.*

**3. PCGS MS-65.** *Ex: J.M. Clapp, who acquired the coin circa 1903, possibly directly from the New Orleans Mint; Clapp estate (1942); The Louis E. Eliasberg, Sr. Collection (Bowers and Merena, 5/1996), lot 1276, where it realized $2,970; The Collection of Dr. Steven L. Duckor (Heritage, 1/2006), lot 1003, where it realized $2,990.*

**4. PCGS MS-65.** *Ex: New York Signature Sale (Heritage, 7/2004), lot 5817, unsold; Palm Beach, FL Signature Sale (Heritage, 11/2004), lot 6281, unsold.*

**5. PCGS MS-65.** *Ex: Long Beach Signature Sale (Heritage, 6/2000), lot 7158, where it realized $4,140; Lake Geneva Sale (Bowers and Merena, 6/2001), lot 286.*

**6. PCGS MS-65.** *Ex: The Benson Collection (Ira & Larry Goldberg, 2/2002), lot 586, where it realized $4,255.*

**7. NGC MS-65.** *Ex: Chicago ANA Signature Sale (Heritage, 8/1999), lot 6867, where it realized $1,438.*

**Total Known in Mint State:** 110-135 Coins

**Total Known and Value Breakdown by Grade:**

| MS-60 to MS-62 | MS-63 | MS-64 | MS-65 |
|---|---|---|---|
| 40-50 Coins | 15-20 Coins | 40-50 Coins | 10-12 Coins |
| N/A | $375-$475 | $900-$1,200 | $3,500-$4,500 |

| MS-66 | MS-67 | MS-68 | MS-69 to MS-70 |
|---|---|---|---|
| 3-4 Coins | 1 Coin | 0 Coins | 0 Coins |
| $5,000-$7,500 | $7,500-$10,000 | -- | -- |

Note: The conclusions presented in the following "Collecting and Investing Strategies" section are drawn in large part from the Investment Potential Ratios that are summarized in Appendices G and H at the end of this book. For a detailed analysis of the formula used to derive these Investment Potential Ratios, please refer to the Introduction of this book.

**Collecting and Investing Strategies:** The 1903-O Barber Dime is a more-or-less underrated issue in MS-64 and MS-65, and both the collector and investor could do well acquiring an example of this issue in one of those grades. Nevertheless, it is at the MS-66 and MS-67 grade levels where I am particularly fond of the investment potential of the 1903. This is the most undervalued New Orleans Mint Barber Dime in the finest Mint State grades. When viewed in the wider context of this series, in fact, only the 1905 is more underrated than the 1903-O in MS-66. And in MS-67, it is only the 1903 and 1907 that offer greater potential for price appreciation than the 1903-O.

The 1903-O is not a particularly challenging issue to find with good eye appeal, providing that you are willing to accept some muting of the luster even through the MS-65 grade level. Your only impediment to finding a pleasing example, therefore, should be the availability of the coins in the market.

Although I am a fan of originally toned coins, this is one issue for which a dipped example might be preferable. Just make sure that the dipping was properly executed and that the surfaces retain some degree of vibrancy to the luster. Do not expect a "blazer," of course, as the 1903-O almost always comes with more-or-less deficient luster. If you do want an originally toned coin, make sure that the surfaces are not too dark.

# 1903-S

## MINTAGE
613,300

Courtesy of David Lawrence

## RARITY RANKINGS

***Overall, Mint State:** 6th of 74 (Tie)*
***High Grade, MS-65 or Finer:** 19th of 74 (Tie)*

### SAN FRANCISCO MINT ISSUES

***Overall, Mint State:** 2nd of 24 (Tie)*
***High Grade, MS-65 or Finer:** 10th of 24 (Tie)*

**Important Varieties:** None.

**General Comments:** A "magic date" in the series, the 1903-S is one of only 13 business strike Barber Dimes with an original mintage of fewer than 1 million coins. The 1903-S is actually not as rare in Mint State as the overlooked 1898-S, but it is tied with the 1901-S as the second-rarest Barber Dime struck in the San Francisco Mint. The 1903-S also just barely makes it into the top ten among S-mint Barber Dimes in the category of high-grade rarity, in which it shares its ranking with the 1893-S, 1896-S and 1902-S.

The 1903-S is actually more common at and above the MS-65 grade level than the higher-mintage 1898-O and 1899-S. Clearly, the low-mintage status of the 1903-S was recognized early, leading to a greater rate of survival for this issue when compared to those of the 1898-O and 1898-S. Even so, the 1903-S is a leading rarity in the Mint State Barber Dime series, and it is tied with the 1899-O and 1901-S as the sixth-rarest issue of the type after the 1894-O, 1895-O, 1896-O, 1898-O and 1898-S.

**Strike:** While a few examples have a touch of softness to the upper-right portion of the reverse wreath and/or the right (facing) bow of the ribbon knot, the 1903-S is an overall sharply struck issue.

**Luster:** This issue is characterized by above-average luster that comes either satiny or, much less frequently, softly frosted in texture.

**Surfaces:** When offered in Mint State at all, the 1903-S is actually much more likely to be in the MS-64 to MS-66 grade range than in the lower reaches of Mint State through MS-63. This is perhaps surprising for such a low-mintage issue, but I believe that this phenomenon is easily explained. With so few Mint State coins known, the 1903-S does not appear to have been saved to a great extent by contemporary dealers or as part of bank reserves. Rather, I believe that most Uncirculated examples have come down to us thanks to the efforts of earlier generations of collectors, who were more likely to take exceptionally good care of their charges than, say, bank employees.

The prevalence of slidemarks among the few lower-grade Mint State survivors that I have seen lends further support for this theory. Distractions such as these are a direct result of long-terms storage in collectors' coin albums and would not be present on coins that spent the majority of their time as part of original rolls.

**Toning:** Richly toned surfaces are the rule for most Mint State 1903-S Barber Dimes, and the widespread practice of dipping and other forms of numismatic conservation have yet to significantly impact this issue. Do not expect to see particularly vivid colors on a 1903-S Dime, however, as many examples display deeper shades such as russet, antique-copper and even charcoal. Toning for the issue is often at least partially mottled in distribution.

**Eye Appeal:** The 1903-S is a well-produced and, for those Mint State pieces that have survived, generally well-preserved issue. As such, I am compelled to assign this issue an above-average eye appeal rating even though dark and/or mottled toning can be a problem even for high-grade examples in MS-66 and MS-67.

**Significant Examples:**

**1. NGC MS-67.** *Ex: The John C. Hugon Collection (Heritage, 1/2005), lot 4035, where it realized $10,638; San Francisco, CA ANA Signature Auction (Heritage, 7/2005), lot 10162, unsold; Long Beach Signature Auction (Heritage, 9/2005), lot 2433, unsold; Dallas Signature Coin Auction (Heritage, 10/2006), lot 760, unsold; Long Beach, CA Signature Coin Auction (Heritage, 2/2007), lot 2947, where it realized $8,338.*

**2. PCGS MS-67.** *Ex: The Wayne S. Rich Collection (Bowers and Merena, 3/2002), lot 2096, where it realized $10,925.*

**3. NGC MS-66.** *Ex: J.M. Clapp, who acquired the coin directly from the San Francisco Mint in October of 1903; Clapp estate (1942); The Louis E. Eliasberg, Sr. Collection (Bowers and Merena, 5/1996), lot 1277, where it realized $3,190; The Richmond Collection (David Lawrence, 3/2005), lot 1322, where it realized $4,370; The Southwest Collection (Heritage, 2/2008), lot 172, where it realized $4,025.*

**4. NGC MS-66.** *Ex: San Francisco Rarities Sale (Bowers and Merena, 7/2005), lot 410, where it realized $3,335; Beverly Hills Rarities Sale (Bowers and Merena, 2/2006), lot 200, where it realized $3,508.*

**5. PCGS MS-66.** *Ex: The Emery and Nichols Collections (Bowers and Merena, 11/1984), lot 405; where it realized $3,740; Atlanta, GA Signature Sale (Heritage, 8/2001), lot 5728, where it realized $3,968; Long Beach Signature Sale (Heritage, 2/2002), lot 5534, where it realized $4,025; New York Rarities Sale (Bowers and Merena, 7/2002), lot 151, unsold; Long Beach Signature Sale (Heritage, 2/2003), lot 6351, where it realized $3,910; The Collection of Dr. Steven L. Duckor (Heritage, 1/2006), lot 1004, where it realized $4,888.*

**6. PCGS MS-66.** *Ex: Auction '82 (Paramount's session, 8/1982), lot 1623, where it realized $1,250; The Frog Run Farm Collection (American Numismatic Rarities, 11/2004), lot 674, where it realized $3,565; Long Beach Signature Sale (Heritage, 2/2005), lot 6286, where it realized $4,083.*

**7. PCGS MS-66.** *Ex: Long Beach Signature Sale (Heritage, 5/2003), lot 5785, where it realized $4,830.*

**8. NGC MS-66.** *Ex: New York ANA Signature Sale (Heritage, 8/1997), lot 6179, where it realized $2,100; Portland ANA Signature Sale (Heritage, 8/1998), lot 6378, where it realized $3,795.*

**9. NGC MS-66.** *Ex: Long Beach Signature Sale (Heritage, 10/1995), lot 5891, where it realized $2,420.*

**Total Known in Mint State:** 65-85 Coins

**Total Known and Value Breakdown by Grade:**

| MS-60 to MS-62 | MS-63 | MS-64 | MS-65 |
|---|---|---|---|
| 15-20 Coins | 6-8 Coins | 20-25 Coins | 7-9 Coins |
| N/A | $1,250-$1,750 | $1,750-$2,250 | $2,250-$2,750 |

| MS-66 | MS-67 | MS-68 | MS-69 to MS-70 |
|---|---|---|---|
| 15-20 Coins | 2-3 Coins | 0 Coins | 0 Coins |
| $4,000-$5,500 | $10,000-$15,000 | -- | -- |

<u>*Note:*</u> The conclusions presented in the following "Collecting and Investing Strategies" section are drawn in large part from the Investment Potential Ratios that are summarized in Appendices G and H at the end of this book. For a detailed analysis of the formula used to derive these Investment Potential Ratios, please refer to the Introduction of this book.

**Collecting and Investing Strategies:** A limited mintage notwithstanding, the 1903-S is an underrated issue in both MS-64 and MS-65. This issue is actually more undervalued in MS-65 than any other Barber Dime with the sole exception of the 1907-S. The numismatic investor and high-grade Barber Dime specialist would both be wise to focus on either of these two grade levels when pursuing this key-date issue. Conversely, I would avoid the 1903-S in MS-66 and MS-67 as such pieces are overpriced relative to their actual rarity. While high-end Gems and Superb Gems are legitimately rare coins when viewed in the wider context of the numismatic market, their prices are inflated due to the overall scarcity of the issue in terms of total number of circulated and Mint State coins known to exist.

The Mint State population of the 1903-S is fairly evenly distributed throughout the MS-60 and MS-66 grade range, which means that you are just as likely to encounter a nearly pristine, premium-quality Gem in today's market than you are to find a low-grade BU with slidemarks or other significant detractions. These facts explain why there is a relatively narrow spread for this issue between all Mint State grades except MS-66 and MS-67. This phenomenon creates a curious situation for the buyer. You must be particularly mindful of examples that grade MS-65 or lower that are billed as premium quality by the seller. Such coins will certainly carry a premium-quality price tag. Chances are pretty good, however, that you will be able to find a middle-of-the road example in the next grade for not much more money. In short, I would not purchase a premium-quality 1903-S in MS-64 unless you could absolutely not afford to stretch for an MS-65. On the other hand, I would acquire a premium-quality Gem in MS-65 since such a piece holds greater investment potential than an overrated MS-66.

# Proof
# 1904

## MINTAGE
670

*Courtesy of Bowers and Merena*

## RARITY
## RANKINGS

*Overall, All Proof Grades: 15th of 25 (Tie)*
*High Grade, Proof-65 or Finer: 8th of 25 (Tie)*
*Overall, Cameo Finish: 6th of 24 (Tie)*
*Deep/Ultra Cameo Finish: Unknown*

**Important Varieties:** None.

**General Comments:** Proof Barber Dime production continued to fall through 1904, the Philadelphia Mint delivering only 670 specimens that year. Continuing the trend begun with the proof 1903, however, the proof 1904 is an easier issue to locate than its immediate predecessor despite having a lower mintage. Obviously, numismatic interest in proof Barber Dimes advanced to a significant degree over what it has been just a year or two earlier.

The 1904 is similar in overall rarity to the 1909, and it falls roughly in the bottom half of the proof Barber Dime series in terms of total number of specimens believed extant. On the other hand, the 1904 vies with the 1908 as the eighth-rarest proof Barber Dime in high grades, indicating that relatively few examples were handled with the utmost care over the years.

In an absolute sense, the proof 1904 is still obtainable with relative ease in grades through Proof-65. Even Proof-66s can only be described as marginally rare when viewed in the wider context of the rare coin market. Superb Gems in Proof-67 and Proof-68 are another matter entirely, however, and it may take some "looking" to procure a specimen in one of those grades.

**Strike:** As befits the method of manufacture, striking quality for the proof 1903 is excellent.

**Finish:** The proof 1904 has a greater number of Cameo-designated examples certified at PCGS and NGC than either the proof 1902 or the proof 1903. Even so, the typical example is all-brilliant in finish or, at best, possessed of minimal field-to-device contrast only on the reverse. Obverse contrast is also likely to be minimal for those coins that PCGS and NGC have deemed worthy of a Cameo designation.

**Surfaces:** While I definitely believe that most proof 1904 Barber Dimes were distributed to collectors either directly from the Mint or through the services of a few contemporary dealers, this issue was not that well cared for over the years. The typical survivor displays a few scattered contact marks that, fortunately, tend to be small, wispy hairlines that are not all that distracting to the eye.

**Toning:** You should expect to see some degree of toning when confronted with an example of this issue in a dealer's inventory or at auction. Colors are usually quite dark, but they also tend to be somewhat iridescent in quality and not all that much of a hindrance to the underlying Mint finish. On the positive side, however, many deeply toned specimens also include more vivid highlights on one or both side of the coin. Often times a strong, direct light source will be required to appreciate the more colorful toning on a proof 1904 Dime.

**Eye Appeal:** The proof 1904 has above-average eye appeal that is certainly superior to that often seen for the proof 1903. Even many deeply toned specimens still retain considerable, if not full vibrancy to the original finish.

**Significant Examples:**

**1. NGC Proof-68.** *Ex: Fort Lauderdale ANA National Money Show Auction (Superior, 3/2000), lot 296, where it realized $6,210.*

**2. NGC Proof-67.** *Ex: Long Beach, CA Signature Coin Auction (Heritage, 9/2007), lot 1050, where it realized $2,645.*

**3. PCGS Proof-67.** *Ex: The Bruce Scher #1 All-Time PCGS Registry Set (Heritage, 2/2005), lot 4064, where it realized $3,502; CSNS Signature Auction (Heritage, 4/2006), lot 1340, unsold.*

**4. NGC Proof-67.** *Ex: The John C. Hugon Collection (Heritage, 1/2005), lot 4088, where it realized $3,335.*

**5. NGC Proof-67.** *Ex: Mid-Winter ANA Signature Sale (Heritage, 3/1999), lot 6351, where it realized $3,335.*

**6. NGC Proof-67 Cameo.** *Ex: The William H. LaBelle, Sr. Collection (American Numismatic Rarities, 7/2005), lot 1019, unsold.*

**7. NGC Proof-67 Cameo.** *Ex: Long Beach, CA Signature Auction (Heritage, 5/2008), lot 158, where it realized $5,750.*

**Total Known:** 360-440 Coins

**Total Known and Value Breakdown by Grade:**

| Brilliant-Finish Coins | | | |
|---|---|---|---|
| **Proof-60-62** | **Proof-63** | **Proof-64** | **Proof-65** |
| 55-65 Coins | 80-95 Coins | 100-125 Coins | 55-65 Coins |
| N/A | $425-$500 | $600-$800 | $1,350-$1,700 |
| **Proof-66** | **Proof-67** | **Proof-68** | **Proof-69-70** |
| 35-45 Coins | 12-15 Coins | 1-2 Coins | 0 Coins |
| $1,500-$2,500 | $3,000-$4,000 | $7,500-$12,000 | -- |

| Cameo Coins | | | |
|---|---|---|---|
| **Proof-60-62 Cameo** | **Proof-63 Cameo** | **Proof-64 Cameo** | **Proof-65 Cameo** |
| 0 Coins | 1-2 Coins | 10-12 Coins | 4-5 Coins |
| -- | $600-$750 | $900-$1,100 | $1,750-$2,750 |
| **Proof-66 Cameo** | **Proof-67 Cameo** | **Proof-68 Cameo** | **Proof-69-70 Cameo** |
| 5-7 Coins | 4-5 Coins | 0 Coins | 0 Coins |
| $2,500-$4,000 | $5,750-$7,750 | -- | -- |

| Deep/Ultra Cameo | | | |
|---|---|---|---|
| **Proof-60-62 Deep/ Ultra Cameo** | **Proof-63 Deep/ Ultra Cameo** | **Proof-64 Deep/ Ultra Cameo** | **Proof-65 Deep/ Ultra Cameo** |
| 0 Coins | 0 Coins | 0 Coins | 0 Coins |
| -- | -- | -- | -- |
| **Proof-66 Deep/ Ultra Cameo** | **Proof-67 Deep/ Ultra Cameo** | **Proof-68 Deep/ Ultra Cameo** | **Proof-69-70 Deep/ Ultra Cameo** |
| 0 Coins | 0 Coins | 0 Coins | 0 Coins |
| -- | -- | -- | -- |

*Note:* The conclusions presented in the following "Collecting and Investing Strategies" section are drawn in large part from the Investment Potential Ratios that are summarized in Appendices G and H at the end of this book. For a detailed analysis of the formula used to derive these Investment Potential Ratios, please refer to the Introduction of this book.

**Collecting and Investing Strategies:** The 1904 is one of the more overrated Barber Dimes in Proof-65, and Proof-64s also do not hold much investment potential even though they are fairly well priced in comparison to their rarity. Proof-66s are underrated, however, and Proof-67s are more so than those of any other Barber Dime with the exception of only the 1902, 1903 and 1912. It is in the finest grades, therefore, where you should concentrate your search for an example of this issue.

As always, a sound strategy for selecting a proof 1904 Barber Dime that will appeal to a maximum number of buyers when the time comes to sell is to focus on acquiring a piece with solid technical quality and strong eye appeal. At the Proof-66 or Proof-67 levels, select a coin with either untoned surfaces or relatively even patination. The toning can be deep (it usually is for this issue), but make sure that it does not obscure the underlying finish and, if possible, includes some more vivid highlights on one or both sides of the coin.

# 1904

## MINTAGE
### 14,600,357

Courtesy of Bowers and Merena

## RARITY RANKINGS

*Overall, Mint State:* 50th of 74
*High Grade, MS-65 or Finer:* 30th of 74 (Tie)

## PHILADELPHIA MINT ISSUES

*Overall, Mint State:* 7th of 25
*High Grade, MS-65 or Finer:* 2nd of 25

**Important Varieties:** None.

**General Comments:** Like the 1902 and 1903, the 1904 is on overlooked Barber Dime that is just not all that common in Mint State for a P-mint issue with a sizeable original mintage. The 1904 is more plentiful than both of those issues, but it is rarer in Mint State than all other P-mint Barber Dimes with the exception of the 1894, 1895, 1896 and 1905. The situation is even more dramatic in high grades, where the 1904 emerges as the second-rarest Philadelphia Mint Barber Dime after the 1895. The 1904 is rarer than the widely saved 1892-O and the lower-mintage 1911-S in all Mint State grades, and it is similar in high-grade rarity to the 1906-D, 1908-S, 1909-O and 1915-S.

**Strike:** Striking quality for the 1904 is usually more-or-less sharp, but there are some noteworthy exceptions that are very surprising for a Philadelphia Mint Barber Dime. I have seen more than a few Mint State examples with noticeable softness of detail over the top of Liberty's portrait on the obverse and/or at isolated portions of the wreath where that device is closest to the reverse border.

**Luster:** The 1904 exhibits both softly frosted and satiny luster to very good effect, and the typical Mint State survivor is very attractive as far as this characteristic is concerned.

**Surfaces:** Scattered abrasions are the norm for this issue, but even in lower grades such distractions are seldom conspicuous to the unaided eye.

**Toning:** Less than one third, if not one quarter of the Mint State examples that I have seen are either mostly or completely brilliant. This observation places the majority of 1904 Dimes in the toned category. The type of patination seen most often for this issue is moderate-to-deep in color with a rich, handsome appearance. Several pieces are quite colorfully toned, even if such colors are confined to the peripheries.

**Eye Appeal:** This issue tends to come very nice, and overall eye appeal for Mint State survivors is well above average.

**Significant Examples:**

**1. NGC MS-66 ★.** *Ex: CSNS Signature Coin Auction (Heritage, 4/2008), lot 620, where it realized $2,300.*

**2. PCGS MS-66.** *Ex: Long Beach Signature Sale (Heritage, 9/2003), lot 6452, where it realized $2,070; The Collection of Dr. Steven L. Duckor (Heritage, 1/2006), lot 1005, where it realized $2,760; Denver ANA Auction (Bowers and Merena, 8/2006), lot 763, unsold; Long Beach, CA Signature Coin Auction (Heritage, 2/2007), lot 2948, where it realized $2,990.*

**3. PCGS MS-66.** *Ex: Dallas Signature Coin Auction (Heritage, 10/2006), lot 761, where it realized $2,760.*

**4. NGC MS-66.** *Ex: CSNS Signature Auction (Heritage, 4/2006), lot 1300, where it realized $1,840.*

**5. PCGS MS-66.** *Ex: San Francisco, CA ANA Signature Auction (Heritage, 7/2005), lot 5893, unsold; Long Beach Signature Auction (Heritage, 9/2005), lot 2434, where it realized $4,313.*

**6. PCGS MS-66.** *Ex: Pre-FUN Orlando Elite Coin Auction (Superior, 1/2004), lot 245, unsold; Portland, OR Signature Sale (Heritage, 3/2004), lot 5538, where it realized $3,105; New York, NY Signature Sale (Heritage, 7/2004), lot 5820, where it realized $2,990.*

**7. PCGS MS-66.** *Ex: CSNS Signature Sale (Heritage, 5/2004), lot 6659, where it realized $3,105.*

**8. PCGS MS-66.** *Ex: Long Beach Signature Sale (Heritage, 9/2003), lot 6451, where it realized $5,980.*

**Total Known in Mint State:** 225-275 Coins

**Total Known and Value Breakdown by Grade:**

| MS-60 to MS-62 | MS-63 | MS-64 | MS-65 |
|---|---|---|---|
| 45-55 Coins | 55-65 Coins | 90-110 Coins | 25-30 Coins |
| N/A | $135-$175 | $300-$400 | $1,250-$1,750 |

| MS-66 | MS-67 | MS-68 | MS-69 to MS-70 |
|---|---|---|---|
| 10-15 Coins | 0 Coins | 0 Coins | 0 Coins |
| $2,000-$3,500 | -- | -- | -- |

*Note:* The conclusions presented in the following "Collecting and Investing Strategies" section are drawn in large part from the Investment Potential Ratios that are summarized in Appendices G and H at the end of this book. For a detailed analysis of the formula used to derive these Investment Potential Ratios, please refer to the Introduction of this book.

**Collecting and Investing Strategies:** I do not recommend acquiring the 1904 Barber Dime in any grade below MS-66 if ROI (read: return on investment) is not at least part of your consideration for pursuing numismatics. Examples in MS-64 and MS-65 are somewhat underrated, nonetheless, but the most undervalued Mint State survivors are those at the MS-66 level.

Emphasize eye appeal above all else when pursuing this issue in the finest Mint State grades. Fortunately, your task will be relatively easy in this regard as most Gem-quality examples that I have seen are either fully brilliant or possessed of handsome, richly original patina. Additionally, the few really softly struck coins are largely concentrated at the lower reaches of Mint State.

# 1904-S

## MINTAGE
## 800,000

Courtesy of David Lawrence

## RARITY RANKINGS

*Overall, Mint State: 19th of 74*
*High Grade, MS-65 or Finer: 10th of 74*

## SAN FRANCISCO MINT ISSUES

*Overall, Mint State: 9th of 24*
*High Grade, MS-65 or Finer: 6th of 24*

**Important Varieties:** None.

**General Comments:** The New Orleans Mint refrained from striking coins of this denomination in 1904, which confirms the 1904-S as the only mintmarked Barber Dime of this date. This issue concludes a run of low-mintage Barber Dimes from the San Francisco Mint that began in 1901 and continued through 1904 with a single interruption in 1902. The 1904-S is highly elusive in all Mint State grades, and it is obvious that few of the 800,000 pieces produced were kept from entering circulation. It is rarer than such other S-mint Barber Dimes as the 1913-S and 1915-S, but is not as elusive in Mint State as the 1896-S, 1901-S, 1903-S or 1909-S. Perhaps even more interesting is the fact that the 1904-S was saved in greater numbers than the higher-mintage 1897-S, 1898-S and 1910-S.

At and above the MS-65 grade level, the situation reverses itself with the 1904-S ranking as the rarest of the low-mintage San Francisco Mint Dimes produced from 1901-1904. Among S-mint Barber Dimes, in fact, only the 1892-S, 1895-S, 1897-S, 1898-S and 1907-S are ranked ahead of the 1904-S in high-grade rarity.

**Strike:** The 1904-S has a very similar quality of strike to the 1904. The vast majority of examples are sharply impressed. On the other hand, the occasional piece is offered on which softness of detail is readily evident over the top of Liberty's portrait and/or in isolated areas of the reverse wreath.

**Luster:** Luster quality for this issue is excellent, the coins almost always displaying a satin or softly frosted texture to the surfaces. NGC has also certified a single Mint State coin with a Prooflike finish (December/2008).

**Surfaces:** A few scattered ticks and abrasions are often present on Mint State 1904-S Barber Dimes, and these can be fairly sizeable even through the MS-64 grade level. This issue is anything but easy to locate with overall smooth surfaces.

**Toning:** Most Mint State coins are originally toned, although pieces that are more-or-less brilliant from dipping are beginning to make an appearance in greater numbers. As far as the toned coins are concerned, they usually possess deep, rich patina that provides an antique appearance to the surfaces. More vividly toned pieces are not unknown, but they are clearly in the minority among the originally preserved examples.

**Eye Appeal:** Eye appeal for the 1904-S is above average, if not downright strong, and the typical Mint State coin is very appealing in the context of the assigned grade.

**Significant Examples:**

**1. NGC MS-66.** *Ex: The Belle Glade Collection (Heritage, 8/2007), lot 574, where it realized $5,750; FUN Signature Coin Auction (Heritage, 1/2008), lot 1034, where it realized $6,325.*

**2. PCGS MS-66.** *Ex: Long Beach Signature Sale (Heritage, 9/1998), lot 6617, unsold; Long Beach Signature Sale (Heritage, 2/1999), lot 5857, where it realized $3,565; The Belle Glade Collection (Heritage, 8/2006), lot 942, where it realized $6,325.*

**3. PCGS MS-66.** *Ex: The Collection of Dr. Steven L. Duckor (Heritage, 1/2006), lot 1006, where it realized $8,625.*

**4. PCGS MS-66.** *Ex: New York, NY Signature Sale (Heritage, 7/2002), lot 7617, where it realized $5,290; FUN Signature Sale (Heritage, 1/2003), lot 6477, where it realized $4,888; CSNS Signature Auction (Heritage, 5/2005), lot 6646, where it realized $9,200.*

**5. PCGS MS-66.** *Ex: The Wayne S. Rich Collection (Bowers and Merena, 3/2002), lot 2099, where it realized $4,830.*

**6. NGC MS-65.** *Ex: Superior's sale of 2/1999, lot 636, where it realized $2,185; Dallas, TX Coin Signature Auction (Heritage, 7/2006), lot 658,* *where it realized $3,968; CSNS Signature Coin Auction (Heritage, 4/2008), lot 621, where it realized $3,450.*

**7. PCGS MS-65.** *Ex: Long Beach, CA Signature Auction (Heritage, 9/2006), lot 1345, unsold; Long Beach, CA Signature Coin Auction (Heritage, 2/2007), lot 2949, where it realized $3,738; CSNS Signature Coin Auction (Heritage, 5/2007), lot 371, unsold.*

**8. PCGS MS-65.** *Ex: The Irving Goodman Collection (Superior, 5/1996), lot 731, where it realized $1,760; The John C. Hugon Collection (Heritage, 1/2005), lot 4037, where it realized $2,875; Dallas, TX Signature Auction (Heritage, 11/2005), lot 1026, where it realized $3,623.*

**9. PCGS MS-65.** *Ex: Law Collection; San Francisco, CA ANA Signature Auction (Heritage, 7/2005), lot 5894, where it realized $4,025.*

**Total Known in Mint State:** 90-105 Coins

**Total Known and Value Breakdown by Grade:**

| MS-60 to MS-62 | MS-63 | MS-64 | MS-65 |
|---|---|---|---|
| 30-35 Coins | 15-20 Coins | 25-30 Coins | 10-12 Coins |
| N/A | $1,100-$1,400 | $2,750-$3,250 | $3,500-$4,000 |

| MS-66 | MS-67 | MS-68 | MS-69 to MS-70 |
|---|---|---|---|
| 6-8 Coins | 1 Coin | 0 Coins | 0 Coins |
| $5,000-$10,000 | $15,000-$25,000 | -- | -- |

*Note:* The conclusions presented in the following "Collecting and Investing Strategies" section are drawn in large part from the Investment Potential Ratios that are summarized in Appendices G and H at the end of this book. For a detailed analysis of the formula used to derive these Investment Potential Ratios, please refer to the Introduction of this book.

**Collecting and Investing Strategies:** I do not advise purchasing a 1904-S that grades lower than MS-65 unless you need such a coin for a complete set of similarly graded Barber Dimes. The 1904-S is underrated only in the MS-65 to MS-67 grade range, with MS-65 and MS-67 being the two most desirable grades for this low-mintage, key-date issue.

Both brilliant and richly toned high-grade 1903-S Barber Dimes have performed well in my experience, so the exact "look" of the piece that you acquire can be dictated by your personal preference. Be wary, however, of the occasional Gem with noticeable softness of strike in isolated areas on the obverse and/or reverse.

# Proof
# 1905

## MINTAGE
727

Courtesy of Bowers and Merena

## RARITY RANKINGS

*Overall, All Proof Grades: 17th of 25*
*High Grade, Proof-65 or Finer: 18th of 25 (Tie)*
*Overall, Cameo Finish: 13th of 24*
*Deep/Ultra Cameo Finish: Unknown*

**Important Varieties:** None.

**General Comments:** The 1905 is one of the more common issues in the proof Barber Dime series—and the most common from the 20th century—but it is rarer than all issues of this type that date to the 1890s with the obvious exception of the 1894-S. The proof 1905 is even more plentiful when we consider only those coins that grade Proof-65 or finer, but high-grade examples are still rarer than those of the proof 1892-1898 issues. This issue is also only a median rarity among proof Barber Dimes with a Cameo finish, but it is unknown as a Deep/Ultra Cameo.

**Strike:** Striking softness is virtually unknown for the proof 1905, and all examples that I have seen display very sharp, if not full definition to even the most intricate elements of the design.

**Finish:** While more plentiful with a Cameo finish than the proof Barber Dimes from 1902-1904, the proof 1905 is still an issue that is usually encountered with an all-brilliant finish. Even most of the specimens that PCGS and NGC have certified as Cameo display only minimal field-to-device contrast that is often a bit more pronounced on the reverse.

**Surfaces:** Many proof 1905 Barber Dimes possess grade-limiting contact marks in the form of wispy hairlines or slidemarks. These blemishes are often small in size and not overly conspicuous, but slidemarks from storage in old coin albums can be very distracting, especially since those features tend to be concentrated on Liberty's cheek.

A fair number of examples are also overall smooth, and the 1905 is definitely not among the more challenging proof Barber Dimes to locate in Proof-65 and Proof-66. Virtually pristine specimens in Proof-67 and Proof-68, however, can be difficult to come by in today's market.

**Toning:** Richly and originally toned proof 1905 Dimes outnumber untoned specimens by a factor of at least three-to-one. The toned specimens tend to display deeper colors but, fortunately, even on those coins the patina is sometimes iridescent in quality and not overly detracting to the underlying finish. I have also seen a few exceptionally vivid examples, and these are among the most beautifully toned proof Barber Dimes of any date known to exist. The untoned coins are largely the result of dipping, although such pieces are usually highly attractive with radiant surfaces.

**Eye Appeal:** As an issue, the proof 1905 has above-average eye appeal that usually applies to deeply toned specimens just as much as it does to coins with brilliant or vividly toned surfaces.

**Significant Examples:**

**1. PCGS Proof-67 Cameo.** *Ex: CSNS Signature Auction (Heritage, 5/2005), lot 6715, where it realized $4,025; FUN Signature Auction (Heritage, 1/2006), lot 1858, where it realized $2,760.*

**2. NGC Proof-67 Cameo.** *Ex: Long Beach Signature Sale (Heritage, 5/2003), lot 5814, where it realized $2,300; The William H. LaBelle, Sr. Collection (American Numismatic Rarities, 7/2005), lot 1020, unsold; Atlanta Sale (American Numismatic Rarities, 10/2005), lot 5212, unsold; The Old Colony Collection (American Numismatic Rarities, 12/2005), lot 512, unsold; The New York Connoisseur's Collection (American Numismatic Rarities, 1/2006), lot 591, unsold; The Old West & Franklinton Collections (American Numismatic Rarities, 8/2006), lot 360, where it realized $3,450.*

**3. NGC Proof-67 Cameo.** *Ex: Dallas Signature Auction (Heritage, 12/2005), lot 519, where it realized $2,990.*

**4. PCGS Proof-67 Cameo.** *Ex: The Bruce Scher #1 All-Time PCGS Registry Set (Heritage, 2/2005), lot 4065, where it realized $4,313.*

**Total Known:** 365-425 Coins

## Total Known and Value Breakdown by Grade:

| Brilliant-Finish Coins | | | |
|---|---|---|---|
| **Proof-60-62** | **Proof-63** | **Proof-64** | **Proof-65** |
| 35-40 Coins | 60-70 Coins | 80-90 Coins | 60-70 Coins |
| N/A | $425-$500 | $600-$800 | $1,400-$1,600 |
| **Proof-66** | **Proof-67** | **Proof-68** | **Proof-69-70** |
| 60-70 Coins | 23-28 Coins | 5-7 Coins | 0 Coins |
| $1,500-$2,000 | $2,500-$5,000 | $7,500-$9,000 | -- |

| Cameo Coins | | | |
|---|---|---|---|
| **Proof-60-62 Cameo** | **Proof-63 Cameo** | **Proof-64 Cameo** | **Proof-65 Cameo** |
| 1-2 Coins | 2-3 Coins | 5-7 Coins | 10-12 Coins |
| N/A | $600-$750 | $900-$1,100 | $1,600-$1,800 |
| **Proof-66 Cameo** | **Proof-67 Cameo** | **Proof-68 Cameo** | **Proof-69-70 Cameo** |
| 14-16 Coins | 8-10 Coins | 1 Coin | 0 Coins |
| $2,000-$3,000 | $3,500-$5,000 | $10,000-$12,000 | -- |

| Deep/Ultra Cameo | | | |
|---|---|---|---|
| **Proof-60-62 Deep/ Ultra Cameo** | **Proof-63 Deep/ Ultra Cameo** | **Proof-64 Deep/ Ultra Cameo** | **Proof-65 Deep/ Ultra Cameo** |
| 0 Coins | 0 Coins | 0 Coins | 0 Coins |
| -- | -- | -- | -- |
| **Proof-66 Deep/ Ultra Cameo** | **Proof-67 Deep/ Ultra Cameo** | **Proof-68 Deep/ Ultra Cameo** | **Proof-69-70 Deep/ Ultra Cameo** |
| 0 Coins | 0 Coins | 0 Coins | 0 Coins |
| -- | -- | -- | -- |

_Note:_ The conclusions presented in the following "Collecting and Investing Strategies" section are drawn in large part from the Investment Potential Ratios that are summarized in Appendices G and H at the end of this book. For a detailed analysis of the formula used to derive these Investment Potential Ratios, please refer to the Introduction of this book.

**Collecting and Investing Strategies:** The 1905 is an accurately priced, if somewhat overrated proof Barber Dime at the Gem and Superb Gem grade levels. It is to the Proof-64 grade level, therefore, where the investor and collector/investor should look to find a desirable example of this issue. Indeed, the 1905 is more underrated in Proof-64 than any other proof Barber Dime with the sole exception of the 1897.

I would not pay a premium for any proof 1905 Barber Dime just because it has received a Cameo designation from PCGS or NGC. I have seen many Cameo-finish specimens sell for less than all-brilliant specimens through auction, and this is even true for coins certified by the same service and sold within a six-to-18 month period. Dark or mottled toning can depress the value of a Cameo-finish specimen, while vivid patination will certainly result in a premium bid for an all-brilliant example.

I have also noticed a wide variation in technical quality among high-grade proofs of this date that further explains the odd pricing structure of this issue beginning in Proof-65. In other words, there are a fair number of high-grade proof Barber Dimes in PCGS and NGC holders that are either unattractive coins due to the presence of dark and/or mottled toning or are simply overgraded in their current holders. This fact adds greater emphasis to my conclusion that you should avoid purchasing a 1905 that grades finer than Proof-64.

# 1905

## MINTAGE
### 14,551,623

Courtesy of David Lawrence

## RARITY RANKINGS

*Overall, Mint State: 49th of 74*
*High Grade, MS-65 or Finer: 37th of 74 (Tie)*

## PHILADELPHIA MINT ISSUES

*Overall, Mint State: 6th of 25*
*High Grade, MS-65 or Finer: 4th of 25 (Tie)*

**Important Varieties:** None.

**General Comments:** The 1905 is rarer than all other P-mint Barber Dimes in Mint State with the exception of just the 1894, 1895, 1896, 1902 and 1903. It is a more challenging coin to locate than an original mintage of 14.5 million pieces might suggest, and it also ranks ahead of such mintmarked issues of the type as the 1892-O, 1911-D and 1911-S. In high grades, the 1905 is similar in rarity to the 1900-S, 1903 and 1914-S, and it is one of the most elusive P-mint Barber Dimes in that category.

**Strike:** The 1905 comes very well struck, and many examples possess virtually full definition to both sides.

**Luster:** Luster for this issue is usually satin or softly frosted in texture. Both luster types are very appealing when found on a Mint State 1905 Barber Dime.

**Surfaces:** While the typical example is marred by at least a few abrasions, these tend to be small in size and well scattered over the surfaces.

**Toning:** Most Mint State 1905 Dimes are toned, if only lightly so in pale silver or gold iridescence. Actually, most pieces that I have handled are extensively toned, the colors often very dark and quite unappealing. Richly original examples with more vibrant patination represent a significant find in today's market, as do dipped pieces with brilliant surfaces that still possess vibrant luster.

**Eye Appeal:** A much more challenging issue to find "nice" than a sizeable original mintage of 14.5 million pieces might imply, the 1905 usually possesses below-average eye appeal even when offered in MS-64 and MS-65. Dark, unsightly toning bears much of the blame for this assessment, although scattered abrasions are also a problem in grades up to and including MS-65.

**Significant Examples:**

**1. PCGS MS-67.** *Ex: The Collection of D. Steven L. Duckor (Heritage, 1/2006), lot 1007, where it realized $9,775.*

**2. NGC MS-67 ★.** *Ex: The John C. Hugon Collection (Heritage, 1/2005), lot 4038, where it realized $5,750.*

**3. NGC MS-67.** *Ex: CSNS Signature Sale (Heritage, 4/2002), lot 5495, unsold; Rarities Sale (Bowers and Merena, 1/2003), lot 225, where it realized $1,898; Elite Coin Auction (Superior, 7/2003), lot 1018, where it realized $2,760.*

**4. NGC MS-66.** *Ex: Long Beach, CA Signature U.S. Coin Auction (Heritage, 5/2007), lot 713, where it realized $920.*

**5. NGC MS-66.** *Ex: Palm Beach, FL Signature Sale (Heritage, 11/2004), lot 6286, unsold.*

**6. NGC MS-66.** *Ex: Auction #1886 (Teletrade, 5/2004), lot 1135, where it realized $1,050.*

**Total Known in Mint State:** 225-260 Coins

**Total Known and Value Breakdown by Grade:**

| MS-60 to MS-62 | MS-63 | MS-64 | MS-65 |
|---|---|---|---|
| 55-65 Coins | 45-55 Coins | 80-90 Coins | 35-40 Coins |
| N/A | $135-$175 | $225-$300 | $600-$800 |

| MS-66 | MS-67 | MS-68 | MS-69 to MS-70 |
|---|---|---|---|
| 4-6 Coins | 3-4 Coins | 0 Coins | 0 Coins |
| $1,000-$2,500 | $6,000-$7,500 | -- | -- |

*Note:* The conclusions presented in the following "Collecting and Investing Strategies" section are drawn in large part from the Investment Potential Ratios that are summarized in Appendices G and H at the end of this book. For a detailed analysis of the formula used to derive these Investment Potential Ratios, please refer to the Introduction of this book.

**Collecting and Investing Strategies:** The 1905 is definitely an underrated P-mint Barber Dime in all grades from MS-64 through MS-67. In MS-66, in fact, this is the most undervalued Barber Dime irrespective of issuing Mint.

In order to maximize your return in a Mint State 1905, I strongly suggest avoiding darkly toned coins as well as dipped pieces with subdued luster. Be selective when pursuing this issue, particularly in the finest Mint State grades, and be patient until the opportunity to purchase an attractively toned, brilliant and/or fully lustrous example becomes available.

# 1905-O

## MINTAGE
3,400,000
(Includes 1905-O Micro O)

Courtesy of David Lawrence

## RARITY RANKINGS

**Overall, Mint State:** *39th of 74 (Tie)*
**High Grade, MS-65 or Finer:** *44th of 74 (Tie)*

## NEW ORLEANS MINT ISSUES

**Overall, Mint State:** *14th of 17*
**High Grade, MS-65 or Finer:** *15th of 17*

**Important Varieties:** The Micro O is the most significant variety of the 1905-O, and it is the subject of the following section.

**General Comments:** After a one-year hiatus, the New Orleans Mint returned to Barber Dime production in 1905 with a mintage of 3.4 million pieces. The year 1905 is a watershed in the Barber Dime series, with relatively fewer coins struck entering circulation and, as a result, a higher percentage of the original mintages surviving in Mint State. This trend continues through the end of the Barber Dime series in 1916, and it helps to explain why many issues struck from 1905-1916 are relatively obtainable in Mint State.

The 1905-O is one of the most plentiful New Orleans Mint Barber Dimes in Mint State. It is rarer than the 1892-O, 1906-O and 1907-O in an absolute sense, nonetheless, and high-grade examples are rarer than those of the 1906-O and 1908-O issues. The 1905-O is similar in overall rarity in Mint State to the 1903, and in high-grade rarity to the 1894 and 1912-S.

Mint State 1905-O Dimes are still relatively scarce coins when viewed in the wider context of U.S. numismatics, and even examples in the MS-60 to MS-64 grade range will require a good bit of patience to procure. Gems in MS-65 and MS-66 are rare, and Superb Gems in MS-67 are very rare.

**Strike:** The difficulty of locating a sharply struck 1905-O has been overstated in the past by catalogers and other numismatic researchers. More than half of the Mint State examples that I have seen are overall sharply defined with no significant lack of detail on either side.

As befits a Barber coin from the New Orleans Mint, of course, there are some softly struck survivors throughout the Mint State grading scale. Those coins will usually display minimal-to-significant lack of detail along Liberty's haircurls and the lowermost leaves in the wreath from above the ear to the top of the brow. The ribbon inscribed LIBERTY and the leaves immediately above that device are also prone to incompleteness of strike. On the reverse, look for striking softness over the lower-right portion of the wreath and/or on the large leaf to the left of the ribbon bow. A minority of Mint State pieces exhibit a curious swelling to the entire wreath that is indicative of a soft strike throughout the reverse.

**Luster:** The 1905-O has above-average luster for a New Orleans Mint Barber Dime, and the finish is usually quite vibrant even in lower Mint State grades such as MS-62 and MS-63. Satiny and softly frosted examples exist is nearly identical numbers, with perhaps a slight edge in availability going to the satin-textured coins.

**Surfaces:** As with most other New Orleans Mint issues in the Barber Dime series, the 1905-O is usually not a heavily abraded coin. Scattered handling marks, although almost always present (even if only in limited numbers), tend to be small in size and relatively inconspicuous.

**Toning:** If you are looking at a Mint State 1905-O Barber Dime, chances are very good that you are also looking at an originally toned coin. Most examples that I have handled possess deep, rich patina, often with more vivid highlights intermingled at and near the borders. Dipped or otherwise brilliant-to-lightly-toned coins remain in the minority among Mint State survivors.

**Eye Appeal:** Overall eye appeal for the 1905-O is surprisingly strong for a New Orleans Mint issue in this series. Enough Mint State examples exist with a relatively sharp strike, good luster and pleasing toning that even a modicum of patience on the part of the buyer will procure an attractive piece.

**Significant Examples:**

1. **PCGS MS-67.** *Ex: The Belle Glade Collection (Heritage, 8/2007), lot 575, where it realized $2,070; Phoenix, AZ ANA Signature Auction (Heritage, 3/2008), lot 418, where it realized $9,200.*

**2. NGC MS-67.** *Ex: Baltimore Auction (Bowers and Merena, 11/2007), lot 835, where it realized $5,290.*

**3. PCGS MS-67.** *Ex: The Collection of Dr. Steven L. Duckor (Heritage, 1/2006), lot 1008, where it realized $10,925.*

**4. PCGS MS-67.** *Ex: The John C. Hugon Collection (Heritage, 1/2005), lot 4039, where it realized $5,463.*

**5. NGC MS-67.** *Ex: The Dr. Robert W. Swan and Rod Sweet Collections (Bowers and Merena, 3/2004), lot 1206, where it realized $4,255.*

**6. PCGS MS-67.** *Ex: The Ronald W. Brown Acadiana Collection (Heritage, 8/1999), lot 6869, where it realized $5,060.*

**7. PCGS MS-66. CAC.** *Ex: Dr. Steven L. Duckor; Long Beach Signature Sale (Heritage, 1/2004), lot 5625, where it realized $2,415; The Southwest Collection (Heritage, 2/2008), lot 175, where it realized $2,300.*

**8. PCGS MS-66.** *Ex: The Frog Run Farm Collection (American Numismatic Rarities, 11/2004), lot 677, where it realized $2,243; CSNS Signature Coin Auction (Heritage, 5/2007), lot 372, unsold.*

**9. PCGS MS-66.** *Ex: CSNS Signature Auction (Heritage, 4/2006), lot 1301, where it realized $2,070.*

**10. PCGS MS-66.** *Ex: Detroit ANA Signature Sale (Heritage, 7/1994), lot 6469, where it realized $2,420.*

**11. PCGS MS-66.** *Ex: Auction '88 (RARCOA's session, 7/1988), lot 1654, where it realized $7,480.*

**Total Known in Mint State:** 165-205 Coins

**Total Known and Value Breakdown by Grade:**

| MS-60 to MS-62 | MS-63 | MS-64 | MS-65 |
|---|---|---|---|
| 30-35 Coins | 40-50 Coins | 50-60 Coins | 25-30 Coins |
| N/A | $300-$400 | $550-$750 | $1,250-$1,500 |

| MS-66 | MS-67 | MS-68 | MS-69 to MS-70 |
|---|---|---|---|
| 15-20 Coins | 8-10 Coins | 0 Coins | 0 Coins |
| $1,750-$2,500 | $5,500-$10,000 | -- | -- |

*Note:* The conclusions presented in the following "Collecting and Investing Strategies" section are drawn in large part from the Investment Potential Ratios that are summarized in Appendices G and H at the end of this book. For a detailed analysis of the formula used to derive these Investment Potential Ratios, please refer to the Introduction of this book.

**Collecting and Investing Strategies:** The 1905-O is far from the most underrated Barber Dime, but it is consistently undervalued in all grades from MS-64 to MS-66. Superb Gems should be avoided, however, as this issue is overrated in MS-67.

Much has been written in the past about the difficulty of locating a sharply struck or otherwise attractive 1905-O Barber Dime. I do not agree with the catalogers and researchers who have put forth those conclusions. While there is no denying that this issue is scarce-to-rare in all Mint State grades, many (but not all!) of the pieces that I have handled are actually very appealing. When we further consider that much of the demand for this issue comes from advanced Barber Dime specialists who are apt to view any purchase with a very critical eye, a situation arises in which you not only can, but must be very selective when it comes to purchasing a 1905-O.

Absolutely avoid those coins that possess readily evident lack of detail on one or both sides. Enough sharply struck Mint State examples exist so that you should not have to settle in this category. Additionally, you should pass on any example that is darkly toned (I have even seen a PCGS MS-65 with surfaces that are nearly black). Chances are good that you will still have to buy a richly toned coin, and I even recommend this as the dipped pieces that I have seen are either subdued in the luster category or retain mottled, hazy remnants of the original patination. When selecting a toned 1905-O, look for a coin with more-or-less even patina and, if possible, some vivid colors intermingled here and there.

# 1905-O Micro O

### MINTAGE
3,400,000
(Includes 1905-O)

*Courtesy of David Lawrence*

### RARITY RANKINGS

*Not Applicable*

**Important Varieties:** This important variety is attributed as Lawrence-101 and Breen-3545.

**General Comments:** Traditional numismatic wisdom has it that the 1905-O Micro O Barber Dime was struck from a reverse die that Mint employees erroneously prepared using a mintmark device punch intended for use in the Barber Quarter series. I see no reason to dispute this theory.

The exact number of 1905-O Micro O Dimes struck can never be known but, judging by the paucity of both circulated and Mint State examples in numismatic circles, the mintage must have been very limited. There are probably fewer than 10 coins known in all Mint State grades, the finest of which are a pair of Gems listed at PCGS (December/2008).

<u>Note:</u> Due to its inclusion in the indispensible numismatic reference *A Guide Book of United States Coins*, 62nd Edition (2009) by R.S. Yeoman, as well as its inclusion on the PCGS Population Report and NGC Census, I have decided to discuss the 1905-O Micro O in considerable detail in this book. Since the 1905-O Micro O is a variety and not a separate issue, however, I have excluded it from the rarity rankings that I have conducted for most other issues in this series.

**Strike:** This is a well-struck variety, and the Mint State coins that I have seen rival the best-produced examples of the 1905-O Normal O.

**Luster:** The 1905-O Micro O is not a particularly lustrous variety, and Mint State survivors display a subdued, satin-to-softly frosted texture.

**Surfaces:** This variety comes either lightly-to-moderately abraded or overall smooth. Examples in the former category usually display both small and moderate-size abrasions, and these can be very distracting in the MS-60 to MS-63 grade range.

**Toning:** The extreme rarity of this variety in Mint State and the fact that the value of Mint State survivors rises dramatically with grade has led to widespread dipping among high-grade 1905-O Micro O Dimes. Most coins that I have seen possess subdued, golden-tinged surfaces that are the result of incomplete removal of the original toning on in the dipping solution. The few examples that are still completely original exhibit deep, rich patination.

**Eye Appeal:** The 1905-O Micro O is decidedly below average in this category, and it is very difficult to locate a truly attractive coin among the Mint State survivors. Subdued surfaces with muted luster are the prime culprits, and these undesirable attributes are usually enhanced, not mitigated by dipping.

**Significant Examples:**

**1. PCGS MS-65.** *The John C. Hugon Collection (Heritage, 1/2005), lot 4040, where it realized $12,650.*

**2. NGC MS-65.** *Ex: Long Beach Sale (Paramount, 8/1975), lot 702; The Allen F. Lovejoy Reference Collection of United States Dimes (Stack's, 10/1990), lot 549; ANA Centennial Auction (Bowers and Merena, 8/1991), lot 316, unsold.*

NGC no longer lists an example of this variety in MS-65 on its Census (November/2008), and I do not believe that the NGC MS-65 referred to above is the same as the PCGS MS-65 example from the Hugon Collection. As such, the NGC MS-65 must have either been removed from a third-party holder entirely or has since been downgraded (unlikely) or upgraded (possible, especially since PCGS does list a single example in MS-66—December/2008—that I have been unable to trace).

**3. NGC MS-64.** *Ex: The Richmond Collection (David Lawrence, 3/2005), lot 1327, where it realized $5,463.*

**4. NGC MS-63.** *Ex: The Southland Collection (Heritage, 5/2007), lot 373, where it realized $4,888.*

**5. PCGS MS-63.** *Ex: FUN Signature Auction (Heritage, 1/2006), lot 1824, where it realized $4,600.*

**6. PCGS MS-63.** *Ex: CSNS Signature Auction (Heritage, 5/2005), lot 6648, where it realized $4,313.*

**Total Known in Mint State:** 8-9 Coins

**Total Known and Value Breakdown by Grade:**

| MS-60 to MS-62 | MS-63 | MS-64 | MS-65 |
|---|---|---|---|
| 1 Coin | 3 Coins | 2-3 Coins | 1 Coin |
| N/A | $4,500-$5,500 | $7,500-$10,000 | $12,500-$17,500 |

| MS-66 | MS-67 | MS-68 | MS-69 to MS-70 |
|---|---|---|---|
| 1 Coin | 0 Coins | 0 Coins | 0 Coins |
| $17,500-$20,000 | -- | -- | -- |

**Collecting and Investing Strategies:** I much prefer originally toned coins for the 1905-O Micro O to pieces that have been dipped and now possess subdued, golden-toned surfaces. Not that this matters much, however, as the extreme rarity of this variety means that all PCGS and NGC-certified examples represent important buying opportunities in today's market. If you are assembling an advanced Barber Dime set or a specialized collection of variety coinage, you should strongly consider acquiring any Mint State example of the 1905-O Micro O that becomes available for purchase. If your sole consideration is return on investment, however, I would pass over this variety and turn your efforts to a Barber Dime that is likely to enjoy strong demand among a wider variety of numismatic buyers.

# 1905-S

**MINTAGE**
6,855,199

Courtesy of David Lawrence

## RARITY RANKINGS

***Overall, Mint State:*** *45th of 74*
***High Grade, MS-65 or Finer:*** *29th of 74*

## SAN FRANCISCO MINT ISSUES

***Overall, Mint State:*** *20th of 24*
***High Grade, MS-65 or Finer:*** *15th of 24*

**Important Varieties:** None.

**General Comments:** S-mint Barber Dime production moved back into the seven-figure range in 1905 after limited totals were reported for both the 1903-S and 1904-S. Enough examples have survived that the 1905-S ranks as the most common San Francisco Mint Barber Dime after only the 1911-S, 1912-S, 1914-S and the final-year 1916-S. The 1905-S is a bit more highly ranked in grades at and above MS-65, at which levels it is also rarer than the 1900-S, 1906-S and 1908-S, as well as the low-mintage 1913-S and 1915-S.

When viewed in the wider context of the U.S. rare coin market, this issue can only be described as moderately scarce in lower Mint State grades through MS-64. Gems are somewhat rare from a condition standpoint, however, and Superb Gems are so elusive as to number only three or four coins.

**Strike:** This is a well-struck issue, and the typical example possesses very sharp, if not full definition.

**Luster:** The 1905-S also has excellent luster that is usually a blend of satin and softly frosted characteristics.

**Surfaces:** Most Mint State examples exhibit grade-limiting abrasions. These are almost always confined to the obverse, where slidemarks and other wispy distractions over Liberty's portrait suggest that many of the Uncirculated 1905-S Dimes in today's market were once stored in albums.

**Toning:** The typical example is richly toned with moderate-to-deep patination throughout. Colors vary from dark to vivid.

**Eye Appeal:** Although well produced, the 1905-S is not a well-preserved issue. This assertion is made despite the fact that the total Mint State population for the issue is generous by the standards of a San Francisco Mint Barber Dime from the earliest years of the 20th century. Expect the typical Mint State 1905-S to display only average eye appeal.

**Significant Examples:**

1. **NGC MS-67.** *Ex: Orlando Sale (Superior, 8/1992), lot 107, where it realized $3,520; Long Beach Signature Auction (Heritage, 6/2005), lot 5831, where it realized $6,038.*

2. **PCGS MS-66.** *Ex: The Collection of Dr. Steven L. Duckor (Heritage, 1/2006), lot 1009, where it realized $3,220.*

3. **PCGS MS-66.** *Ex: The John C. Hugon Collection (Heritage, 1/2005), lot 4041, where it realized $2,990.*

4. **PCGS MS-66.** *Ex: New York, NY Signature Sale (Heritage, 7/2004), lot 5822, where it realized $2,588.*

5. **NGC MS-66.** *Ex: Philadelphia Signature Sale (Heritage, 8/2000), lot 6967, where it realized $863; Santa Clara Signature Sale (Heritage, 11/2000), lot 6838, where it realized $891.*

**Total Known in Mint State:** 200-235 Coins

**Total Known and Value Breakdown by Grade:**

| MS-60 to MS-62 | MS-63 | MS-64 | MS-65 |
|---|---|---|---|
| 55-65 Coins | 50-60 Coins | 60-70 Coins | 25-30 Coins |
| N/A | $225-$325 | $400-$550 | $575-$700 |

| MS-66 | MS-67 | MS-68 | MS-69 to MS-70 |
|---|---|---|---|
| 6-8 Coins | 3-4 Coins | 0 Coins | 0 Coins |
| $2,500-$4,500 | $5,000-$10,000 | -- | -- |

<u>Note:</u> The conclusions presented in the following "Collecting and Investing Strategies" section are drawn in large part from the Investment Potential Ratios that are summarized in Appendices G and H at the end of this book. For

a detailed analysis of the formula used to derive these Investment Potential Ratios, please refer to the Introduction of this book.

**Collecting and Investing Strategies:** I am particularly fond of the 1905-S in MS-65 and MS-66, although this issue is also underrated to a greater or lesser extent in MS-64 and MS-67. MS-66 is probably the most desirable grade for this issue in terms of investment potential, for the 1905-S is more undervalued at that level than any other Barber Dime with the exception of the 1903-O and 1905.

# Proof
# 1906

## MINTAGE
675

Courtesy of Bowers and Merena

## RARITY RANKINGS

*Overall, All Proof Grades: 9th of 25*
*High Grade, Proof-65 or Finer: 12th of 25*
*Overall, Cameo Finish: 9th of 24 (Tie)*
*Overall, Deep/Ultra Cameo Finish: 1st of 12 (Tie)*

**Important Varieties:** None.

**General Comments:** The 1906 is an overlooked issue in the proof Barber Dime series. It is actually in the top ten for the series in terms of overall rarity, ranking ahead of even the lower-mintage proof 1911 and proof 1913. In high grades, the 1906 is only a median rarity for its type. It is more challenging to locate as a Gem than all 1890s issues in this series (except, of course, the 1894-S), as well as the 1900, 1901, 1905, 1909 and 1911.

The 1906 is similar in rarity to the 1912 and 1913 as a Cameo, which means that it is among the more elusive proof Barber Dimes with that finish. It is tied with the 1894, 1910 and 1911 as the rarest collectible proof Dime of this type with a Deep/Ultra Cameo finish.

**Strike:** I cannot recall ever handling a proof 1906 Barber Dime that was less than sharply struck, and the typical specimen actually possesses full definition to both the obverse and the reverse.

**Finish:** The vast majority of examples display an all-brilliant finish with no appreciable field-to-device contrast. Even so, a handful of coins have received a Cameo designation from PCGS and NGC, although such pieces do not display near the boldness of contrast that characterizes Cameo-finish examples from the 1890s. Surprisingly for an issue that was produced using all-brilliant proofing techniques, there is a single specimen certified Proof-65 Deep Cameo at PCGS (December/2008).

**Surfaces:** Contact marks and other blemishes are usually present on the obverse of a proof 1906 but, fortunately, such distractions tend to be small in size and singularly inconspicuous. There is also a generous number of specimens known whose surfaces are overall smooth, if not virtually pristine.

**Toning:** This issue is one of the easier proof Barber Dimes to locate with colorful, iridescent toning. Many specimens that I have seen possess vivid multicolored toning to one or both sides, although the most attractive colors are sometimes only appreciable when the coin is held at direct angles to a good light source. Minimally toned and brilliant examples are not unknown, but they are in the minority among survivors.

**Eye Appeal:** Overall eye appeal for the proof 1906 is well above average, if not downright strong. This issue comes with expert striking quality, and many pieces also exhibit very pretty toning.

### Significant Examples:

**1. NGC Proof-67 Cameo.** *Ex: Long Beach, CA Signature Auction (Heritage, 5/2008), lot 159, where it realized $3,738.*

**2. NGC Proof-67 Cameo.** *Ex: Long Beach, CA Signature Coin Auction (Heritage, 2/2007), lot 2966, where it realized $3,220.*

**3. PCGS Proof-67 Cameo.** *Ex: Dallas Signature Auction (Heritage, 12/2005), lot 507, where it realized $6,038.*

**4. NGC Proof-67 Cameo.** *Ex: CSNS Signature Sale (Heritage, 5/2003), lot 5959, where it realized $3,000; Classics Sale (American Numismatic Rarities, 1/2004), lot 1389, where it realized $2,760.*

**5. PCGS Proof-65 Deep Cameo.** *Ex: CSNS Signature Sale (Heritage, 5/2003), lot 5960, where it realized $2,703.*

**Total Known:** 300-375 Coins

### Total Known and Value Breakdown by Grade:

| Brilliant-Finish Coins | | | |
|---|---|---|---|
| **Proof-60-62** | **Proof-63** | **Proof-64** | **Proof-65** |
| 30-40 Coins | 55-65 Coins | 85-100 Coins | 45-55 Coins |
| N/A | $425-$500 | $650-$800 | $1,250-$1,500 |
| **Proof-66** | **Proof-67** | **Proof-68** | **Proof-69-70** |
| 35-45 Coins | 18-22 Coins | 3-4 Coins | 0 Coins |
| $1,750-$3,000 | $2,750-$5,500 | $7,500-$15,000 | -- |

| Cameo Coins | | | |
|---|---|---|---|
| **Proof-60-62 Cameo** | **Proof-63 Cameo** | **Proof-64 Cameo** | **Proof-65 Cameo** |
| 0 Coins | 4-5 Coins | 7-9 Coins | 6-8 Coins |
| -- | $600-$750 | $900-$1,100 | $2,000-$2,500 |
| **Proof-66 Cameo** | **Proof-67 Cameo** | **Proof-68 Cameo** | **Proof-69-70 Cameo** |
| 8-10 Coins | 5-7 Coins | 0 Coins | 0 Coins |
| $2,500-$3,500 | $3,500-$8,000 | -- | -- |

| Deep/Ultra Cameo | | | |
|---|---|---|---|
| **Proof-60-62 Deep/ Ultra Cameo** | **Proof-63 Deep/ Ultra Cameo** | **Proof-64 Deep/ Ultra Cameo** | **Proof-65 Deep/ Ultra Cameo** |
| 0 Coins | 0 Coins | 0 Coins | 1 Coin |
| -- | -- | -- | $5,000-$10,000 |
| **Proof-66 Deep/ Ultra Cameo** | **Proof-67 Deep/ Ultra Cameo** | **Proof-68 Deep/ Ultra Cameo** | **Proof-69-70 Deep/ Ultra Cameo** |
| 0 Coins | 0 Coins | 0 Coins | 0 Coins |
| -- | -- | -- | -- |

<u>*Note:*</u> The conclusions presented in the following "Collecting and Investing Strategies" section are drawn in large part from the Investment Potential Ratios that are summarized in Appendices G and H at the end of this book. For a detailed analysis of the formula used to derive these Investment Potential Ratios, please refer to the Introduction of this book.

**Collecting and Investing Strategies:** The 1906 offers relatively good value in most grades, and I can only describe this issue as somewhat underrated at the Proof-65 level. This is an issue that is not likely to appreciate much in value but, on the other hand, the proof 1906 is not overvalued in light of its rarity. I would only consider the proof 1906 for inclusion in a complete set of proof Barber Dimes or a proof date set. Skip this issue for proof type purposes or pure investment purposes.

While I cannot deny the existence of many vividly toned proof 1906 Barber Dimes, you should refrain from buying such pieces based solely upon the images presented in auction catalogs and/or on the Internet. Professional numismatic photographers are trained to image coins in the best light possible (no pun intended), and the pictures that they produce for many proof 1906 Dimes are taken at angles that call forth the most vivid colors possible. The coins almost certainly display those colors, but chances are also good that their surfaces will present a much darker appearance when turned away from a direct light source. Make sure you evaluate all richly toned examples of this issue in person to ascertain whether or not you find the toning attractive at all angles. Closer inspection can also weed out coins that are so darkly toned that the underlying Mint finish is subdued, if not outright impaired.

# 1906

### MINTAGE
### 19,957,731

Courtesy of David Lawrence

### RARITY
### RANKINGS

**Overall, Mint State:** *63rd of 74*
**High Grade, MS-65 or Finer:** *59th of 74 (Tie)*

## PHILADELPHIA MINT ISSUES

**Overall, Mint State:** *15th of 25*
**High Grade, MS-65 or Finer:** *13th of 25 (Tie)*

**Important Varieties:** A Repunched Date variety is known with repunching evident on the final two digits. This RPD is attributed alternately as FS-301, FS-010.085, Lawrence-301 and Breen-3548.

**General Comments:** In Mint State, the 1906 is among the more readily obtainable Barber Dimes. This issue is still rarer than the 1897, 1898, 1907, 1914-D and 1910, to say nothing of the truly common Barber Dimes such as the 1892, 1911 and 1916. The 1906 is only marginally less plentiful when we consider only the finer Mint State grades, and it compares favorably to the 1907 in terms of high-grade rarity. Beginning in MS-66, nonetheless, the 1906 does develop into a conditionally rare issue. It is unobtainable any finer than MS-67.

**Strike:** The typical example is sharply struck throughout, sometimes with just a touch of softness to the detail at the right (facing) bow ribbon knot on the reverse. Every once in a long while, however, a Mint State 1906 comes along with noticeable lack of detail on the obverse immediately above the ribbon inscribed LIBERTY and/or on the reverse over the lower-right portion of the wreath.

**Luster:** Luster for the 1906 is only average to slightly above average, and the typical example will not be all that radiant in appearance. I have seen examples with both a satiny finish from the dies and a softly frosted texture.

**Surfaces:** Overall smooth-looking examples in MS-65 can be had without undue difficulty, but the truth is that most 1906 Barber Dimes exhibit at least a few noticeable abrasions. These can be quite severe in lower grades through MS-63 where sizeable distractions such as slidemarks become most prevalent.

**Toning:** Mint State survivors generally come with rich toning that is usually the result of long-term storage in cardboard coin albums. Such toning is either more-or-less evenly distributed over the surfaces or confined to the areas at and near the rims. Colors tend to be concentrated toward the darker end of the spectrum, although more vivid highlights are usually intermingled, sometimes to the extent of dominating the overall appearance.

A smaller number of completely original coins with minimally toned or fully brilliant surfaces are known. On the other hand, I have not encountered too many dipped examples of this issue.

**Eye Appeal:** Eye appeal for the 1906 varies considerably with grade but, as long as you do not mind richly original toning, the typical example will be pleasing to the eye.

**Significant Examples:**

**1. NGC MS-67.** *Ex: Long Beach Signature Auction (Heritage, 6/2005), lot 5832, where it realized $2,530; Dallas, TX Signature Auction (Heritage, 11/2005), lot 1027, where it realized $2,415; The Southwest Collection (Heritage, 2/2008), lot 177, where it realized $2,760.*

**2. PCGS MS-67.** *Ex: Long Beach, CA Signature Auction (Heritage, 9/2006), lot 1347, where it realized $6,325.*

**3. PCGS MS-67.** *Ex: The Boys Town and Charles S. Mamiye Collections (Bowers and Merena, 3/1998), lot 615, where it realized $1,045; The John C. Hugon Collection (Heritage, 1/2005), lot 4042, where it realized $6,900.*

**4. PCGS MS-67.** *Ex: Elite Coin Auction (Superior, 7/2003), lot 1020, where it realized $5,980.*

**5. NGC MS-67.** *Ex: Mid-Winter ANA Signature Sale (Heritage, 3/1999), lot 6338, where it realized $2,013.*

**Total Known in Mint State:** 440-530 Coins

### Total Known and Value Breakdown by Grade:

| MS-60 to MS-62 | MS-63 | MS-64 | MS-65 |
|---|---|---|---|
| 100-125 Coins | 115-140 Coins | 145-170 Coins | 60-70 Coins |
| N/A | $125-$165 | $225-$300 | $500-$650 |

| MS-66 | MS-67 | MS-68 | MS-69 to MS-70 |
|---|---|---|---|
| 12-15 Coins | 7-9 Coins | 0 Coins | 0 Coins |
| $850-$1,250 | $2,750-$7,500 | -- | -- |

*Note:* The conclusions presented in the following "Collecting and Investing Strategies" section are drawn in large part from the Investment Potential Ratios that are summarized in Appendices G and H at the end of this book. For a detailed analysis of the formula used to derive these Investment Potential Ratios, please refer to the Introduction of this book.

**Collecting and Investing Strategies:** In MS-64 and MS-65 the 1906 is neither overrated nor particularly underrated, and such coins offer solid-enough value as to be appealing to date collectors and those assembling complete Barber Dime sets in Choice-to-Gem grades. MS-67s are genuinely overvalued and should be avoided if possible. MS-66s, however, are more underrated than similarly graded examples of all but a handful of other issues in this series, and that is the grade level upon which you should direct your resources of time and money for the 1906 Barber Dime.

Concentrate on finding an example that is sharply struck throughout, free of individually distracting abrasions and possessed of uncommonly vibrant luster. The toned examples that I have seen are mostly attractive, although experience has taught me that even patination rather than mottled color tends to be looked upon more favorably in the market. Brilliant coins are also highly desirable, of course, particularly if they are naturally untoned as opposed to having been dipped.

# 1906-D

## MINTAGE
4,060,000

*Courtesy of Bowers and Merena*

## RARITY RANKINGS

*Overall, Mint State: 32nd of 74 (Tie)*
*High Grade, MS-65 or Finer: 30th of 74 (Tie)*

## DENVER MINT ISSUES

*Overall, Mint State: 4th of 8*
*High Grade, MS-65 or Finer: 3rd of 8*

**Important Varieties:** There are three significant varieties known for the 1906-D Barber Dime:

- Repunched Date and Repunched Mintmark: attributed FS-301 and FS-010.088

- Repunched Date and Repunched Mintmark: attributed as FS-302 and FS-010.89

- Repunched Date and Misplaced Date: attributed as FS-303 and FS-010.089

**General Comments:** An extremely popular issue for first-year mintmarked type purposes, the 1906-D is the premier Dime struck in the Denver Mint. Unfortunately for later generations of numismatists, the historical significance of this issue seems to have been lost on the contemporary public. The result of this circumstance is that relatively few Mint State examples of the '06-D have survived. Although only a median rarity among Denver Mint Barber Dimes, the 1906-D is an elusive issue in an absolute sense that compares favorably to the 1908-O in terms of total number of Mint State coins believed to exist. This issue is actually rarer than the low-mintage 1913-S and 1915-S, as well as the challenging 1894 and 1896 from the Philadelphia Mint. High-grade 1906-D Dimes are very elusive, and the issue compares favorably to the 1904, 1908-S, 1909-O and 1915-S in that category.

**Strike:** Great care seems to have been taken in the production of this issue, and virtually all Mint State examples are razor sharp-to-full in strike.

**Luster:** Luster is also a strong suit for the 1906-D, and examples vary in finish from satin to softly frosted. Satiny coins are encountered more often in numismatic circles.

**Surfaces:** Excessive abrasions are seldom a problem for this issue, although you should expect the typical Mint State survivor to possess at least a few distracting marks. Only a small percentage of survivors approach perfection in the area of surface preservation.

**Toning:** The 1906-D comes brilliant and deeply toned, dark and vivid, as well as uniformly patinated and peripherally toned. Attractive coins exist in all categories with the exception of darkly toned.

**Eye Appeal:** This is an overall pleasing issue that usually possesses above-average eye appeal either in an absolute sense or within the context of the assigned grade.

**Significant Examples:** Although PCGS has certified two 1906-D Barber Dimes as MS-67 (December/2008), I have been unable to locate an auction appearance for either of those coins during the nine-year period from 2000-2008.

**1. NGC Specimen MS-64:** *Walter Breen (*Walter Breen's Encyclopedia of United States and Colonial Proof Coins, *1977) reports having seen a branch mint proof 1906-D Barber Dime at a San Francisco convention held in September of 1976, although I have no way of knowing whether that coin is the piece that has since been certified Specimen MS-64 at NGC. I have also not seen the examples that NGC has certified as Specimen MS-64 and, thus, cannot offer an opinion regarding the validity of the Specimen designation on the insert. The possibility exists that one or more specimen strikings of the 1906-D Barber Dime were produced to commemorate the beginning of coinage operations at the Denver Mint.*

**Total Known in Mint State:** 135-170 Coins

**Total Known and Value Breakdown by Grade:**

| MS-60 to MS-62 | MS-63 | MS-64 | MS-65 |
|---|---|---|---|
| 30-35 Coins | 25-30 Coins | 45-55 Coins | 20-25 Coins |
| N/A | $250-$350 | $750-$850 | $1,250-$1,500 |

**Total Known and Value Breakdown by Grade (cont.):**

| MS-66 | MS-67 | MS-68 | MS-69 to MS-70 |
|-------|-------|-------|----------------|
| 15-20 Coins | 1-2 Coins | 0 Coins | 0 Coins |
| $1,500-$2,500 | $7,500-$8,500 | -- | -- |

*Note:* The conclusions presented in the following "Collecting and Investing Strategies" section are drawn in large part from the Investment Potential Ratios that are summarized in Appendices G and H at the end of this book. For a detailed analysis of the formula used to derive these Investment Potential Ratios, please refer to the Introduction of this book.

**Collecting and Investing Strategies:** While the 1906-D is not the most underrated issue in the D-mint Barber Dime series, it is still undervalued in all grades from MS-64 through MS-67. MS-67s offer particularly high investment potential, although I admit that the paucity of examples known in that grade will exclude most numismatists from even seeing (let alone owning!) a 1906-D at that level of preservation. A more realistic strategy, of course, would be to acquire a lower-grade piece in MS-64, MS-65 or MS-66.

Do not underestimate the difficulty of locating an attractive, high-grade 1906-D Barber Dime. Writing in the 1991 book The Complete Guide to Barber Dimes, David Lawrence states of this issue: "Quite a few coins were saved because this was the first year of the Denver Mint." This statement is just not true, as the estimated Mint State population that I have provided makes clear. The 1906-D, in fact, has even fewer survivors in Mint State than the lower-mintage 1905-O. There is a fairly sizeable concentration of coins at the MS-66 grade level, nonetheless, and perhaps those are the coins that were saved to which Lawrence refers.

# 1906-O

## MINTAGE
2,610,000

Courtesy of David Lawrence

## RARITY RANKINGS

*Overall, Mint State: 43rd of 74 (Tie)*
*High Grade, MS-65 or Finer: 53rd of 74 (Tie)*

## NEW ORLEANS MINT ISSUES

*Overall, Mint State: 15th of 17 (Tie)*
*High Grade, MS-65 or Finer: 17th of 17*

**Important Varieties:** I know of a very interesting variety for the 1906-O that combines a Repunched Date with a Misplaced Date. It is attributed as FS-301.

**General Comments:** Despite a lower mintage, the 1906-O is more plentiful in Mint State than the 1905-O. Obviously, more examples of this 2.6 million-piece delivery were kept from entering circulation, probably by contemporary dealers but also perhaps by banks and other financial institutions. The 1906-O, in fact, vies with the 1907-O as the second most-common New Orleans Mint Barber Dime in Mint State after the 1892-O. At and above the MS-65 grade level, the 1906-O is actually the most frequently encountered O-mint issue in this series. The '06-O is still rarer in high grades than many other issues in the Barber Dime series, including the 1911-D, 1911-S, 1914-D and the final-year 1916-S.

**Strike:** The 1906-O comes with an exceptional quality of strike for an O-mint Barber Dime, and the typical example is overall sharply defined. Lack of detail is still present on most coins, nonetheless, but it tends to be very minor and confined to the olive leaves at the top of the obverse and/or over the right (facing) bow of the ribbon knot on the reverse.

**Luster:** I have seen both satin and softly frosted examples, the former perhaps a bit more frequently over the years.

**Surfaces:** Most Mint State '06-O Dimes are minimally abraded, at most, and even on such coins distractions tend to be small in size and not overly conspicuous. Chances are also very good that if you locate an Uncirculated example it will be overall smooth in outward appearance.

**Toning:** Toned coins are in the majority among Mint State survivors, and these are usually evenly patinated throughout as opposed to being peripherally toned. The appearance of these pieces ranges from quite dark to relatively vivid, although the colors usually have a rich antique "look" in both cases.

**Eye Appeal:** The 1906-O is one of the most consistently attractive New Orleans Mint Barber Dimes produced up until that point in time, and you should have little difficulty locating an attractive coin among the Mint State survivors.

### Significant Examples:

**2. NGC MS-68.** *Ex: Michael Keith Ruben; The Leonard J. Torok, M.D. Collection (Bowers and Merena, 9/1998), lot 437, where it realized $6,900. This coin was featured in the article "68" by Scott Travers that appeared in the December, 1991 issue of COINage magazine.*

**3. NGC MS-67.** *Ex: The Benson Collection (Ira & Larry Goldberg, 2/2003), lot 347; Dallas, TX Coin Signature Auction (Heritage, 7/2006), lot 663, unsold; Dallas Signature Coin Auction (Heritage, 11/2006), lot 539, where it realized $2,530; CSNS Signature Coin Auction (Heritage, 4/2008), lot 627, unsold.*

**4. NGC MS-67 ★.** *Ex: The Belle Glade Collection (Heritage, 8/2007), lot 581, where it realized $4,025.*

**5. PCGS MS-67.** *Ex: Denver ANA Auction (Bowers and Merena, 8/2006), lot 764, where it realized $5,750.*

**6. NGC MS-67.** *Ex: FUN Signature Sale (Heritage, 1/1997), lot 5922, unsold; Mid-Winter ANA Signature Sale (Heritage, 3/1998), lot 5677, where it realized $2,415; The John C. Hugon Collection (Heritage, 1/2005), lot 4044, where it realized $4,140; CSNS Signature Auction (Heritage, 5/2005), lot 6658, where it realized $2,990.*

**7. NGC MS-67.** *Ex: FUN Signature Sale (Heritage, 1/1998), lot 6691, where it realized $1,840; The Bradley Bloch Collection (Ira & Larry Goldberg, 9/1999), lot 1201, where it realized $2,875; Long Beach Signature Sale (Heritage, 10/2001), lot 6093, unsold.*

**8. NGC MS-67.** *Ex: Detroit ANA Signature Sale (Heritage, 7/1994), lot 6472, where it realized $1,925.*

**Total Known in Mint State:** 185-225 Coins

**Total Known and Value Breakdown by Grade:**

| MS-60 to MS-62 | MS-63 | MS-64 | MS-65 |
|---|---|---|---|
| 20-25 Coins | 35-45 Coins | 65-75 Coins | 35-45 Coins |
| N/A | $200-$300 | $450-$550 | $975-$1,250 |

| MS-66 | MS-67 | MS-68 | MS-69 to MS-70 |
|---|---|---|---|
| 20-25 Coins | 8-10 Coins | 1 Coin | 0 Coins |
| $1,300-$2,000 | $3,000-$6,000 | $7,000-$9,000 | -- |

*Note:* The conclusions presented in the following "Collecting and Investing Strategies" section are drawn in large part from the Investment Potential Ratios that are summarized in Appendices G and H at the end of this book. For a detailed analysis of the formula used to derive these Investment Potential Ratios, please refer to the Introduction of this book.

**Collecting and Investing Strategies:** Offering good value in MS-65 and MS-67, the 1906-O is certainly not a bad buy in either of those grades. The truly underrated grades for this issue are MS-64 and MS-66, however, and it is to those levels that you should look for a 1906-O Barber Dime that has the greatest potential to increase in value in the coming years.

This is one New Orleans Mint issue in the Barber Dime series for which you should have little difficulty locating an attractive Mint State example. Whether you choose to acquire a satiny or frosty example, a richly toned coin or one of the few untoned pieces, the 1906-O that you select is apt to be well struck, lustrous and relatively abrasion free in the context of the assigned grade.

# 1906-S

## MINTAGE
3,136,640

Courtesy of David Lawrence

## RARITY RANKINGS

*Overall, Mint State: 31st of 74*
*High Grade, MS-65 or Finer: 52nd of 74*

### SAN FRANCISCO MINT ISSUES

*Overall, Mint State: 16th of 24*
*High Grade, MS-65 or Finer: 22nd of 24*

**Important Varieties:** As with the year's Philadelphia, Denver and New Orleans Mint issues, the 1906-S has contributed a significant variety to the Barber Dime series. It is a combination Repunched Date and Repunched Mintmark variety with the attribution FS-301.

**General Comments:** The San Francisco Mint struck less than half as many Barber Dimes in 1906 as it did in 1905. While most examples were almost certainly distributed into circulation at or near the time of striking, enough coins were set aside that the 1906-S now ranks as one of the more readily obtainable San Francisco Mint issues of its type in Mint State. Since most of the coins that have survived are relatively high grade, it should come as no surprise to read that the 1906-S is actually the most plentiful S-mint Barber Dime in Gem Mint State after only the 1911-S and 1916-S. Such coins, however, are still rare when viewed in the wider context of the Barber Dime series. As a Superb Gems, the 1906-S is very rare and seldom encountered in numismatic circles.

**Strike:** The 1906-S is not among the more sharply struck San Francisco Mint issues in the Barber Dime series. The typical example presents much like a 1906-O with softness of definition at the top of Liberty's portrait on the reverse and over and around the right bow of the ribbon on the reverse. Lack of detail even in those areas is usually minor, however, and most Mint State examples still present as overall sharply struck.

**Luster:** Unlike strike, luster quality for the 1905-S is consistent with that seen for most other issues in the San Francisco Mint Barber Dime series. Most Mint State examples are highly lustrous with a radiant sheen that can be either satiny or softly frosted in texture.

**Surfaces:** This issue is usually offered with few, if any, abrasions. When such distractions are present they tend to be small in size, singularly inconspicuous and, as such, not overly bothersome to the unaided eye.

**Toning:** Examples run the gamut from brilliant to richly toned. The former are largely dipped, although a few fully original pieces exhibit only minimal peripheral toning with the result that their surfaces present as predominantly brilliant. The toned coins are generally attractive with rich patina that is usually only moderately deep in hue.

**Eye Appeal:** The 1906-S is very strong in the eye appeal category, such is the care with which most Mint States examples were produced and subsequently preserved.

**Significant Examples:**

**1. PCGS MS-67.** *Ex: The Southwest Collection (Heritage, 2/2008), lot 180, where it realized $19,550.*

**2. PCGS MS-67.** *Ex: Chicago 1991 Sale (RARCOA and David W. Akers, 8/1991), lot 305, where it realized $5,250.*

**3. NGC MS-67.** *Ex: Auction '90 (Superior's session, 7/1990), lot 1053, where it realized $10,500.*

**Total Known in Mint State:** 135-165 Coins

**Total Known and Value Breakdown by Grade:**

| MS-60 to MS-62 | MS-63 | MS-64 | MS-65 |
|---|---|---|---|
| 25-30 Coins | 18-22 Coins | 35-45 Coins | 35-40 Coins |
| N/A | $375-$500 | $650-$800 | $950-$1,200 |

| MS-66 | MS-67 | MS-68 | MS-69 to MS-70 |
|---|---|---|---|
| 20-25 Coins | 3-4 Coins | 0 Coins | 0 Coins |
| $1,750-$3,500 | $17,500-$22,500 | -- | -- |

*Note:* The conclusions presented in the following "Collecting and Investing Strategies" section are drawn in large part from the Investment Potential Ratios that are summarized in Appendices G and H at the end of this book. For a detailed analysis of the formula used to derive these Investment Potential Ratios, please refer to the Introduction of this book.

**Collecting and Investing Strategies:** The 1906-S is one of the more underrated S-mint Barber Dimes in MS-64, and such pieces seem particularly attractive for numismatic investment purposes. The high-grade date and mint collector could also do well acquiring a 1906-S in MS-65 or MS-66, for the issue offers good value (if not much investment potential) in those grades. On the other hand, I would stay away from this issue in MS-67 as it is one of the six most overrated Barber Dimes as a Superb Gem.

An accurately graded 1906-S in MS-64, MS-65 or MS-66 will allow you to fully appreciate the strong technical and aesthetic merits for which this issue is known. Being a proponent of originality, my personal penchant is for richly toned coins, but dipped pieces are also quite pleasing with radiant, brilliant-surfaces and vibrant mint luster.

# Proof
# 1907

## MINTAGE
575

*Courtesy of Bowers and Merena*

## RARITY RANKINGS

*Overall, All Proof Grades: 5th of 25*
*High Grade, Proof-65 or Finer: 11th of 25*
*Overall, Cameo Finish: 4th of 24 (Tie)*
*Deep/Ultra Cameo Finish: Unknown*

**Important Varieties:** None.

**General Comments:** With the sole exception of the 1908, the 1907 boasts the lowest mintage of any proof Barber Dime struck during the first decade of the 20th century. It is the rarest issue in the entire proof Barber Dime series discounting only the 1908, 1914 and 1915, as well as the 1894-S. The 1907 does have a higher incidence of Gem-quality coins among the survivors than many other proof Barber Dimes, however, and it does not have as impressive a ranking in terms of high-grade rarity. Nevertheless, the 1907 is rarer in high grades than all proof Barber Dimes from the 1890s save for only the 1894-S, as well as the 1900, 1901, 1906 and 1911.

The proof 1907 is one of the rarest Barber Dimes with a Cameo finish, and it compares favorably in this regard with the proof 1908. This issue is unknown with a Deep/Ultra Cameo finish.

**Strike:** The proof 1907 is seldom offered with anything less than a very sharp strike, and most examples possess full definition to all elements of the design.

**Finish:** An all-brilliant finish is the norm for this issue, although many examples do possess the beginnings of Cameo contrast on the reverse. True obverse and reverse Cameos are elusive, and such pieces seldom display more than the bare minimum of field-to-device contrast to secure this designation from PCGS or NGC.

**Surfaces:** Wispy hairlines and other small contact marks are seen on many proof 1907 Barber Dimes, but even so the issue is not particularly challenging to locate with overall smooth surfaces. Pristine-looking specimens in Proof-66 and Proof-67 are also encountered on a fairly regular basis as part of the offerings in major auctions and on the bourse floor at national conventions.

**Toning:** While brilliant and minimally toned pieces are becoming more prevalent due to dipping and other forms of numismatic conservation, richly toned coins are still dominant among survivors of this issue. The toned specimens often display handsome, antique colors that yield to more vivid undertones when the surfaces dip into a light.

**Eye Appeal:** The proof 1907 tends to come very nice, and most examples are well above average as far as eye appeal is concerned.

**Significant Examples:**

**1. PCGS Proof-68.** *Ex: New York, NY ANA Signature Sale (Heritage, 8/1997), lot 6191, where it realized $5,290.*

**2. NGC Proof-67 Cameo.** *Ex: FUN Signature Coin Auction (Heritage, 1/2007), lot 2690, where it realized $4,255; Summer FUN Signature Coin Auction (Heritage, 6/2008), lot 762, where it realized $4,888.*

**3. NGC Proof-66 Cameo.** *Ex: Milwaukee, WI ANA Signature Coin Auction (Heritage, 8/2007), lot 600, where it realized $1,610.*

**4. PCGS Proof-66 Cameo.** *Ex: Dallas Signature Auction (Heritage, 12/2005), lot 508, where it realized $2,070.*

**5. PCGS Proof-66 Cameo.** *Ex: CSNS Signature Sale (Heritage, 5/2004), lot 6703, where it realized $3,450.*

**Total Known:** *280-350 Coins*

**Total Known and Value Breakdown by Grade:**

| Brilliant-Finish Coins | | | |
|---|---|---|---|
| **Proof-60-62** | **Proof-63** | **Proof-64** | **Proof-65** |
| 30-35 Coins | 40-50 Coins | 85-100 Coins | 45-55 Coins |
| N/A | $425-$500 | $650-$800 | $1,000-$1,500 |
| **Proof-66** | **Proof-67** | **Proof-68** | **Proof-69-70** |
| 40-50 Coins | 20-25 Coins | 1 Coin | 0 Coins |
| $1,750-$2,250 | $2,500-$5,750 | $10,000-$15,000 | -- |

| Cameo Coins | | | |
|---|---|---|---|
| **Proof-60-62 Cameo** | **Proof-63 Cameo** | **Proof-64 Cameo** | **Proof-65 Cameo** |
| 0 Coins | 2-3 Coins | 6-8 Coins | 3-4 Coins |
| -- | $600-$750 | $900-$1,100 | $2,000-$2,500 |
| **Proof-66 Cameo** | **Proof-67 Cameo** | **Proof-68 Cameo** | **Proof-69-70 Cameo** |
| 8-10 Coins | 3-4 Coins | 0 Coins | 0 Coins |
| $2,750-$3,500 | $4,750-$8,500 | -- | -- |

| Deep/Ultra Cameo | | | |
|---|---|---|---|
| **Proof-60-62 Deep/ Ultra Cameo** | **Proof-63 Deep/ Ultra Cameo** | **Proof-64 Deep/ Ultra Cameo** | **Proof-65 Deep/ Ultra Cameo** |
| 0 Coins | 0 Coins | 0 Coins | 0 Coins |
| -- | -- | -- | -- |
| **Proof-66 Deep/ Ultra Cameo** | **Proof-67 Deep/ Ultra Cameo** | **Proof-68 Deep/ Ultra Cameo** | **Proof-69-70 Deep/ Ultra Cameo** |
| 0 Coins | 0 Coins | 0 Coins | 0 Coins |
| -- | -- | -- | -- |

*Note:* The conclusions presented in the following "Collecting and Investing Strategies" section are drawn in large part from the Investment Potential Ratios that are summarized in Appendices G and H at the end of this book. For a detailed analysis of the formula used to derive these Investment Potential Ratios, please refer to the Introduction of this book.

**Collecting and Investing Strategies:** I do not recommend this issue for investment purposes as it is fairly accurately priced in most grades in light of its rarity. On the other hand, there is nothing wrong with adding a 1907 to a proof type set. This issue is particularly attractive for such purposes since it offers not only the allure of a relatively limited mintage, but also the technical merits of expert striking quality and overall careful surface preservation.

All-brilliant specimens of the 1907 are best purchased with richly original toning as these often display very vivid undertones that, in the finer grades, enhance already strong eye appeal. Many of the dipped coins have since been certified as Cameo at PCGS and NGC, and the lack of toning is preferred on those coins as it allows full appreciation of field-to-device contrast.

# 1907

**MINTAGE**
22,220,000

Courtesy of David Lawrence

## RARITY RANKINGS

*Overall, Mint State:* 64th of 74
*High Grade, MS-65 or Finer:* 59th of 74 (Tie)

## PHILADELPHIA MINT ISSUES

*Overall, Mint State:* 16th of 25
*High Grade, MS-65 or Finer:* 13th of 25 (Tie)

**Important Varieties:** I am aware of a Repunched Date variety for this issue that is known by the attributions FS-301 and Lawrence-103.

**General Comments:** The 1907 is one of the most plentiful Barber Dimes in all Mint State grades, but it is still not the most common issue of the type. In terms of total number of Mint State examples known, the 1907 is rarer than the 1897, 1898, 1910 and 1914-D, and it is much rarer than issues such as the 1892, 1911 and 1916. In high grades, the 1907 is similar in rarity to the 1906. This issue is rarer as a Gem than such others in the Barber Dime series as the 1893, 1908, 1911-D and 1911-S, to say nothing of the likes of the 1892 and 1911.

**Strike:** Striking quality for the 1907 is usually very sharp, and many examples are virtually fully detailed on both sides. Softness of strike, when present at all, is apt to be extremely minor and confined to the reverse at the upper-left portion of the wreath and/or the right (facing) loop of the ribbon knot.

**Luster:** As an issue, the 1907 has much better luster than the 1906. The typical Mint State example is very vibrant with either a frosty or, less frequently, satin texture.

**Surfaces:** Scattered distractions in the form of wispy slidemarks and hairline-type abrasions are the norm for Mint State 1907 Barber Dimes, and these are often concentrated on the obverse over Liberty's cheek and neck. Even so, the 1907 is easier to obtain with overall smooth-looking surfaces that most other issues in this series. On the other hand, coins that approach perfection in the area of surface preservation are very difficult to obtain.

**Toning:** The vast majority of examples that I have handled are toned. While some coins display toning only around the peripheries, more are known with either even toning throughout or mottled patination. Colors range from quite dark to moderately vivid, the latter often confined only to the areas at and near the rims.

**Eye Appeal:** A well-produced issue, the 1907 possesses above-average eye appeal. The typical Mint State example is apt to be pleasing, if not highly attractive either in an absolute sense or within the context of the assigned grade.

**Significant Examples:** As of December 2008, PCGS has certified a single 1907 Barber Dime as MS-67. I have been unable to find an auction appearance for that coin during the nine-year period from 2000-2008.

**Total Known in Mint State:** 480-570 Coins

**Total Known and Value Breakdown by Grade:**

| MS-60 to MS-62 | MS-63 | MS-64 | MS-65 |
|---|---|---|---|
| 100-125 Coins | 150-175 Coins | 150-175 Coins | 55-65 Coins |
| N/A | $125-$165 | $225-$300 | $500-$650 |

| MS-66 | MS-67 | MS-68 | MS-69 to MS-70 |
|---|---|---|---|
| 25-30 Coins | 1 Coin | 0 Coins | 0 Coins |
| $850-$1,250 | $5,000-$10,000 | -- | -- |

*Note:* The conclusions presented in the following "Collecting and Investing Strategies" section are drawn in large part from the Investment Potential Ratios that are summarized in Appendices G and H at the end of this book. For a detailed analysis of the formula used to derive these Investment Potential Ratios, please refer to the Introduction of this book.

**Collecting and Investing Strategies:** The 1907 is only slightly undervalued in MS-65 and MS-66, and it would be a stretch to describe it as such in MS-64. The lone MS-67 known to PCGS and NGC is actually the most undervalued Barber Dime at that grade level, although its unique status rules it out as a realistic candidate for inclusion in most investment portfolios. Instead, I would overlook this issue for investment purposes and leave MS-64s, MS-65s and MS-66s to type or date collectors.

Strike, luster and (at the Gem grade level) abrasions should pose no problem in your quest for an attractive 1907 Barber Dime. Toning is also generally attractive, but I have seen a few pieces with streaks and/or spots of deeper color on one or both sides that should be avoided due to below-average eye appeal.

# 1907-D

## MINTAGE
4,080,000

## RARITY RANKINGS

*Overall, Mint State:* 14th of 74 (Tie)
*High Grade, MS-65 or Finer:* 25th of 74 (Tie)

## DENVER MINT ISSUES

*Overall, Mint State:* 1st of 8
*High Grade, MS-65 or Finer:* 2nd of 8

**Important Varieties:** The FS-301, Lawrence-101 Repunched Date variety for this issue is gaining in popularity among specialists.

**General Comments:** Despite a nearly identical mintage, the 1907-D is rarer in Mint State than the 1906-D. Apparently, what little public interest there was in the first-year Denver Mint Dime had faded by the time the 1907-D was released into commercial channels. As a result, nearly the entire mintage of 1907-D Dimes served its intended role as a circulating medium of exchange. This issue, in fact, is the rarest Denver Mint Barber Dime in terms of total number of Mint State examples known to exist. The 1907-D is also a leading Denver Mint Barber Dime in terms of high-grade rarity, but Gems are not quite as elusive as those of the 1910-D. When viewed in the wider context of this series, the 1907-D emerges as similar in overall rarity to the 1901-O and nearly identical in high-grade rarity to the 1900-O. This issue is rarer in all grades than such others as the 1896, 1913-S and 1915-S.

**Strike:** The 1907-D is not as sharply struck as the 1906-D. Expect to see softness of detail on the obverse at the top of Liberty's portrait and on the reverse at the upper-right portion of the wreath and/or over the lower-right portion of the same device. Even with these deficiencies, however, the typical 1907-D presents as overall bold after a cursory glance at the surfaces.

**Luster:** This issue is only average in the luster category, and most Mint State examples are not overly vibrant in finish. A satin texture is the norm for the '07-D.

**Surfaces:** Despite their overall rarity, Mint State 1907-D Dimes are generally well preserved with few, if any wispy abrasions.

**Toning:** There is a nearly 50-50 mix of brilliant and richly toned coins among Mint State examples, with perhaps a slight edge in availability going to the toned pieces. Most of the toned coins that I have seen are very attractive with vivid colors either dominating the outward appearance or enhancing deeper patination. Even those pieces with mottled toning are still pleasing to the eye.

Brilliant examples of the 1907-D are largely the result of dipping. Those coins are also highly desirable, nonetheless, with bright, lustrous surfaces that are free of the hazy patina that is sometimes seen on coins that were too deeply toned before being dipped.

**Eye Appeal:** Deficiencies with the strike notwithstanding, the 1907-D is an attractive issue that is almost always a delight to behold when encountered in Mint State.

### Significant Examples:

**1. NGC MS-68.** *Ex: Portland, OR ANA Signature Sale (Heritage, 8/1998), lot 6380, where it realized $5,060; Chicago ANA Signature Sale (Heritage, 8/1999), lot 6871, unsold; New York ANA Sale (Superior, 8/2002), lot 758, unsold; Atlanta, GA ANA Signature Auction (Heritage, 4/2006), lot 438, where it realized $17,250; Baltimore Auction (Bowers and Merena, 2/2008), lot 437, where it realized $24,150.*

**2. PCGS MS-67.** *Ex: Bay Area Collection (Heritage, 3/2003), lot 5572, where it realized $20,125.*

**3. NGC MS-66.** *Ex: The Charles S. Mamiye Collection (Bowers and Merena, 3/1998), lot 620, where it realized $1,870; The John C. Hugon Collection (Heritage, 1/2005), lot 4047, where it realized $3,910; New York, NY Signature Auction (Heritage, 6/2005), lot 5403, where it realized $4,313; Dallas, TX Signature Auction (Heritage, 11/2005), lot 1032, unsold; Long Beach Signature Auction (Heritage, 2/2006), lot 796, where it realized $3,594; Baltimore Auction (Bowers and Merena, 11/2007), lot 838, where it realized $4,025; CSNS Signature Auction (Heritage, 4/2008), lot 629, where it realized $4,313.*

**4. PCGS MS-66.** *Ex: The Louis E. Eliasberg, Sr. Collection (Bowers and Merena, 5/1996), lot 1289, where it realized $2,200; The Collection of Dr. Steven L. Duckor (Heritage, 1/2006), lot 1015, where it realized $8,625; Pre-Long Beach Auction (Ira & Larry Goldberg, 5/2006), lot 1710, where it realized $8,625; Chicago Rarities Sale (Bowers and Merena, 4/2008), lot 254, unsold.*

**5. NGC MS-66.** *Ex: FUN Signature Sale (Heritage, 1/2000), lot 6588, where it realized $4,025; Dallas Signature Coin Auction (Heritage, 10/2006), lot 763, where it realized $4,370.*

**6. NGC MS-66.** *Ex: The Clifford Columbus Collection (Heritage, 6/2005), lot 5834, where it realized $4,025.*

**7. PCGS MS-66.** *Ex: Long Beach Signature Sale (Heritage, 9/2003), lot 6456, where it realized $5,980; CSNS Signature Auction (Heritage, 5/2005), lot 6660, where it realized $7,475.*

**8. NGC MS-66.** *Ex: Atlanta Rarities Sale (Bowers and Merena, 8/2001), lot 115, where it realized $3,220.*

**Total Known in Mint State:** 80-100 Coins

**Total Known and Value Breakdown by Grade:**

| MS-60 to MS-62 | MS-63 | MS-64 | MS-65 |
|---|---|---|---|
| 15-20 Coins | 10-15 Coins | 25-30 Coins | 15-18 Coins |
| N/A | $625-$800 | $1,750-$2,500 | $2,750-$4,000 |

| MS-66 | MS-67 | MS-68 | MS-69 to MS-70 |
|---|---|---|---|
| 10-12 Coins | 1-2 Coins | 1 Coin | 0 Coins |
| $3,000-$10,000 | $8,000-$20,000 | $25,000-$27,500 | -- |

*Note:* The conclusions presented in the following "Collecting and Investing Strategies" section are drawn in large part from the Investment Potential Ratios that are summarized in Appendices G and H at the end of this book. For a detailed analysis of the formula used to derive these Investment Potential Ratios, please refer to the Introduction of this book.

**Collecting and Investing Strategies:** The 1907-D is a very attractive issue in Mint State that is sure to be of particular interest to collectors and investors that appreciate richly toned coins. That being said, the investment potential for this issue is just not all that favorable. MS-64s, MS-65s and MS-66s are actually overrated and should be not be considered for inclusion in numismatic holdings other than complete sets of high-grade Barber Dimes. The 1907-D is a genuinely underrated issue as a Superb Gem, but I admit that such coins are very rare in an absolute sense and just do not trade all that often in the numismatic market. If and when an MS-67 or MS-68 does become available for sale, I suggest snapping it up at a price as close to the levels reported in this book as possible. Such an investment could pay strong dividends in the future.

# 1907-O

## MINTAGE
5,058,000

Courtesy of David Lawrence

## RARITY RANKINGS

**Overall, Mint State:** *43rd of 74 (Tie)*
**High Grade, MS-65 or Finer:** *41st of 74 (Tie)*

### NEW ORLEANS MINT ISSUES

**Overall, Mint State:** *15th of 17 (Tie)*
**High Grade, MS-65 or Finer:** *13th of 17 (Tie)*

**Important Varieties:** There is a widely spaced Repunched Mintmark variety for the 1907-O with the attribution FS-501.

**General Comments:** As the Denver Mint started to assume more responsibility for providing circulating coinage in the Western United States, commercial demand for O-mint Barber Dimes diminished. Since the 1907-O also has the benefit of a generous mintage, it is easy to understand why a relatively large number of Mint State examples have survived. This issue, in fact, is one of the most common New Orleans Mint Barber Dimes in Mint State. It is surpassed in an absolute sense by only the 1892-O, and in high grades by just the 1905-O, 1907-O and 1908-O.

In Mint State, nonetheless, the 1907-O still ranks as a median rarity when viewed in the wider context of the Barber Dime series. It is rarer than such issues as the 1905-S, 1912-S and 1914-S in terms of total number of Mint State coins known to exist. The 1907-O is similar in high-grade rarity to the 1908-D and rarer at and above the MS-65 level than even the lower-mintage 1906-S, 1911-S, 1912-S and 1913-S.

**Strike:** This issue is not known for sharp striking detail, and the typical Mint State example is softly struck in one or more of the following areas: the haircurls above Liberty's brow; the ribbon upon which the word LIBERTY is inscribed; the olive leaves immediately above the headband; the upper right and left portions of the reverse wreath; the lower right and left portions of the reverse wreath; the right (facing) loop of the ribbon knot at the base of the reverse wreath.

**Luster:** In sharp contrast to the quality of strike that characterizes this issue, the 1907-O typically displays good-to-excellent luster. Most examples are satiny in texture, while softly frosted pieces are encountered much less often in the market.

**Surfaces:** Scattered abrasions, while often present, are usually small in size and not overly conspicuous. The 1907-O is also not a particularly challenging New Orleans Mint Barber Dime to locate with overall smooth-looking surfaces, although pieces that approach perfection in this category are rare.

**Toning:** The typical example will possess a generous amount of toning, the colors seldom vivid and often quite dark.

**Eye Appeal:** This is not an easy issue to locate with strong eye appeal, this despite a relatively generous Mint State population by the standards of the O-mint Barber Dime series. Inadequacies with the strike, as well as unappealing toning, can both be significant hurdles to overcome in your search for an attractive '07-O.

**Significant Examples:** Although PCGS and NGC have each certified a single 1907-O Dime as MS-67 (December/2008), I have been unable to find an auction appearance for either of those coins during the nine-year period from 2000-2008.

**Total Known in Mint State:** 185-225 Coins

**Total Known and Value Breakdown by Grade:**

| MS-60 to MS-62 | MS-63 | MS-64 | MS-65 |
|---|---|---|---|
| 30-40 Coins | 50-60 Coins | 60-70 Coins | 25-30 Coins |
| N/A | $225-$325 | $450-$650 | $1,000-$1,250 |

| MS-66 | MS-67 | MS-68 | MS-69 to MS-70 |
|---|---|---|---|
| 20-25 Coins | 1-2 Coins | 0 Coins | 0 Coins |
| $1,500-$3,000 | $8,000-$12,500 | -- | -- |

*Note:* The conclusions presented in the following "Collecting and Investing Strategies" section are drawn in large part from the Investment Potential Ratios that are summarized in Appendices G and H at the end of this book. For

a detailed analysis of the formula used to derive these Investment Potential Ratios, please refer to the Introduction of this book.

**Collecting and Investing Strategies:** The 1907-O may not be grossly undervalued relative to many other Barber Dimes, but examples in the MS-64 to MS-67 grade range are still underrated to one degree or another. As such, both the collector and the investor could do well acquiring an example of this issue in one of those grades.

The real key to realizing the full potential of the 1907-O is to recognize that this is a very difficult issue to find "nice." Many Mint State examples are just not attractive coins, the strike often noticeably deficient and the toning usually dark and/or mottled in distribution. You are going to have to select one of the more attractive survivors in order to have a coin that has the best chance to appreciate in value in the coming years.

As far as mitigating the striking problem is concerned, I advise holding out for one of the overall sharp-looking survivors. Such pieces are not unknown, and they do trade fairly regularly in most Mint State grades. The toning issue may be a tougher nut to crack, but my experience suggests that many (but not all!) of the more attractive pieces are those on which the toning is confined to the peripheries. Avoid dipped coins as these have a tendency to look washed out and somewhat flat in the luster category.

# 1907-S

## MINTAGE
3,178,470

Courtesy of David Lawrence

## RARITY RANKINGS

*Overall, Mint State: 20th of 74*
*High Grade, MS-65 or Finer: 3rd of 74*

### SAN FRANCISCO MINT ISSUES

*Overall, Mint State: 10th of 24*
*High Grade, MS-65 or Finer: 2nd of 24*

**Important Varieties:** None.

**General Comments:** The 1907-S is a surprisingly rare issue in Mint State for a late-date Barber Dime with a respectable total of 3.1 million pieces produced. It is rarer in an absolute sense than the 1892-S, 1893-S, 1895-S and 1899-S, as well as such 20th century issues in this series as the 1906-S, 1908-S and 1913-S. In high grades, the 1907-S is actually the second-rarest San Francisco Mint issue in the Barber Dime series, outstripping even the vaunted 1898-S and the low-mintage 1901-S, 1903-S, 1904-S, 1909-S, 1913-S and 1915-S for this honor.

The 1907-S is solidly in the upper third among all Barber Dime issues in terms of overall rarity. And only the 1894-O and the 1895-S are being rarer than this issue in high grades.

**Strike:** A few examples have a bit of striking softness confined to the top of Liberty's portrait on the obverse and the lower-right portion of the reverse wreath. Otherwise, the 1907-S is a well-produced issue with sharp-to-full striking detail.

**Luster:** The 1907-S is not among the more lustrous S-mint Barber Dimes, and the typical example exhibits a satiny texture to the surfaces that is often a bit subdued.

**Surfaces:** A very rare issue in Gem Mint State, the 1907-S is almost always offered with scattered, grade-defining abrasions. These distractions are usually most prevalent on the obverse over Liberty's portrait, and they are usually fairly plentiful in number and/or relatively large in size.

**Toning:** Richly toned coins outnumber brilliant examples, but not by a substantial margin. Toning for this issue is usually quite deep and seldom possessed of vivid color. On the other hand, toning for this issue it is often confined to the peripheries, thus leaving the centers more-or-less bright. Examples with little-to-no-toning are largely the result of dipping.

**Eye Appeal:** The 1907-S is one of the most consistently unattractive San Francisco Mint issues in the Barber Dime series. A combination of subdued luster, significant abrasions and/or relatively dark toning limits the eye appeal for the majority of Mint State survivors.

**Significant Examples:**

1. **PCGS MS-66.** *Ex: Long Beach Signature Sale (Heritage, 2/2005), lot 6294, where it realized $5,750; The Collection of Dr. Steven L. Duckor (Heritage, 1/2006), lot 1017, where it realized $4,025.*

2. **PCGS MS-66.** *Ex: The John C. Hugon Collection (Heritage, 1/2005), lot 4049, where it realized $7,188.*

3. **NGC MS-66.** *Ex: Long Beach Signature Sale (Heritage, 6/2000), lot 7174, where it realized $2,415.*

4. **PCGS MS-66.** *Ex: The Louis E. Eliasberg, Sr. Collection (Bowers and Merena, 5/1996), lot 1291, where it realized $2,750; Orlando Rarities Sale (Bowers and Merena, 1/1997), lot 100, where it realized0 $2,310; The Charles S. Mamiye Collection (Bowers and Merena, 3/1998), lot 623, where it realized $4,180.*

5. **PCGS MS-66.** *Ex: Detroit ANA Signature Sale (Heritage, 8/1994), lot 6473, where it realized $2,310.*

6. **NGC MS-65.** *Ex: The Southwest Collection (Heritage, 2/2008), lot 184, where it realized $1,955.*

7. **NGC MS-65.** *Ex: Charlotte ANA National Money Signature Sale (Heritage, 3/2003), lot 5575, where it realized $1,380; Long Beach Signature Sale (Heritage, 1/2004), lot 5626, where it realized $1,380.*

**8. NGC MS-65.** *Ex: The Charles S. Mamiye Collection (Bowers and Merena, 3/1998), lot 624, where it realized $1,540; FUN Signature Sale (Heritage, 1/2001), lot 6798, unsold; Long Beach Signature Sale (Heritage, 2/2001), lot 5690, unsold; FUN Signature Sale (Heritage, 1/2002), lot 5929, unsold; CSNS Signature Sale (Heritage, 4/2002), lot 5497, where it realized $1,380; FUN Signature Sale (Heritage, 1/2004), lot 5675, where it realized $1,006.*

**9. PCGS MS-65.** *Ex: The Alex Highland Collection (Heritage, 6/2001), lot 6226, where it realized $1,668; The Frog Run Farm Collection (American Numismatic Rarities, 11/2004), lot 685, where it realized $2,070.*

**10. NGC MS-65.** *Ex: Long Beach Signature Sale (Heritage, 9/1998), lot 6620, where it realized $1,610; FUN Signature Sale (Heritage, 1/2000), lot 6589, unsold; Central States Signature Sale (Heritage, 5/2000), lot 7223, where it realized $1,610.*

**Total Known in Mint State:** 95-110 Coins

**Total Known and Value Breakdown by Grade:**

| MS-60 to MS-62 | MS-63 | MS-64 | MS-65 |
|---|---|---|---|
| 25-30 Coins | 30-35 Coins | 25-30 Coins | 6-8 Coins |
| N/A | $575-$700 | $1,200-$1,400 | $1,800-$2,200 |

| MS-66 | MS-67 | MS-68 | MS-69 to MS-70 |
|---|---|---|---|
| 6-8 Coins | 0 Coins | 0 Coins | 0 Coins |
| $4,000-$6,000 | -- | -- | -- |

*Note:* The conclusions presented in the following "Collecting and Investing Strategies" section are drawn in large part from the Investment Potential Ratios that are summarized in Appendices G and H at the end of this book. For a detailed analysis of the formula used to derive these Investment Potential Ratios, please refer to the Introduction of this book.

**Collecting and Investing Strategies:** The 1907-S is one of the most underrated Barber Dimes in the finer Mint State grades, and it is the most undervalued issue of the type in MS-65. As such, I would make the acquisition of one of the rare MS-65s your highest priority as far as this issue is concerned.

The 1907-S is an issue that will almost certainly require that you compromise in at least one area lest you run the risk of never making a purchase. You can realistically hold out for a sharply struck coin, and smooth-looking Gems in MS-65 and MS-66 are available as long as you have the funds. As far as luster and toning are concerned, however, I would just not be too picky when it comes to this very challenging issue. Try to find a coin with at least above-average vibrancy to the surfaces, and stay away from examples that are deeply toned throughout. It is also a good idea to avoid dipped coins when pursuing the 1907-S as such pieces tend to be even more subdued in the luster category.

# Proof

# 1908

## MINTAGE
545

Courtesy of David Lawrence

## RARITY
## RANKINGS

*Overall, All Proof Grades: 4th of 25*
*High Grade, Proof-65 or Finer: 8th of 25 (Tie)*
*Overall, Cameo Finish: 4th of 24 (Tie)*
*Deep/Ultra Cameo Finish: Unknown*

**Important Varieties:** None.

**General Comments:** The 1908 has the third-lowest mintage in the entire proof Barber Dime series, excluding (of course) the branch mint proof 1894-S. As this fact might suggest, the 1908 is one of the rarer proofs of this type, ranking behind only the 1894-S, 1914 and 1915 in this regard. The 1908 is also one of the rarer proof Barber Dimes in high grades, and it is equally as elusive above the Proof-64 grade level as the proof 1904.

The proof 1908 is similar in rarity to the proof 1914 as a Cameo, which means that it is a highly elusive issue with that finish. Like most proof Barber Dimes produced during the 20th century, the 1908 is unknown with a Deep/Ultra Cameo finish.

**Strike:** All examples that I have handled are fully struck, and I doubt that the proof 1908 exists with anything less than razor-sharp definition.

**Finish:** The proof 1908 seldom displays more than trivial field-to-device contrast that is not strong enough to support a Cameo designation from PCGS or NGC. The typical example is actually uniformly brilliant in finish.

**Surfaces:** Hairlines and other contact marks are almost always small and well scattered when present on an example of the proof 1908 Barber Dime.

Many specimens are also carefully preserved with a virtually pristine "look" to the surfaces.

**Toning:** This issue is available with a wide range of visual appearances that run the gamut from fully brilliant to darkly toned. The most attractively toned specimens usually display rather deep patination that does, however, yield to colorful undertones as the coin is held at direct angles to a good light source. Most of the brilliant specimens that I have seen are also highly desirable.

**Eye Appeal:** Eye appeal for the proof 1908 is very good, if not excellent, and there are attractive examples available in virtually all grades at which this issue is represented.

**Significant Examples:**

1. **PCGS Proof-68.** *Ex: New York ANA Signature Sale (Heritage, 8/1997), lot 6192, unsold.*

2. **NGC Proof-67 Cameo.** *Ex: Long Beach, CA Signature Auction (Heritage, 5/2008), lot 161, where it realized $4,313.*

3. **PCGS Proof-67 Cameo.** *Ex: Long Beach Signature Auction (Heritage, 5/2006), lot 1145, where it realized $6,900.*

4. **PCGS Proof-67 Cameo.** *Ex: Dallas Signature Auction (Heritage, 12/2005), lot 509, where it realized $6,325.*

5. **NGC Proof-66 Cameo.** *Ex: Baltimore, MD ANA U.S. Coin Signature Auction (Heritage, 7/2008), lot 130, where it realized $2,760.*

6. **PCGS Proof-66 Cameo.** *Ex: Long Beach, CA Signature U.S. Coin Auction (Heritage, 6/2007), 742, unsold; Dallas, TX U.S. Coin Signature Auction (Heritage, 11/2007), lot 450, where it realized $2,760.*

7. **PCGS Proof-66 Cameo.** *Ex: Palm Beach, FL Signature Sale (Heritage, 11/2004), lot 6309, where it realized $2,876.*

**Total Known:** 275-340 Coins

**Total Known and Value Breakdown by Grade:**

| Brilliant-Finish Coins | | | |
|---|---|---|---|
| **Proof-60-62** | **Proof-63** | **Proof-64** | **Proof-65** |
| 30-35 Coins | 40-50 Coins | 80-95 Coins | 40-50 Coins |
| N/A | $425-$500 | $650-$800 | $1,000-$1,500 |
| **Proof-66** | **Proof-67** | **Proof-68** | **Proof-69-70** |
| 40-50 Coins | 20-25 Coins | 4-5 Coins | 0 Coins |
| $1,750-$2,750 | $3,000-$5,750 | $6,500-$10,000 | -- |

| Cameo Coins | | | |
|---|---|---|---|
| **Proof-60-62 Cameo** | **Proof-63 Cameo** | **Proof-64 Cameo** | **Proof-65 Cameo** |
| 1 Coin | 4-5 Coins | 4-6 Coins | 4-6 Coins |
| N/A | $600-$750 | $1,000-$1,500 | $1,750-$2,500 |
| **Proof-66 Cameo** | **Proof-67 Cameo** | **Proof-68 Cameo** | **Proof-69-70 Cameo** |
| 4-5 Coins | 3-4 Coins | 1-2 Coins | 0 Coins |
| $2,750-$3,750 | $4,500-$8,000 | $7,500-$9,000 | -- |

| Deep/Ultra Cameo | | | |
|---|---|---|---|
| **Proof-60-62 Deep/ Ultra Cameo** | **Proof-63 Deep/ Ultra Cameo** | **Proof-64 Deep/ Ultra Cameo** | **Proof-65 Deep/ Ultra Cameo** |
| 0 Coins | 0 Coins | 0 Coins | 0 Coins |
| -- | -- | -- | -- |
| **Proof-66 Deep/ Ultra Cameo** | **Proof-67 Deep/ Ultra Cameo** | **Proof-68 Deep/ Ultra Cameo** | **Proof-69-70 Deep/ Ultra Cameo** |
| 0 Coins | 0 Coins | 0 Coins | 0 Coins |
| -- | -- | -- | -- |

_Note:_ The conclusions presented in the following "Collecting and Investing Strategies" section are drawn in large part from the Investment Potential Ratios that are summarized in Appendices G and H at the end of this book. For a detailed analysis of the formula used to derive these Investment Potential Ratios, please refer to the Introduction of this book.

**Collecting and Investing Strategies:** Also somewhat underrated in Proof-64, the 1908 is the most undervalued Barber Dime in Proof-65 after only the 1915. Proof-66s are fairly accurately priced, which means that they do not hold much potential to appreciate in value in coming years. This issue is a bit overrated in Proof-67 and should be avoided in that grade.

There are some really pretty proof 1908 Barber Dimes in numismatic circles, and you should have no difficulty finding such a piece regardless of whether your preference is for brilliance or original toning. Be wary of images in auction catalogs or on numismatic websites that show extremely vivid colors on examples of this issue. Those coins are usually shot at direct angles to bring out the full vividness of the underlying patina; the outward appearance is usually one of significantly deeper toning. Not that such a coin is unattractive, for it will almost certainly be looked upon quite favorably by the toning enthusiast, but just make sure that you know exactly what you are purchasing before writing out the check. On the other hand, you should avoid any proof 1908 Barber Dime with mottled toning as those coins tend to be quite splotchy in appearance and often possess distracting toning spots on one or both sides.

# 1908

## MINTAGE
### 10,600,000

Courtesy of Bowers and Merena

## RARITY RANKINGS

*Overall, Mint State: 62nd of 74*
*High Grade, MS-65 or Finer: 62nd of 74 (Tie)*

## PHILADELPHIA MINT ISSUES

*Overall, Mint State: 14th of 25*
*High Grade, MS-65 or Finer: 15th of 25 (Tie)*

**Important Varieties:** Several Repunched Date varieties have been confirmed for the 1908 Barber Dime, and these are known by the following attributions:

- FS-301, Lawrence-101

- FS-302

- FS-303

**General Comments:** As with the 1907, the 1908 is one of the more plentiful issues in the business strike Barber Dime series. It is actually a bit rarer than both the 1906 and 1907 in terms of total number of Mint State examples known to exist, and it is also less common than issues such as the 1897, 1898, 1910 and 1914-D. The 1908 compares favorably in high-grade rarity to the 1893, and it is rarer in that regard than such other issues in this series as the 1911-D, 1911-S, 1912, 1913, 1914 and 1916.

**Strike:** The 1908 is a well-produced issue, and most examples exhibit more-or-less sharp striking definition to both sides. A few pieces, nonetheless, display softness of detail here and there around the peripheries on one or both sides.

**Luster:** This issue also has very-good-to-excellent luster that is almost always of a frosty texture.

**Surfaces:** Mint State examples vary from moderately abraded to virtually pristine, although the typical piece is apt to display very few, if any distractions. When present, abrasions on a 1908 Barber Dime are usually small in size and not overly detracting to the eye.

**Toning:** Although brilliant examples are becoming a bit more prevalent due to the widespread practice of dipping and other forms of numismatic conservation, the typical 1908 is still a toned coin. Toning for this issue is usually light-to-moderate in depth, and the color is often quite pleasing, even if it seldom possessed of truly vivid color.

**Eye Appeal:** An attractive issue, the 1908 is usually a delightful coin to behold, especially at or above the MS-64 grade level.

**Significant Examples:**

**1. NGC MS-67.** *Ex: Long Beach Signature Sale (Heritage, 2/2003), lot 6356, unsold; CSNS Signature Sale (Heritage, 5/2003), lot 5949, where it realized $2,070; The Southwest Collection (Heritage, 2/2008), lot 185, where it realized $2,530.*

**2. PCGS MS-67.** *Ex: The John C. Hugon Collection (Heritage, 1/2005), lot 4050, where it realized $3,738; The Greenhill Collection (Ira & Larry Goldberg, 9/2006), lot 1507, where it realized $2,070; FUN Signature Coin Auction (Heritage, 1/2007), lot 2655, where it realized $17,250.*

**3. NGC MS-67.** *Ex: The Richard C. Jewell Collection (American Numismatic Rarities, 3/2005), lot 1622, where it realized $3,220.*

**4. NGC MS-67.** *Ex: New York Rarities Sale (Bowers and Merena, 7/2002), lot 153, unsold.*

**5. NGC MS-67.** *Ex: Elite Sale (Superior, 1/2002), lot 1118, where it realized $1,955.*

**Total Known in Mint State:** 420-510 Coins

**Total Known and Value Breakdown by Grade:**

| MS-60 to MS-62 | MS-63 | MS-64 | MS-65 |
|---|---|---|---|
| 80-100 Coins | 105-130 Coins | 140-165 Coins | 60-70 Coins |
| N/A | $125-$175 | $225-$300 | $500-$650 |

| MS-66 | MS-67 | MS-68 | MS-69 to MS-70 |
|---|---|---|---|
| 30-40 Coins | 5 Coins | 0 Coins | 0 Coins |
| $850-$1,000 | $3,000-$17,500 | -- | -- |

*Note:* The conclusions presented in the following "Collecting and Investing Strategies" section are drawn in large part from the Investment Potential Ratios that are summarized in Appendices G and H at the end of this book. For a detailed analysis of the formula used to derive these Investment Potential Ratios, please refer to the Introduction of this book.

**Collecting and Investing Strategies:** The 1908 is one of the more accurately priced Barber Dimes in most Mint State grades, and examples in the MS-64 to MS-66 range are only marginally underrated. In MS-67, however, the 1908 is the most overrated P-mint Barber Dime after only the 1895. As such, I do not recommend Superb Gems for this issue unless you are assembling a top-ranked Barber Dime set on the PCGS or NGC registries.

In an absolute sense, the 1908 is a plentiful issue that is both well produced and well preserved. As such, you should experience no difficulty locating an attractive coin in most Mint State grades. I do advise being selective when it comes to strike, however, as there are too many sharply struck examples of the 1908 to settle for a coin with even minor lack of detail. Pay particular attention to the left-obverse border and upper-reverse periphery as, when present at all, lack of detail for this issue is usually confined to one or both of those areas.

# 1908-D

**MINTAGE**
7,490,000

Courtesy of Bowers and Merena

**RARITY RANKINGS**

*Overall, Mint State: 41st of 74*
*High Grade, MS-65 or Finer: 41st of 74 (Tie)*

## DENVER MINT ISSUES

*Overall, Mint State: 5th of 8*
*High Grade, MS-65 or Finer: 5th of 8*

**Important Varieties:** The 1908-D has more significant varieties than any other issue in the Barber Dime series:

- Repunched Mintmark: attributed as FS-301 and FS-010.220
- Repunched Date: attributed as FS-302 and FS-010.210
- Repunched Date: attributed as FS-303, FS-010.200 and Lawrence-104
- Repunched Date: attributed as FS-304, FS-010.225 and Lawrence-105
- Repunched Date: attributed as FS-305, FS-010.230 and Lawrence-101
- Repunched Date: attributed as FS-306 and FS-010.235
- Repunched Date: attributed as FS-307 and FS-010.240

**General Comments:** For the first time since opening its doors as a coinage facility, the Denver Mint produced more than 5 million Dimes in 1908. The 1908-D is the first Denver Mint issue in this series that will not present a significant obstacle to the completion of a Mint State set. On the other hand, the 1908-D does not have a much greater Mint State population than the 1906-D, and it is appreciably rarer in all Mint State grades than the 1911-D, 1912-D and 1914-D. This issue is also rarer in an absolute sense than such others in the Barber Dime series as the 1894, 1905-S, 1906-O, 1912-S and 1914-S. In high-grade rarity, the 1908-D is very similar to the lower-mintage 1907-O.

**Strike:** The 1908-D is usually more than adequate as far as strike is concerned, but you should not expect this issue to display the same exactness of detail as the typical 1906-D. There is usually a touch of softness to the strike on the obverse at the top of Liberty's portrait and/or on the reverse at the upper or lower-left portions of the wreath.

**Luster:** Most examples exhibit pleasing, if not overly vibrant luster. I have seen coins with both satin and softly frosted textures, and these seem to account for nearly identical percentages of the Mint State population.

**Surfaces:** Abrasions are seldom a significant impediment to the eye appeal of a Mint State '08-D. Distractions are usually present, nonetheless, even if only in minimal numbers.

**Toning:** The majority of examples that I have handled are originally toned, often quite extensively with rich, antique colors. A much smaller number of Mint State survivors are toned only around the peripheries. Brilliant examples are starting to make an appearance as more and more silver coins of all types are subjected to dipping and other forms of numismatic conservation.

**Eye Appeal:** The 1908-D has above-average, although not excellent eye appeal. This issue is generally well produced, and enough MS-64s and MS-65s exist that you should not have too much difficulty locating a relatively smooth-looking example.

**Significant Examples:**

1. **PCGS MS-67.** *Ex: The Bradley Bloch Collection (Ira & Larry Goldberg, 9/1999), lot 1203, where it realized $2,530; The John C. Hugon Collection (Heritage, 1/2005), lot 4051, where it realized $4140; The Collection of Dr. Steven L. Duckor (Heritage, 1/2006), lot 1019, where it realized $4,600.*

2. **NGC MS-67.** *Ex: The Lindesmith Collection (Bowers and Merena, 3/2000), lot 405, unsold; CSNS Signature Auction (Heritage, 5/2005), lot 6665, where it realized $3,738.*

This coin is an example of the Repunched Date variety with the attributions FS-303, FS-010.200 and Lawrence-104.

3. **NGC MS-66. CAC.** *Ex: Pre-Long Beach Elite Coin Auction (Superior, 5/2003), lot 2385, unsold; Long Beach Signature Sale (Heritage, 9/2003), lot 6459, where it realized $1,093; CSNS Signature Auction (Heritage, 5/2005), lot 6664, where it realized $1,553; Baltimore Auction (Bowers*

*and Merena, 7/2006), lot 1023, unsold; Baltimore Auction (Heritage, 3/2006), lot 612, unsold; Baltimore, MD ANA U.S. Coin Signature Auction (Heritage, 7/2008), lot 117, where it realized $1,610.*

**4. PCGS MS-66. CAC.** *Ex: Auction '89 (RARCOA's session, 7/1989), lot 129, where it realized $5,500; Dr. Steven L. Duckor; Palm Beach, FL Signature Sale (Heritage 3/2005), 5483, where it realized $1,236; The Southwest Collection (Heritage, 2/2008), lot 186, where it realized $2,300.*

**5. NGC MS-66.** *Ex: FUN Signature Sale (Heritage, 1/2004), lot 5676, where it realized $1,035.*

**6. NGC MS-66.** *Ex: The Bay Area Collection (Heritage, 3/2003), lot 5577, where it realized $776; November Signature Sale (Heritage, 11/2003), lot 6026, where it realized $1,035.*

**7. NGC MS-66.** *Ex: Long Beach Signature Sale (Heritage, 5/2001), lot 8036, where it realized $1,984; The Benson Collection (Ira & Larry Goldberg, 2/2002), lot 594, where it realized $1,035*

**8. NGC MS-66.** *Ex: Pre-Long Beach Elite Coin Auction (Superior, 10/2001), lot 1805, where it realized $1,495.*

**Total Known in Mint State:** 170-210 Coins

**Total Known and Value Breakdown by Grade:**

| MS-60 to MS-62 | MS-63 | MS-64 | MS-65 |
|---|---|---|---|
| 35-45 Coins | 45-55 Coins | 45-55 Coins | 25-30 Coins |
| N/A | $200-$300 | $550-$700 | $800-$1,000 |

| MS-66 | MS-67 | MS-68 | MS-69 to MS-70 |
|---|---|---|---|
| 12-15 Coins | 8-10 Coins | 0 Coins | 0 Coins |
| $1,500-$2,500 | $4,000-$5,000 | -- | -- |

<u>Note:</u> The conclusions presented in the following "Collecting and Investing Strategies" section are drawn in large part from the Investment Potential Ratios that are summarized in Appendices G and H at the end of this book. For a detailed analysis of the formula used to derive these Investment Potential Ratios, please refer to the Introduction of this book.

**Collecting and Investing Strategies:** After only the 1910-D, the 1908-D is the most underrated Barber Dime in MS-64, MS-65 and MS-66. Such coins are attractive not only for inclusion in a high-grade Barber Dime set, but also for mintmarked type collecting as well as more generalized numismatic investing. Superb Gems in MS-67 could also do well in a high-ranked set, but investors should probably avoid the 1908-D in that grade since such coins are a bit overrated at the values given in this book.

Most 1908-D Dimes are attractive coins, if not in an absolute sense then at least in the context of their assigned grade. Both the originally toned examples and the bright, brilliant-white pieces are attractive, but I would pass on any example with noticeable softness of strike. Enough well-struck coins are obtainable that you should insist on adding one of those coins to your collection or portfolio.

# 1908-O

## MINTAGE
### 1,789,000

Courtesy of David Lawrence

## RARITY RANKINGS

*Overall, Mint State: 32nd of 74 (Tie)*
*High Grade, MS-65 or Finer: 50th of 74 (Tie)*

## NEW ORLEANS MINT ISSUES

*Overall, Mint State: 12th of 17*
*High Grade, MS-65 or Finer: 16th of 17*

**Important Varieties**: I am aware of two Repunched Date varieties for the 1908-O that have drawn the attention of variety specialists. The attributions for these varieties are FS-301, FS-010.250 and FS-302, FS-010.260, respectively.

**General Comments:** As a much lower-mintage might suggest, the 1908-O is more elusive than the 1907-O in terms of total number of Mint State coins believed extant. This issue is also ranked ahead of the 1892-O, 1893-O, 1905-O and 1906-O in this regard. A sizeable percentage of Mint State survivors are high grade, however, with the result that the 1908-O is actually the most common O-mint Barber in Gem after only the 1906-O. The 1908-O is similar in overall rarity to the 1906-D, and it compares favorably with the low-mintage 1913-S in high-grade rarity.

**Strike:** For a product of the New Orleans Mint, the 1908-O is a rather well-struck issue. There are certainly Mint State survivors that are free of bothersome lack of detail, although you will also be confronted with coins that are a bit softly impressed over the top of Liberty's portrait, at the upper-right portion of the reverse wreath and/or over the lower-right portion of the same device.

**Luster:** The 1908-O has above-average, if not downright strong luster. There are some satiny pieces in the market, but most examples that I have seen are decidedly frosty in texture.

**Surfaces:** Distracting abrasions for this issue tend to be small in size and relatively few in number, although low-end Mint State coins can display noticeable slidemarks and other significant distractions.

**Toning:** There is not much middle ground in this category as far as the 1908-O is concerned, and examples tend to be either richly toned or fully brilliant. Coins in the former category tend to have deeper, more antique-looking colors as opposed to vivid patination. Most of the brilliant pieces have been dipped.

**Eye Appeal:** Overall eye appeal for the 1908-O is surprisingly strong for a New Orleans Mint Barber Dime, and most Mint State examples are quite pleasing to the eye.

**Significant Examples:**

1. **NGC MS-67.** *Ex: Dallas, TX U.S. Coin Signature Auction (Heritage, 11/2007), lot 433, where it realized $3,450; Baltimore Auction (Bowers and Merena, 6/2007), lot 676, unsold.*

2. **PCGS MS-67.** *Ex: Denver ANA Auction (Bowers and Merena, 8/2006), lot 766, where it realized $6,210.*

3. **PCGS MS-67.** *Ex: Long Beach Signature Sale (Heritage, 2/2005), lot 6299, where it realized $6,210.*

4. **NGC MS-67.** *Ex: The John C. Hugon Collection (Heritage, 1/2005), lot 4052, where it realized $6,095.*

**Total Known in Mint State:** 135-170 Coins

**Total Known and Value Breakdown by Grade:**

| MS-60 to MS-62 | MS-63 | MS-64 | MS-65 |
|---|---|---|---|
| 15-18 Coins | 30-35 Coins | 35-45 Coins | 35-45 Coins |
| N/A | $450-$550 | $650-$750 | $1,000-$1,500 |

| MS-66 | MS-67 | MS-68 | MS-69 to MS-70 |
|---|---|---|---|
| 15-20 Coins | 5-7 Coins | 0 Coins | 0 Coins |
| $1,500-$2,000 | $3,500-$7,500 | -- | -- |

*Note:* The conclusions presented in the following "Collecting and Investing Strategies" section are drawn in large part from the Investment Potential Ratios that are summarized in Appendices G and H at the end of this book. For a detailed analysis of the formula used to derive these Investment Potential Ratios, please refer to the Introduction of this book.

**Collecting and Investing Strategies:** Even though the 1908-O is a very scarce-to-rare issue in all Mint State grades, the issue has just not garnered the attention that it deserves in MS-64 and MS-66. Such pieces are underrated and stand to increase in value as the market takes more notice of the conditionally challenging nature of this issue. MS-65s and MS-67s are more appropriately priced at the levels given in this book and, as such, the 1908-O will probably not see much price appreciation in those grades.

Do not settle for an average example of the 1908-O since many of the Mint State survivors are sharply struck, highly lustrous and attractively toned. Take advantage of these desirable traits, especially since they are missing in examples of so many other O-mint issues in the Barber Dime series.

# 1908-S

### MINTAGE
3,220,000

Courtesy of David Lawrence

### RARITY RANKINGS

*Overall, Mint State: 24th of 74 (Tie)*
*High Grade, MS-65 or Finer: 30th of 74 (Tie)*

## SAN FRANCISCO MINT ISSUES

*Overall, Mint State: 12th of 24*
*High Grade, MS-65 or Finer: 16th of 24 (Tie)*

**Important Varieties:** None.

**General Comments:** A median rarity in the S-mint Barber Dime series, the 1908-S is more challenging to locate in Mint State than the 1900-S, 1906-S, 1911-S, 1912-S, 1913-S, 1914-S and 1916-S. This issue is similar in high-grade rarity to the low-mintage 1915-S, as well as the 1904, 1906-D and 1909-O from the other coinage facilities that contributed to the Barber Dime series.

The 1908-S is very scarce in Mint State grades through MS-65. High-end Gems in MS-66 are very rare, while only three MS-67s are known to PCGS. NGC has yet to certify a single 1908-S Barber Dime as a Superb Gem (December/2008).

**Strike:** The typical example is sharply, if not fully struck. There are exceptions, of course, and these come in the form of coins on which the top of Liberty's portrait and/or the lower portion of the reverse wreath are a bit softly impressed.

**Luster:** Luster quality for the 1908-S is usually excellent, and most examples have a bright, satiny sheen to the surfaces.

**Surfaces:** Mint State survivors range from noticeably abraded to virtually pristine. The typical piece that you are likely to encounter in the market will not be too heavily abraded, however, but rather will display only a few wispy distractions, most of which will probably be confined to the obverse.

**Toning:** The majority of coins that I have handled are richly toned, the colors usually moderate-to-deep as opposed to vivid. A few completely original pieces with light, iridescent toning are known, one of which is the Pittman specimen (David W. Akers, 5/1997, lot 715). Most such examples, however, have been dipped, a practice that also explains the existence of most of the brilliant coins that I have seen.

**Eye Appeal:** This is an attractive issue, although the 1908-S is not quite as strong in the eye appeal category as the 1907-S. The toning can be a bit dark for some buyers, and it takes an advanced numismatist who values originality to appreciate many Mint State 1908-S Barber Dimes.

**Significant Examples:**

**1. NGC MS-67.** *Ex: Chicago '96 Sale (RARCOA and David W. Akers, 7/1996), lot 205, where it realized $2,750; The Oliver Jung Collection (American Numismatic Rarities, 7/2004), lot 43, where it realized $6,440.*

**2. PCGS MS-67.** *Ex: The Wayne S. Rich Collection (Bowers and Merena, 3/2002), lot 2110, where it realized $5,750.*

**Total Known in Mint State:** 110-135 Coins

**Total Known and Value Breakdown by Grade:**

| MS-60 to MS-62 | MS-63 | MS-64 | MS-65 |
|---|---|---|---|
| 25-30 Coins | 20-25 Coins | 30-35 Coins | 25-30 Coins |
| N/A | $550-$700 | $1,250-$1,400 | $1,500-$2,000 |

| MS-66 | MS-67 | MS-68 | MS-69 to MS-70 |
|---|---|---|---|
| 10-12 Coins | 2-3 Coins | 0 Coins | 0 Coins |
| $2,500-$4,000 | $5,000-$8,000 | -- | -- |

*Note:* The conclusions presented in the following "Collecting and Investing Strategies" section are drawn in large part from the Investment Potential Ratios that are summarized in Appendices G and H at the end of this book. For a detailed analysis of the formula used to derive these Investment Potential Ratios, please refer to the Introduction of this book.

**Collecting and Investing Strategies:** The 1908-S is among the more underrated Barber Dimes in MS-64, MS-66 and MS-67, and the issue should be seriously considered for its investment potential in those grades. MS-65s offer solid value in light of their rarity, but I would not expect this issue to see an appreciable price increase in that grade.

Your only significant impediment to obtaining an attractive Mint State 1908-S Barber Dime should be the prevalence of more-or-less deeply toned coins among the high-grade survivors. I happen to appreciate richly original silver coins, but I am also a realist who understands that the market usually discounts such pieces because they can be difficult to sell. With this in mind, I suggest obtaining a 1908-S that is either completely brilliant or, if you are really patient, lightly toned in more iridescent shades. The latter are among the most highly desirable examples within the context of their assigned grade, but they are rare in an absolute sense and almost always command a strong premium when offered through auction or for outright purchase.

# Proof
# 1909

## MINTAGE
650

Courtesy of David Lawrence

## RARITY RANKINGS

*Overall, All Proof Grades: 15th of 25 (Tie)*
*High Grade, Proof-65 or Finer: 16th of 25*
*Overall, Cameo Finish: 8th of 24*
*Deep/Ultra Cameo Finish: Unknown*

**Important Varieties:** None.

**General Comments:** Produced in greater numbers than the proof 1907, proof 1908, proof 1910 and proof 1911, the proof 1909 is an easier issue to obtain in all grades. This is actually the most common proof Barber Dime from the 20th century with the sole exception of the 1905. Examples that grade up to an including Proof-66 are plentiful, and even Superb Gems in Proof-67 can only really be described as scarce. Proof-68s, however, are very rare coins.

With a Cameo finish, the 1909 is a rare issue that is more challenging to locate than such other proof Barber Dimes from the 20th century as the 1905, 1906, 1910, 1911, 1912 and 1913. This issue is unknown with a Deep/Ultra Cameo finish.

**Strike:** The proof 1909 comes sharply-to-fully struck with pinpoint definition to all elements of the design.

**Finish:** The proof 1909 almost always display an all-brilliant finish with little, if any evidence of field-to-device contrast. The few Cameo specimens that have been graded by PCGS and NGC usually offer only moderate contrast on the obverse with a much bolder Cameo finish to the reverse.

**Surfaces:** Hairlines and other distractions tend to be minor for this issue, and there are many examples that are overall smooth, if not virtually pristine.

**Toning:** I have seen examples that are both fully brilliant and deeply toned. The majority of pieces, nonetheless, display at least some degree of patination to the surfaces. Toning for this issue tends to be quite deep, and the colors are usually fairly dark and sometimes mottled in distribution.

**Eye Appeal:** Overly dark and/or splotchy-looking examples aside, the proof 1909 has strong eye appeal. This is an expertly produced issue, and enough examples have been carefully preserved over the years that you should have no difficulty locating an attractive, smooth-looking specimen.

**Significant Examples:**

**1. PCGS Proof-68.** *Ex: Las Vegas Auction (Bowers and Merena, 10/2006), lot 5316, where it realized $7,906.*

**2. NGC Proof-68.** *Ex: CSNS Signature Auction (Heritage, 5/2005), lot 6718, where it realized $5,175; Long Beach Signature Auction (Heritage, 9/2005), lot 2474, unsold; Long Beach Signature Auction (Heritage, 2/2006), lot 817, unsold.*

**3. NGC Proof-68 ★ Cameo.** *Ex: C.F. Childs, who is believed to have purchased the coin directly from the Philadelphia Mint in 1909; The Walter H. Childs Collection (Bowers and Merena, 8/1999), lot 228, where it realized $8,625; The John C. Hugon Collection (Heritage, 1/2005), lot 4093, where it realized $8,913.*

**4. NGC Proof-67 ★ Cameo.** *Ex: Baltimore, MD ANA U.S. Coin Signature Auction (Heritage, 7/2008), lot 131, where it realized $4,025.*

**5. NGC Proof-67 Cameo.** *Ex: Dallas, TX Signature Coin Auction (Heritage, 4/2007), lot 565, where it realized $3,450.*

**Total Known:** 360-440 Coins

**Total Known and Value Breakdown by Grade:**

| Brilliant-Finish Coins | | | |
|---|---|---|---|
| **Proof-60-62** | **Proof-63** | **Proof-64** | **Proof-65** |
| 30-40 Coins | 55-65 Coins | 95-120 Coins | 60-70 Coins |
| N/A | $425-$500 | $650-$800 | $1,000-$1,500 |
| **Proof-66** | **Proof-67** | **Proof-68** | **Proof-69-70** |
| 60-70 Coins | 30-40 Coins | 2-3 Coins | 0 Coins |
| $1,750-$2,750 | $2,500-$4,000 | $6,000-$10,000 | -- |

| Cameo Coins | | | |
|---|---|---|---|
| Proof-60-62 Cameo | Proof-63 Cameo | Proof-64 Cameo | Proof-65 Cameo |
| 1 Coin | 3-4 Coins | 2-3 Coins | 4-6 Coins |
| N/A | $600-$750 | $1,000-$1,500 | $1,750-$2,500 |
| Proof-66 Cameo | Proof-67 Cameo | Proof-68 Cameo | Proof-69-70 Cameo |
| 10-12 Coins | 4-5 Coins | 1-2 Coins | 0 Coins |
| $3,000-$4,500 | $3,500-$5,500 | $7,500-$9,000 | -- |

| Deep/Ultra Cameo | | | |
|---|---|---|---|
| Proof-60-62 Deep/ Ultra Cameo | Proof-63 Deep/ Ultra Cameo | Proof-64 Deep/ Ultra Cameo | Proof-65 Deep/ Ultra Cameo |
| 0 Coins | 0 Coins | 0 Coins | 0 Coins |
| -- | -- | -- | -- |
| Proof-66 Deep/ Ultra Cameo | Proof-67 Deep/ Ultra Cameo | Proof-68 Deep/ Ultra Cameo | Proof-69-70 Deep/ Ultra Cameo |
| 0 Coins | 0 Coins | 0 Coins | 0 Coins |
| -- | -- | -- | -- |

*Note:* The conclusions presented in the following "Collecting and Investing Strategies" section are drawn in large part from the Investment Potential Ratios that are summarized in Appendices G and H at the end of this book. For a detailed analysis of the formula used to derive these Investment Potential Ratios, please refer to the Introduction of this book.

**Collecting and Investing Strategies:** In lower grades through Proof-64, the 1909 is very close to the median for rarity and price among proof Barber Dimes. Such coins, therefore, offer solid value at reported price levels, but they should not be expected to advance much in price in the coming years. In Proof-66 the 1909 is the most overrated proof Barber Dime after only the 1895. Since Proof-67s are also overrated, I just do not like the 1909 for inclusion in most numismatic collections and portfolios. In fact, I would avoid this issue in all grades unless you are assembling a complete set of proof Barber Dimes.

# 1909

## MINTAGE
10,240,000

Courtesy of David Lawrence

## RARITY RANKINGS

*Overall, Mint State: 58th of 74*
*High Grade, MS-65 or Finer: 53rd of 74 (Tie)*

## PHILADELPHIA MINT ISSUES

*Overall, Mint State: 10th of 25*
*High Grade, MS-65 or Finer: 9th of 25 (Tie)*

**Important Varieties:** None.

**General Comments:** One of the scarcer P-mint issues from its era, the 1909 is more elusive in Mint State than the 1906, 1907, 1908, 1910 and, of course, the 1911. It is also rarer than the 1897, 1898, 1901 and 1914-D in terms of total number of Mint State coins known to exist. Along with the 1901, 1906-O, 1915 and 1916-S, the 1909 ranks ahead of such issues as the 1899, 1906, 1907, 1911-D, 1911-S and 1914-D in terms of high-grade rarity.

**Strike:** Striking quality for the 1909 is usually beyond reproach, and the typical example exhibits sharp-to-full definition on both sides. A few pieces do reveal some trivial lack of detail on the reverse either at the upper-right portion of the wreath or at the right (facing) bow of the ribbon knot. Even on such coins, however, softness of strike is usually so minimal as to be easily overlooked.

**Luster:** The 1909 is also known for excellent luster, and the vast majority of examples that I have handled are softly frosted in texture.

**Surfaces:** Examples vary from noticeably abraded to virtually pristine, although coins in the latter category are nowhere near as plentiful as one might assume given the relatively high mintage. Most Mint State 1909 Barber Dimes display at least a few scattered abrasions that, fortunately, tend to be small in size and not individually distracting to the unaided eye.

**Toning:** This is not one of the more extensively toned issues in the Barber Dime series, and you have a greater probability of locating an example with brilliant or lightly patinated surfaces than a coin with deep, rich toning. Some of the pieces in the former category are naturally brilliant or lightly toned, while others have been dipped.

**Eye Appeal:** Overall eye appeal for the 1909 is quite strong, the care with which this issue was struck and a generous Mint State population ensuring that there is a substantial number of attractive coins from which to choose.

**Significant Examples:**

**1. PCGS MS-67.** *Ex: The Collection of Dr. Steven L. Duckor (Heritage, 1/2006), lot 1022, where it realized $8,625.*

**2. PCGS MS-66.** *Ex: The Bell Collection (Heritage, 9/2008), lot 1718, where it realized $1,093.*

**3. PCGS MS-66.** *Ex: CSNS Signature Auction (Heritage, 4/2006), lot 1310, where it realized $891; Long Beach, CA Signature U.S. Coin Auction (Heritage 6/2007), 721, where it realized $920.*

**4. PCGS MS-66.** *Ex: Long Beach Signature Auction (Heritage, 5/2006), lot 1115, where it realized $1,006.*

**5. NGC MS-66.** *Ex: Pre-Long Beach Auction (Ira & Larry Goldberg, 9/2003), lot 269, where it realized $719.*

**6. PCGS MS-66.** *Ex: Auction '90 (Superior's session, 8/1990), lot 1054, where it realized $6,000.*

**Total Known in Mint State:** 375-450 Coins

**Total Known and Value Breakdown by Grade:**

| MS-60 to MS-62 | MS-63 | MS-64 | MS-65 |
|---|---|---|---|
| 85-95 Coins | 100-125 Coins | 125-150 Coins | 50-60 Coins |
| N/A | $125-$175 | $225-$300 | $500-$600 |

| MS-66 | MS-67 | MS-68 | MS-69 to MS-70 |
|---|---|---|---|
| 12-15 Coins | 2-3 Coins | 0 Coins | 0 Coins |
| $950-$1,150 | $5,000-$10,000 | -- | -- |

*Note:* The conclusions presented in the following "Collecting and Investing Strategies" section are drawn in large part from the Investment Potential Ratios that are summarized in Appendices G and H at the end of this book. For a detailed analysis of the formula used to derive these Investment Potential Ratios, please refer to the Introduction of this book.

**Collecting and Investing Strategies:** The 1909 is somewhat underrated in MS-64 and MS-65, but the real potential for this issue lies at the MS-66 and MS-67 grade levels. In MS-66, in fact, the 1909 is the most undervalued Philadelphia Mint Barber Dime after only the 1905 and 1906. Take advantage of the underrated nature of this issue in MS-66 before market values for such coins rise appreciably above the $1,200 mark.

Given the rarity of the 1909 in MS-66, I would approach purchase opportunities with a less critical eye. On the other hand, you should definitely avoid coins that are so darkly toned that the eye appeal is diminished. I have seen a few such pieces in MS-66 holders, and the careful buyer would be wise to be wary of those coins.

# 1909-D

## MINTAGE
954,000

Courtesy of Bowers and Merena

## RARITY RANKINGS

**Overall, Mint State:** *21st of 74*
**High Grade, MS-65 or Finer:** *35th of 74 (Tie)*

## DENVER MINT ISSUES

**Overall, Mint State:** *2nd of 8*
**High Grade, MS-65 or Finer:** *4th of 8*

**Important Varieties:** None.

**General Comments:** Based on mintage figures, the Denver Mint's primary concern in 1909 was obviously in the striking of Quarters and Half Eagles. No Half Dollars or Quarter Eagles were struck in that facility throughout 1909, and the year's production of Dimes, Eagles and Double Eagles was very limited.

The 1909-D trails only the 1907-D as the rarest Denver Mint issue in the Barber Dime series. It is only a median rarity in this mintmarked series when we consider high-grade examples at and above the MS-65 level, but the 1909-D does have a much smaller population of Gems than the relatively common 1911-D and 1914-D. The 1908-D and 1912-D are also more plentiful than the 1909-D in high grades, as are many Barber Dimes from other Mints including the 1892-O, 1900-S, 1903, 1905 and 1907-O.

The population of 1909-D Dimes certified by PCGS and NGC is fairly well distributed, and Gems in MS-65 are not much rarer than lower-grade examples in, say, MS-63 or MS-64. For this reason I believe that most Mint State 1909-D Dimes that have survived did so as part of numismatic collections and not as part of bank reserves or some other kind of financial medium. In MS-66 the 1909-D is very rare, nonetheless, and in MS-67 it is all but unknown.

**Strike:** The 1909-D usually comes well struck with overall bold, if not sharp definition. Nevertheless, there is often a touch of softness to the detail at the top of Liberty's portrait on the obverse as well as on the reverse at the upper and/or lower-right portion of the wreath.

**Luster:** Luster for this issue is usually frosty, less often satiny, and it is almost always high in quality.

**Surfaces:** Perhaps surprisingly for an issue that is so rare in Mint State, the 1909-D is seldom encountered with sizeable or otherwise individually distracting abrasions. You should expect to see at least a couple of wispy marks on a Mint State '09-D Dime, however, and these are just as likely to be present in MS-65 as they are in MS-64.

**Toning:** Most Mint State examples are very attractive in this area, their surfaces either richly patinated throughout, peripherally toned or fully brilliant. Colors tend to be moderate or light, and it is not often that I have encountered a darkly toned piece in the market.

**Eye Appeal:** This is an attractive issue that was both well made and carefully preserved over the years. Your only impediment to locating an attractive Mint State piece, in fact, should be the paucity of such survivors in numismatic circles.

**Significant Examples:**

**1. NGC MS-67.** *Ex: Denver ANA Signature Sale (Heritage, 8/1996), lot 6987, where it realized $5,775; Long Beach Signature Sale (Heritage, 9/2003), lot 6460, where it realized $6,900; The Phelan Collection (Bowers and Merena, 7/2008), lot 475, unsold.*

**2. PCGS MS-66.** *Ex: CSNS Signature Coin Auction (Heritage, 4/2008), lot 632, where it realized $6,325.*

**3. PCGS MS-66.** *Ex: The John C. Hugon Collection (Heritage, 1/2005), lot 4055, where it realized $6,900.*

**4. PCGS MS-66.** *Ex: Chicago 1991 Sale (RARCOA and David W. Akers, 8/1991), lot 309, where it realized $3,850; The Bay Area Collection (Heritage, 3/2003), lot 5580, where it realized $14,950.*

**Total Known in Mint State:** 105-125 Coins

### Total Known and Value Breakdown by Grade:

| MS-60 to MS-62 | MS-63 ~ | MS-64 | MS-65 |
|---|---|---|---|
| 20-25 Coins | 15-20 Coins | 30-35 Coins | 30-35 Coins |
| N/A | $700-$900 | $1,250-$1,500 | $2,500-$3,500 |

| MS-66 | MS-67 | MS-68 | MS-69 to MS-70 |
|---|---|---|---|
| 8-10 Coins | 1 Coin | 0 Coins | 0 Coins |
| $5,000-$15,000 | $7,500-$10,000 | -- | -- |

*Note:* The conclusions presented in the following "Collecting and Investing Strategies" section are drawn in large part from the Investment Potential Ratios that are summarized in Appendices G and H at the end of this book. For a detailed analysis of the formula used to derive these Investment Potential Ratios, please refer to the Introduction of this book.

**Collecting and Investing Strategies:** One of the "magic dates" in the Barber Dime series, the 1909-D also attracts the attention of more generalized numismatists because of its status as low-mintage silver coin from the 20th century. This issue is certainly underrated in MS-64, but MS-65s and MS-66s are just valued too high in relation to their actual rarity. The lone MS-67 known to NGC represents an excellent value in the $7,500-$10,000 range. As a Superb Gem, in fact, the 1909-D is tied with the 1903 and 1903-O as the most underrated Barber Dime after only the 1907.

# 1909-O

**MINTAGE**
2,287,000

Courtesy of David Lawrence

**RARITY RANKINGS**

*Overall, Mint State: 28th of 74*
*High Grade, MS-65 or Finer: 30th of 74 (Tie)*

## NEW ORLEANS MINT ISSUES

*Overall, Mint State: 11th of 17*
*High Grade, MS-65 or Finer: 12th of 17*

**Important Varieties:** None.

**General Comments:** The 1909-O is the final Dime struck in the New Orleans Mint, the facility having ceased coinage operations by the end of that year. Despite a mintage that is nearly twice as large, the 1909-O is rarer than the 1908-O from both overall and high-grade standpoints. It is also rarer than the 1893-O in an absolute sense, as well as the 1892-O, 1905-O, 1906-O and 1907-O in all Mint State grades. The 1909-O is more elusive than the low-mintage 1895, 1913-S and 1915-S in terms of total number of Mint State coins known to exist, and it compares favorably with the 1904, 1906-D, 1908-S and 1915-S in high-grade rarity.

**Strike:** The difficulty of locating a well-struck example of the 1909-O Barber Dime has been overstated in the past. Most examples are no more softly defined than other poorly struck New Orleans Mint Barber Dimes, and the 1909-O is actually better produced than the 1898-O. Still, you will seldom encounter a truly sharply struck 1909-O as the typical example will be a bit blunt on the obverse at the top of Liberty's portrait and on the reverse over the upper and lower-right portions of the wreath.

**Luster:** The 1909-O has above-average luster for a New Orleans Mint issue of this type, and most Mint State examples that I have handled are actually quite vibrant. Expect to see a satiny finish, although a few pieces do have more of a softly frosted texture.

**Surfaces:** You are just as likely to encounter a noticeably abraded 1909-O Dime in the market as an overall smooth-looking example. Abrasions, when present, are usually small in size, although some lower-end pieces are marred by detracting slidemarks on the obverse over Liberty's cheek and/or neck.

**Toning:** A richly toned 1909-O is a rare coin, as most examples are either fully brilliant or more lightly patinated. Additionally, many of the coins that do display deeper colors tend to be peripherally toned, their centers retaining partial-to-full brilliance.

**Eye Appeal:** While the 1909-O is not as easy to locate with strong eye appeal as the 1908-O, the issue is still above average in this regard. Luster and surface preservation are particularly strong attributes, and the strike is usually not all that bad by New Orleans Mint standards.

### Significant Examples:

**1. PCGS MS-67.** *Ex: The John C. Hugon Collection (Heritage, 1/2005), lot 4056, where it realized $13,800.*

**2. NGC MS-67.** *Ex: The Cabinet of Lucien M. LaRiviere (Bowers and Merena, 3/2001), lot 1556, where it realized $2,300.*

**3. PCGS MS-67.** *Ex: The Time Capsule Collection (Bowers and Merena, 11/1998), lot 1417, where it realized $12,075.*

**Total Known in Mint State:** 120-145 Coins

**Total Known and Value Breakdown by Grade:**

| MS-60 to MS-62 | MS-63 | MS-64 | MS-65 |
|---|---|---|---|
| 25-30 Coins | 30-35 Coins | 30-35 Coins | 20-25 Coins |
| N/A | $350-$550 | $1,000-$1,250 | $1,500-$2,000 |

| MS-66 | MS-67 | MS-68 | MS-69 to MS-70 |
|---|---|---|---|
| 10-15 Coins | 3-4 Coins | 0 Coins | 0 Coins |
| $3,500-$6,500 | $5,000-$15,000 | -- | -- |

*Note:* The conclusions presented in the following "Collecting and Investing Strategies" section are drawn in large part from the Investment Potential Ratios that are summarized in Appendices G and H at the end of this book. For a detailed analysis of the formula used to derive these Investment Potential Ratios, please refer to the Introduction of this book.

**Collecting and Investing Strategies:** This is a solidly underrated issue in MS-64 and MS-65, the two grade levels at which I believe the 1909-O deserves the most serious consideration among numismatic collectors and investors. On the other hand, the 1909-O should be avoided in MS-66 and MS-67 as the issue is a bit overrated in those grades.

Do not be taken in by auction catalog descriptions or other numismatic marketing pieces that are touting a specific 1909-O as having an exceptional strike for the issue. As previously stated, many Mint State examples are overall boldly defined, and the lack of detail that is present is usually not all that distracting to the eye.

# 1909-S

**MINTAGE**
1,000,000

Courtesy of David Lawrence

**RARITY
RANKINGS**

*Overall, Mint State:* 12th of 74 (Tie)
*High Grade, MS-65 or Finer:* 12th of 74 (Tie)

## SAN FRANCISCO MINT ISSUES

*Overall, Mint State:* 5th of 24 (Tie)
*High Grade, MS-65 or Finer:* 7th of 24 (Tie)

**Important Varieties:** None.

**General Comments:** Another low-mintage, heavily circulated Barber Dime from the early 20th century, the 1909-S is a highly elusive issue in all Mint State grades. The 1909-S is similar in overall rarity in Mint State to the 1896-S, 1901-O and 1907-D. It even ranks ahead of the highly regarded 1895-S, 1897-O and 1909-D, as well as the lower-mintage 1904-S, 1913-S and 1915-S, in this regard. In fact, the 1909-S is tied with the 1896-S as the fifth-rarest San Francisco Mint Barber Dime.

In terms of high-grade rarity, the 1909-S vies with the 1899-S and 1901-S as the seventh-rarest issue in this mintmarked series. The only S-mint issues of the type that are more elusive than the 1909-S in Gem Mint State are the 1892-S, 1895-S, 1897-S, 1904-S and 1907-S. Barber Dimes from other Mints that compare favorably with the 1909-S in high-grade rarity are the 1898-O, 1899-O and 1910-D.

Several of the Gem 1909-S Barber Dimes that I have seen possess similar toning, an observation that suggests that a small number of high-quality examples were kept intact for many years before being dispersed into the numismatic market. Exactly when this dispersal took place is unknown, but it almost certainly occurred sometime during the mid-to-late 20th century.

**Strike:** The 1909-S is one of the more softly struck S-mint Barber Dimes, but to describe the typical example as poorly struck would be doing the issue a great injustice. Most examples actually present as overall boldly defined, although you should expect to see minor lack of detail in a few isolated areas. The top of Liberty's portrait is usually the feature that is most significantly affected by softness of strike, but lack of detail can also be present on the reverse at the top of the wreath and/or over and around the right (facing) bow of the ribbon knot.

**Luster:** Luster for this issue is adequate, not excellent, and it can either be satiny or softly frosted in texture. In my experience, the satiny pieces are a bit easier to obtain.

**Surfaces:** Most of the Mint State 1909-S Barber Dimes that have survived have done so without acquiring a significant number of abrasions. The typical piece that is offered in the market is apt to be overall smooth, and the abrasions that are usually associated with this issue tend to be small in size and singularly inconspicuous.

**Toning:** The 1909-S is usually offered with rich, original toning that is usually quite vivid in color. There are exceptions, of course, and I have seen completely original coins that are either lightly patinated or brilliant. Of course, there are also a few dipped pieces among the Mint State examples that have been certified by PCGS and NGC.

**Eye Appeal:** Overall eye appeal for this issue is still above average despite the fact that the strike is apt to be a trifle soft here and there. The luster on many examples could also be more vibrant by San Francisco Mint standards.

**Significant Examples:**

**1. PCGS MS-66.** *Ex: California Sale (Ira & Larry Goldberg, 10/2000), lot 1646, where it realized $4,140; The Belle Glade Collection (Heritage, 8/2007), lot 1634, where it realized $24,150.*

**2. PCGS MS-66.** *Ex: The John C. Hugon Collection (Heritage, 1/2005), lot 4057, where it realized $12,075.*

**3. NGC MS-66.** *Ex: Elite Coin Auction (Superior, 1/2003), lot 470, where it realized $3,163.*

**4. PCGS MS-66.** *Ex: Albert F. Holden, who obtained the coin directly from the San Francisco Mint in 1909; The Norweb Collection (Bowers and Merena, 10/1987), lot 629; Long Beach Signature Sale (Heritage, 10/1994), lot 5244, where it realized $3,080.*

**5. NGC MS-65.** *Ex: Baltimore Rarities Sale (Bowers and Merena, 7/2008), lot 476, unsold; The Southwest Collection (Heritage, 2/2008), lot 194, where it realized $2,300.*

**6. NGC MS-65.** *Ex: Baltimore Auction (Heritage, 6/2008), lot 644, where it realized $2,300.*

**7. PCGS MS-65.** *Ex: CSNS Signature Coin Auction (Heritage, 4/2008), lot 633, where it realized $2,760.*

**8. NGC MS-65.** *Ex: Orlando Rarities Sale (Bowers and Merena, 1/1997), lot 101, unsold; The Frog Run Farm Collection (American Numismatic Rarities, 11/2004), lot 689, where it realized $2,185.*

**9. NGC MS-65.** *Ex: Long Beach Signature Sale (Heritage, 2/2003), lot 6359, where it realized $1,495.*

**10. PCGS MS-65.** *Ex: The ANA Sale of the Millennium (Bowers and Merena, 8/2000), lot 1173, where it realized $1,610; The Benson Collection (Ira & Larry Goldberg, 2/2002), lot 598, where it realized $2,415.*

**Total Known in Mint State:** 80-95 Coins

**Total Known and Value Breakdown by Grade:**

| MS-60 to MS-62 | MS-63 | MS-64 | MS-65 |
|---|---|---|---|
| 15-20 Coins | 15-20 Coins | 25-30 Coins | 10-12 Coins |
| N/A | $800-$1,200 | $1,450-$1,600 | $2,250-$3,000 |

| MS-66 | MS-67 | MS-68 | MS-69 to MS-70 |
|---|---|---|---|
| 10-12 Coins | 0 Coins | 0 Coins | 0 Coins |
| $5,000-$15,000 | -- | -- | -- |

*Note*: The conclusions presented in the following "Collecting and Investing Strategies" section are drawn in large part from the Investment Potential Ratios that are summarized in Appendices G and H at the end of this book. For a detailed analysis of the formula used to derive these Investment Potential Ratios, please refer to the Introduction of this book.

**Collecting and Investing Strategies:** Collectors of high-quality Barber Dimes should focus on the MS-64 and MS-65 grade levels for the 1909-S. This issue is decidedly underrated in those grades. MS-66s, on the other hand, are overvalued in light of their true rarity.

Pay special attention to the strike when searching for a 1909-S Barber Dime in MS-64 or MS-65. Try to acquire a coin with above-average definition, particularly on the obverse at the top of Liberty's portrait. Do not be obsessed with finding a coin that is 100% fully struck or else you will probably never make a purchase. I personally like those coins that possess richly original toning, although the more lightly patinated examples also tend to be very attractive.

# Proof
# 1910

## MINTAGE
551

Courtesy of David Lawrence

## RARITY RANKINGS

*Overall, All Proof Grades:* 6th of 25
*High Grade, Proof-65 or Finer:* 10th of 25
*Overall, Cameo Finish:* 12th of 24
*Overall, Deep/Ultra Cameo Finish:* 1st of 12 (Tie)

**Important Varieties:** None.

**General Comments:** At just 551 pieces produced, the 1910 boasts one of the most limited press runs for a proof coin of this type. This issue is one of the rarest in the proof Barber Dime series, ranking behind only the 1894-S, 1907, 1908, 1914 and 1915. The proof 1910 is not as favorably disposed when we consider only the extant population in high grades, but it is still in the top ten in that category. In fact, the proof 1910 is only marginally less rare than the proof 1904 and proof 1908 in high grades, and it handily outdistances all of the 1890s issues in this series (except, of course, the 1894-S) in the finest proof grades.

The 1910 is a median rarity in the proof Barber Dime series with a Cameo finish, ranking ahead of all of the 1890s issues save for the 1894-S, as well as the 1900, 1901, 1905 and 1911. Along with the 1894, 1906 and 1911, the 1910 is the rarest collectible proof Barber Dime with a Deep/Ultra Cameo finish.

**Strike:** Strike for the proof 1910 ranges from razor sharp to full.

**Finish:** This issue is usually encountered with an all-brilliant finish that includes only minimal field-to-device contrast. Specimens certified as Cameo at PCGS and NGC are only really cameos on the reverse, but they have secured that designation because they possess above-average contrast for an example of this issue. PCGS has graded a single example with a Deep Cameo finish (December/2008), however, and that coin possesses remarkable field-to-device contrast on both sides.

**Surfaces:** The typical proof 1910 is either moderately hairlined or overall smooth. There are also a fair number of virtually pristine specimens in numismatic circles, but the 1910 is not as easy to locate at that level of preservation as most of the preceding proof issues in the Barber Dime series.

**Toning:** Most specimens that I have seen are toned to one degree or another, and the patination is often quite deep with more vivid undertones that are only readily evident as the coin dips into a light. Dipped pieces tend to be very vibrant and free of detracting haziness to the surfaces.

**Eye Appeal:** Overall eye appeal for the proof 1910 is quite strong, and there are many attractive specimens irrespective of finish or manner of toning.

**Significant Examples:**

**1. NGC Proof-68.** *Ex: FUN Signature Coin Auction (Heritage, 1/2007), lot 2692, unsold; St. Louis Rarities Sale (Bowers and Merena, 5/2007), lot 50, where it realized $4,830; Dallas, TX U.S. Coin Signature Auction (Heritage, 11/2007), lot 452, where it realized $5,750.*

**2. NGC Proof-68.** *Ex: Orlando Rarities Sale (Bowers and Merena, 1/1997), lot 102, where it realized $4,400.*

**3. NGC Proof-68 Cameo.** *Ex: C.F. Childs, who is believed to have purchased the coin directly from the Philadelphia Mint in 1910; The Walter H. Childs Collection (Bowers and Merena, 8/1999), lot 229, $8,625; The John C. Hugon Collection (Heritage, 1/2005), lot 4094, where it realized $7,763.*

**4. PCGS Proof-67 Cameo.** *Ex: Long Beach Signature Auction (Heritage, 5/2006), lot 1148, where it realized $4,600; Long Beach, CA Signature Coin Auction (Heritage, 5/2008), lot 164, where it realized $4,888.*

**5. NGC Proof-67 Cameo.** *Ex: Phoenix, AZ ANA Signature Auction (Heritage, 5/2008), lot 432, where it realized $4,025.*

**6. NGC Proof-67 Cameo.** *Ex: The J.B. Worthington Collection (American Numismatic Rarities, 5/2005), lot 187, where it realized $2,530.*

**7. PCGS Proof-66 Cameo.** *Ex: Milwaukee, WI ANA Signature Coin Auction (Heritage, 8/2007), lot 602, where it realized $2,530.*

**8. PCGS Proof-66 Cameo.** *Ex: Dallas Signature Auction (Heritage, 12/2005), lot 510, where it realized $2,300.*

**9. PCGS Proof-66 Cameo.** *Ex: The Official Auction of the ANA Las Vegas Coin Show (Bowers and Merena, 10/2005), lot 5423, where it realized $2,070.*

**10. PCGS Proof-66 Deep Cameo.** *Ex: The Bruce Scher #1 All-Time PCGS Registry Set (Heritage, 2/2005), lot 4070, where it realized $4,600.*

**Total Known:** 285-340 Coins

**Total Known and Value Breakdown by Grade:**

| Brilliant-Finish Coins | | | |
|---|---|---|---|
| **Proof-60-62** | **Proof-63** | **Proof-64** | **Proof-65** |
| 20-25 Coins | 45-55 Coins | 85-95 Coins | 55-65 Coins |
| N/A | $425-$500 | $650-$800 | $1,000-$1,500 |
| **Proof-66** | **Proof-67** | **Proof-68** | **Proof-69-70** |
| 25-30 Coins | 15-20 Coins | 4-6 Coins | 0 Coins |
| $2,000-$3,500 | $4,000-$5,000 | $5,500-$8,500 | -- |

| Cameo Coins | | | |
|---|---|---|---|
| **Proof-60-62 Cameo** | **Proof-63 Cameo** | **Proof-64 Cameo** | **Proof-65 Cameo** |
| 1 Coin | 6-8 Coins | 10-12 Coins | 7-9 Coins |
| N/A | $575-$750 | $1,000-$1,200 | $1,750-$2,250 |
| **Proof-66 Cameo** | **Proof-67 Cameo** | **Proof-68 Cameo** | **Proof-69-70 Cameo** |
| 5-7 Coins | 4-5 Coins | 3-4 Coins | 0 Coins |
| $2,500-$3,500 | $4,000-$5,000 | $8,500-$15,000 | -- |

| Deep/Ultra Cameo Coins | | | |
|---|---|---|---|
| **Proof-60-62 Deep/ Ultra Cameo** | **Proof-63 Deep/ Ultra Cameo** | **Proof-64 Deep/ Ultra Cameo** | **Proof-65 Deep/ Ultra Cameo** |
| 0 Coins | 0 Coins | 0 Coins | 0 Coins |
| -- | -- | -- | -- |
| **Proof-66 Deep/ Ultra Cameo** | **Proof-67 Deep/ Ultra Cameo** | **Proof-68 Deep/ Ultra Cameo** | **Proof-69-70 Deep/ Ultra Cameo** |
| 1 Coin | 0 Coins | 0 Coins | 0 Coins |
| $5,000-$10,000 | -- | -- | -- |

*Note:* The conclusions presented in the following "Collecting and Investing Strategies" section are drawn in large part from the Investment Potential Ratios that are summarized in Appendices G and H at the end of this book. For a detailed analysis of the formula used to derive these Investment Potential Ratios, please refer to the Introduction of this book.

**Collecting and Investing Strategies:** The 1910 should be a safe purchase in all grades from Proof-64 through Proof-66. The issue is underrated in Proof-64 and Proof-66, and fairly accurately priced in Proof-65 and Proof-67. With a limited mintage to boot, the 1910 is certainly among the more desirable Barber Dimes for better-date proof type purposes.

# 1910

## MINTAGE
11,520,000

Courtesy of Bowers and Merena

## RARITY RANKINGS

*Overall, Mint State: 67th of 74*
*High Grade, MS-65 or Finer: 67th of 74*

### PHILADELPHIA MINT ISSUES

*Overall, Mint State: 18th of 25*
*High Grade, MS-65 or Finer: 18th of 25*

**Important Varieties:** None.

**General Comments:** The 1910 is among the most common Barber Dimes in Mint State, ranking behind all of the mintmarked issues of the type from both absolute and high-grade standpoints. Most P-mint Barber Dimes are also rarer than the 1910, but this issue is more challenging to locate in all Mint State grades than the 1892, 1898, 1911, 1912, 1913, 1914 and 1916. The 1910 is not all that difficult to locate even in MS-66, although such coins are genuinely scarce when viewed in the wider context of the numismatic market. Superb Gems in MS-67 are very rare in an absolute sense, and the 1910 is all but unobtainable in MS-68.

**Strike:** The 1910 almost always displays sharp striking detail to both the obverse and the reverse. Lack of detail, when present at all, is apt to be light and confined to the portion of the wreath that is closest to the upper-reverse border.

**Luster:** This issue has very good, if not excellent luster. Softly frosted surfaces are the norm for the 1910, although I have seen a few Mint State pieces with more of a satiny texture.

**Surfaces:** Scattered abrasions are almost always present on examples of this issue, and this even includes many coins that have been certified as MS-65 by PCGS and NGC. Abrasions range from small to moderate in size. This issue is surprisingly difficult to locate with overall smooth-looking surfaces for a high-mintage, late-date Barber Dime from the Philadelphia Mint.

**Toning:** Mint State examples range from fully brilliant to richly toned, but the typical example will possess either untoned surfaces or only light patination. Toning for this issue tends to be iridescent or light, a fact that confirms the 1910 as one of the more attractive Barber Dimes in this category.

**Eye Appeal:** The 1910 has very good, but not excellent eye appeal, the limitation in my assessment stemming solely from the paucity of minimally abraded examples among the Mint State survivors.

**Significant Examples:**

1. **NGC MS-67.** *Ex: The Phelan Collection (Bowers and Merena, 7/2008), lot 477, unsold; The Phelan Collection (Bowers and Merena, 11/2008), lot 1925, where it realized $1,440.*

2. **PCGS MS-67.** *Ex: The Collection of Dr. Steven L. Duckor (Heritage, 1/2006), lot 1025, where it realized $4,313.*

3. **PCGS MS-67.** *Ex: Orlando Rarities Sale (Bowers and Merena, 1/2003), lot 228, unsold; The John C. Hugon Collection (Heritage, 1/2005), lot 4058, where it realized $7,188; The Official Auction of the ANA Las Vegas Coin Show (Bowers and Merena, 10/2005), lot 5424, where it realized $4,485.*

4. **NGC MS-67 ★.** *Ex: San Francisco, CA ANA Signature Auction (Heritage, 7/2005), lot 5903, where it realized $2,760.*

5. **PCGS MS-67.** *Ex: Long Beach Signature Sale (Heritage, 9/2002), lot 6291, where it realized $3,105; Charlotte ANA National Money Signature Sale (Heritage, 5581), where it realized $2,703; Baltimore, MD Signature Sale (Heritage, 7/2003), lot 6623, where it realized $3,335.*

**Total Known in Mint State:** 560-695 Coins

**Total Known and Value Breakdown by Grade:**

| MS-60 to MS-62 | MS-63 | MS-64 | MS-65 |
|---|---|---|---|
| 100-125 Coins | 135-160 Coins | 190-240 Coins | 95-115 Coins |
| N/A | $125-$175 | $250-$350 | $475-$575 |

**Total Known and Value Breakdown by Grade (cont.):**

| MS-66 | MS-67 | MS-68 | MS-69 to MS-70 |
|---|---|---|---|
| 30-40 Coins | 10-12 Coins | 1 Coin | 0 Coins |
| $750-$850 | $3,000-$8,000 | $15,000-$25,000 | -- |

*Note:* The conclusions presented in the following "Collecting and Investing Strategies" section are drawn in large part from the Investment Potential Ratios that are summarized in Appendices G and H at the end of this book. For a detailed analysis of the formula used to derive these Investment Potential Ratios, please refer to the Introduction of this book.

**Collecting and Investing Strategies:** The 1910 is valued fairly close to the mean in MS-64 and MS-65, which means that such coins are fairly accurately priced at the levels provided in this book. MS-66s are more underrated and, as such, they offer the best investment opportunities for this issue in Mint State. This issue is overrated in MS-67.

Several 1910 Barber Dimes in PCGS and NGC MS-65 holders that I have seen exhibit noticeable abrasions such as reeding marks or even light slidemarks. These are sometimes even present in prime focal areas including Liberty's neck or cheek on the obverse. An MS-65 should not have a sizeable, outwardly distracting abrasion such as this, particularly in a prime focal area and on a coin of this size. Be sure to carefully evaluate all high-grade 1910 Barber Dimes that you encounter and make sure that the coin is accurately graded before including it among your numismatic holdings.

# 1910-D

### MINTAGE
3,490,000

Courtesy of David Lawrence

### RARITY RANKINGS

*Overall, Mint State:* 22nd of 74 (Tie)
*High Grade, MS-65 or Finer:* 12th of 74 (Tie)

## DENVER MINT ISSUES

*Overall, Mint State:* 3rd of 8
*High Grade, MS-65 or Finer:* 1st of 8

**Important Varieties:** None.

**General Comments:** The 1910-D is an overlooked issue that is actually among the rarest Barber Dimes from the Denver Mint. In terms of total number of Mint State coins believed to exist, in fact, only the 1907-D and 1909-D from this coinage facility are more challenging to locate than the 1910-D. This issue is similar in overall rarity to the 1892-S.

In high grades, the 1910-D is the rarest Denver Mint Barber Dime, and it compares favorably to the 1898-O, 1899-O and 1899-S, as well as the low-mintage 1901-S and 1909-S, in this regard. Even low-grade Mint State 1910-D Dimes through MS-64 are very scarce coins, while any example that grades MS-65 or finer must be regarded as a rare piece.

**Strike:** Strike varies considerably for this issue and, as a whole, the 1910-D is not as poorly struck as some numismatic writers have claimed in the past. True, there are plenty of Mint State examples with soft striking detail on the obverse at the top of Liberty's portrait and/or along the entire hairline down to the ear. The reverse impression is also sometimes uneven with lack of definition over the upper-left or upper-right portions of the wreath and/or in the lower-right area of the same device. On the other hand, I have also seen quite a few Mint State pieces that are sharply struck throughout and free of bothersome lack of detail.

**Luster:** This issue has inferior luster that almost always exhibits a subdued, satiny texture.

**Surfaces:** The 1910-D is also a heavily abraded issue, the typical Mint State survivor displaying significant handling marks on both the obverse and the reverse. Abrasions tend to be small in size, but they are usually plentiful and can be particularly distracting on the obverse over and around Liberty's portrait.

**Toning:** Mint State examples tend to come either brilliant or moderately-to-deeply toned with few coins occupying the middle ground between these two extremes. Toning for this issue is rarely, if ever, vivid in color, and sometimes it is also quite mottled in distribution.

**Eye Appeal:** Overall eye appeal for the 1910-D is well below average, and there are very few Mint State examples that, on their own, would merit even an average rating in this category.

**Significant Examples:**

**1. PCGS MS-67.** *Ex: The Collection of Dr. Steven L. Duckor (Heritage, 1/2006), lot 1026, where it realized $16,100.*

**2. NGC MS-67.** *Ex: The John C. Hugon Collection (Heritage, 1/2005), lot 4059, where it realized $5,175.*

**3. PCGS MS-66.** *Ex: CSNS Signature Auction (Heritage, 5/2005), lot 6671, where it realized $1,840.*

**4. NGC MS-66.** *Ex: FUN Signature Sale (Heritage, 1/2004), lot 5681, unsold.*

**5. NGC MS-66.** *Ex: Chicago 1991 Sale (RARCOA and David W. Akers, 8/1991), lot 311, where it realized $2,860; Bay Area Collection (Heritage, 3/2003), lot 5582, where it realized $1,380.*

**6. PCGS MS-66.** *Ex: Anaheim ANA Sale (Heritage, 8/1995), lot 6052, where it realized $2,970; CSNS Signature Sale (Heritage, 4/2002), lot 5498, where it realized $1,208; Long Beach Signature Sale (Heritage, 9/2002), lot 6292, where it realized $1,553.*

**7. NGC MS-66.** *Ex: Chicago ANA Signature Sale (Heritage, 8/1999), lot 6873, where it realized $949.*

**8. NGC MS-65.** *Ex: The Southwest Collection (Heritage, 2/2008), lot 196, where it realized $1,610.*

**9. PCGS MS-65.** *Ex: Palm Beach, FL Signature Auction (Heritage, 3/2006), lot 490, where it realized $2,530.*

**10. NGC MS-65.** *Ex: Dallas, TX Signature Auction (Heritage, 11/2005), lot 1038, where it realized $978.*

**11. NGC MS-65.** *Ex: Long Beach Signature Sale (Heritage, 6/2000), lot 7185, where it realized $921.*

**12. PCGS MS-65.** *Ex: The Louis E. Eliasberg, Sr. Collection (Bowers and Merena, 5/1996), lot 1301, where it realized $715; The Boyd E. Hayward, M.D. Collection (Bowers and Merena, 9/1997), lot 610, where it realized $1,320.*

**Total Known in Mint State:** 105-135 Coins

**Total Known and Value Breakdown by Grade:**

| MS-60 to MS-62 | MS-63 | MS-64 | MS-65 |
|---|---|---|---|
| 20-25 Coins | 30-40 Coins | 35-45 Coins | 10-12 Coins |
| N/A | $325-$400 | $450-$650 | $1,250-$1,750 |

| MS-66 | MS-67 | MS-68 | MS-69 to MS-70 |
|---|---|---|---|
| 7-9 Coins | 2-3 Coins | 0 Coins | 0 Coins |
| $2,000-$3,000 | $6,000-$17,500 | -- | -- |

*Note:* The conclusions presented in the following "Collecting and Investing Strategies" section are drawn in large part from the Investment Potential Ratios that are summarized in Appendices G and H at the end of this book. For a detailed analysis of the formula used to derive these Investment Potential Ratios, please refer to the Introduction of this book.

**Collecting and Investing Strategies:** The 1910-D is the most underrated Denver Mint Barber Dime in MS-64, MS-65 and MS-66. Since this issue is also one of the more underrated coins of the type in those grades, I see real potential for the 1910-D to increase in value. The one exception to this conclusion in the finer Mint State grades comes at the MS-67 level, where the 1910-D is actually a somewhat overrated Barber Dime.

Despite its obvious potential in the MS-64 to MS-66 grade range, the 1910-D is one of the most consistently unattractive issues in the entire Barber Dime series—a fact that is not widely known throughout the general collecting and investing communities. Expect most 1Mint State examples to have below-average luster. The toning, if there is any, is also apt to be more-or-less deep in color and not especially vibrant. On the other hand, you can be selective in the areas of strike and, for a coin that grades MS-65 or MS-66, surface preservation. Try to find one of the more sharply struck examples, and insist on a lack of individually distracting abrasions for a coin that grades MS-65 or finer.

# 1910-S

**MINTAGE**
1,240,000

Courtesy of David Lawrence

**RARITY RANKINGS**

*Overall, Mint State: 17th of 74*
*High Grade, MS-65 or Finer: 28th of 74*

### SAN FRANCISCO MINT ISSUES

*Overall, Mint State: 8th of 24*
*High Grade, MS-65 or Finer: 14th of 24*

**Important Varieties:** None.

**General Comments:** The original mintage of the 1910-S is not much greater than that of the 1909-S, and it is also a leading condition rarity in the San Francisco Mint Barber Dime series. In terms of total number of Mint State coins believed to exist, the 1910-S ranks ahead of such other issues as the 1892-S, 1895-S, 1904-S, 1913-S and 1915-S. Issues form other Mints that cannot compare with the 1910-S in this regard include the 1897-O, 1909-D and 1895.

The 1910-S is not ranked as high when we consider only those coins extant in MS-65 and finer grades, but it is still rarer as a Gem than the 1905-S, 1908-S, 1913-S and 1915-S, to name just a few other S-mint Barber Dimes. The 1910-S is also rarer in high grades than the 1896, 1906-D and 1909-O, among numerous other issues in this series.

**Strike:** This is a well-produced issue, and the vast majority of Mint State survivors exhibit sharp striking detail to all elements of the design. On the few exceptions, there is only a touch of softness to the strike over those elements of the wreath that are closest to the upper-reverse border.

**Luster:** As an issue, the 1910-S possesses excellent, satin-to-softly frosted luster. There is, nonetheless, a single example certified as MS-64 Prooflike on the NGC Census (Decemebr/2008).

**Surfaces:** Abrasions are not a significant problem for this issue, and chances are good that if you can locate a Mint State coin it will possess overall smooth surfaces. Those abrasions that I have seen on examples of this issue tend to be small in size and not overly distracting to the naked eye.

**Toning:** While there are a few brilliant examples known to exist, the typical 1910-S Barber Dime is toned in light-to-deep patination. Colors tend to be either soft or quite vivid and, as a rule, an originally toned '10-S Dime is an attractive coin.

**Eye Appeal:** This issue tends to come "nice," and the overall eye appeal is usually very strong.

**Significant Examples:**

**1. PCGS MS-67.** *Ex: Long Beach, CA Signature Coin Auction (Heritage, 2/2007), lot 2951, where it realized $20,700.*

**2. NGC MS-67.** *Ex: Chicago Rarities Sale (Bowers and Merena, 8/1999), lot 123; The Bradley Bloch Collection (Ira & Larry Goldberg, 9/1999), lot 1205, where it realized $2,990; The Dr. Jon Kardatzke Collection (Ira & Larry Goldberg, 2/2000), lot 656, where it realized $1,025.*

**3. PCGS MS-66.** *Ex: Summer FUN Signature Coin Auction (Heritage, 7/2007), lot 552, where it realized $4,025; Long Beach, CA Signature Coin Auction (Heritage, 9/2007), lot 1030, where it realized $3,968.*

**4. PCGS MS-66.** *Ex: FUN Signature Sale (Heritage, 1/1998), lot 6693, where it realized $1,323; Philadelphia 2000 Signature Sale (Heritage, 8/2000), lot 6975, where it realized $1,725; Dallas, TX Signature Coin Auction (Heritage, 4/2007), lot 559, unsold.*

**5. PCGS MS-66.** *Ex: The Haig A. Koshkarian Collection (American Numismatic Rarities, 3/2004), lot 512, where it realized $3,220; The Collection of Dr. Steven L. Duckor (Heritage, 1/2006), lot 1027, where it realized $4,600.*

**6. PCGS MS-66.** *Ex: Long Beach Signature Sale (Heritage, 9/2002), lot 6294, where it realized $2,185.*

**7. PCGS MS-66.** *Ex: The Collections of Phillip Flanagan, Dr. Robert I. Hinkley, Dr. John C. Wong and Tree Many Feathers (Bowers and Merena, 11/2001), lot 6173, unsold.*

**Total Known in Mint State:** 80-110 Coins

## Total Known and Value Breakdown by Grade:

| MS-60 to MS-62 | MS-63 | MS-64 | MS-65 |
|---|---|---|---|
| 12-15 Coins | 15-20 Coins | 25-30 Coins | 20-25 Coins |
| N/A | $525-$625 | $950-$1,100 | $1,900-$2,100 |

| MS-66 | MS-67 | MS-68 | MS-69 to MS-70 |
|---|---|---|---|
| 6-8 Coins | 3-4 Coins | 0 Coins | 0 Coins |
| $4,000-$5,000 | $8,000-$22,500 | -- | -- |

*Note:* The conclusions presented in the following "Collecting and Investing Strategies" section are drawn in large part from the Investment Potential Ratios that are summarized in Appendices G and H at the end of this book. For a detailed analysis of the formula used to derive these Investment Potential Ratios, please refer to the Introduction of this book.

**Collecting and Investing Strategies:** The 1910-S is one of the most undervalued Barber Dimes in MS-64 and MS-66, and the issue is also underrated in MS-65. MS-64s seem like a particularly good buy since the 1910-S is the most underrated Barber Dime in that grade after only the 1898-O and 1902-S. Only in MS-67 would I avoid the 1910-S, for the issue is overvalued in that grade at the prices given in this book. This issue comes nice, so your only impediment to locating an attractive Mint State example in MS-64, MS-65 or MS-66 should be your ability to pay for the coin.

# Proof
# 1911

## MINTAGE
543

Courtesy of Bowers and Merena

## RARITY RANKINGS

**Overall, All Proof Grades:** *12th of 25*
**High Grade, Proof-65 or Finer:** *14th of 25 (Tie)*
**Overall, Cameo Finish:** *16th of 24*
**Overall, Deep/Ultra Cameo Finish:** *1st of 12 (Tie)*

**Important Varieties:** None.

**General Comments:** The 1911 is only a median rarity in the proof Barber Dime series despite a relatively limited mintage of 543 pieces. In an absolute sense, the 1911 is rarer than most proof Barber Dimes from the 1890s, as well as the 1900, 1901, 1904, 1905 and 1909. In high grades, the 1911 is similar in rarity to the 1914 and more challenging to locate than the 1905, 1909 and all proofs from the 1890s with the obvious exception of the 1894-S.

By proof Barber Dime standards, the 1911 is a relatively plentiful issue as a Cameo, but it is still rarer with that finish than the 1892, 1895 and 1900, to name just a few other proofs of this type. The 1910 vies with the 1894, 1906 and 1910 as the rarest collectible proof Barber Dime with a Deep/Ultra Cameo finish.

**Strike:** This is a sharply struck issue, and most examples even possess full definition to the devices.

**Finish:** The vast majority of proof 1911 Dimes display little, if any field-to-device contrast, particularly on the obverse. Even on such examples the reverse is still apt to possess modest contrast, but few examples possess enough of a satin texture over the devices to secure a Cameo designation from PCGS or NGC.

**Surfaces:** The proof 1911 typically displays scattered hairlines and other small contact marks, although the issue is really not all that challenging to locate with overall smooth-looking surfaces.

**Toning:** This issue is available from deeply toned to fully brilliant. Examples that are toned throughout tend to be very handsome with vivid undertones that are best appreciated when the coin dips into a light. Interestingly, those pieces that display more mottled toning schemes also tend to have deeper patination that is much less vivid. Several of the all-brilliant and golden-toned pieces have been dipped.

**Eye Appeal:** As a whole, this issue has above-average-to-strong eye appeal. There are exceptions, however, and these include those coins with mottled toning as well as those dipped pieces where some of the original patina remains in the form of hazy-gold highlights.

**Significant Examples:**

**1. PCGS Proof-68.** *Ex: Long Beach Signature Sale (Heritage, 1/2004), lot 5646, where it realized $13,800; The Bruce Scher #1 All-Time PCGS Registry Set (Heritage, 2/2005), lot 4071, where it realized $17,250.*

**2. NGC Proof-68.** *Ex: Pre-Long Beach Elite Coin Auction (Superior, 5/2003), lot 2388, where it realized $12,075.*

**3. NGC Proof-68 Cameo.** *Ex: Dallas Signature Auction (Heritage, 12/2005), lot 524, where it realized $6,325.*

**4. NGC Proof-68 Cameo.** *Ex: CSNS Signature Auction (Heritage, 5/2005), lot 6722, where it realized $5,750.*

**5. NGC Proof-67 Cameo.** *Ex: Palm Beach, FL Signature Auction (Heritage, 3/2006), lot 506, where it realized $2,990.*

**6. PCGS Proof-67 Cameo.** *Ex: Dallas Signature Auction (Heritage, 12/2005), lot 511, where it realized $4,313.*

**7. NGC Proof-67 Cameo.** *Ex: Long Beach Signature Auction (Heritage, 9/2005), lot 2475, where it realized $2,760.*

**8. NGC Proof-68 Ultra Cameo.** *Ex: C.L. Lee Sale (American Numismatic Rarities, 9/2005), lot 277, where it realized $10,925.*

**Total Known:** 325-405 Coins

## Total Known and Value Breakdown by Grade:

| Brilliant-Finish Coins | | | |
|---|---|---|---|
| **Proof-60-62** | **Proof-63** | **Proof-64** | **Proof-65** |
| 25-30 Coins | 30-40 Coins | 90-110 Coins | 55-65 Coins |
| N/A | $425-$500 | $650-$800 | $1,100-$1,500 |
| **Proof-66** | **Proof-67** | **Proof-68** | **Proof-69-70** |
| 40-50 Coins | 20-25 Coins | 10-12 Coins | 1 Coin |
| $1,600-$2,000 | $3,000-$5,000 | $8,000-$25,000 | N/A |

| Cameo Coins | | | |
|---|---|---|---|
| **Proof-60-62 Cameo** | **Proof-63 Cameo** | **Proof-64 Cameo** | **Proof-65 Cameo** |
| 1 Coin | 4-5 Coins | 15-20 Coins | 12-15 Coins |
| N/A | $650-$750 | $1,000-$1,200 | $1,500-$2,000 |
| **Proof-66 Cameo** | **Proof-67 Cameo** | **Proof-68 Cameo** | **Proof-69-70 Cameo** |
| 10-12 Coins | 8-10 Coins | 4-5 Coins | 1 Coin |
| $2,000-$3,000 | $3,500-$5,000 | $8,500-$30,000 | -- |

| Deep/Ultra Cameo Coins | | | |
|---|---|---|---|
| **Proof-60-62 Deep/ Ultra Cameo** | **Proof-63 Deep/ Ultra Cameo** | **Proof-64 Deep/ Ultra Cameo** | **Proof-65 Deep/ Ultra Cameo** |
| 0 Coins | 0 Coins | 0 Coins | 0 Coins |
| -- | -- | -- | -- |
| **Proof-66 Deep/ Ultra Cameo** | **Proof-67 Deep/ Ultra Cameo** | **Proof-68 Deep/ Ultra Cameo** | **Proof-69-70 Deep/ Ultra Cameo** |
| 0 Coins | 0 Coins | 1 Coin | 0 Coins |
| -- | -- | $10,000-$15,000 | -- |

*Note:* The conclusions presented in the following "Collecting and Investing Strategies" section are drawn in large part from the Investment Potential Ratios that are summarized in Appendices G and H at the end of this book. For a detailed analysis of the formula used to derive these Investment Potential Ratios, please refer to the Introduction of this book.

**Collecting and Investing Strategies:** Valued very close to the optimum level for proof Barber Dimes, the 1911 is neither significantly underrated nor appreciably overrated in the grades that are most popular with numismatic buyers. While there is certainly no danger in adding such an issue to a type set or complete collection, I do not like the proof 1911 for investment purposes. This issue is just not likely to increase much in value in the coming years.

Avoid any proof 1911 Dime with mottled toning, as well as those pieces that have been dipped but still retain remnants of the original toning in the form of hazy-gold overtones. Examples in both categories are visually unappealing and, while you will probably be able to acquire such a piece at a discount, chances are also good that you will not realize a strong price when the time comes to sell.

# 1911

**MINTAGE**
18,870,000

Courtesy of David Lawrence

## RARITY RANKINGS

*Overall, Mint State: 72nd of 74*
*High Grade, MS-65 or Finer: 73rd of 74*

## PHILADELPHIA MINT ISSUES

*Overall, Mint State: 23rd of 25*
*High Grade, MS-65 or Finer: 24th of 25*

**Important Varieties:** None.

**General Comments:** This is obviously a common issue, and it is plentiful in all grades through MS-65. Even in MS-66 the 1911 cannot really be described as a scarce coin, and enough pieces exist in that grade that acquiring one should prove an easy task. The 1911 has one of the more generous populations of MS-67s at PCGS and NGC, but the issue is still rare at that level of preservation when viewed in the wider context of U.S numismatics. MS-68s are very rare and seldom encountered in the market.

The only Barber Dimes that are more plentiful than the 1911 in terms of total number of Mint State coins known to exist are the first-year 1892 and the final-year 1916. In high grades, only the 1892 is more common than the 1911.

**Strike:** This is a high-mintage issue with a large number of Mint State survivors, so it should come as no surprise to read that striking quality varies somewhat for the 1911. Nonetheless, the majority of examples are sharply defined on both the obverse and the reverse. When lack of detail is present, it is usually confined to the top of Liberty's portrait, the top of the reverse wreath and/or the lower-right portion of the reverse wreath.

**Luster:** Luster for this issue is almost always excellent, the typical example displaying a richly frosted finish from the dies.

**Surfaces:** While most Mint State examples are marred by grade-limiting abrasions, enough Gems are known that the 1911 is one of the easiest Barber Dimes to locate with overall smooth surfaces. Coins that approach perfection in the area of surface preservation are surprisingly rare for a late-date, high-mintage Barber Dime from the Philadelphia Mint.

**Toning:** The large number of Mint State survivors come with all manner of appearances, including richly toned, moderately patinated and fully brilliant. Toning for this issue ranges from smooth to mottled, dark to very vivid in color.

**Eye Appeal:** The 1911 has strong eye appeal, and there are many attractive examples from which to choose in most Mint State grades.

**Significant Examples:**

**1. NGC MS-68 ★.** *Ex: Long Beach Signature Auction (Heritage, 5/2006), lot 1116, where it realized $9,775.*

**2. NGC MS-68 ★.** *Ex: Pre-Long Beach Elite Coin Auction (Superior, 5/2003), lot 2389, where it realized $20,700.*

**Total Known in Mint State:** 1,135-1,360 Coins

**Total Known and Value Breakdown by Grade:**

| MS-60 to MS-62 | MS-63 | MS-64 | MS-65 |
|---|---|---|---|
| 200-250 Coins | 270-320 Coins | 360-410 Coins | 190-240 Coins |
| N/A | $125-$150 | $200-$275 | $475-$650 |

| MS-66 | MS-67 | MS-68 | MS-69 to MS-70 |
|---|---|---|---|
| 95-110 Coins | 20-25 Coins | 3-4 Coins | 0 Coins |
| $800-$950 | $2,500-$3,500 | $10,000-$20,000 | -- |

*Note:* The conclusions presented in the following "Collecting and Investing Strategies" section are drawn in large part from the Investment Potential Ratios that are summarized in Appendices G and H at the end of this book. For a detailed analysis of the formula used to derive these Investment Potential Ratios, please refer to the Introduction of this book.

**Collecting and Investing Strategies:** The 1911 is a bit overrated in the MS-64 to MS-67 grade range, but not excessively so by the standards of the Barber Dime series. Still, I would avoid this issue for any purpose other than inclusion in a complete set of Mint State Barber Dimes.

# 1911-D

## MINTAGE
11,209,000

## RARITY RANKINGS

**Overall, Mint State:** *54th of 74*
**High Grade, MS-65 or Finer:** *64th of 74*

### DENVER MINT ISSUES

**Overall, Mint State:** *6th of 8*
**High Grade, MS-65 or Finer:** *8th of 8*

**Important Varieties:** None.

**General Comments:** The 1911-D is one of the most common Denver Mint issues in the Barber Dime series, although it is not as plentiful in Mint State as such P-mint coins as the 1893, 1899, 1891 and 1909, to say nothing of the 1892, 1911 and 1916. The 1911-D is also rarer than the 1912-D, 1914-D and 1916-S in terms of total number of Mint State coins believed to exist.

In grades at and above the MS-65 level, the 1911-D is actually the most common Denver Mint issue in the Barber Dime series. The '11-D, however, is still rarer in high grades than the 1897, 1898 and 1911-S, to name just a few other issues.

**Strike:** This is a well-struck issue, and the Mint State coins that I have seen possess sharp-to-full definition throughout.

**Luster:** The 1911-D also comes with very good-to-excellent luster that is almost always of a softly frosted type.

**Surfaces:** Most Mint State examples vary in surface preservation from lightly abraded to overall smooth. Locating a truly superb coin, therefore, is not an easy task.

**Toning:** The 1911-D has a large-enough Mint State population that you should be able to find coins that run the gamut from richly toned to completely untoned. There are some really handsome examples among the toned coins, and the naturally brilliant pieces are also highly attractive with bright, radiant surfaces.

**Eye Appeal:** This is a well-produced issue with overall eye appeal that is above average, if not downright strong.

**Significant Examples:**

1. **NGC MS-67.** *Ex: Milwaukee, WI ANA Signature Coin Auction (Heritage, 8/2007), lot 586, where it realized $2,300; Long Beach, CA Signature Auction (Heritage, 5/2008), lot 137, where it realized $2,760.*

2. **NGC MS-67.** *Ex: Palm Beach, FL Signature Sale (Heritage, 11/2004), lot 6293, where it realized $5,290; Palm Beach, FL Signature Auction (Heritage, 5/2006), lot 493, where it realized $2,530; The Southwest Collection (Heritage, 2/2008), lot 202, where it realized $2,990.*

3. **PCGS MS-67.** *Ex: Long Beach, CA Signature U.S. Coin Auction (Heritage, 726, where it realized $5,175.*

4. **NGC MS-67.** *Ex: CSNS Signature Coin Auction (Heritage, 5/2007), lot 380, where it realized $2,300.*

5. **PCGS MS-67.** *Ex: The Collection of Dr. Steven L. Duckor (Heritage, 1/2006), lot 1029, where it realized $10,350.*

6. **NGC MS-67.** *Ex: Dallas Signature Sale (Heritage, 12/2004), lot 5777, where it realized $4,543.*

7. **NGC MS-67.** *Ex: Milwaukee Rarities Sale (Bowers and Merena, 5/2004), lot 141, where it realized $2,530.*

8. **NGC MS-67.** *Ex: Atlanta, GA ANA Signature Sale (Heritage, 8/2001), lot 5734, where it realized $1,725.*

9. **PCGS MS-67.** *Ex: Long Beach Signature Sale (Heritage, 2/2000), lot 5502, where it realized $2,760.*

10. **PCGS MS-67.** *Ex: ANA Signature Sale (Heritage, 8/1995), lot 6053, where it realized $3,410.*

**Total Known in Mint State:** 305-365 Coins

**Total Known and Value Breakdown by Grade:**

| MS-60 to MS-62 | MS-63 | MS-64 | MS-65 |
|---|---|---|---|
| 45-55 Coins | 50-60 Coins | 95-110 Coins | 70-80 Coins |
| N/A | $125-$175 | $250-$350 | $475-$675 |

**Total Known and Value Breakdown by Grade (cont.):**

| MS-66 | MS-67 | MS-68 | MS-69 to MS-70 |
|---|---|---|---|
| 35-45 Coins | 10-12 Coins | 0 Coins | 0 Coins |
| $850-$1,500 | $2,500-$10,000 | -- | -- |

*Note:* The conclusions presented in the following "Collecting and Investing Strategies" section are drawn in large part from the Investment Potential Ratios that are summarized in Appendices G and H at the end of this book. For a detailed analysis of the formula used to derive these Investment Potential Ratios, please refer to the Introduction of this book.

**Collecting and Investing Strategies:** In the MS-64 to MS-66 grade range, the 1911-D is an excellent mintmarked type candidate for the collector or investor that is looking for a representative of Barber Dime production in the Denver Mint. Such coins offer fairly solid value in light of the number of coins extant, although you should not expect much price appreciation for the 1911-D in these grades. In MS-67 the 1911-D is overrated and should be avoided unless you are competing for top honors on the PCGS or NGC registries in one of the Barber Dime categories.

I particularly like originally toned examples of the 1911-D, as long as they are not dark and/or splotchy in appearance. The dipped pieces tend to be a little subdued in the luster category, and some of them retain irregular splashes of toning that can be a bit distracting to the eye.

# 1911-S

## MINTAGE
3,520,000

Courtesy of David Lawrence

## RARITY RANKINGS

**Overall, Mint State:** *53rd of 74*
**High Grade, MS-65 or Finer:** *65th of 74*

### SAN FRANCISCO MINT ISSUES

**Overall, Mint State:** *23rd of 24*
**High Grade, MS-65 or Finer:** *24th of 24*

**Important Varieties:** None.

**General Comments:** The 1911-S is only marginally rarer than the 1911-D in terms of total number of Mint State coins known to exist, and it is actually the more common of the two issues in high grades. These are particularly interesting facts when we consider that the 1911-D has a mintage that is more than three times greater than that of its S-mint counterpart. Clearly, a sizeable number of 1911-S Barber Dimes must have been set aside at the time of delivery and subsequently preserved in Mint State.

The 1911-S is actually the second most common S-mint Barber Dime in Mint State after only the 1916-S, and it is the most common issue from this coinage facility in high grades. Several P-mint issues in this series are still easier to obtain than the 1911-S in all Mint State grades, among which are the 1897, 1898, 1910 and 1913. Some really spectacular 1911-S Dimes have survived in MS-67 and even MS-68, but this issue is clearly an important condition rarity as a Superb Gem.

**Strike:** The 1911-S is usually offered with a very sharp strike, and there are few exceptions to this rule. On those coins that are a bit softly struck, expect to see minor lack of detail on the obverse at the top of Liberty's portrait and/or on the reverse over the upper-right and lower-right portions of the wreath.

**Luster:** This issue typically comes with excellent luster, and I have seen examples with both satiny and softly frosted textures.

**Surfaces:** There are definitely some moderately-to-lightly abraded coins among Mint State 1911-S Dimes, but this issue is seen nearly as frequently with overall smooth-looking surfaces. Pieces that are virtually abrasion free are very rare.

**Toning:** The typical Mint State example is lightly toned or fully brilliant, although there are some richly toned coins known to exist. Color for this issue tends to be toward the deeper end of the spectrum, although it is seldom so dark that the eye appeal is impaired.

**Eye Appeal:** The 1911-S is an overall attractive issue that is extremely pretty when encountered in the finer Mint State grades.

**Significant Examples:**

**1. NGC MS-68.** *Ex: Long Beach Signature Sale (Heritage, 5/2003), lot 5796, where it realized $3,450; The James W. Lull Collection (Bowers and Merena, 1/2005), lot 675, where it realized $8,625; CSNS Signature Auction (Heritage, 5/2005), lot 6678, unsold; Dallas, TX Signature Auction (Heritage, 11/2005), lot 2076, unsold; FUN Signature Auction (Heritage, 1/2006), lot 3132, where it realized $8,050; The Southwest Collection (Heritage, 2/2008), lot 204, where it realized $9,200.*

**2. PCGS MS-67.** *Ex: The Collection of Dr. Steven L. Duckor (Heritage, 1/2006), lot 1030, where it realized $7,188.*

**3. NGC MS-67.** *Ex: Dallas, TX Signature Auction (Heritage, 11/2005), lot 1042, where it realized $2,070.*

**4. PCGS MS-67.** *Ex: Long Beach Signature Auction (Heritage, 6/2005), lot 5841, where it realized $3,450; San Francisco, CA ANA Signature Auction (Heritage, 7/2005), lot 5906, where it realized $3,450.*

**5. NGC MS-67.** *Ex: CSSN Signature Auction (Heritage, 5/2005), lot 6677, where it realized $2,530.*

**6. PCGS MS-67.** *Ex: The John C. Hugon Collection (Heritage, 1/2005), lot 4063, where it realized $3,910.*

**7. PCGS MS-67.** *Ex: CSNS Signature Sale (Heritage, 4/2002), lot 5500, where it realized $2,875.*

**8. PCGS MS-67.** *Ex: Atlanta, GA ANA Signature Sale (Heritage, 8/2001), lot 5736, where it realized $2,875.*

**Total Known in Mint State:** 290-345 Coins

**Total Known and Value Breakdown by Grade:**

| MS-60 to MS-62 | MS-63 | MS-64 | MS-65 |
|---|---|---|---|
| 55-65 Coins | 50-60 Coins | 65-75 Coins | 55-65 Coins |
| N/A | $250-$325 | $600-$750 | $800-$950 |

| MS-66 | MS-67 | MS-68 | MS-69 to MS-70 |
|---|---|---|---|
| 55-65 Coins | 10-12 Coins | 1 Coin | 0 Coins |
| $1,000-$1,500 | $2,500-$8,500 | $10,000-$12,500 | -- |

*Note:* The conclusions presented in the following "Collecting and Investing Strategies" section are drawn in large part from the Investment Potential Ratios that are summarized in Appendices G and H at the end of this book. For a detailed analysis of the formula used to derive these Investment Potential Ratios, please refer to the Introduction of this book.

**Collecting and Investing Strategies:** This is another issue that I do not recommend from the standpoint of investment potential. The collector need not fear the 1911-S in MS-64, MS-65 or MS-66 because such pieces offer fairly solid value relative to their rarity. It is just that the issue is not underrated in those grades (if anything, MS-66s are a bit overrated), and the market is unlikely to witness significant price gains for these coins over a period of even five-to-10 years. In MS-67 the 1911-S is an overrated issue that should be avoided unless you are assembling a high-ranked Registry Set of this series.

There are enough attractive 1911-S Barber Dimes in both the brilliant and toned categories that a choice between the two should be based on your personal preference. The only exceptions here are those examples on which the toning is mottled in distribution. Skip those coins as they are not among the more attractive examples of this issue in the market.

# Proof
# 1912

## MINTAGE
### 700

Courtesy of Bowers and Merena

## RARITY
## RANKINGS

***Overall, All Proof Grades:*** *7th of 25*
***High Grade, Proof-65 or Finer:*** *6th of 25 (Tie)*
***Overall, Cameo Finish:*** *9th of 24 (Tie)*
***Deep/Ultra Cameo Finish:*** *Unknown*

**Important Varieties:** None.

**General Comments:** The 1912 has one of the higher mintages in the 20th century portion of the proof Barber Dime series, but it is still among the rarest issues of its type. Many proof 1912 Dimes may have been destroyed in the Mint when they failed to sell by the end of that year, and most of those coins that have survived do not appear to have been handled with the utmost care by their previous owners.

In an absolute sense, the 1912 is rarer than even the lower-mintage 1909, 1911 and 1913, to say nothing of the common proof Barber Dimes from the 1890s. The proof 1912 is similar in high-grade rarity to the proof 1903, and it is more elusive in this regard than such other issues as the proof 1906, proof 1907 and proof 1910.

**Strike:** The proof 1912 is a carefully produced issue that almost always displays a razor sharp, if not 100% full strike.

**Finish:** This issue is hardly ever offered with a Cameo designation from PCGS or NGC. Rather, the vast majority of survivors have been struck using all-brilliant proofing techniques and display little, if any, field-to-device contrast.

**Surfaces:** This is not a well-preserved issue, and most pieces that I have encountered are marred by at least a few noticeable hairlines, contact marks or other signs of mishandling.

**Toning:** The proof 1912 is usually offered with moderate-to-heavy toning, the colors sometimes so deep and/or mottled in distribution that they can inhibit the grade, the eye appeal or both. I have not encountered all that many dipped pieces—an indication of the depth of toning that is usually associated with this issue.

**Eye Appeal:** Eye appeal for this issue is decidedly below average, and most pieces are noticeably marked, darkly toned or both. The truly attractive proof 1912 Barber Dimes that I have seen—and these have been very few in number—possess overall smooth surfaces and more colorful toning.

**Significant Examples:**

1. **NGC Proof-68.** *Ex: Atlanta, GA ANA Signature Sale (Heritage, 8/2001), lot 5753, where it realized $5,463; The J.B. Worthington Collection (American Numismatic Rarities, 5/2005), lot 189, where it realized $5,290; San Francisco, CA ANA Signature Auction (Heritage, 7/2005), lot 5928, where it realized $5,463.*

2. **NGC Proof-67.** *Ex: FUN Signature Sale (Heritage, 1/2005), lot 6221, where it realized $2,990; Dallas Signature Coin Auction (Heritage, 10/2006), lot 776, where it realized $2,990.*

3. **PCGS Proof-67 Cameo.** *Ex: The Bruce Scher #1 All-Time PCGS Registry Set (Heritage, 2/2005), lot 4072, where it realized $9,775; The Michael Casper Collection (Heritage, 1/2006), lot 314, unsold; The Michael Casper Collection (Heritage, 3/2006), lot 507, unsold; The Michael Casper Collection (Heritage, 8/2006), lot 5148, unsold; FUN Signature Coin Auction (Heritage, 1/2007), lot 2694, unsold.*

4. **PCGS Proof-67 Cameo.** *Ex: Dallas Signature Auction (Heritage, 12/2005), lot 512, where it realized $6,325.*

**Total Known:** 300-365 Coins

**Total Known and Value Breakdown by Grade:**

| Brilliant-Finish Coins | | | |
|---|---|---|---|
| **Proof-60-62** | **Proof-63** | **Proof-64** | **Proof-65** |
| 30-35 Coins | 55-65 Coins | 90-110 Coins | 55-65 Coins |
| N/A | $425-$500 | $650-$800 | $1,100-$1,500 |
| **Proof-66** | **Proof-67** | **Proof-68** | **Proof-69-70** |
| 30-40 Coins | 8-10 Coins | 1-2 Coins | 0 Coins |
| $1,600-$2,000 | $2,500-$3,500 | $5,500-$6,000 | N/A |

| Cameo Coins | | | |
|---|---|---|---|
| **Proof-60-62 Cameo** | **Proof-63 Cameo** | **Proof-64 Cameo** | **Proof-65 Cameo** |
| 1 Coin | 4-5 Coins | 6-8 Coins | 8-10 Coins |
| N/A | $625-$775 | $1,000-$1,200 | $1,500-$2,000 |
| **Proof-66 Cameo** | **Proof-67 Cameo** | **Proof-68 Cameo** | **Proof-69-70 Cameo** |
| 8-10 Coins | 3-4 Coins | 0 Coins | 0 Coins |
| $2,000-$3,000 | $5,000-$10,000 | -- | -- |

| Deep/Ultra Cameo Coins | | | |
|---|---|---|---|
| **Proof-60-62 Deep/ Ultra Cameo** | **Proof-63 Deep/ Ultra Cameo** | **Proof-64 Deep/ Ultra Cameo** | **Proof-65 Deep/ Ultra Cameo** |
| 0 Coins | 0 Coins | 0 Coins | 0 Coins |
| -- | -- | -- | -- |
| **Proof-66 Deep/ Ultra Cameo** | **Proof-67 Deep/ Ultra Cameo** | **Proof-68 Deep/ Ultra Cameo** | **Proof-69-70 Deep/ Ultra Cameo** |
| 0 Coins | 0 Coins | 0 Coins | 0 Coins |
| -- | -- | -- | -- |

*Note:* The conclusions presented in the following "Collecting and Investing Strategies" section are drawn in large part from the Investment Potential Ratios that are summarized in Appendices G and H at the end of this book. For a detailed analysis of the formula used to derive these Investment Potential Ratios, please refer to the Introduction of this book.

**Collecting and Investing Strategies:** In Proof-64 and Proof-65 the 1912 is valued very close to the mean for proof Barber Dimes, and such coins would make a wise choice for inclusion in a better-date proof type set. The numismatic investor, on the other hand, should look to the Proof-66 and Proof-67 grade levels for a better return from a proof 1912 Dime. This issue is underrated in the finest grades, and in Proof-67 the 1912 is actually the most undervalued issue in the entire proof Barber Dime series. (This statement does not take into consideration the 1894-S which, as a branch mint proof with only a handful of coins known, is in a category all its own.)

The proof 1912 is an issue that is going to test your patience. So many examples in numismatic circles are noticeably hairlined with dark, mottled or otherwise unsightly toning. You need to focus on finding a coin with relatively light, even patination. If you can locate a colorfully toned piece, so much the better, but you should anticipate paying a significant premium for such an example in all grades beginning at the Proof-65 level.

# 1912

## MINTAGE
19,349,300

Courtesy of David Lawrence

## RARITY RANKINGS

*Overall, Mint State: 71st of 74*
*High Grade, MS-65 or Finer: 71st of 74*

## PHILADELPHIA MINT ISSUES

*Overall, Mint State: 22nd of 25*
*High Grade, MS-65 or Finer: 22nd of 25*

**Important Varieties:** None.

**General Comments:** With the exception of only the 1892, 1911 and 1916, the 1912 is the most common Barber Dime in Mint State. The 1912 is also the fourth most common Barber Dime in high grades, although in that category the 1914 takes the place of the 1916 alongside the 1892 and 1911. This issue is available in quantity in all grades up to and including MS-65. Not even MS-66s can be described as rare, for they exist in large enough numbers that the buyer should find procuring one to be a fairly easy task. Superb Gems are still conditionally rare coins, however, and the 1912 is unknown in any grade above MS-67.

**Strike:** There are far fewer 1912 Barber Dimes with noticeable softness of detail than there are for the 1911. The typical 1912 is a sharply struck coin with crisp delineation between even the more intricate elements of the design. Softness of strike, when present at all, is usually extremely minor and confined to the top of the wreath on the reverse.

**Luster:** The 1912 has good, not excellent luster that is usually of a satin or softly frosted type.

**Surfaces:** With a large mintage and a relatively sizeable population of Mint State survivors, surface preservation varies widely for the 1912. The typical example encountered in today's market is lightly-to-moderately abraded, but there are enough Gems in MS-65 and MS-66 that you should have little difficulty obtaining an overall smooth-looking coin. On the other hand, examples that approach perfection are rare and seldom offered at even the largest numismatic gatherings.

**Toning:** Mint State survivors range from brilliant to deeply toned. Many of the coins in the former category have been dipped, while a few of the more deeply toned pieces that I have seen are actually artificially toned. The latter situation is very curious inasmuch as the 1912 is not a rare issue in most Mint State grades, so there seems to be little incentive to apply toning to, say a lightly cleaned example for the sake of getting it into a PCGS or NGC holder.

**Eye Appeal:** Overall eye appeal for the 1912 is only average—a surprising rating for a late-date, P-mint Barber Dime with such a large number of Mint State coins known to exist. The luster quality for this issue could be better, and then there is the prevalence of abrasions and unattractive toning among the survivors.

**Significant Examples:**

**1. NGC MS-67.** *Ex: Long Beach Signature Sale (Heritage, 2/2005), lot 6303, where it realized $2,760; Baltimore Rarities Sale (Bowers and Merena, 7/2008), lot 480, unsold.*

**2. NGC MS-67.** *Ex: Drew St. John Sale (American Numismatic Rarities, 6/2005), lot 1458, unsold; The Southwest Collection (Heritage, 2/2008), lot 205, where it realized $2,300.*

**3. NGC MS-67.** *Ex: The Greenhill Collection (Ira & Larry Goldberg, 9/2006), lot 1510, where it realized $2,185.*

**4. PCGS MS-67.** *Ex: The Collection of Dr. Steven L. Duckor (Heritage, 1/2006), lot 1031, where it realized $4,888.*

**5. PCGS MS-67.** *Ex: The Michael Casper Collection (Heritage, 1/2006), lot 1835, where it realized $4,888.*

**6. PCGS MS-67.** *Ex: The John C. Hugon Collection (Heritage, 1/2005), lot 4064, where it realized $8,050.*

**Total Known in Mint State:** 1,135-1,300 Coins

## Total Known and Value Breakdown by Grade:

| MS-60 to MS-62 | MS-63 | MS-64 | MS-65 |
| --- | --- | --- | --- |
| 200-250 Coins | 300-350 Coins | 375-425 Coins | 195-245 Coins |
| N/A | $125-$175 | $225-$275 | $475-$650 |

| MS-66 | MS-67 | MS-68 | MS-69 to MS-70 |
| --- | --- | --- | --- |
| 60-70 Coins | 8-10 Coins | 0 Coins | 0 Coins |
| $825-$975 | $2,500-$8,500 | -- | -- |

*Note:* The conclusions presented in the following "Collecting and Investing Strategies" section are drawn in large part from the Investment Potential Ratios that are summarized in Appendices G and H at the end of this book. For a detailed analysis of the formula used to derive these Investment Potential Ratios, please refer to the Introduction of this book.

**Collecting and Investing Strategies:** The 1912 is a bit overrated in MS-64, MS-65 and MS-67, but not by a wide enough margin for me to dislike the issue for type or date purposes. In MS-66 this issue offers even more solid value, and the buyer would probably be best served by selecting an example in that grade.

The 1912 is a much more challenging issue to locate with strong eye appeal for a P-mint Barber Dime with a relatively large number of Mint State survivors. This fact, coupled with the reality that the 1912 does not offer much potential for price appreciation, seems to argue against including this issue in an investment portfolio. If you must or choose to purchase a 1912 Barber Dime, insist on a coin with vibrant luster and original surfaces that have neither been dipped nor retoned. Be wary of an over concentration of abrasions at the MS-65, MS-66 and MS-67 grade levels as I have seen a few examples in high-grade holders that were a bit too baggy for my liking.

# 1912-D

**MINTAGE**
11,760,000

Courtesy of Bowers and Merena

## RARITY RANKINGS

*Overall, Mint State: 55th of 74*
*High Grade, MS-65 or Finer: 47th of 74 (Tie)*

### DENVER MINT ISSUES

*Overall, Mint State: 7th of 8*
*High Grade, MS-65 or Finer: 6th of 8*

**Important Varieties:** None.

**General Comments:** After only the 1914-D, the 1912-D is the most common Denver Mint Barber Dime in terms of total number of Mint State coins known to exist. In high grades, however, the 1912-D is also rarer than the 1911-D, and it is an overlooked issue in Gem Mint State. It is also rarer in high grades than the 1906-O, 1906-S, 1908-O, 1911-S, 1913-S and 1916-S, as well as such P-mint issues as the 1900, 1901 and 1916.

**Strike:** The 1912-D is a generally well-produced issue, and the typical example is overall sharply struck. When present at all, lack of detail is usually minor and confined to the haircurls above Liberty's brow on the obverse and/ or the top of the reverse wreath.

**Luster:** Most Mint State examples are very attractive in the luster category, the surfaces possessing a vibrant sheen in either a satin or frosty texture. There are exceptions, however, and some lower-grade coins through MS-64 are a bit subdued in finish.

**Surfaces:** Scattered small and moderate-size abrasions accompany most Mint State 1912-D Barber Dimes, and these features can be quite troublesome in lower grades through MS-63. Locating a smooth (to say nothing of virtually pristine) example is not an easy task.

**Toning:** The 1912-D is available both brilliant and extensively toned. The typical piece, however, is lightly-to-moderately patinated, which is fortunate since the more widely toned pieces that I have seen tend to display dark and/or mottled patination to the surfaces that is not particularly attractive.

**Eye Appeal:** This issue has slightly above-average eye appeal that, as a rule, is stronger than that which one is likely to see in an example of the 1912-P. Scattered abrasions, subdued luster and unsightly toning can still be a problem for the 1912-D, however, so it will pay to be selective when pursuing this issue.

**Significant Examples:** Although PCGS reports having certified a single 1912-D Barber Dime as MS-67 (December/2008), I have been unable to locate an auction appearance for that coin during the nine-year period from the turn of the 21st century to the end of 2008.

**Total Known in Mint State:** 325-395 Coins

**Total Known and Value Breakdown by Grade:**

| MS-60 to MS-62 | MS-63 | MS-64 | MS-65 |
|---|---|---|---|
| 80-90 Coins | 90-110 Coins | 105-130 Coins | 35-45 Coins |
| N/A | $125-$175 | $250-$300 | $550-$700 |

| MS-66 | MS-67 | MS-68 | MS-69 to MS-70 |
|---|---|---|---|
| 15-18 Coins | 1 Coin | 0 Coins | 0 Coins |
| $1,500-$5,000 | $10,000-$15,000 | -- | -- |

*Note:* The conclusions presented in the following "Collecting and Investing Strategies" section are drawn in large part from the Investment Potential Ratios that are summarized in Appendices G and H at the end of this book. For a detailed analysis of the formula used to derive these Investment Potential Ratios, please refer to the Introduction of this book.

**Collecting and Investing Strategies:** The 1912-D is a more-or-less underrated issue in the finer Mint State grades, with the lone MS-67 listed at PCGS being more undervalued than examples in MS-64, MS-65 or MS-66. This is a potentially attractive issue for mintmarked type purposes, inasmuch as it also has a relatively sizeable Mint State population for a Denver Mint Barber Dime. I do believe that the '12-D could serve effectively in this manner, but in order to do so you should be in the market for a coin that grades MS-65 or MS-66. In MS-64 and lower grades distracting abrasions and subdued luster can be significant stumbling blocks to locating a desirable example. Additionally, you should also avoid Gems in MS-65 and MS-66 with dark and/or mottled toning that inhibits the eye appeal. A coin with lighter and/or more evenly distributed patina is a much better bet for protecting your investment in this issue.

# 1912-S

## MINTAGE
3,420,000

Courtesy of Bowers and Merena

## RARITY RANKINGS

*Overall, Mint State:* 47th of 74
*High Grade, MS-65 or Finer:* 44th of 74 (Tie)

## SAN FRANCISCO MINT ISSUES

*Overall, Mint State:* 22nd of 24
*High Grade, MS-65 or Finer:* 20th of 24

**Important Varieties:** A minor Doubled Die Obverse error is known, and it is known by the attributions FS-010.25 and FS-101.

**General Comments:** The 1912-S ranks behind only the 1911-S and 1916-S as the most common S-mint Barber Dime in Mint State, although the 1906-S and the low-mintage 1913-S are also more plentiful than this issue in high grades. These facts belie the true rarity of the 1912-S in the context of the Barber Dime series as a whole. This issue is one of the rarer Barber Dimes from the 1910s, and it is more challenging to locate in Mint State than the 1911, 1911-D, 1911-S, 1912, 1912-D, 1913, 1914, 1914-D, 1915, 1916 and 1916-S. In high grades, the 1912-S is also rarer than the low-mintage 1913-S, as well as such earlier-date issues in this series as the 1893, 1900, 1908-O and 1909.

Nevertheless, the 1912-S is obtainable with patience in Mint State grades through MS-64. As a Gem, however, the 1912-S is a conditionally rare issue. MS-66s are very rare, and Superb Gems in MS-67 exist to the extent of just three coins (December/2008).

**Strike:** This is a vey well-produced issue that is almost always offered with razor sharp-to-full striking detail.

**Luster:** Luster is also a strong suit for the 1912-S, although most examples tend toward a satiny texture that is not as vibrant as the frosty mint luster that is seen on many Barber Dimes from the Philadelphia and Denver Mints. NGC has even certified a single MS-67 with a Prooflike finish (December/2008).

**Surfaces:** Abrasions are almost always present on the surfaces of a 1912-S Barber Dime, but they tend to be small in size and not overly distracting to the eye.

**Toning:** Mint State examples run the gamut from untoned to deeply patinated, but the vast majority of pieces are either lightly toned or fully brilliant. A fair number of coins have been dipped, a practice that for this issue at least tends to subdue the luster to a greater or lesser extent.

**Eye Appeal:** The typical 1912-S possesses either average or above-average eye appeal, the variation stemming from the lack or presence of deeper toning and/or subdued luster.

**Significant Examples:**

**1. NGC MS-67.** *Ex: The John Jay Pittman Collection (David W. Akers, 10/1997), lot 724, where it realized $2,420; The Collection of Dr. Steven L. Duckor (Heritage, 1/2006), lot 1033, where it realized $1,495; Denver ANA Auction (Bowers and Merena, 8/2006), lot 771, where it realized $7,763.*

**2. PCGS MS-67.** *Ex: Long Beach Signature Sale (Heritage, 9/2003), lot 6463, where it realized $12,075.*

**3. NGC MS-67 Prooflike.** *Ex: The Southwest Collection (Heritage, 2/2008), lot 207, where it realized $8,625.*

**4. PCGS MS-66.** *Ex: The John C. Hugon Collection (Heritage, 1/2005), lot 4066, where it realized $2,990; CSNS Signature Auction (Heritage, 5/2005), lot 6682, where it realized $2,760.*

**5. NGC MS-66.** *Ex: FUN Signature Sale (Heritage, 1/2004), lot 5687, unsold.*

**6. PCGS MS-66.** *Ex: The Benson Collection (Ira & Larry Goldberg, 2/2002), lot 608, where it realized $2,070; Pre-Long Beach Auction (Ira & Larry Goldberg, 1/2004), lot 1927, where it realized $1,955.*

**Total Known in Mint State:** 215-250 Coins

## Total Known and Value Breakdown by Grade:

| MS-60 to MS-62 | MS-63 | MS-64 | MS-65 |
|---|---|---|---|
| 45-55 Coins | 50-60 Coins | 70-80 Coins | 35-40 Coins |
| N/A | $200-$250 | $350-$400 | $600-$675 |

| MS-66 | MS-67 | MS-68 | MS-69 to MS-70 |
|---|---|---|---|
| 12-15 Coins | 3 Coins | 0 Coins | 0 Coins |
| $1,750-$3,000 | $8,000-$12,500 | -- | -- |

*Note:* The conclusions presented in the following "Collecting and Investing Strategies" section are drawn in large part from the Investment Potential Ratios that are summarized in Appendices G and H at the end of this book. For a detailed analysis of the formula used to derive these Investment Potential Ratios, please refer to the Introduction of this book.

**Collecting and Investing Strategies:** The 1912-S is among the more underrated Barber Dimes in the finer Mint State grades, although MS-67s are valued so close to the mean for the series that they probably do not offer much potential for future price appreciation. Examples in the MS-64 to MS-66 grade range are another matter entirely, and such pieces are undervalued relative to their true rarity at the price levels provided in this book. Just be sure to avoid darkly toned coins and you could do very well by adding a Choice or Gem-quality '12-S Dime to your numismatic holdings.

# Proof
# 1913

## MINTAGE
### 622

Courtesy of David Lawrence

## RARITY RANKINGS

***Overall, All Proof Grades:*** *10th of 25 (Tie)*
***High Grade, Proof-65 or Finer:*** *4th of 25*
*Overall, Cameo Finish: 9th of 24 (Tie)*
***Deep/Ultra Cameo Finish:*** *Unknown*

**Important Varieties:** None.

**General Comments:** Similar in overall rarity to the 1903, the 1913 is one of the rarer proof Barber Dimes. It is more challenging to locate than the 1900, 1901, 1904, 1905, 1909 and 1911, as well as all proof Barber Dimes from the 1890s with the sole exception of the 1894-S. In high grades, the 1913 is actually the rarest proof Dime of this type after only the branch mint 1894-S, the 1902 and the low-mintage 1915.

A Cameo proof 1913 is a rare coin that is on par with a proof 1906 and proof 1912 Barber Dime with that finish. There are no Deep/Ultra Cameo 1913 proof Dimes known to PCGS or NGC (December/2008).

**Strike:** A sharp strike is the norm for this issue, and most examples are actually fully defined throughout both sides.

**Finish:** The vast majority of proof 1913 Barber Dimes display an all-brilliant finish with little, if any contrast between the fields and devices. If present at all, Cameo contrast for this issue is usually confined to only one side of the coin.

**Surfaces:** The proof 1913 is a bit easier to locate with overall smooth-looking surfaces than the proof 1912, but the typical specimen that appears in the market is still apt to display scattered hairlines. A high-quality, pristine-looking proof 1913 Dime is a rare coin that is few and far between in numismatic circles.

**Toning:** Few examples display more than light-to-moderate toning, and there is a fair number of virtually brilliant coins due to the widespread practice of dipping and other methods of numismatic conservation. Those coins that display deeper patination tend to be attractive, the colors sometimes even quite vivid in appearance.

**Eye Appeal:** The 1913 is not the most consistently attractive issue in the proof Barber Dime series, but it does have better-than-average eye appeal. High-quality specimens with minimal or colorful toning are usually very pretty coins.

**Significant Examples:**

**1. NGC Proof-68 ★.** *Ex: The John C. Hugon Collection (Heritage, 1/2005), lot 4097, where it realized $6,325.*

**2. NGC Proof-67.** *Ex: Long Beach Signature Sale (Heritage, 9/2003), lot 6476, where it realized $2,645; CSNS Signature Auction (Heritage, 5/2005), lot 6724, where it realized $2,530; Baltimore Auction (Bowers and Merena, 8/2005), lot 1124, unsold; Beverly Hills Rarities Sale (Bowers and Merena, 2/2006), lot 207, where it realized $2,185.*

**3. NGC Proof-68 Cameo.** *Ex: The J.B. Worthington Collection (American Numismatic Rarities, 5/2005), lot 190, where it realized $5,520.*

**4. NGC Proof-67 Cameo.** *Ex: Long Beach, CA Signature Coin Auction (Heritage, 2/2007), lot 2970, where it realized $4,025.*

**5. NGC Proof-66 Cameo.** *Ex: Milwaukee, WI ANA Coin Signature Auction (Heritage, 8/2007), lot 605, unsold; Dallas, TX U.S. Coin Signature Auction (Heritage, 11/2007), lot 453, unsold.*

**6. PCGS Proof-66 Cameo.** *Ex: November Signature Sale (Heritage, 11/2003), lot 6048, where it realized $2,070; The Bruce Scher #1 All-Time PCGS Registry Set (Heritage, 2/2005), lot 4073, where it realized $2,530; Long Beach Signature Auction (Heritage, 5/2006), lot 1153, where it realized $2,070.*

**7. PCGS Proof-66 Cameo.** *Ex: The Law Collection; CSNS Signature Auction (Heritage, 4/2006), lot 1349, where it realized $2,530.*

**8. PCGS Proof-66 Cameo.** *Ex: Long Beach Signature Sale (Heritage, 9/2003), lot 6477, where it realized $3,795.*

**Total Known:** 320-395 Coins

## Total Known and Value Breakdown by Grade:

| Brilliant-Finish Coins | | | |
|---|---|---|---|
| **Proof-60-62** | **Proof-63** | **Proof-64** | **Proof-65** |
| 45-55 Coins | 65-75 Coins | 105-130 Coins | 40-50 Coins |
| N/A | $425-$500 | $650-$800 | $1,100-$1,500 |
| **Proof-66** | **Proof-67** | **Proof-68** | **Proof-69-70** |
| 20-25 Coins | 12-15 Coins | 1 Coin | 1 Coin |
| $1,700-$2,000 | $3,000-$4,000 | $5,500-$8,500 | $10,000-$15,000 |

| Cameo Coins | | | |
|---|---|---|---|
| **Proof-60-62 Cameo** | **Proof-63 Cameo** | **Proof-64 Cameo** | **Proof-65 Cameo** |
| 1 Coin | 1-2 Coins | 11-15 Coins | 8-10 Coins |
| N/A | $625-$775 | $1,000-$1,200 | $1,400-$1,700 |
| **Proof-66 Cameo** | **Proof-67 Cameo** | **Proof-68 Cameo** | **Proof-69-70 Cameo** |
| 7-9 Coins | 1-2 Coins | 1 Coin | 0 Coins |
| $2,000-$4,000 | $5,000-$10,000 | $10,000-$15,000 | -- |

| Deep/Ultra Cameo Coins | | | |
|---|---|---|---|
| **Proof-60-62 Deep/ Ultra Cameo** | **Proof-63 Deep/ Ultra Cameo** | **Proof-64 Deep/ Ultra Cameo** | **Proof-65 Deep/ Ultra Cameo** |
| 0 Coins | 0 Coins | 0 Coins | 0 Coins |
| -- | -- | -- | -- |
| **Proof-66 Deep/ Ultra Cameo** | **Proof-67 Deep/ Ultra Cameo** | **Proof-68 Deep/ Ultra Cameo** | **Proof-69-70 Deep/ Ultra Cameo** |
| 0 Coins | 0 Coins | 0 Coins | 0 Coins |
| -- | -- | -- | -- |

*Note:* The conclusions presented in the following "Collecting and Investing Strategies" section are drawn in large part from the Investment Potential Ratios that are summarized in Appendices G and H at the end of this book. For a detailed analysis of the formula used to derive these Investment Potential Ratios, please refer to the Introduction of this book.

**Collecting and Investing Strategies:** With the sole exception of examples at the Proof-64 level, the 1913 is among the more underrated proof Barber Dimes in higher grades. This issue is particularly undervalued in Proof-66, being second only to the 1915 in that category. Since it is also among the rarer proof Barber Dimes, the 1913 comes highly recommended for inclusion in an advanced collection or portfolio in grades at and above the Proof-65 level.

Most proof 1913 Dimes possess strong eye appeal and solid technical merits for the assigned grade. As such, you can relax your standards somewhat when searching for a Gem or Superb-quality example. Pleasing examples exist in all of the finer grades, and these coins range in appearance from fully brilliant to extensively toned.

# 1913

**MINTAGE**
19,760,000

Courtesy of Bowers and Merena

**RARITY RANKINGS**

*Overall, Mint State: 69th of 74*
*High Grade, MS-65 or Finer: 69th of 74*

## PHILADELPHIA MINT ISSUES

*Overall, Mint State: 20th of 25*
*High Grade, MS-65 or Finer: 20th of 25*

**Important Varieties:** None.

**General Comments:** The 1913 is a very common Barber Dime in an absolute sense, although it is not quite as plentiful in Mint State as the 1892, 1911, 1912, 1914 or 1916. Examples are readily obtainable in all grades through MS-65. MS-66s are somewhat scarce, but even in that grade the 1913 is available with patience. As a Superb Gem, however, this issue is genuinely rare and seldom encountered in numismatic circles.

**Strike:** The 1913 is rarely offered with anything less than sharp striking detail. When softness of strike is present on an example of this issue, it is usually extremely minor and confined to the uppermost portions of the reverse wreath.

**Luster:** Luster quality for this issue is very good, if not downright excellent. The majority of examples are frosty in texture, although the occasional satiny piece is encountered in the market.

**Surfaces:** Mint State survivors range in appearance from noticeably abraded to virtually pristine. The typical piece will display at least a few grade-limiting abrasions, although these will tend to be small in size and singularly inconspicuous, except perhaps in lower Mint State grades through MS-62.

**Toning:** I have seen 1913 Dimes that are both deeply toned and fully brilliant. The majority of coins that have passed through my hands, however, are ether lightly toned or brilliant. More and more of the lightly toned pieces are being dipped, thus increasing the number of brilliant coins among the survivors.

**Eye Appeal:** The typical Mint State example is an attractive coin for its respective grade, the strike, luster and surface preservation almost always technically sound and aesthetically pleasing.

**Significant Examples:**

1. **NGC MS-67.** *Ex: CSNS Signature Sale (Heritage, 5/2004), lot 6677, unsold; Pittsburgh, PA Signature Sale (Heritage, 8/2004), lot 5711, unsold.*

**Total Known in Mint State:** 950-1,140 Coins

**Total Known and Value Breakdown by Grade:**

| MS-60 to MS-62 | MS-63 | MS-64 | MS-65 |
|---|---|---|---|
| 200-250 Coins | 260-310 Coins | 325-375 Coins | 125-150 Coins |
| N/A | $125-$175 | $225-$275 | $475-$650 |

| MS-66 | MS-67 | MS-68 | MS-69 to MS-70 |
|---|---|---|---|
| 35-45 Coins | 3-4 Coins | 0 Coins | 0 Coins |
| $825-$975 | $2,500-$5,000 | -- | -- |

*Note:* The conclusions presented in the following "Collecting and Investing Strategies" section are drawn in large part from the Investment Potential Ratios that are summarized in Appendices G and H at the end of this book. For a detailed analysis of the formula used to derive these Investment Potential Ratios, please refer to the Introduction of this book.

**Collecting and Investing Strategies:** The 1913 offers fairly solid value for the price in MS-64, MS-65 and MS-66, and such examples would do well in most numismatic collections. This issue is definitely underrated in MS-67, being more so than any other P-mint Barber Dime save for only the 1896, 1902, 1903 and 1907.

The 1913 is a well-produced and generally well-preserved issue that is a more appealing Mint State type candidate than the 1912. Since the more extensively toned pieces that I have seen tend to be quite dark, I would opt for a brilliant 1913 Barber Dime. My personal preference is for original coins, but the dipped pieces are usually also appealing with good luster and no unsightly haziness to the surfaces.

# 1913-S

## MINTAGE
### 510,000

Courtesy of David Lawrence

## RARITY RANKINGS

*Overall, Mint State: 34th of 74*
*High Grade, MS-65 or Finer: 50th of 74 (Tie)*

## SAN FRANCISCO MINT ISSUES

*Overall, Mint State: 17th of 24*
*High Grade, MS-65 or Finer: 21st of 24*

**Important Varieties:** None.

**General Comments:** The 1913-S is the first in a run of low-mintage San Francisco Mint Barber Dimes that continues through 1915. This issue actually has the second-lowest mintage in the entire business strike Barber Dime series after only the 1895-O, and it is a genuinely scarce, if not rare issue in all Mint State grades. On the other hand, the 1913-S was saved in much greater numbers at the time of issue than many other Barber Dimes—a fact that had led many numismatists to overstate the rarity of this issue. In terms of total number of Mint State coins known to exist, the 1913-S is nowhere near as rare as the 1894-O, 1895-O 1896-O or 1898-S, and it is also more plentiful than issues such as the 1892-S, 1895, 1895-S, 1897-O, 1899-S, 1907-D, 1909-D and 1909-O. In high grades, the 1913-S is on par with the 1908-O and less rare than even many higher-mintage issues form its era such as the 1910-D, 1910-S, 1912-D, 1912-S, 1914-S and 1915-S.

The 1913-S is still far from the most common S-mint Barber Dime in Mint State, and it is more challenging to locate in an absolute sense than the 1900-S, 1905-S, 1911-S, 1912-S, 1914-S, 1915-S and 1916-S. On the other hand, the

1913-S is rarer in high grades than only the 1906-S, 1911-S and 1916-S from the San Francisco Mint. Barber Dimes from other Mints that are more plentiful than the 1913-S in high grades include the 1901, 1906-O, 1909, 1911-D, 1914-D and 1915. With only a handful of Superb Gems known to exist, this issue is clearly a major rarity at the top of the grading scale.

**Strike:** The 1913-S is a well-produced issue that almost always displays razor-sharp, if not full striking detail.

**Luster:** The typical example possesses excellent, vibrant luster that is usually satiny in texture.

**Surfaces:** This issue seldom has problems with significant abrasions, and most Mint State survivors are either overall smooth or possessed of only a few small, wispy marks.

**Toning:** I have yet to encounter a deeply and/or extensively toned Mint State example of this issue. Most pieces are brilliant or, at best, lightly patinated. The few coins with deeper colors to one or both sides tend to be toned only around the peripheries.

**Eye Appeal:** Eye appeal for this issue is excellent, the coins almost universally sharp in strike, vibrant in luster and well preserved.

**Significant Examples:**

**1. NGC MS-67.** *Ex: The Southwest Collection (Heritage, 2/2008), lot 209, where it realized $6,900; Baltimore, MD ANA U.S. Coin Signature Auction (Heritage, 7/2008), lot 121.*

**2. PCGS MS-67.** *Ex: Long Beach Signature Auction (Heritage, 6/2005), lot 5842, where it realized $10,925.*

**3. PCGS MS-67.** *Ex: FUN Signature Sale (Heritage, 1/2005), lot 4068, where it realized $10,350.*

**Total Known in Mint State:** 145-185 Coins

**Total Known and Value Breakdown by Grade:**

| MS-60 to MS-62 | MS-63 | MS-64 | MS-65 |
|---|---|---|---|
| 20-25 Coins | 30-40 Coins | 40-50 Coins | 30-40 Coins |
| N/A | $550-$700 | $850-$1,100 | $1,500-$2,500 |

| MS-66 | MS-67 | MS-68 | MS-69 to MS-70 |
|---|---|---|---|
| 20-25 Coins | 4-5 Coins | 0 Coins | 0 Coins |
| $2,500-$4,000 | $7,000-$12,500 | -- | -- |

<u>Note:</u> The conclusions presented in the following "Collecting and Investing Strategies" section are drawn in large part from the Investment Potential Ratios that are summarized in Appendices G and H at the end of this book. For a detailed analysis of the formula used to derive these Investment Potential Ratios, please refer to the Introduction of this book.

**Collecting and Investing Strategies:** The 1913-S is a decidedly overrated issue in the MS-65 to MS-67 grade range, a limited mintage resulting in overly aggressive pricing on the part of the market despite the fact that this issue was saved in relatively large numbers. MS-64s are a bit underrated, however, and it is to those pieces that I would look to maximize ROI in an example of this key-date issue.

Beware of values reported for this issue in many general numismatic price guides—they tend to be lower than what you should expect to pay for an example either through auction or from a dealer. On the positive side, you can relax your standards for quality and eye appeal when pursuing this issue. The typical 1913-S is a highly attractive coin in the context of its assigned grade, and you should not have to compromise in any area when selecting a coin for inclusion in your collection or portfolio.

# Proof
# 1914

## MINTAGE
### 425

## RARITY RANKINGS

*Overall, All Proof Grades: 3rd of 25*
*High Grade, Proof-65 or Finer: 5th of 25*
*Overall, Cameo Finish: 6th of 24 (Tie)*
*Deep/Ultra Cameo Finish: Unknown*

**Important Varieties:** None.

**General Comments:** The penultimate issue in the proof Barber Dime series, the 1914 has the lowest mintage of the type after that of only the branch mint 1894-S. The 1914 is the rarest proof Barber Dime behind the 1894-S and 1915, although the 1902 and 1913 are also rarer than this issue in high grades. Survivors in lower grades are on the scarce side, and you may have to exercise some patience even to acquire a 1914 in Proof-64 or Proof-65. Examples that grade any finer are rare.

As a Cameo proof, the 1914 is similar in rarity to the 1904, and it is among the more challenging proof Barber Dimes to locate with that finish. There are no Deep/Ultra Cameo specimens known to exist.

**Strike:** The proof 1914 comes fully struck with pinpoint definition to all devices.

**Finish:** Very few specimens display more than the barest trace of mint frost to the devices, and most examples are uniformly brilliant in finish. Even the handful of coins that have received a Cameo designation from PCGS and NGC are not all that impressive in the area of field-to-device contrast—they are simply more Cameo in finish that the typical proof 1914 Barber Dime.

**Surfaces:** Expect to see at least a few scattered hairlines on examples of this issue, and these tend to be concentrated on the obverse over and around Liberty's portrait. The 1914 is one of the most challenging proof Barber Dimes to locate with carefully preserved surfaces.

**Toning:** Many examples are rather deeply toned, and these tend to be quite dark in appearance and not all that attractive. The more attractive of those pieces display vivid, multicolored undertones that are best appreciated when the coin is held at a direct angle to a good light source. Lightly toned coins are not seen all that often, although brilliant pieces are becoming more prevalent as more and more proof 1914 Dimes are dipped.

**Eye Appeal:** Overall eye appeal for the proof 1914 is only average. While the coins are sharply struck with deep mirrors in the fields, many examples are noticeably marked, and more than a few are darkly toned. As well, this issue generally lacks the strength of field-to-device contrast that is so appealing in early-date proof Barber Dimes.

### Significant Examples:

**1. PCGS Proof-67.** *Ex: The Bruce Scher #1 All-Time PCGS Registry Set (Heritage, 2/2005), lot 4074, where it realized $3,738.*

**2. NGC Proof-67.** *Ex: The John C. Hugon Collection (Heritage, 1/2005), lot 4098, where it realized $5,463.*

**3. NGC Proof-67.** *Ex: New York, NY Signature Sale (Heritage, 7/2004), lot 5838, where it realized $3,163.*

**4. PCGS Proof-67.** *Ex: The Haig A. Koshkarian Collection (American Numismatic Rarities, 3/2004), lot 513, where it realized $3,220.*

**5. NGC Proof-67.** *Ex: Pre-FUN Elite Coin Auction (Superior, 1/2004), lot 246, where it realized $2,530.*

**6. NGC Proof-67.** *Ex: Mid-Winter ANA Signature Sale (Heritage, 3/1997), lot 5936, unsold; November Signature Sale (November, 11/2003), lot 6049, where it realized $2,185.*

**7. PCGS Proof-67 Cameo.** *Ex: The J.B. Worthington Collection (American Numismatic Rarities, 5/2005), lot 191, where it realized $3,680; Dallas, TX Signature Auction (Heritage, 11/2005), lot 1060, where it realized $6,325.*

**8. NGC Proof-67 Cameo.** *Ex: Dallas, TX Signature Auction (Heritage, 11/2005), lot 1061, where it realized $3,220.*

**9. NGC Proof-67 Cameo.** *Ex: Long Beach Signature Sale (Heritage, 6/2004), lot 8103, where it realized $3,105.*

**10. NGC Proof-66 Cameo.** *Ex: The Mulholland Collection (Heritage, 8/2006), lot 966, unsold; FUN Signature Coin Auction (Heritage, 1/2007), lot 2696, where it realized $2,415.*

**Total Known:** 265-315 Coins

**Total Known and Value Breakdown by Grade:**

| Brilliant-Finish Coins | | | |
|---|---|---|---|
| **Proof-60-62** | **Proof-63** | **Proof-64** | **Proof-65** |
| 25-30 Coins | 65-75 Coins | 70-80 Coins | 40-50 Coins |
| N/A | $475-$600 | $750-$900 | $1,100-$1,500 |
| **Proof-66** | **Proof-67** | **Proof-68** | **Proof-69-70** |
| 30-35 Coins | 10-15 Coins | 1-2 Coins | 0 Coins |
| $1,250-$2,000 | $4,000-$6,000 | $7,500-$10,000 | -- |

| Cameo Coins | | | |
|---|---|---|---|
| **Proof-60-62 Cameo** | **Proof-63 Cameo** | **Proof-64 Cameo** | **Proof-65 Cameo** |
| 0 Coins | 2-3 Coins | 5-7 Coins | 10-12 Coins |
| N/A | $650-$800 | $1,000-$1,500 | $1,750-$2,000 |
| **Proof-66 Cameo** | **Proof-67 Cameo** | **Proof-68 Cameo** | **Proof-69-70 Cameo** |
| 4-5 Coins | 2-3 Coins | 0 Coins | 0 Coins |
| $2,500-$5,000 | $5,000-$10,000 | -- | -- |

| Deep/Ultra Cameo Coins | | | |
|---|---|---|---|
| **Proof-60-62 Deep/ Ultra Cameo** | **Proof-63 Deep/ Ultra Cameo** | **Proof-64 Deep/ Ultra Cameo** | **Proof-65 Deep/ Ultra Cameo** |
| 0 Coins | 0 Coins | 0 Coins | 0 Coins |
| -- | -- | -- | -- |
| **Proof-66 Deep/ Ultra Cameo** | **Proof-67 Deep/ Ultra Cameo** | **Proof-68 Deep/ Ultra Cameo** | **Proof-69-70 Deep/ Ultra Cameo** |
| 0 Coins | 0 Coins | 0 Coins | 0 Coins |
| -- | -- | -- | -- |

*Note:* The conclusions presented in the following "Collecting and Investing Strategies" section are drawn in large part from the Investment Potential Ratios that are summarized in Appendices G and H at the end of this book. For a detailed analysis of the formula used to derive these Investment Potential Ratios, please refer to the Introduction of this book.

**Collecting and Investing Strategies:** The 1914 is in the top five among underrated Barber Dimes in the Proof-64 to Proof-66 grade range, and in Proof-67 it is among the ten most undervalued issues of the type. Whether you are assembling a complete Barber Dime set, a better date proof type collection or a diversified numismatic portfolio, a high-grade proof 1914 would make a potentially lucrative addition to your holdings.

Beware of values provided for the proof 1914 in standard references such as the book A Guide Book of United States Coins by R.S. Yeoman and The Coin Dealer Newsletter CDN Quarterly II. Such sources price the 1914 identically to most other proof Barber Dimes even though the issue almost always commands a premium in the market. Be sure to check recent auction prices realized data to determine exactly what you should expect to pay for a proof 1914 Barber Dime in the current market.

Regardless of what grade level for the proof 1914 fits best with your numismatic budget, try to acquire a coin with brilliant, lightly toned or colorfully toned surfaces. Absolutely avoid darkly toned examples of this issue as these tend to be unattractive and will almost always trade at a discount in the market.

# 1914

### MINTAGE
17,360,230

Courtesy of Bowers and Merena

### RARITY RANKINGS

*Overall, Mint State: 70th of 74*
*High Grade, MS-65 or Finer: 72nd of 74*

## PHILADELPHIA MINT ISSUES

*Overall, Mint State: 21st of 25*
*High Grade, MS-65 or Finer: 23rd of 25*

**Important Varieties:** None.

**General Comments:** A late-date Philadelphia Mint issue with a high mintage, the 1914 is one of the most common issues in the Barber Dime series. Only the 1892, 1911, 1912 and 1916 are more plentiful in terms of total number of Mint State coins known. In high grades, the list of more common Barber Dimes dwindles to just two: the first-year 1892 and the 1911.

The 1914 is easy to obtain in all grades up to and including MS-65. Premium-quality Gems in MS-66, while not really common in an absolute sense, are still plentiful by the standards of this type. Very few MS-67s are known, however, and neither PCGS nor NGC has certified a single 1914 in a higher grade (December/2008).

**Strike:** The typical example is sharply struck throughout, and many pieces are fully defined. Nevertheless, occasional softness of strike is noted for the 1914, and this is usually confined to the reverse at the upper portion of the wreath.

**Luster:** Mint State 1914 Barber Dimes also come with very good-to-excellent luster. While a few satiny pieces are known, the typical example is decidedly frosty in finish.

**Surfaces:** Most Mint State survivors are scattered throughout the grading scale from MS-60 to MS-66, and these coins range in appearance from noticeably abraded to virtually pristine.

**Toning:** While there are some moderately-to-deeply toned examples known, the 1914 is usually encountered with only minimal patination to the surfaces. Many brilliant coins also exist, many of which are original and others of which have been dipped at one time or another.

**Eye Appeal:** The 1914 has above average-to-strong eye appeal. Despite the fact that many Mint State survivors display considerable abrasions, enough high-quality pieces are known that you should have little difficulty locating an overall smooth-looking coin with a sharp strike, strong luster and attractive surfaces.

**Significant Examples:**

1. **PCGS MS-67.** *Ex: The Collection of Dr. Steven L. Duckor (Heritage, 1/2006), lot 1036, where it realized $4,888.*

2. **NGC MS-67.** *Ex: Pre-Long Beach Elite Coin Auction (Superior, 5/2003), lot 2390, where it realized $3,048; The John C. Hugon Collection (Heritage, 1/2005), lot 4069, where it realized $2,530.*

**Total Known in Mint State:** 1,080-1,320 Coins

**Total Known and Value Breakdown by Grade:**

| MS-60 to MS-62 | MS-63 | MS-64 | MS-65 |
|---|---|---|---|
| 140-165 Coins | 250-300 Coins | 425-525 Coins | 200-250 Coins |
| N/A | $125-$175 | $250-$350 | $500-$600 |

| MS-66 | MS-67 | MS-68 | MS-69 to MS-70 |
|---|---|---|---|
| 65-75 Coins | 4-6 Coins | 0 Coins | 0 Coins |
| $800-$1,100 | $3,000-$5,000 | -- | -- |

*Note:* The conclusions presented in the following "Collecting and Investing Strategies" section are drawn in large part from the Investment Potential Ratios that are summarized in Appendices G and H at the end of this book. For a detailed analysis of the formula used to derive these Investment Potential Ratios, please refer to the Introduction of this book.

**Collecting and Investing Strategies:** If possible, avoid the 1914 in MS-64 and MS-65 as the issue is overrated in those grades. MS-66s offer solid-enough value and could be a good buy, but only in MS-67 is this issue truly underrated. Be selective with this relatively common issue and insist on locating a coin with vibrant luster, a sharp-to-full strike, a minimum number of abrasions and attractive surfaces (they will probably be brilliant or lightly toned).

# 1914-D

## MINTAGE
11,908,000

*Courtesy of David Lawrence*

## RARITY RANKINGS

*Overall, Mint State: 66th of 74*
*High Grade, MS-65 or Finer: 61st of 74*

## DENVER MINT ISSUES

*Overall, Mint State: 8th of 8*
*High Grade, MS-65 or Finer: 7th of 8*

**Important Varieties:** None.

**General Comments:** The final D-mint Barber Dime, the 1914-D is the most common mintmarked issue of the type in Mint State. In an absolute sense, however, the 1914-D is rarer than such P-mint issues in this series as the 1892, 1898, 1910 and 1913. In high grades, the 1914-D is actually not the most common Denver Mint Barber Dime. That honor goes to the 1911-D. The 1914-D is also rarer as a Gem than the 1893, 1908 and 1911-S, among other issues.

**Strike:** This is a carefully produced issue, and most examples that I have seen are sharply or fully struck. When present at all, lack of detail is almost always minor and confined to either the top of the reverse wreath or the ribbon knot at the base of that device.

**Luster:** Luster quality for the 1914-D is good, although not outstanding, and it is usually of a satin or softly frosted type. Lower-grade examples through MS-64 are usually a tad subdued, but Gems and Superb Gems tend to be much more vibrant in finish.

**Surfaces:** The typical Mint State 1914-D will display a few grade-limiting abrasions, and these tend to be most noticeable on the obverse over Liberty's cheek.

**Toning:** Most Mint State survivors are moderately-to-deeply toned, seldom with particularly vivid color. Instead, the 1914-D is characterized by darker patination that also has the tendency to be mottled or speckled in distribution. Bright, untoned coins are in the minority, and most of those pieces have been dipped at one time.

**Eye Appeal:** Eye appeal for this issue is only average, especially in lower grades through MS-64 where abrasions and sub-par luster are often a problem. The handful of high-grade survivors in MS-66 and MS-67, however, are very attractive coins.

### Significant Examples:

**1. NGC MS-67.** *Ex: The Southwest Collection (Heritage, 2/2008), lot 211, where it realized $3,450.*

**2. PCGS MS-67.** *Ex: The Collection of Dr. Steven L. Duckor (Heritage, 1/2006), lot 1037, where it realized $8,050.*

**3. NGC MS-67.** *Ex: The Louis E. Eliasberg, Sr. Collection (Bowers and Merena, 5/1996), lot 1312, where it realized $2,750; The Leonard J. Torok, M.D. and Nathan R. and Barbara J. Sonnheim Collections (Bowers and Merena, 9/1998), lot 439, where it realized $2,760; The John C. Hugon Collection (Heritage, 1/2005), lot 4070, where it realized $4,888.*

**Total Known in Mint State:** 500-610 Coins

**Total Known and Value Breakdown by Grade:**

| MS-60 to MS-62 | MS-63 | MS-64 | MS-65 |
|---|---|---|---|
| 135-160 Coins | 125-150 Coins | 160-190 Coins | 60-70 Coins |
| N/A | $125-$175 | $250-$300 | $500-$650 |

| MS-66 | MS-67 | MS-68 | MS-69 to MS-70 |
|---|---|---|---|
| 25-30 Coins | 4-6 Coins | 0 Coins | 0 Coins |
| $750-$1,250 | $3,500-$8,500 | -- | -- |

*Note:* The conclusions presented in the following "Collecting and Investing Strategies" section are drawn in large part from the Investment Potential Ratios that are summarized in Appendices G and H at the end of this book. For a detailed analysis of the formula used to derive these Investment Potential Ratios, please refer to the Introduction of this book.

**Collecting and Investing Strategies:** This is a very attractive issue from a valuation standpoint. The 1914-D offer relatively solid value in MS-64, while Gems and Superb Gem through MS-67 are more-or-less underrated coins. This issue, therefore, should be attractive to a wide variety of buyers from dedicated Barber Dime specialists to pure numismatic investors.

The 1914-D is plagued by the same problems of distracting abrasions and unsightly toning as the 1912-D. Bright, brilliant Mint State examples do exist, however, and such is the desirability of those coins with many buyers that they almost always command a strong premium over what you should expect to pay for a coin with dark and/or mottled toning. Due to problems with abrasions and luster, as well as greater potential for price appreciation, I would also select a 1914-D that grades MS-65, MS-66 or MS-67 over an MS-64.

# 1914-S

**MINTAGE**
2,100,000

Courtesy of David Lawrence

**RARITY RANKINGS**

*Overall, Mint State: 46th of 74*
*High Grade, MS-65 or Finer: 37th of 74 (Tie)*

## SAN FRANCISCO MINT ISSUES

*Overall, Mint State: 21st of 24*
*High Grade, MS-65 or Finer: 18th of 24 (Tie)*

**Important Varieties:** None.

**General Comments:** This issue has a higher mintage than the 1913-S and 1915-S, and it is more similar in rarity to the 1912-S in terms of total number of Mint State coins known to exist. The 1914-S is actually a bit rarer than the 1912-S, and it is also more elusive than the 1911-S and 1916-S. This issue is rarer than the 1911-S, 1912-S and 1916-S in high grades, as well as the 1906-S and even the low-mintage 1913-S. Among issues from other Mints, the 1914-S is rarer in all Mint State grades than the 1892-O, 1893, 1901, 1902, 1911-D, 1912-D and 1914-D.

**Strike:** As is the case with most S-mint issues in the Barber Dime series, the 1914-S usually comes well struck with sharp-to-full definition.

**Luster:** The 1914-S is also a highly lustrous issue, and most Mint State survivors possess a vibrant, satiny finish from the dies.

**Surfaces:** Expect to see at least a few abrasions on the typical 1914-S Dime offered in today's market. These are a bit larger than usually seen in S-mint Dimes of this type, at least in lower Mint State grades through MS-63. As with most other issues in this series, the 1914-S is far more likely to display grade-limiting abrasions on the obverse over Liberty's cheek than it is in other areas of the design.

**Toning:** Most Mint State 1914-S Barber Dimes that I have handled are lightly toned or fully brilliant, the latter sometimes due to dipping and other forms of numismatic conservation. There are some moderately toned survivors in numismatic circles that are neither vivid nor particularly dark but somewhere in the middle.

**Eye Appeal:** This is a generally attractive issue, and a bit of diligence on the part of the buyer should turn up a pleasing coin even in lower Mint State grades such as MS-62 and MS-63. Gems in MS-65, MS-66 and MS-67 are usually very attractive coins regardless of whether they are brilliant or toned.

**Significant Examples:**

1. **PCGS MS-67.** *Ex: FUN Signature Sale (Heritage, 1/2004), lot 5690, where it realized $9,775.*

**Total Known in Mint State:** 210-255 Coins

**Total Known and Value Breakdown by Grade:**

| MS-60 to MS-62 | MS-63 | MS-64 | MS-65 |
|---|---|---|---|
| 45-55 Coins | 60-70 Coins | 65-75 Coins | 25-30 Coins |
| N/A | $200-$300 | $575-$650 | $800-$1,000 |

| MS-66 | MS-67 | MS-68 | MS-69 to MS-70 |
|---|---|---|---|
| 15-20 Coins | 1-2 Coins | 0 Coins | 0 Coins |
| $2,000-$3,500 | $7,500-$12,500 | -- | -- |

*Note:* The conclusions presented in the following "Collecting and Investing Strategies" section are drawn in large part from the Investment Potential Ratios that are summarized in Appendices G and H at the end of this book. For a detailed analysis of the formula used to derive these Investment Potential Ratios, please refer to the Introduction of this book.

**Collecting and Investing Strategies:** The 1914-S is an underrated Barber Dime in the finer Mint State grades, with MS-65s and MS-67s being particularly noteworthy in this regard. Like the 1914-D, the 1914-S is an issue that I wholeheartedly recommend to both collectors and numismatic investors.

Avoid 1914-S Barber Dimes with relatively large, singularly distracting abrasions. Even if your numismatic budget forces you down to the MS-64 grade level for this issue, be patient until you locate an example with only small, wispy abrasions to define the grade. Such pieces definitely exist, and they will fit more comfortably into a Mint State Barber Dime set alongside examples of the series' other S-mint issues. Otherwise, the 1914-S should be an easy issue to find "nice" relative to its lower-mintage, semi key-date status.

# Proof
# 1915

## MINTAGE
450

Courtesy of David Lawrence

## RARITY
## RANKINGS

*Overall, All Proof Grades:* 2nd of 25
*High Grade, Proof-65 or Finer:* 2nd of 25
*Overall, Cameo Finish:* 3rd of 24
*Deep/Ultra Cameo Finish:* Unknown

**Important Varieties:** None.

**General Comments:** The 1915 is not only the final issue in the proof Barber Dime series, but it is also the last regular-issue proof Dime struck in the United States Mint prior to 1936. With just 450 pieces produced, the 1915 has the third-lowest mintage among proof Barbers after the 1894-S and 1914. The 1915 is actually more elusive than the lower-mintage 1914, and it is the rarest proof in the Barber Dime series after only the 1894-S. Waning interest in proof coinage among the contemporary public probably resulted in the destruction of many examples of this issue in the Mint, thus explaining its rarity in today's market.

The proof 1915 is the third-rarest collectible issue of the type with a Cameo finish, ranking behind the proof 1902 and proof 1903. It is unknown with a Deep/Ultra Cameo finish.

**Strike:** A full strike is the order of the day for the proof 1915.

**Finish:** All but a handful of specimens emerged from the dies with little, if any contrast between the fields and devices.

**Surfaces:** Most examples that I have handled display at least a few wispy, grade-limiting blemishes. Those features sometimes take the form of slidemarks that point to a coin's long-term storage in some kind of numismatic album. Otherwise, contact marks and other blemishes for the proof 1915 tend to be small in size and singularly inconspicuous.

**Toning:** With only a few exceptions allowed for pieces that have been dipped, the typical proof 1915 displays moderate-to-deep toning to the surfaces. The colors that are usually seen for this issue tend to be toward the darker end of the spectrum. Even deeply toned specimens, however, often reveal brighter, more vivid undertones as the coin is observed with the aid of a strong light source. Truly vivid pieces are not unknown, but they are rare and seldom encountered in numismatic circles.

**Eye Appeal:** The proof 1915 is a generally attractive issue, and most examples that I have seen possess above-average eye appeal in the context of the assigned grade.

**Significant Examples:**

1. **PCGS Proof-67.** *Ex: New York, NY Signature Sale (Heritage, 7/2002), lot 7643, where it realized $2,530; Long Beach Signature Sale (Heritage, 9/2002), lot 6316, unsold; Long Beach Signature Auction (Heritage, 6/2006), lot 1155, where it realized $2,760.*

2. **NGC Proof-67.** *Ex: The John C. Hugon Collection (Heritage, 1/2005), lot 4099, where it realized $2,990; The Official Auction of the ANA Las Vegas Coin Show (Bowers and Merena, 10/2005), lot 5429, where it realized $3,048; Baltimore Auction (Bowers and Merena, 3/2006), lot 614, where it realized $2,990.*

3. **PCGS Proof-67.** *Ex: Long Beach Signature Sale (Heritage, 6/2004), lot 8104, where it realized $2,818.*

4. **PCGS Proof-67.** Ex: C.F. Childs, who is believed to have purchased the coin directly from the Philadelphia Mint in 1915; The Walter H. Childs Collection (Bowers and Merena, 8/1999), lot 233, where it realized $7,475.

5. **NGC Proof-67 Cameo.** *Ex: The BRS Legacy Collection; FUN Signature Auction (Heritage, 1/2006), lot 1865, where it realized $3,220.*

**Total Known:** 220-275 Coins

## Total Known and Value Breakdown by Grade:

| Brilliant-Finish Coins | | | |
|---|---|---|---|
| **Proof-60-62** | **Proof-63** | **Proof-64** | **Proof-65** |
| 35-45 Coins | 35-45 Coins | 75-85 Coins | 35-45 Coins |
| N/A | $475-$600 | $750-$900 | $1,100-$1,500 |
| **Proof-66** | **Proof-67** | **Proof-68** | **Proof-69-70** |
| 12-15 Coins | 18-22 Coins | 1 Coin | 0 Coins |
| $1,500-$2,500 | $3,000-$4,000 | $7,500-$10,000 | -- |

| Cameo Coins | | | |
|---|---|---|---|
| **Proof-60-62 Cameo** | **Proof-63 Cameo** | **Proof-64 Cameo** | **Proof-65 Cameo** |
| 0 Coins | 1 Coin | 1-2 Coins | 4-6 Coins |
| -- | $750-$1,000 | $1,250-$1,500 | $1,750-$2,000 |
| **Proof-66 Cameo** | **Proof-67 Cameo** | **Proof-68 Cameo** | **Proof-69-70 Cameo** |
| 2-3 Coins | 3-4 Coins | 0 Coins | 0 Coins |
| $2,500-$3,500 | $3,250-$5,000 | -- | -- |

| Deep/Ultra Cameo Coins | | | |
|---|---|---|---|
| **Proof-60-62 Deep/ Ultra Cameo** | **Proof-63 Deep/ Ultra Cameo** | **Proof-64 Deep/ Ultra Cameo** | **Proof-65 Deep/ Ultra Cameo** |
| 0 Coins | 0 Coins | 0 Coins | 0 Coins |
| -- | -- | -- | -- |
| **Proof-66 Deep/ Ultra Cameo** | **Proof-67 Deep/ Ultra Cameo** | **Proof-68 Deep/ Ultra Cameo** | **Proof-69-70 Deep/ Ultra Cameo** |
| 0 Coins | 0 Coins | 0 Coins | 0 Coins |
| -- | -- | -- | -- |

*Note:* The conclusions presented in the following "Collecting and Investing Strategies" section are drawn in large part from the Investment Potential Ratios that are summarized in Appendices G and H at the end of this book. For a detailed analysis of the formula used to derive these Investment Potential Ratios, please refer to the Introduction of this book.

**Collecting and Investing Strategies:** Despite its limited mintage and key-date status, the 1915 is one of the most underrated proof Barber Dimes in higher grades. This issue is actually the most undervalued Barber Dime in Proof-65 and Proof-66, these grades holding particular appeal for numismatic investment purposes.

As with the proof 1914, the proof 1915 is undervalued in many popular and widely used price guides for United States coins. Consult current prices realized data from leading auction houses or a trusted, reputable dealer in order to help determine exactly how much you should pay for a proof 1915 Barber Dime in any given market.

Although a very scarce-to-rare issue that can be difficult to locate in all grades, the proof 1915 tends to come "nice." Whether originally toned or dipped to full brilliance, most examples that I have seen are aesthetically pleasing. I would be cautious with lower-grade examples through Proof-64, however, as these sometimes possess slidemarks or other noticeable distractions. If your numismatic budget dictates that you must purchase a proof 1915 that grades lower than Proof-64, try to find a coin with relatively small, inconspicuous blemishes that will not be too detrimental when the time comes to sell.

# 1915

### MINTAGE
### 5,620,000

Courtesy of David Lawrence

### RARITY
### RANKINGS

*Overall, Mint State: 60th of 74*
*High Grade, MS-65 or Finer: 53rd of 74 (Tie)*

## PHILADELPHIA MINT ISSUES

*Overall, Mint State: 12th of 25*
*High Grade, MS-65 or Finer: 9th of 25 (Tie)*

**Important Varieties:** None.

**General Comments**: Although widely regarded as one of the most common issues in the Barber Dime series, the 1915 is actually scarcer than many numismatists realize. A mintage of 5.6 million pieces represents a significant reduction from the totals that the Philadelphia Mint achieved for this type every year from 1897 through 1914. The result is that the 1915 is offered in Mint State much less frequency such other P-mint issues in this series as the 1911, 1912, 1913 and 1914, as well as the final-year 1916. It is also rarer than the 1914-D in terms of total number of Mint State coins believed extant. In high grades, the 1915 is similar in rarity to the 1901, 1906-O, 1909 and 1916-S, and it is more challenging to locate as a Gem than the 1893, 1897, 1898, 1911-D and 1911-S, among other issues.

Enough 1915 Dimes were set aside at the time of issue, however, that this issue is still readily obtainable in all grades through MS-64. Gems in MS-65 are genuinely scarce, while those that grade MS-66 are very rare from a condition standpoint. The 1915 is unknown as a Superb Gem.

**Strike:** The 1915 is a generally well-struck issue, and most examples possess overall bold-to-sharp definition. There are exceptions, however, and I have seen more than a few pieces with noticeable softness of detail to the haircurls over Liberty's brow on the obverse and on the reverse at the top or bottom of the wreath.

**Luster:** Luster quality for this issue varies for average to excellent, satiny to richly frosted. The typical example is more than adequate in this area with plenty of "flash" to the surfaces.

**Surfaces:** You should expect to see at least a few grade-limiting abrasions when confronted with a Mint State 1915 Barber Dime in the numismatic market. This is a surprisingly difficult issue to locate with overall smooth-looking surfaces for a late-date Barber Dime struck in the Philadelphia Mint. I have never seen an example that approaches perfection in the area of surface preservation.

**Toning:** Mint State survivors range in appearance from fully brilliant to richly toned, sometimes even with vivid patination to one or both sides. Coins in the brilliant category include both original and dipped pieces.

**Eye Appeal:** This is a generally attractive issue with an overall eye appeal rating that is well above average.

**Significant Examples:**

**1. NGC MS-66.** *Ex: Long Beach, CA Signature U.S. Coin Auction (Heritage, 6/2007), 733, where it realized $748.*

**2. PCGS MS-66.** *Ex: The Old West & Franklinton Collections (American Numismatic Rarities, 8/2006), lot 367, where it realized $1,380.*

**3. PCGS MS-66.** *Ex: The Collection of Dr. Steven L. Duckor (Heritage, 1/2006), lot 1039, where it realized $2,760.*

**4. NGC MS-66.** *Ex: Long Beach Signature Sale (Heritage, 2/2005), lot 6306, where it realized $1,265; Long Beach Signature Auction (Heritage, 9/2005), lot 2452, unsold.*

**5. PCGS MS-66.** *Ex: The John C. Hugon Collection (Heritage, 1/2005), lot 4072, where it realized $1,955.*

**6. PCGS MS-66.** *Ex: Palm Beach, FL Signature Auction (Heritage, 11/2004), lot 6299, where it realized $1,840.*

**7. NGC MS-66.** *Ex: Long Beach Signature Sale (Heritage, 6/2000), lot 7204, where it realized $776.*

**Total Known in Mint State:** 400-480 Coins

### Total Known and Value Breakdown by Grade:

| MS-60 to MS-62 | MS-63 | MS-64 | MS-65 |
|---|---|---|---|
| 95-115 Coins | 100-125 Coins | 135-160 Coins | 55-65 Coins |
| N/A | $125-$175 | $250-$350 | $500-$600 |

| MS-66 | MS-67 | MS-68 | MS-69 to MS-70 |
|---|---|---|---|
| 12-15 Coins | 0 Coins | 0 Coins | 0 Coins |
| $1,000-$3,000 | -- | -- | -- |

*Note:* The conclusions presented in the following "Collecting and Investing Strategies" section are drawn in large part from the Investment Potential Ratios that are summarized in Appendices G and H at the end of this book. For a detailed analysis of the formula used to derive these Investment Potential Ratios, please refer to the Introduction of this book.

**Collecting and Investing Strategies:** The 1915 is a highly desirable issue among late-date Barber Dimes from a valuation standpoint. The issue offers solid value in MS-64, it is undervalued in MS-65 and it is even more undervalued in MS-66.

Although the 1915 is an overall attractive issue, you should be on the lookout for a few potential pitfalls that could hurt your investment potential with this issue. For starters, avoid pieces with dark and/or mottled toning—I have seen some original 1915 Barber Dimes that are just not attractive coins. Second, emphasize strike and luster quality when searching for a suitable example. Insist on a coin with at least overall sharp striking and vibrant luster, be it satiny or frosty. Finally, be wary of overgraded coins in MS-66. With no examples certified as MS-67 or finer at PCGS and NGC, there is a tendency to graduate some MS-65s to the MS-66 level when they should have been left behind. If an MS-66 looks too baggy to you, pass on it and wait for a more solidly graded example to become available for purchase.

# 1915-S

## MINTAGE
960,000

Courtesy of Bowers and Merena

## RARITY RANKINGS

**Overall, Mint State:** *37th of 74*
**High Grade, MS-65 or Finer:** *30th of 74 (Tie)*

## SAN FRANCISCO MINT ISSUES

**Overall, Mint State:** *18th of 24*
**High Grade, MS-65 or Finer:** *16th of 24 (Tie)*

**Important Varieties:** None.

**General Comments:** With a limited mintage of fewer than 1 million coins, the 1915-S is an understandably rare issue when viewed in the context of the entire Barber Dime series. It is rarer than the 1900-S, 1905-S, 1911-S, 1912-S, 1914-S and 1916-S in terms of total number of Mint State coins known. The high-grade rarity of this issue is similar to that of the 1908-S and greater than that of the 1900-S, 1906-S, 1911-S, 1912-S, 1914-S, 1916-S and even the lower-mintage 1913-S. Among Barber Dimes from other Mints, the 1915-S is rarer in all Mint State grades than the 1892-O, 1905-O, 1906-O, 1907-O and 1908-D, as well as numerous P-mint issues including the 1893 and 1899.

**Strike:** The 1915-S is almost always offered with a sharp-to-full strike.

**Luster:** Luster quality for the 1915-S is very good, although not excellent, and the typical piece exhibits a satiny finish from the dies.

**Surfaces:** Mint State examples usually possess at least a few scattered abrasions, and these tend to be small in size with little effect on the coin other than to preclude a grade above the MS-64 level. The only exception here is slidemarks, which can be quite distracting when they are present on Liberty's portrait and/or in the obverse field.

**Toning:** Many 1915-S Dimes are brilliant, more are lightly toned and a smaller percentage of Mint State survivors are deeply patinated. Toning for this issue is seldom comprised of spectacularly vivid colors, but rather richer shades such as copper-russet and lavender-gray.

**Eye Appeal:** As a rule, a Mint State 1915-S Barber Dime is an attractive coin either in an absolute sense or in the context of the assigned grade.

### Significant Examples:

**1. NGC MS-67.** *Ex: Baltimore Auction (Bowers and Merena, 3/2007), lot 1997, where it realized $3,738.*

**2. NGC MS-67.** *Ex: San Francisco, CA ANA Signature Auction (Heritage, 7/2005), lot 5911, where it realized $2,645; Dallas, TX Signature Auction (Heritage, 11/2005), lot 1046, unsold; Long Beach Signature Auction (Heritage, 2/2006), lot 808, where it realized $4,198.*

**3. PCGS MS-67.** *Ex: The Collection of Dr. Steven L. Duckor (Heritage, 1/2006), lot 1040, where it realized $9,775.*

**4. NGC MS-67.** *Ex: The John C. Hugon Collection (Heritage, 1/2005), lot 4073, where it realized $5,175.*

**5. NGC MS-67.** *Ex: The Medio and Da Costa Gomez Collections (Stack's/American Numismatic Rarities, 6/2004), lot 2660, where it realized $5,750.*

**Total Known in Mint State:** 160-190 Coins

**Total Known and Value Breakdown by Grade:**

| MS-60 to MS-62 | MS-63 | MS-64 | MS-65 |
|---|---|---|---|
| 25-30 Coins | 35-40 Coins | 65-75 Coins | 20-25 Coins |
| N/A | $325-$375 | $475-$575 | $1,250-$1,500 |

| MS-66 | MS-67 | MS-68 | MS-69 to MS-70 |
|---|---|---|---|
| 12-15 Coins | 5 Coins | 0 Coins | 0 Coins |
| $1,750-$2,500 | $5,000-$12,500 | -- | -- |

*Note:* The conclusions presented in the following "Collecting and Investing Strategies" section are drawn in large part from the Investment Potential Ratios that are summarized in Appendices G and H at the end of this book. For a detailed analysis of the formula used to derive these Investment Potential Ratios, please refer to the Introduction of this book.

**Collecting and Investing Strategies:** Despite its low-mintage, key-date status, the 1915-S is an underrated Barber Dime in the MS-64 to MS-66 grade range. Examples in such grades, therefore, come highly recommended for inclusion in a wide variety of numismatic holdings. On the other hand, I do not like the 1915-S in MS-67 because the issue is overrated at that level based on the prices listed in this book.

The 1915-S is not a particularly difficult issue to find with strong eye appeal. Chances are good that if you succeed in locating a Mint State coin for purchase, it will be an attractive piece with a sharp strike, vibrant luster and pleasing surfaces. Be wary of toning for this issue, however, as it is often toward the deeper end of the color spectrum. This can still be a desirable trait as long as the buyer avoids pieces that are overly dark and/or possessed of excessive mottling to the toning.

# 1916

## MINTAGE
18,490,000

Courtesy of Bowers and Merena

## RARITY RANKINGS

*Overall, Mint State: 73rd of 74*
*High Grade, MS-65 or Finer: 70th of 74*

### PHILADELPHIA MINT ISSUES

*Overall, Mint State: 24th of 25*
*High Grade, MS-65 or Finer: 21st of 25*

**Important Varieties:** None.

**General Comments:** After only the first-year 1892, the final-year 1916 is the most plentiful Barber Dime in terms of total number of Mint State coins known to exist. Obviously, many 1916 Barber Dimes were kept from entering circulation—an action that may have been particularly widespread late in the year when the new Mercury Dime made the outgoing type popular as a numismatic keepsake. It is likely, however, that many 1916 Barer Dimes were saved by the general public as opposed to collectors, thus explaining why the 1916 is rarer in high grades than not only the 1892, but also the 1911, 1912 and 1914. In an absolute sense, of course, the 1916 is very common in all grades through MS-65, marginally scarce in MS-66 and only truly rare in MS-67.

**Strike:** Striking quality varies considerably among Mint State survivors of this issue. Most examples are well made with overall sharp, if not full definition to both sides. A few pieces, however, are noticeably deficient in detail over the highpoints of the obverse portrait and/or reverse wreath.

**Luster:** The 1916 has very good, although not outstanding luster that can be either satiny or frosty in texture.

**Surfaces:** Mint State Barber Dimes can be found at all levels of preservation from heavily abraded to virtually pristine. The typical piece offered in the market will be either lightly abraded or overall smooth.

**Toning:** Once again due to the large number of Mint State survivors known, the 1916 ranges in appearance from deeply toned to fully brilliant. Expect to see at least some toning on originally preserved examples, the colors usually moderate or deep and sometimes even quite vivid in shade.

**Eye Appeal:** While there is also much variance among the eye appeal of Mint State 1916 Barber Dimes, the typical example is above average, if not strong in this area.

### Significant Examples:

**1. PCGS MS-67.** *Ex: The Collection of Dr. Steven L. Duckor (Heritage, 1/2006), lot 1041, where it realized $8,050; The Joshua Collection (Heritage, 8/2008), lot 123, where it realized $4,600.*

**2. PCGS MS-67.** *Ex: FUN Signature Coin Auction (Heritage, 1/2007), lot 2669, where it realized $6,900.*

**3. NGC MS-67.** *Ex: CSNS Signature Auction (Heritage, 4/2006), lot 1322, unsold.*

**4. NGC MS-67.** *Ex: Orlando Rarities Sale (Bowers and Merena, 1/2003), lot 230, where it realized $776.25; Long Beach Signature Auction (Heritage, 9/2005), lot 2454, unsold; Dallas Signature Auction (Heritage, 12/2005), lot 493, unsold.*

**5. NGC MS-67.** *Ex: Ft. Lauderdale Rarities Sale (Bowers and Merena, 1/2005), lot 381, where it realized $3,048.*

**Total Known in Mint State:** 1,520-1,710 Coins

**Total Known and Value Breakdown by Grade:**

| MS-60 to MS-62 | MS-63 | MS-64 | MS-65 |
|---|---|---|---|
| 375-425 Coins | 450-500 Coins | 450-500 Coins | 175-200 Coins |
| N/A | $125-$175 | $200-$325 | $450-$600 |

| MS-66 | MS-67 | MS-68 | MS-69 to MS-70 |
|---|---|---|---|
| 60-70 Coins | 10-12 Coins | 0 Coins | 0 Coins |
| $750-$1,500 | $4,500-$8,500 | -- | -- |

*Note:* The conclusions presented in the following "Collecting and Investing Strategies" section are drawn in large part from the Investment Potential Ratios that are summarized in Appendices G and H at the end of this book.

For a detailed analysis of the formula used to derive these Investment Potential Ratios, please refer to the Introduction of this book.

**Collecting and Investing Strategies:** The final-year 1916 is an overrated issue in MS-64 and MS-65, and it is actually the most overrated P-mint Barber Dime in MS-67 after only the 1895 and 1908. I do, however, recommend MS-66s for type purposes or inclusion in a complete Barber Dime set. But as such pieces are already solidly valued at the price levels given in this book, I would on the 1916 even in MS-66 if your primary goal as a numismatic buyer is return on investment.

There are certainly many 1916 Barber Dimes to choose from in all grades from MS-60 to MS-66, so you can afford to be highly selective when pursuing this issue. This is very important because the 1916 is not always up to standard in the areas of strike and luster. Make sure the coin you choose is both sharply struck and highly lustrous. Also try to locate a piece with either brilliant or attractively toned surfaces.

# 1916-S

**MINTAGE**
5,820,000

*Courtesy of David Lawrence*

## RARITY RANKINGS

**Overall, Mint State:** *57th of 74*
**High Grade, MS-65 or Finer:** *53rd of 74 (Tie)*

## SAN FRANCISCO MINT ISSUES

**Overall, Mint State:** *24th of 24*
**High Grade, MS-65 or Finer:** *23rd of 24*

**Important Varieties:** None.

**General Comments:** Dime production in the San Francisco Mint skyrocketed in this, the final year of the Barber series and the first year of the Mercury series. The 1916-S Barber has a higher mintage than any other S-mint issue of the type with the sole exception of the 1905-S. Such a large production is obviously an indication of growth in the United States' economy due to the needs of the Allied powers fighting World War I in Europe.

The 1916-S is the single most common San Francisco Mint Barber Dime in terms of total number of Mint State coins extant, but it was not saved to anywhere near the same extent as the 1911, 1912, 1913, 1916, or even the 1909 or 1914-D. As with the 1916, many examples of the 1916-S may have been saved by the general public as opposed to collectors. Indeed, this issue is similar in high-grade rarity to the 1901, 1906-O, 1909 and 1915. The 1916-S is more challenging to locate as a Gem than such other issues as the 1911-D, 1911-S and 1914-D, to say nothing of the 1898, 1913 or even the 1916.

Enough coins have survived, nonetheless, that locating a 1916-S Barber Dime that grades MS-60 to MS-64 should prove to be a relatively easy task.

On the other hand, and as implied in the foregoing discussion, this issue is quite scarce in MS-65 and genuinely rare in MS-66. The 1916-S is unknown as a Superb Gem.

**Strike:** Although I have heard and read some opinions to the contrary, my experience suggests that the 1916-S is a well-produced issue. Virtually all Mint State coins that I have seen are sharply-to-fully impressed from the dies. Exceptions are few and far between, and those coins seldom possess more than trivial softness of strike to the higher elements of the obverse portrait and/or reverse wreath.

**Luster:** The 1916-S is unusual for a San Francisco Mint Barber Dime in that the luster is sometimes indifferent. While most examples are at least adequate in this regard, and many display a vibrant satin texture, others are quite subdued with almost lifeless surfaces.

**Surfaces:** Scattered small and moderate-size abrasions are often present on one or both sides of Mint State 1916-S Barber Dimes. Minimally marked pieces can be elusive, while virtually pristine pieces are seldom encountered at even the largest numismatic gatherings.

**Toning:** Light-to-moderate toning is the rule for Mint State survivors of this issue, although brilliant coins are becoming more prevalent due to the widespread practice of dipping and other forms of numismatic conservation. Vividly toned 1916-S Barber Dimes are seen much less often than those of the 1916-P.

**Eye Appeal:** The 1916-S has only average eye appeal, a rating that is due primarily to the difficultly of locating highly lustrous, minimally abraded coins among the Mint State survivors.

**Significant Examples:**

    **1. PCGS MS-66.** *Ex: Long Beach, CA Signature U.S. Coin Auction (Heritage, 6/2007), lot 734, where it realized $1,725.*

    **2. PCGS MS-66.** *Ex: The Belle Glade Collection (Heritage, 8/2006), lot 955, where it realized $3,738.*

    **3. PCGS MS-66.** *Ex: The Collection of Dr. Steven L. Duckor (Heritage, 1/2006), lot 1042, where it realized $3,220.*

    **4. PCGS MS-66.** *Ex: The John C. Hugon Collection (Heritage, 1/2005), lot 4075, where it realized $1,725.*

    **5. PCGS MS-66.** *Ex: Chicago 1991 Sale (RARCOA and David W. Akers, 8/1991), lot 318, where it realized $3,850.*

**Total Known in Mint State:** 345-425 Coins

### Total Known and Value Breakdown by Grade:

| MS-60 to MS-62 | MS-63 | MS-64 | MS-65 |
|---|---|---|---|
| 80-95 Coins | 100-125 Coins | 100-125 Coins | 45-55 Coins |
| N/A | $150-$200 | $225-$325 | $525-$700 |

| MS-66 | MS-67 | MS-68 | MS-69 to MS-70 |
|---|---|---|---|
| 20-25 Coins | 0 Coins | 0 Coins | 0 Coins |
| $2,000-$4,000 | -- | -- | -- |

*Note:* The conclusions presented in the following "Collecting and Investing Strategies" section are drawn in large part from the Investment Potential Ratios that are summarized in Appendices G and H at the end of this book. For a detailed analysis of the formula used to derive these Investment Potential Ratios, please refer to the Introduction of this book.

**Collecting and Investing Strategies:** For a final-year issue with a relatively high mintage, the 1916-S is surprisingly underrated in MS-64 and MS-65. It is far from the most undervalued Barber Dime in those grades, however, and MS-66s are actually overrated.

The difficulty of locating an attractive Mint State 1916-S Barber Dime might surprise some buyers. Nevertheless, you must anticipate a struggle with this issue and be prepared to pass up many coins as you wait for a truly desirable piece to make its appearance in the market. Do not settle for an example with subdued luster, noticeable softness of strike and/or individually distracting abrasions. Be mindful of toning, as well, since original examples of the 1916-S can be somewhat dark with a mottled distribution to the toning. Do not make the mistake that I have seen many buyers make in assuming that the 1916-S is a "common date" to be represented by the first Mint State coin that comes their way. Such a strategy is likely to find you placing a mediocre coin with below-average desirability into your collection or portfolio.

# Appendix A

## *Rarity Summary for Proof Barber Dimes: 1892-1915*

| Overall Rarity, All Proof Grades | | |
|---|---|---|
| Rank | Issue | Coins Known |
| 1st | 1894-S | 9 |
| 2nd | 1915 | 220-275 |
| 3rd | 1914 | 265-315 |
| 4th | 1908 | 275-340 |
| 5th | 1907 | 280-350 |
| 6th | 1910 | 285-340 |
| 7th | 1912 | 300-365 |
| 8th | 1902 | 300-370 |
| 9th | 1906 | 300-375 |
| 10th (Tie) | 1903 | 320-395 |
| 10th (Tie) | 1913 | 320-395 |
| 12th | 1911 | 325-405 |
| 13th | 1900 | 340-410 |
| 14th | 1901 | 360-435 |
| 15th (Tie) | 1904 | 360-440 |
| 15th (Tie) | 1909 | 360-440 |
| 17th | 1905 | 365-425 |
| 18th | 1893 | 365-440 |
| 19th | 1897 | 365-445 |
| 20th | 1899 | 375-460 |
| 21st | 1896 | 395-485 |
| 22nd | 1898 | 410-480 |
| 23rd | 1892 | 455-530 |
| 24th | 1895 | 455-550 |
| 25th | 1894 | 500-600 |

# Appendix A

## Rarity Summary for
## Proof Barber Dimes: 1892-1915 (cont.)

| High-Grade Rarity, Proof-65 or Finer | | |
|---|---|---|
| Rank | Issue | Coins Known |
| 1st | 1894-S | 3 |
| 2nd | 1915 | 75-95 |
| 3rd | 1902 | 80-100 |
| 4th | 1913 | 90-115 |
| 5th | 1914 | 100-120 |
| 6th (Tie) | 1903 | 115-140 |
| 6th (Tie) | 1912 | 115-140 |
| 8th (Tie) | 1904 | 115-145 |
| 8th (Tie) | 1908 | 115-145 |
| 10th | 1910 | 120-145 |
| 11th | 1907 | 120-150 |
| 12th | 1906 | 120-155 |
| 13th | 1900 | 150-190 |
| 14th (Tie) | 1901 | 165-195 |
| 14th (Tie) | 1911 | 165-195 |
| 16th | 1909 | 170-210 |
| 17th | 1899 | 175-215 |
| 18th | 1905 | 180-215 |
| 19th | 1896 | 200-235 |
| 20th | 1897 | 200-245 |
| 21st | 1892 | 205-240 |
| 22nd | 1893 | 210-260 |
| 23rd | 1898 | 225-270 |
| 24th | 1895 | 235-290 |
| 25th | 1894 | 250-300 |

# Appendix A

# *Rarity Summary for Proof Barber Dimes: 1892-1915 (cont.)*

| Overall Rarity, Cameo Finish | | |
|---|---|---|
| **Rank** | **Issue** | **Coins Known** |
| 1st | 1902 | 2 |
| 2nd | 1903 | 5-7 |
| 3rd | 1915 | 10-15 |
| 4th (Tie) | 1907 | 20-30 |
| 4th (Tie) | 1908 | 20-30 |
| 6th (Tie) | 1904 | 25-30 |
| 6th (Tie) | 1914 | 25-30 |
| 8th | 1909 | 25-35 |
| 9th (Tie) | 1906 | 30-40 |
| 9th (Tie) | 1912 | 30-40 |
| 9th (Tie) | 1913 | 30-40 |
| 12th | 1910 | 35-45 |
| 13th | 1905 | 40-50 |
| 14th | 1899 | 40-55 |
| 15th | 1901 | 45-60 |
| 16th | 1911 | 60-70 |
| 17th | 1900 | 60-75 |
| 18th | 1895 | 60-80 |
| 19th | 1892 | 65-85 |
| 20th | 1896 | 70-90 |
| 21st | 1897 | 75-90 |
| 22nd (Tie) | 1894 | 75-95 |
| 22nd (Tie) | 1898 | 75-95 |
| 24th | 1893 | 80-105 |
| Unknown | 1894-S | -- |

# Appendix A

## *Rarity Summary for Proof Barber Dimes: 1892-1915 (cont.)*

| Overall Rarity, Deep/Ultra Cameo Finish | | |
|---|---|---|
| Rank | Issue | Coins Known |
| 1st (Tie) | 1894 | 1 |
| 1st (Tie) | 1906 | 1 |
| 1st (Tie) | 1910 | 1 |
| 1st (Tie) | 1911 | 1 |
| 5th | 1892 | 3-4 |
| 6th (Tie) | 1895 | 3-5 |
| 6th (Tie) | 1897 | 3-5 |
| 8th | 1893 | 6-9 |
| 9th | 1900 | 7-9 |
| 10th | 1896 | 9-12 |
| 11th | 1899 | 10-15 |
| 12th | 1898 | 15-20 |
| Unknown | 1894-S | -- |
| Unknown | 1901 | -- |
| Unknown | 1902 | -- |
| Unknown | 1903 | -- |
| Unknown | 1904 | -- |
| Unknown | 1905 | -- |
| Unknown | 1907 | -- |
| Unknown | 1908 | -- |
| Unknown | 1909 | -- |
| Unknown | 1912 | -- |
| Unknown | 1913 | -- |
| Unknown | 1914 | -- |
| Unknown | 1915 | -- |

# Appendix B

## *Rarity Summary for*
## *Barber Dimes: 1892-1916*

| Overall Rarity in Mint State | | |
|---|---|---|
| **Rank** | **Issue** | **Coins Known** |
| 1st | 1895-O | 40-50 |
| 2nd | 1894-O | 40-55 |
| 3rd | 1896-O | 50-60 |
| 4th | 1898-S | 60-75 |
| 5th | 1898-O | 65-80 |
| 6th (Tie) | 1899-O | 65-85 |
| 6th (Tie) | 1901-S | 65-85 |
| 6th (Tie) | 1903-S | 65-85 |
| 9th | 1900-O | 70-90 |
| 10th | 1902-O | 70-95 |
| 11th | 1902-S | 75-95 |
| 12th (Tie) | 1896-S | 80-95 |
| 12th (Tie) | 1909-S | 80-95 |
| 14th (Tie) | 1901-O | 80-100 |
| 14th (Tie) | 1907-D | 80-100 |
| 16th | 1897-S | 80-105 |
| 17th | 1910-S | 80-110 |
| 18th | 1897-O | 85-105 |
| 19th | 1904-S | 90-105 |
| 20th | 1907-S | 95-110 |
| 21st | 1909-D | 105-125 |
| 22nd (Tie) | 1892-S | 105-135 |
| 22nd (Tie) | 1910-D | 105-135 |
| 24th (Tie) | 1903-O | 110-135 |
| 24th (Tie) | 1908-S | 110-135 |

# Appendix B

## *Rarity Summary for Barber Dimes: 1892-1916 (cont.)*

| Overall Rarity in Mint State (Cont.) | | |
|---|---|---|
| **Rank** | **Issue** | **Coins Known** |
| 26th | 1895-S | 110-140 |
| 27th | 1899-S | 115-140 |
| 28th | 1909-O | 120-145 |
| 29th | 1895 | 120-150 |
| 30th | 1893-S | 130-160 |
| 31st | 1906-S | 135-165 |
| 32nd (Tie) | 1906-D | 135-170 |
| 32nd (Tie) | 1908-O | 135-170 |
| 34th | 1913-S | 145-185 |
| 35th (Tie) | 1893-O | 150-190 |
| 35th (Tie) | 1896 | 150-190 |
| 37th | 1915-S | 160-190 |
| 38th | 1900-S | 160-200 |
| 39th (Tie) | 1903 | 165-205 |
| 39th (Tie) | 1905-O | 165-205 |
| 41st | 1908-D | 170-210 |
| 42nd | 1894 | 175-220 |
| 43rd (Tie) | 1906-O | 185-225 |
| 43rd (Tie) | 1907-O | 185-225 |
| 45th | 1905-S | 200-235 |
| 46th | 1914-S | 210-255 |
| 47th | 1912-S | 215-250 |
| 48th | 1902 | 215-260 |
| 49th | 1905 | 225-260 |
| 50th | 1904 | 225-275 |

# Rarity Summary for
# Barber Dimes: 1892-1916 (cont.)

| Overall Rarity in Mint State (Cont.) | | |
|---|---|---|
| Rank | Issue | Coins Known |
| 51st | 1892-O | 240-285 |
| 52nd | 1900 | 275-340 |
| 53rd | 1911-S | 290-345 |
| 54th | 1911-D | 305-365 |
| 55th | 1912-D | 325-395 |
| 56th | 1893 | 335-400 |
| 57th | 1916-S | 325-425 |
| 58th | 1909 | 375-450 |
| 59th | 1901 | 390-475 |
| 60th | 1915 | 400-480 |
| 61st | 1899 | 400-485 |
| 62nd | 1908 | 420-510 |
| 63rd | 1906 | 440-530 |
| 64th | 1907 | 480-570 |
| 65th | 1897 | 500-605 |
| 66th | 1914-D | 500-610 |
| 67th | 1910 | 560-695 |
| 68th | 1898 | 580-715 |
| 69th | 1913 | 950-1,140 |
| 70th | 1914 | 1,080-1,320 |
| 71st | 1912 | 1,135-1,300 |
| 72nd | 1911 | 1,135-1,360 |
| 73rd | 1916 | 1,520-1,710 |
| 74th | 1892 | 1,550-1,800 |

# Appendix B

## *Rarity Summary for Barber Dimes: 1892-1916 (cont.)*

| High-Grade Rarity, MS-65 or Finer | | |
|---|---|---|
| Rank | Issue | Coins Known |
| 1st | 1894-O | 7-10 |
| 2nd | 1895-S | 9-12 |
| 3rd | 1907-S | 12-16 |
| 4th | 1902-O | 13-16 |
| 5th | 1895-O | 13-17 |
| 6th | 1903-O | 14-18 |
| 7th (Tie) | 1892-S | 15-20 |
| 7th (Tie) | 1898-S | 15-20 |
| 9th | 1897-S | 15-25 |
| 10th | 1904-S | 17-21 |
| 11th | 1896-O | 17-22 |
| 12th (Tie) | 1898-O | 20-25 |
| 12th (Tie) | 1899-O | 20-25 |
| 12th (Tie) | 1899-S | 20-25 |
| 12th (Tie) | 1901-S | 20-25 |
| 12th (Tie) | 1909-S | 20-25 |
| 12th (Tie) | 1910-D | 20-25 |
| 18th | 1893-O | 20-35 |
| 19th (Tie) | 1893-S | 25-30 |
| 19th (Tie) | 1896-S | 25-30 |
| 19th (Tie) | 1897-O | 25-30 |
| 19th (Tie) | 1901-O | 25-30 |
| 19th (Tie) | 1902-S | 25-30 |
| 19th (Tie) | 1903-S | 25-30 |

# Rarity Summary for
# Barber Dimes: 1892-1916 (cont.)

| High-Grade Rarity, MS-65 or Finer (Cont.) | | |
|---|---|---|
| Rank | Issue | Coins Known |
| 25th (Tie) | 1895 | 25-35 |
| 25th (Tie) | 1900-O | 25-35 |
| 25th (Tie) | 1907-D | 25-35 |
| 28th | 1910-S | 30-40 |
| 29th | 1905-S | 35-40 |
| 30th (Tie) | 1904 | 35-45 |
| 30th (Tie) | 1906-D | 35-45 |
| 30th (Tie) | 1908-S | 35-45 |
| 30th (Tie) | 1909-O | 35-45 |
| 30th (Tie) | 1915-S | 35-45 |
| 35th (Tie) | 1896 | 40-45 |
| 35th (Tie) | 1909-D | 40-45 |
| 37th (Tie) | 1900-S | 40-50 |
| 37th (Tie) | 1903 | 40-50 |
| 37th (Tie) | 1905 | 40-50 |
| 37th (Tie) | 1914-S | 40-50 |
| 41st (Tie) | 1892-O | 45-55 |
| 41st (Tie) | 1907-O | 45-55 |
| 41st (Tie) | 1908-D | 45-55 |
| 44th (Tie) | 1894 | 50-60 |
| 44th (Tie) | 1905-O | 50-60 |
| 44th (Tie) | 1912-S | 50-60 |
| 47th (Tie) | 1902 | 50-65 |
| 47th (Tie) | 1912-D | 50-65 |
| 49th | 1900 | 55-65 |

# Appendix B

## *Rarity Summary for Barber Dimes: 1892-1916 (cont.)*

| High-Grade Rarity, MS-65 or Finer (cont.) | | |
|---|---|---|
| Rank | Issue | Coins Known |
| 50th (Tie) | 1908-O | 55-70 |
| 50th (Tie) | 1913-S | 55-70 |
| 52nd | 1906-S | 60-70 |
| 53rd (Tie) | 1901 | 65-80 |
| 53rd (Tie) | 1906-O | 65-80 |
| 53rd (Tie) | 1909 | 65-80 |
| 53rd (Tie) | 1915 | 65-80 |
| 53rd (Tie) | 1916-S | 65-80 |
| 58th | 1899 | 75-90 |
| 59th (Tie) | 1906 | 80-95 |
| 59th (Tie) | 1907 | 80-95 |
| 61st | 1914-D | 90-105 |
| 62nd (Tie) | 1893 | 95-115 |
| 62nd (Tie) | 1908 | 95-115 |
| 64th | 1911-D | 115-135 |
| 65th | 1911-S | 120-145 |
| 66th | 1897 | 125-155 |
| 67th | 1910 | 135-170 |
| 68th | 1898 | 145-180 |
| 69th | 1913 | 165-200 |
| 70th | 1916 | 245-280 |
| 71st | 1912 | 265-325 |
| 72nd | 1914 | 270-330 |
| 73rd | 1911 | 305-380 |
| 74th | 1892 | 325-395 |

# Appendix C

## *Rarity Summary for Philadelphia Mint Barber Dimes: 1892-1916*

| Overall Rarity in Mint State | | |
|---|---|---|
| Rank | Issue | Coins Known |
| 1st | 1895 | 120-150 |
| 2nd | 1896 | 150-190 |
| 3rd | 1903 | 165-205 |
| 4th | 1894 | 175-220 |
| 5th | 1902 | 215-260 |
| 6th | 1905 | 225-260 |
| 7th | 1904 | 225-275 |
| 8th | 1900 | 275-340 |
| 9th | 1893 | 335-400 |
| 10th | 1909 | 375-450 |
| 11th | 1901 | 390-475 |
| 12th | 1915 | 400-480 |
| 13th | 1899 | 400-485 |
| 14th | 1908 | 420-510 |
| 15th | 1906 | 440-530 |
| 16th | 1907 | 480-570 |
| 17th | 1897 | 500-605 |
| 18th | 1910 | 560-695 |
| 19th | 1898 | 580-715 |
| 20th | 1913 | 950-1,140 |
| 21st | 1914 | 1,080-1,320 |
| 22nd | 1912 | 1,135-1,300 |
| 23rd | 1911 | 1,135-1,360 |
| 24th | 1916 | 1,520-1,710 |
| 25th | 1892 | 1,550-1,800 |

# Appendix C

## *Rarity Summary for Philadelphia Mint Barber Dimes: 1892-1916 (cont.)*

| Rank | Issue | Coins Known |
|------|-------|-------------|
| **High-Grade Rarity, MS-65 or Finer** | | |
| 1st | 1895 | 25-35 |
| 2nd | 1904 | 35-45 |
| 3rd | 1896 | 40-45 |
| 4th (Tie) | 1903 | 40-50 |
| 4th (Tie) | 190 | 40-50 |
| 6th | 1894 | 50-60 |
| 7th | 1902 | 50-65 |
| 8th | 1900 | 55-65 |
| 9th (Tie) | 1901 | 65-80 |
| 9th (Tie) | 1909 | 65-80 |
| 9th (Tie) | 1915 | 65-80 |
| 12th | 1899 | 75-90 |
| 13th (Tie) | 1906 | 80-95 |
| 13th (Tie) | 1907 | 80-95 |
| 15th (Tie) | 1893 | 95-115 |
| 15th (Tie) | 1908 | 95-115 |
| 17th | 1897 | 125-155 |
| 18th | 1910 | 135-170 |
| 19th | 1898 | 145-180 |
| 20th | 1913 | 165-200 |
| 21st | 1916 | 245-280 |
| 22nd | 1912 | 265-325 |
| 23rd | 1914 | 270-330 |
| 24th | 1911 | 305-380 |
| 25th | 1892 | 325-395 |

# Rarity Summary for Denver Mint Barber Dimes: 1906-1914

| Overall Rarity in Mint State | | |
|---|---|---|
| **Rank** | **Issue** | **Coins Known** |
| 1st | 1907-D | 80-100 |
| 2nd | 1909-D | 105-125 |
| 3rd | 1910-D | 105-135 |
| 4th | 1906-D | 135-170 |
| 5th | 1908-D | 170-210 |
| 6th | 1911-D | 305-365 |
| 7th | 1912-D | 325-395 |
| 8th | 1914-D | 500-610 |

| High-Grade Rarity, MS-65 or Finer | | |
|---|---|---|
| **Rank** | **Issue** | **Coins Known** |
| 1st | 1910-D | 20-25 |
| 2nd | 1907-D | 25-35 |
| 3rd | 1906-D | 35-45 |
| 4th | 1909-D | 40-45 |
| 5th | 1908-D | 45-55 |
| 6th | 1912-D | 50-65 |
| 7th | 1914-D | 90-105 |
| 8th | 1911-D | 115-135 |

# Appendix E

## Rarity Summary for New Orleans Mint Barber Dimes: 1892-1909

| Overall Rarity in Mint State | | |
|---|---|---|
| **Rank** | **Issue** | **Coins Known** |
| 1st | 1895-O | 40-50 |
| 2nd | 1894-O | 40-55 |
| 3rd | 1896-O | 50-60 |
| 4th | 1898-O | 65-80 |
| 5th | 1899-O | 65-85 |
| 6th | 1900-O | 70-90 |
| 7th | 1902-O | 70-95 |
| 8th | 1901-O | 80-100 |
| 9th | 1897-O | 85-105 |
| 10th | 1903-O | 110-135 |
| 11th | 1909-O | 120-145 |
| 12th | 1908-O | 135-170 |
| 13th | 1893-O | 150-190 |
| 14th | 1905-O | 165-205 |
| 15th (Tie) | 1906-O | 185-225 |
| 15th (Tie) | 1907-O | 185-225 |
| 17th | 1892-O | 240-285 |

# Rarity Summary for New Orleans Mint Barber Dimes: 1892-1909 (cont.)

| High-Grade Rarity, MS-65 or Finer | | |
|---|---|---|
| Rank | Issue | Coins Known |
| 1st | 1894-O | 7-10 |
| 2nd | 1902-O | 13-16 |
| 3rd | 1895-O | 13-17 |
| 4th | 1903-O | 14-18 |
| 5th | 1896-O | 17-22 |
| 6th (Tie) | 1898-O | 20-25 |
| 6th (Tie) | 1899-O | 20-25 |
| 8th | 1893-O | 20-35 |
| 9th (Tie) | 1897-O | 25-30 |
| 9th (Tie) | 1901-O | 25-30 |
| 11th | 1900-O | 25-35 |
| 12th | 1909-O | 35-45 |
| 13th (Tie) | 1892-O | 45-55 |
| 13th (Tie) | 1907-O | 45-55 |
| 15th | 1905-O | 50-60 |
| 16th | 1908-O | 55-70 |
| 17th | 1906-O | 65-80 |

# Appendix F

## *Rarity Summary for San Francisco Mint Barber Dimes: 1892-1916*

| Overall Rarity in Mint State | | |
|---|---|---|
| **Rank** | **Issue** | **Coins Known** |
| 1st | 1898-S | 60-75 |
| 2nd (Tie) | 1901-S | 65-85 |
| 2nd (Tie) | 1903-S | 65-85 |
| 4th | 1902-S | 75-97 |
| 5th (Tie) | 1896-S | 80-95 |
| 5th (Tie) | 1909-S | 80-95 |
| 7th | 1897-S | 80-105 |
| 8th | 1910-S | 80-110 |
| 9th | 1904-S | 90-105 |
| 10th | 1907-S | 95-110 |
| 11th | 1892-S | 105-135 |
| 12th | 1908-S | 110-135 |
| 13th | 1895-S | 110-140 |
| 14th | 1899-S | 115-140 |
| 15th | 1893-S | 130-160 |
| 16th | 1906-S | 135-165 |
| 17th | 1913-S | 145-185 |
| 18th | 1915-S | 160-190 |
| 19th | 1900-S | 160-200 |
| 20th | 1905-S | 200-235 |
| 21st | 1914-S | 210-255 |
| 22nd | 1912-S | 215-250 |
| 23rd | 1911-S | 290-345 |
| 24th | 1916-S | 345-425 |

# *Rarity Summary for San Francisco Mint Barber Dimes: 1892-1916 (cont.)*

| High-Grade Rarity, MS-65 or Finer | | |
|---|---|---|
| **Rank** | **Issue** | **Coins Known** |
| 1st | 1895-S | 9-12 |
| 2nd | 1907-S | 12-16 |
| 3rd (Tie) | 1892-S | 15-20 |
| 3rd (Tie) | 1898-S | 15-20 |
| 5th | 1897-S | 15-25 |
| 6th | 1904-S | 17-21 |
| 7th (Tie) | 1899-S | 20-25 |
| 7th (Tie) | 1901-S | 20-25 |
| 7th (Tie) | 1909-S | 20-25 |
| 10th (Tie) | 1893-S | 25-30 |
| 10th (Tie) | 1896-S | 25-30 |
| 10th (Tie) | 1902-S | 25-30 |
| 10th (Tie) | 1903-S | 25-30 |
| 14th | 1910-S | 30-40 |
| 15th | 1905-S | 35-40 |
| 16th (Tie) | 1908-S | 35-45 |
| 16th (Tie) | 1915-S | 35-45 |
| 18th (Tie) | 1900-S | 40-50 |
| 18th (Tie) | 1914-S | 40-50 |
| 20th | 1912-S | 50-60 |
| 21st | 1913-S | 55-70 |
| 22nd | 1906-S | 60-70 |
| 23rd | 1916-S | 65-80 |
| 24th | 1911-S | 120-145 |

# Appendix G

## *Investment Potential Ratio Summary for Proof Barber Dimes: 1892-1915*

| | Proof-64 | | |
|---|---|---|---|
| Issue | Approx. Pop. Proof-64 | Approx. Value Proof-64 | Investment Potential Ratio |
| 1897 | 80 | $675.00 | -33.33% |
| 1905 | 85 | $700.00 | -22.58% |
| 1914 | 75 | $825.00 | -21.29% |
| 1898 | 90 | $675.00 | -19.44% |
| 1893 | 80 | $800.00 | -16.35% |
| 1908 | 88 | $725.00 | -15.17% |
| 1915 | 80 | $825.00 | -12.95% |
| 1910 | 90 | $725.00 | -12.65% |
| 1900 | 85 | $788.00 | -10.63% |
| 1906 | 93 | $725.00 | -9.06% |
| 1907 | 93 | $725.00 | -9.06% |
| 1892 | 103 | $700.00 | -2.02% |
| 1911 | 100 | $725.00 | -1.53% |
| 1912 | 100 | $725.00 | -1.53% |
| 1896 | 108 | $675.00 | -0.92% |
| 1899 | 93 | $788.00 | -0.51% |
| 1903 | 113 | $688.00 | 4.94% |
| 1909 | 108 | $725.00 | 5.87% |
| 1904 | 113 | $700.00 | 6.57% |
| 1901 | 105 | $750.00 | 6.62% |
| 1902 | 117 | $713.00 | 11.37% |
| 1913 | 118 | $725.00 | 13.72% |
| 1894 | 148 | $700.00 | 27.50% |
| 1895 | 128 | $900.00 | 44.11% |

*Key:* Negative numbers represent underrated issues; positive numbers represent overrated issues.

# Investment Potential Ratio Summary
# for Proof Barber Dimes: 1892-1915 (cont.)

| Issue | Approx. Pop. Proof-65 | Approx. Value Proof-65 | Investment Potential Ratio |
|-------|-----------------------|------------------------|----------------------------|
| 1915 | 40 | $1,300.00 | -53.47% |
| 1908 | 45 | $1,250.00 | -40.52% |
| 1900 | 40 | $1,475.00 | -40.48% |
| 1914 | 45 | $1,300.00 | -36.81% |
| 1913 | 45 | $1,300.00 | -36.81% |
| 1907 | 50 | $1,250.00 | -27.18% |
| 1902 | 45 | $1,525.00 | -20.10% |
| 1906 | 50 | $1,375.00 | -17.90% |
| 1898 | 60 | $1,250.00 | -7.18% |
| 1910 | 60 | $1,250.00 | -7.18% |
| 1911 | 60 | $1,300.00 | -3.47% |
| 1912 | 60 | $1,300.00 | -3.47% |
| 1897 | 65 | $1,250.00 | 0.51% |
| 1893 | 65 | $1,250.00 | 0.51% |
| 1896 | 65 | $1,250.00 | 0.51% |
| 1909 | 65 | $1,250.00 | 0.51% |
| 1899 | 60 | $1,400.00 | 3.95% |
| 1892 | 75 | $1,250.00 | 12.82% |
| 1904 | 60 | $1,525.00 | 13.23% |
| 1905 | 65 | $1,500.00 | 19.07% |
| 1901 | 70 | $1,425.00 | 20.10% |
| 1903 | 65 | $1,525.00 | 20.93% |
| 1894 | 103 | $1,300.00 | 38.28% |
| 1895 | 93 | $1,500.00 | 46.86% |

*Key:* Negative numbers represent underrated issues; positive numbers represent overrated issues.

# Investment Potential Ratio Summary
## for Proof Barber Dimes: 1892-1915 (cont.)

| | Proof-66 | | |
|---|---|---|---|
| Issue | Approx. Pop. Proof-66 | Approx. Value Proof-66 | Investment Potential Ratio |
| 1915 | 14 | $2,000.00 | -243.54% |
| 1913 | 23 | $1,850.00 | -116.83% |
| 1914 | 33 | $1,625.00 | -64.76% |
| 1902 | 30 | $2,125.00 | -54.48% |
| 1912 | 35 | $1,800.00 | -47.76% |
| 1910 | 28 | $2,750.00 | -34.87% |
| 1904 | 40 | $2,000.00 | -20.69% |
| 1911 | 45 | $1,800.00 | -17.28% |
| 1897 | 50 | $1,750.00 | -9.10% |
| 1907 | 45 | $2,000.00 | -7.35% |
| 1906 | 40 | $2,375.00 | -2.06% |
| 1900 | 45 | $2,125.00 | -1.15% |
| 1903 | 45 | $2,125.00 | -1.15% |
| 1908 | 45 | $2,250.00 | 5.06% |
| 1894 | 65 | $1,625.00 | 6.85% |
| 1893 | 60 | $1,750.00 | 6.90% |
| 1899 | 55 | $1,925.00 | 8.32% |
| 1905 | 65 | $1,750.00 | 13.05% |
| 1898 | 60 | $2,125.00 | 25.52% |
| 1901 | 60 | $2,125.00 | 25.52% |
| 1892 | 70 | $1,975.00 | 29.50% |
| 1896 | 70 | $2,125.00 | 36.95% |
| 1909 | 65 | $2,250.00 | 37.88% |
| 1895 | 65 | $2,300.00 | 40.37% |

_Key:_ Negative numbers represent underrated issues; positive numbers represent overrated issues.

# Investment Potential Ratio Summary
## for Proof Barber Dimes: 1892-1915 (cont.)

| | Proof-67 | | |
|---|---|---|---|
| Issue | Approx. Pop. Proof-67 | Approx. Value Proof-67 | Investment Potential Ratio |
| 1912 | 9 | $3,000.00 | -178.34% |
| 1902 | 14 | $3,250.00 | -80.63% |
| 1903 | 14 | $3,500.00 | -74.20% |
| 1904 | 14 | $3,500.00 | -74.20% |
| 1913 | 14 | $3,500.00 | -74.20% |
| 1914 | 13 | $5,000.00 | -48.22% |
| 1896 | 17 | $3,500.00 | -45.21% |
| 1901 | 18 | $3,750.00 | -31.25% |
| 1915 | 20 | $3,500.00 | -24.91% |
| 1892 | 28 | $2,500.00 | -17.79% |
| 1893 | 28 | $2,500.00 | -17.79% |
| 1910 | 18 | $4,500.00 | -11.95% |
| 1906 | 20 | $4,125.00 | -8.82% |
| 1900 | 26 | $3,500.00 | 1.63% |
| 1911 | 23 | $4,000.00 | 2.96% |
| 1907 | 23 | $4,125.00 | 6.18% |
| 1897 | 28 | $3,500.00 | 7.95% |
| 1905 | 26 | $3,750.00 | 8.06% |
| 1908 | 23 | $4,375.00 | 12.61% |
| 1909 | 35 | $3,250.00 | 17.94% |
| 1894 | 40 | $3,750.00 | 39.02% |
| 1895 | 40 | $4,375.00 | 55.11% |
| 1898 | 33 | $5,500.00 | 71.87% |
| 1899 | 35 | $5,500.00 | 75.85% |

*Key:* Negative numbers represent underrated issues; positive numbers represent overrated issues.

# Appendix H

## *Investment Potential Ratio Summary for Barber Dimes: 1892-1916*

| | MS-64 | | |
|---|---|---|---|
| Issue | Approx. Pop. MS-64 | Approx. Value MS-64 | Investment Potential Ratio |
| 1898-O | 14 | $2,250.00 | -261.99% |
| 1902-S | 20 | $1,500.00 | -197.51% |
| 1910-S | 28 | $1,025.00 | -149.83% |
| 1910-D | 40 | $550.00 | -136.42% |
| 1898-S | 18 | $2,125.00 | -133.15% |
| 1903 | 50 | $325.00 | -130.79% |
| 1896 | 45 | $525.00 | -114.46% |
| 1899-O | 18 | $2,250.00 | -109.60% |
| 1901-O | 18 | $2,250.00 | -109.60% |
| 1908-O | 40 | $700.00 | -108.17% |
| 1906-S | 40 | $725.00 | -103.47% |
| 1907-S | 28 | $1,300.00 | -98.04% |
| 1902 | 70 | $300.00 | -80.65% |
| 1909-O | 33 | $1,125.00 | -79.04% |
| 1901-S | 23 | $1,800.00 | -78.41% |
| 1908-D | 50 | $625.00 | -74.30% |
| 1900-S | 50 | $638.00 | -71.85% |
| 1905 | 85 | $263.00 | -63.41% |
| 1905-S | 65 | $475.00 | -58.24% |
| 1912-S | 75 | $375.00 | -57.38% |
| 1909-S | 28 | $1,525.00 | -55.66% |
| 1893 | 88 | $300.00 | -52.59% |
| 1905-O | 55 | $650.00 | -52.13% |
| 1900 | 90 | $300.00 | -50.17% |
| 1907-O | 65 | $550.00 | -44.11% |

*Key:* Negative numbers represent underrated issues; positive numbers represent overrated issues.

# Appendix H

# *Investment Potential Ratio Summary for Barber Dimes: 1892-1916 (cont.)*

| | MS-64 (cont.) | | |
|---|---|---|---|
| Issue | Approx. Pop. MS-64 | Approx. Value MS-64 | Investment Potential Ratio |
| 1906-O | 70 | $500.00 | -42.98% |
| 1908-S | 33 | $1,325.00 | -41.38% |
| 1906-D | 50 | $800.00 | -41.34% |
| 1903-S | 23 | $2,000.00 | -40.74% |
| 1915-S | 70 | $525.00 | -38.27% |
| 1911-D | 103 | $300.00 | -36.71% |
| 1916-S | 113 | $275.00 | -33.17% |
| 1909-D | 33 | $1,375.00 | -31.96% |
| 1900-O | 23 | $2,050.00 | -31.33% |
| 1904 | 100 | $350.00 | -30.09% |
| 1913-S | 45 | $975.00 | -29.72% |
| 1912-D | 118 | $275.00 | -29.57% |
| 1892-O | 88 | $425.00 | -29.05% |
| 1894 | 55 | $775.00 | -28.59% |
| 1914-S | 70 | $613.00 | -21.70% |
| 1909 | 138 | $263.00 | -20.04% |
| 1903-O | 45 | $1,050.00 | -15.59% |
| 1908 | 153 | $263.00 | -13.22% |
| 1901 | 138 | $300.00 | -13.07% |
| 1906 | 158 | $263.00 | -11.23% |
| 1899 | 148 | $288.00 | -10.63% |
| 1911-S | 70 | $675.00 | -10.02% |
| 1907 | 163 | $263.00 | -9.37% |
| 1915 | 148 | $300.00 | -8.37% |
| 1897 | 168 | $275.00 | -5.35% |

*Key:* Negative numbers represent underrated issues; positive numbers represent overrated issues.

# Appendix H

## Investment Potential Ratio Summary for Barber Dimes: 1892-1916 (cont.)

| | MS-64 (cont.) | | |
|---|---|---|---|
| Issue | Approx. Pop. MS-64 | Approx. Value MS-64 | Investment Potential Ratio |
| 1898 | 175 | $263.00 | -5.33% |
| 1914-D | 175 | $275.00 | -3.07% |
| 1893-S | 38 | $1,375.00 | 6.31% |
| 1910 | 215 | $300.00 | 11.85% |
| 1913 | 350 | $250.00 | 19.65% |
| 1911 | 385 | $238.00 | 19.89% |
| 1912 | 400 | $250.00 | 23.08% |
| 1893-O | 55 | $1,075.00 | 27.90% |
| 1916 | 475 | $263.00 | 29.32% |
| 1892 | 510 | $275.00 | 32.97% |
| 1902-O | 30 | $1,875.00 | 33.11% |
| 1914 | 475 | $300.00 | 36.29% |
| 1892-S | 40 | $1,500.00 | 42.49% |
| 1895 | 50 | $1,250.00 | 43.40% |
| 1899-S | 40 | $1,550.00 | 51.90% |
| 1907-D | 28 | $2,125.00 | 57.33% |
| 1897-O | 28 | $2,500.00 | 127.95% |
| 1897-S | 40 | $2,125.00 | 160.19% |
| 1895-S | 40 | $2,375.00 | 207.27% |
| 1904-S | 28 | $3,000.00 | 222.11% |
| 1896-S | 33 | $2,750.00 | 226.98% |
| 1896-O | 20 | $4,250.00 | 320.38% |
| 1894-O | 13 | $6,250.00 | 438.56% |
| 1895-O | 11 | $12,500.00 . | 1481.32% |

*Key:* Negative numbers represent underrated issues; positive numbers represent overrated issues.

# Investment Potential Ratio Summary
# for Barber Dimes: 1892-1916 (cont.)

| | MS-65 | | |
|---|---|---|---|
| Issue | Approx. Pop. MS-65 | Approx. Value MS-65 | Investment Potential Ratio |
| 1907-S | 7 | $2,000.00 | -481.24% |
| 1903-S | 8 | $2,500.00 | -355.12% |
| 1894-O | 3 | $13,750.00 | -324.01% |
| 1910-D | 11 | $1,500.00 | -286.26% |
| 1898-S | 9 | $3,125.00 | -236.27% |
| 1899-S | 9 | $3,125.00 | -236.27% |
| 1902-O | 9 | $3,625.00 | -192.29% |
| 1909-S | 11 | $2,625.00 | -187.31% |
| 1905-S | 28 | $638.00 | -108.17% |
| 1897-S | 11 | $3,625.00 | -99.36% |
| 1904-S | 11 | $3,750.00 | -88.37% |
| 1903 | 28 | $900.00 | -85.13% |
| 1908-D | 28 | $900.00 | -85.13% |
| 1914-S | 28 | $900.00 | -85.13% |
| 1902 | 35 | $588.00 | -79.71% |
| 1906-D | 23 | $1,375.00 | -79.07% |
| 1915-S | 23 | $1,375.00 | -79.07% |
| 1893-O | 15 | $2,625.00 | -75.80% |
| 1903-O | 11 | $4,000.00 | -66.38% |
| 1907-O | 28 | $1,125.00 | -65.34% |
| 1912-S | 38 | $638.00 | -64.94% |
| 1895-S | 7 | $6,750.00 | -63.48% |
| 1900 | 40 | $625.00 | -60.03% |
| 1912-D | 40 | $625.00 | -60.03% |
| 1905 | 38 | $700.00 | -59.49% |

*Key:* Negative numbers represent underrated issues; positive numbers represent overrated issues.

# Appendix H

## Investment Potential Ratio Summary for Barber Dimes: 1892-1916 (cont.)

| | MS-65 (cont.) | | |
|---|---|---|---|
| Issue | Approx. Pop. MS-65 | Approx. Value MS-65 | Investment Potential Ratio |
| 1896 | 28 | $1,250.00 | -54.35% |
| 1901-O | 14 | $3,125.00 | -53.73% |
| 1895 | 18 | $2,375.00 | -46.67% |
| 1909-O | 23 | $1,750.00 | -46.09% |
| 1905-O | 28 | $1,375.00 | -43.35% |
| 1902-S | 14 | $3,250.00 | -42.73% |
| 1901 | 50 | $588.00 | -40.28% |
| 1916-S | 50 | $613.00 | -38.09% |
| 1909 | 55 | $550.00 | -35.26% |
| 1904 | 28 | $1,500.00 | -32.36% |
| 1892-O | 38 | $1,025.00 | -30.90% |
| 1915 | 60 | $550.00 | -28.29% |
| 1906-S | 38 | $1,075.00 | -26.51% |
| 1899 | 60 | $575.00 | -26.09% |
| 1907 | 60 | $575.00 | -26.09% |
| 1910-S | 23 | $2,000.00 | -24.10% |
| 1899-O | 11 | $4,500.00 | -22.40% |
| 1906 | 65 | $575.00 | -20.20% |
| 1908 | 65 | $575.00 | -20.20% |
| 1914-D | 65 | $575.00 | -20.20% |
| 1906-O | 40 | $1,113.00 | -17.11% |
| 1897 | 78 | $538.00 | -11.66% |
| 1901-S | 11 | $4,625.00 | -11.41% |
| 1911-D | 75 | $575.00 | -10.76% |
| 1908-S | 28 | $1,750.00 | -10.37% |

Key: Negative numbers represent underrated issues; positive numbers represent overrated issues.

# Investment Potential Ratio Summary
# for Barber Dimes: 1892-1916 (cont.)

| Issue | Approx. Pop. MS-65 | Approx. Value MS-65 | Investment Potential Ratio |
|---|---|---|---|
| 1908-O | 40 | $1,250.00 | -5.06% |
| 1911-S | 60 | $875.00 | 0.29% |
| 1898-O | 14 | $3,750.00 | 1.24% |
| 1910 | 105 | $525.00 | 2.36% |
| 1900-S | 33 | $1,625.00 | 3.53% |
| 1893 | 65 | $850.00 | 3.99% |
| 1894 | 40 | $1,375.00 | 5.93% |
| 1898 | 113 | $575.00 | 9.86% |
| 1892-S | 15 | $3,625.00 | 12.15% |
| 1913 | 138 | $563.00 | 16.18% |
| 1916 | 188 | $525.00 | 21.71% |
| 1907-D | 17 | $3,375.00 | 26.25% |
| 1914 | 225 | $550.00 | 27.93% |
| 1911 | 215 | $563.00 | 28.12% |
| 1912 | 220 | $563.00 | 28.61% |
| 1892 | 210 | $625.00 | 33.06% |
| 1913-S | 35 | $2,000.00 | 44.47% |
| 1896-S | 14 | $4,250.00 | 45.22% |
| 1893-S | 23 | $2,875.00 | 52.86% |
| 1909-D | 33 | $3,000.00 | 124.46% |
| 1896-O | 9 | $7,500.00 | 148.52% |
| 1897-O | 14 | $5,500.00 | 155.16% |
| 1900-O | 20 | $4,750.00 | 187.77% |
| 1895-O | 13 | $27,500.00 | 2064.80% |

*Key:* Negative numbers represent underrated issues; positive numbers represent overrated issues.

# Appendix H

## Investment Potential Ratio Summary for Barber Dimes: 1892-1916 (cont.)

| | MS-66 | | |
|---|---|---|---|
| Issue | Approx. Pop. MS-66 | Approx. Value MS-66 | Investment Potential Ratio |
| 1905 | 5 | $1,750.00 | -358.15% |
| 1903-O | 4 | $6,250.00 | -304.12% |
| 1905-S | 7 | $3,500.00 | -176.31% |
| 1910-D | 8 | $2,500.00 | -174.15% |
| 1910-S | 7 | $4,500.00 | -140.96% |
| 1907-S | 7 | $5,000.00 | -123.29% |
| 1906 | 14 | $1,050.00 | -112.89% |
| 1909 | 14 | $1,050.00 | -112.89% |
| 1897-S | 5 | $8,750.00 | -110.76% |
| 1900 | 13 | $1,800.00 | -97.92% |
| 1902-O | 5 | $9,250.00 | -93.09% |
| 1908-D | 14 | $2,000.00 | -79.32% |
| 1915 | 14 | $2,000.00 | -79.32% |
| 1908-S | 11 | $3,250.00 | -76.05% |
| 1915-S | 14 | $2,125.00 | -74.90% |
| 1901 | 17 | $1,575.00 | -67.87% |
| 1912-S | 14 | $2,375.00 | -66.06% |
| 1894 | 13 | $2,750.00 | -64.35% |
| 1904 | 13 | $2,750.00 | -64.35% |
| 1908-O | 18 | $1,750.00 | -54.82% |
| 1899 | 18 | $1,875.00 | -50.40% |
| 1903 | 17 | $2,125.00 | -48.43% |
| 1906-D | 18 | $2,000.00 | -45.98% |
| 1905-O | 18 | $2,125.00 | -41.57% |
| 1914-D | 28 | $1,000.00 | -39.66% |

Key: Negative numbers represent underrated issues; positive numbers represent overrated issues.

# Investment Potential Ratio Summary
# for Barber Dimes: 1892-1916 (cont.)

| | MS-66 (cont.) | | |
|---|---|---|---|
| Issue | Approx. Pop. MS-66 | Approx. Value MS-66 | Investment Potential Ratio |
| 1907 | 28 | $1,050.00 | -37.89% |
| 1904-S | 7 | $7,500.00 | -34.94% |
| 1906-O | 23 | $1,650.00 | -32.99% |
| 1892-O | 11 | $4,500.00 | -31.87% |
| 1893-O | 11 | $4,500.00 | -31.87% |
| 1910 | 35 | $800.00 | -31.73% |
| 1896 | 14 | $3,375.00 | -30.72% |
| 1908 | 35 | $925.00 | -27.31% |
| 1913 | 40 | $900.00 | -20.69% |
| 1914-S | 18 | $2,750.00 | -19.48% |
| 1907-O | 23 | $2,250.00 | -11.79% |
| 1911-D | 40 | $1,175.00 | -10.97% |
| 1912-D | 17 | $3,250.00 | -8.67% |
| 1898 | 40 | $1,375.00 | -3.91% |
| 1912 | 65 | $900.00 | -0.50% |
| 1906-S | 23 | $2,625.00 | 1.47% |
| 1893-S | 6 | $10,000.00 | 3.41% |
| 1914 | 70 | $950.00 | 3.57% |
| 1895-S | 4 | $15,000.00 | 5.12% |
| 1893 | 33 | $2,000.00 | 7.05% |
| 1916 | 65 | $1,125.00 | 7.45% |
| 1911-S | 60 | $1,250.00 | 9.18% |
| 1911 | 103 | $875.00 | 10.54% |
| 1899-S | 11 | $5,750.00 | 12.30% |
| 1902 | 23 | $3,000.00 | 14.72% |

Key: Negative numbers represent underrated issues; positive numbers represent overrated issues.

# Appendix H

## Investment Potential Ratio Summary for Barber Dimes: 1892-1916 (cont.)

| | MS-66 (cont.) | | |
|---|---|---|---|
| Issue | Approx. Pop. MS-66 | Approx. Value MS-66 | Investment Potential Ratio |
| 1916-S | 23 | $3,000.00 | 14.72% |
| 1909-O | 13 | $5,000.00 | 15.17% |
| 1897 | 55 | $1,550.00 | 16.60% |
| 1892 | 123 | $1,050.00 | 20.04% |
| 1900-S | 11 | $6,000.00 | 21.14% |
| 1902-S | 11 | $6,000.00 | 21.14% |
| 1901-S | 9 | $7,250.00 | 22.89% |
| 1913-S | 23 | $3,250.00 | 23.55% |
| 1907-D | 11 | $6,500.00 | 38.81% |
| 1903-S | 18 | $4,750.00 | 51.20% |
| 1901-O | 14 | $6,000.00 | 62.05% |
| 1899-O | 9 | $8,500.00 | 67.07% |
| 1897-O | 9 | $8,750.00 | 75.90% |
| 1900-O | 9 | $9,000.00 | 84.74% |
| 1892-S | 4 | $18,000.00 | 111.14% |
| 1909-D | 9 | $10,000.00 | 120.08% |
| 1896-S | 13 | $8,750.00 | 147.70% |
| 1909-S | 11 | $10,000.00 | 162.50% |
| 1898-S | 8 | $12,500.00 | 179.26% |
| 1895 | 9 | $11,750.00 | 181.93% |
| 1898-O | 6 | $17,500.00 | 268.47% |
| 1896-O | 9 | $15,000.00 | 296.78% |
| 1894-O | 5 | $27,500.00 | 551.88% |
| 1895-O | 3 | $57,500.00 | 1332.12% |

Key: Negative numbers represent underrated issues; positive numbers represent overrated issues.

# Appendix H

## Investment Potential Ratio Summary for Barber Dimes: 1892-1916 (cont.)

| Issue | Approx. Pop. MS-67 | Approx. Value MS-67 | Investment Potential Ratio |
|---|---|---|---|
| **MS-67** | | | |
| 1907 | 1 | $7,500.00 | -308.99% |
| 1903 | 1 | $8,750.00 | -293.82% |
| 1903-O | 1 | $8,750.00 | -293.82% |
| 1909-D | 1 | $8,750.00 | -293.82% |
| 1902 | 1 | $9,000.00 | -290.79% |
| 1900-O | 1 | $12,500.00 | -248.31% |
| 1901-O | 1 | $12,500.00 | -248.31% |
| 1912-D | 1 | $12,500.00 | -248.31% |
| 1902-O | 1 | $13,750.00 | -233.15% |
| 1896 | 1 | $15,000.00 | -217.98% |
| 1900-S | 1 | $17,500.00 | -187.64% |
| 1904-S | 1 | $20,000.00 | -157.30% |
| 1906-D | 2 | $8,000.00 | -102.92% |
| 1914-S | 2 | $10,000.00 | -78.65% |
| 1902-S | 2 | $10,250.00 | -75.62% |
| 1907-O | 2 | $10,250.00 | -75.62% |
| 1913 | 4 | $3,750.00 | -54.49% |
| 1908-S | 3 | $6,500.00 | -54.46% |
| 1909 | 3 | $7,500.00 | -42.32% |
| 1898-S | 1 | $30,000.00 | -35.96% |
| 1914 | 5 | $4,000.00 | -31.46% |
| 1907-D | 2 | $14,000.00 | -30.11% |
| 1905 | 4 | $6,750.00 | -18.09% |
| 1914-D | 5 | $5,500.00 | -13.26% |
| 1892-O | 3 | $10,000.00 | -11.99% |

_Key:_ Negative numbers represent underrated issues; positive numbers represent overrated issues.

# Investment Potential Ratio Summary for Barber Dimes: 1892-1916 (cont.)

| | MS-67 (cont.) | | |
|---|---|---|---|
| Issue | Approx. Pop. MS-67 | Approx. Value MS-67 | Investment Potential Ratio |
| 1894 | 4 | $7,500.00 | -8.99% |
| 1905-S | 4 | $7,500.00 | -8.99% |
| 1912-S | 3 | $10,250.00 | -8.95% |
| 1897-S | 2 | $16,250.00 | -2.81% |
| 1908-O | 6 | $5,500.00 | 0.07% |
| 1898 | 9 | $3,750.00 | 1.06% |
| 1901 | 5 | $6,750.00 | 1.91% |
| 1897 | 8 | $4,625.00 | 6.12% |
| 1910-D | 3 | $11,750.00 | 9.25% |
| 1906-O | 9 | $4,500.00 | 10.16% |
| 1908-D | 9 | $4,500.00 | 10.16% |
| 1906 | 8 | $5,125.00 | 12.19% |
| 1903-S | 3 | $12,500.00 | 18.35% |
| 1911 | 23 | $3,000.00 | 19.01% |
| 1893-O | 4 | $10,000.00 | 21.35% |
| 1909-O | 4 | $10,000.00 | 21.35% |
| 1893 | 6 | $7,500.00 | 24.34% |
| 1899-S | 4 | $10,250.00 | 24.38% |
| 1899 | 5 | $8,750.00 | 26.18% |
| 1915-S | 5 | $8,750.00 | 26.18% |
| 1910 | 11 | $5,500.00 | 30.38% |
| 1911-S | 11 | $5,500.00 | 30.38% |
| 1912 | 11 | $5,500.00 | 30.38% |
| 1892 | 28 | $3,750.00 | 31.22% |
| 1913-S | 5 | $9,750.00 | 38.31% |

Key: Negative numbers represent underrated issues; positive numbers represent overrated issues.

# Investment Potential Ratio Summary
# for Barber Dimes: 1892-1916 (cont.)

| MS-67 (cont.) | | | |
|---|---|---|---|
| Issue | Approx. Pop. MS-67 | Approx. Value MS-67 | Investment Potential Ratio |
| 1911-D | 11 | $6,250.00 | 39.48% |
| 1900 | 7 | $8,125.00 | 41.45% |
| 1916 | 11 | $6,500.00 | 42.51% |
| 1899-O | 2 | $20,000.00 | 42.70% |
| 1908 | 5 | $10,250.00 | 44.38% |
| 1905-O | 9 | $7,750.00 | 49.60% |
| 1898-O | 1 | $37,500.00 | 55.06% |
| 1910-S | 4 | $15,250.00 | 85.06% |
| 1896-O | 2 | $25,000.00 | 103.37% |
| 1906-S | 4 | $20,000.00 | 142.70% |
| 1894-O | 1 | $45,000.00 | 146.07% |
| 1901-S | 4 | $22,500.00 | 173.03% |
| 1897-O | 5 | $22,500.00 | 193.03% |
| 1895 | 4 | $27,500.00 | 233.71% |
| 1893-S | 1 | $62,500.00 | 358.43% |

*Key:* Negative numbers represent underrated issues; positive numbers represent overrated issues.

# Glossary

**About Good:** The descriptive term associated with the numeric designation of 3 on the 70-point grading scale for United States coins. The abbreviation for About Good is AG.

**About Uncirculated:** The descriptive term associated with the numeric designations of 50, 53, 55 and 58 on the 70-point grading scale for United States coins. The abbreviation for About Uncirculated is AU.

**American Numismatic Association:** Chartered by Congress in 1891, the American Numismatic Association is the leading hobby organization in U.S. numismatics. The American Numismatic Association is often referred to by the abbreviation ANA. It is a non-profit organization.

**Brilliant Uncirculated:** The descriptive term that corresponds to the MS-60, MS-61 and MS-62 grade levels. Brilliant Uncirculated is abbreviated as BU.

**Business Strike:** A regular-issue con struck on normally prepared planchets by dies that are also given normal preparation. Business strikes coins can also be referred to as circulation strikes, and they are coins that the Mint produces for use in commerce.

**Cameo:** Coins that display noticeable contrast between frosty devices/lettering and mirror-finish fields. Both PCGS and NGC use this term as a component of the grade assigned to certain proof coins.

**Certified:** A coin that has been submitted to a third-party grading service and returned to the submitter in a sonically sealed, tamper-evident holder. Coins certified by PCGS and NGC enjoy nearly universal acceptance in the U.S. rare coin market of the early 21st century.

**Certified Acceptance Corporation:** An independent, third-party numismatic authentication service that renders an opinion on the validity of grades assigned to coins that have been certified by PCGS and NGC. CAC affixes green stickers to PCGS and NGC holders when the coin in question meets their strict grading criteria. Gold-label stickers are affixed to coins that exceed CAC's expectations in light of the grade assigned by PCGS or NGC.

**Choice AU:** The descriptive term that corresponds to the AU-55 and, to a lesser extant, AU-58 grade levels.

**Choice Proof:** Descriptive term that correspond to the Proof-63 and Proof-64 grade levels.

**Choice Uncirculated/Choice Mint State/Choice BU:** Descriptive terms that correspond to the MS-63 and MS-64 grade levels.

**Clashmarks:** Impressions from the devices, legends or other features from one die into the surface of the opposing die. Clashmarks are imparted when a pair of dies comes together in the coinage press in the absence of an intervening planchet. Once they become part of a die, clashmarks are transferred to the surface of a coin during the striking process.

**Cleaning:** The use of an abrasive substance or device to alter the surfaces of a coin. Cleaned coins often display numerous scattered hairlines on one or both sides and, as impaired examples, are usually not eligible for certification at the major third-party grading services.

**Deep Cameo:** A proof coin certified by PCGS that has especially bold field-to-device contrast. The corresponding designation at NGC is Ultra Cameo.

**Die Polish Lines:** See Striations.

**Dime:** A United States coins with a face value of 10 cents. Dimes have been struck in the United States Mint since 1796.

**Dipped:** A coin that has been immersed in a weak acid solution to remove toning from the surfaces. Coins that are dipped also lose the outermost layers of metal, which means that the original mint luster will become less vibrant with each subsequent immersion in the dipping solution. Additionally, and also due to the loss of the outermost layers of metal, silver coins that have been dipped will rarely, if ever, reacquire the depth and variety of toning seen on original examples.

**Extremely Fine:** The descriptive term associated with the numeric designations of 40 and 45 on the 70-point grading scale for United States coins. Abbreviations for Extremely Fine include EF and XF.

**Fair:** The descriptive term associated with the designation 2 on the 70-point grading scale for United States coins. Fair is sometimes abbreviated as FR.

**Fine:** The descriptive term associated with the numeric designations of 12 and 15 on the 70-point grading scale for United States coins. Fine is sometimes abbreviated as F.

**Gem Proof:** The descriptive term that corresponds to the Proof-65 and Proof-66 grade levels. Often times only the word Gem is needed to convey the same meaning.

**Gem Uncirculated/Gem Mint State/Gem BU:** The descriptive terms that correspond to the MS-65 and MS-66 grade levels. Often times only the word Gem is needed to convey the same meaning.

**Good:** The descriptive term associated with the numeric designations of 4 and 6 on the 70-point grading scale for United States coins. Good is sometimes abbreviated as G.

**Hairlines:** Thin lines on a coin's surfaces that, when use in reference to a business strike example, are indicative of cleaning or another form of mishandling. Hairlines are also used to describe light handling marks on proof coins and, in this case, are not always the result of cleaning. Unlike die polish lines, hairlines are set below the surface of a coin.

**Hub:** A master die from which working dies are created.

**Impaired:** A descriptive term for coins that have been cleaned, damaged, whizzed, repaired or otherwise mishandled to the point where they will trade at a discounted price. It is the stated policy of major third-party grading services such as PCGS and NGC that impaired coins are not eligible for certification and will be returned to the submitter without being mounted in a plastic holder.

**Insert:** The small piece of paper included in the holder with coins certified by PCGS, NGC and other third-party grading services. Upon the insert are found such important information as the coin's date, denomination, grade and, if applicable, variety.

**Lintmark:** An as-struck depression on a coin's surface, usually thin and curly in shape, caused by a thread that adhered to the die during the striking process. Lintmarks are usually found on proof coins, whose dies are wiped with a cloth during the preparation process. These cloths sometimes leave behind tiny threads that adhere to the die.

**Luster:** The original finish imparted to a coin at the time of striking. Or, the amount and intensity of light reflected from the surface of a coin.

**Mint State:** A coin struck for circulation that does not display any evidence of wear. Mint State coins are graded on a numeric scale from 60-70. The term Uncirculated also describes a Mint State coin.

**Near-Gem:** The descriptive term that corresponds to the MS-64 and Proof-64 grade levels.

**Near-Mint:** The descriptive term that corresponds to the AU-58 grade level.

**NGC Census:** A listing of all coins certified by Numismatic Guaranty Corporation. Up-to-date versions of the NGC Census are available for viewing through the firm's website, www.ngccoin.com.

**Numismatic Guaranty Corporation:** Founded in 1987, NGC authenticates, grades and encapsulates coins for a fee. Along with PCGS, it is the leading third-party certification service in the U.S. rare coin market of the early 21st century.

**Numismatics:** The study or collection of rare coins. A person who studies, collects or invests in rare coins is known as a numismatist.

**PCGS Population Report:** A listing of all coins certified by Professional Coin Grading Service. Up-to-date versions of the PCGS Population Report are accessible for a fee through the firm's website, www.pcgs.com.

**Planchet Flaw:** An as-struck, usually irregular-shaped hole in a coin's surface. Planchet flaws are usually caused by impurities in the alloy that cause a piece of the planchet to break away under the extreme pressure imparted during the striking process. Unlike a scrape or other type of abrasion, the interior of a planchet flaw will appear rough and irregular.

**Polishing:** An especially severe form of cleaning. Coins that have been polished display unnaturally bright and/or glossy-textured surfaces. Technically impaired, polished coins are not eligible for certification at the major third-party grading services.

**Poor:** The descriptive term associated with the numeric designation of 1 on the 70-point grading scale for United States coins. Poor is sometimes abbreviated as PO.

**Prime Focal Areas:** The most important surface areas of a coin when evaluating eye appeal and/or technical grade. Examples of prime focal areas are Liberty's cheek, the date and the mintmark. Abrasions or other distractions in prime focal areas will have a more profound effect on a coin's eye appeal than if they were located in a less-critical area.

**Professional Coin Grading Service:** Founded in 1986, PCGS authenticates, grades and encapsulates coins for a fee. Along with NGC, it is the leading third-party certification service in the U.S. rare coin market of the early 21st century.

**Professional Numismatists Guild:** An organization of rare coin and paper money experts whose members are held to high standards of integrity and professionalism. The abbreviation for the Professional Numismatists Guild is PNG. It is a non-profit organization.

**Proof:** A coin struck with specially prepared dies on a specially prepared planchet. Proof coins are usually struck with two or more blows from the dies, the presses simultaneously operating at slower speeds and higher striking pressures. This extra care is designed to impart uncommonly sharp striking detail to the devices on both sides of the coin. Proof coins are usually not intended for circulation but, rather, are prepared by the Mint for sale to collectors as well as presentation and other special purposes.

*Note:* The term Proof is not a grade like Extremely Fine, About Uncirculated or even Mint State. Instead, the term Proof refers to a method of manufacture.

**Resubmissions:** A term that professional numismatists use to describe coins that are removed from PCGS and NGC holders and submitted to these services at least one more time in the hopes of securing a higher grade. Resubmissions skew the number of coins listed in the PCGS Population Report and NGC Census when the submitter does not return the old insert(s) to the grading services.

**ROI:** Return on investment. The ratio of money gained or lost on an investment relative to the amount of money invested. Return on investment is also known as rate of return, or ROR.

**Striations:** Incuse lines on the surface of a die that result from polishing during the preparation process. When transferred to a coin during striking, striations will appear as raised lines. Since these features are as struck, striations will not result in a lower numeric grade from PCGS or NGC.

**Superb Gem:** The descriptive term that corresponds to the MS-67, MS-68, MS-69, Proof-67, Proof-68 and Proof-69 grade levels.

**Toning:** The color or colors seen on one or both sides of many coins. The intensity and variety of toning that a coin displays is a function of how, where and how long it was stored.

**Ultra Cameo:** A proof coin certified by NGC that has especially bold field-to-device contrast. The corresponding designation at PCGS is Deep Cameo.

**Very Fine:** The descriptive term associated with the numeric designations of 20, 25, 30 and 35 on the 70-point grading scale for United States coins. The abbreviation for Very Fine is VF.

**Very Good:** The descriptive term associated with the numeric designations of 8 and 10 on the 70-point grading scale for United States coins. The abbreviation for Very Good is VG.

**Whizzing:** An attempt to simulate original luster on a coin's surface through the use of a wire brush or similar device. Whizzed coins are considered to be impaired and are not eligible for certification at the major third-party grading services.

# Bibliography

Ambio, Jeff. *Collecting & Investing Strategies for Walking Liberty Half Dollars*. Irvine, California: Zyrus Press, 2008.

Bowers and Merena Auctions. http://www.bowersandmerena.com/. Prices realized archives, various sales, accessed January-December, 2008.

Breen , Walter. *Walter Breen's Complete Encyclopedia of U.S. and Colonial Coins*. New York, New York: Doubleday, 1988.

Breen, Walter. *Walter Breen's Encyclopedia of United States and Colonial Proof Coins: 1722-1977*. New York, New York: FCI Press, Inc., 1977.

Certified Acceptance Corporation. http://www.cacoin.com/. "What's New at CAC" archives, accessed December, 2008.

Coin Dealer Newsletter, The. *The Coin Dealer Newsletter Monthly Supplement, Vol. XXXIII, No. 10*. Torrance, California: October 10, 2008.

Coin Dealer Newsletter, The. *The Coin Dealer Newsletter CDN Quarterly II, Vol. XVII, No. 8*. Torrance, California, August 8, 2008.

Coin Facts. http://www.coinfacts.com/. Barber Dimes section, accessed December, 2008.

Dannreuther, John and Garrett, Jeff. *The Official Red Book of Auction Records: 1995-2004, U.S. Small Cents-Silver Dollars*. Atlanta, Georgia: Whitman Publishing, LLC, 2005.

David Lawrence Rare Coins. http://www.davidlawrence.com/. Prices realized archives, Richmond Collection Part III, accessed January-December, 2008.

Feigenbaum, David and John. *The Complete Guide to Certified Barber Coinage*. Virginia Beach, Virginia: DLRC Press, 1999.

Fivaz, Bill and Stanton, J. T. *Cherrypickers' Guide to Rare Die Varieties of United States Coins, Fourth Edition, Volume II*. Atlanta, Georgia: Whitman Publishing, LLC, 2006.

Flynn, Kevin. *The 1894-S Dime: A Mystery Unraveled*. Rancocas, New Jersey: Kevin Flynn, 2005.

Garrett, Jeff and Guth, Ron. *100 Greatest U.S. Coins, Second Edition*. Atlanta, Georgia: Whitman Publishing, LLC, 2005.

Heritage Auction Galleries. http://coins.ha.com/. Prices realized archives, various sales, accessed January-December, 2008.

Ira & Larry Goldberg Auctioneers, http://www.goldbergcoins.com/index.shtml. Prices realized archives, various sales, accessed January-December, 2008.

Lawrence, David. *The Complete Guide to Barber Dimes*. Virginia Beach, Virginia: DLRC Press, 1991.

Miller, Wayne. *The Morgan and Peace Dollar Textbook*. Helena, Montana: Wayne Miller, no date given.

Numismatic Guaranty Corporation. *Census & Price Guide*. http://www.ngccoin.com/. Accessed January-December, 2008.

Professional Coin Grading Service. *Official Guide to Coin Grading and Counterfeit Detection*. New York, New York: House of Collectibles, 1997.

Professional Coin Grading Service. *PCGS Population Report*. http://www.pcgs.com/. Accessed January-December, 2008.

Stack's. http://www.stacks.com/. Prices realized archives, various sales, accessed January-December, 2008.

Superior Galleries. http://www.sgbh.com/Shop/home/index/html/Prices realized archives, various sales, accessed January-December, 2008.

Yeoman, R.S. *A Guide Book of Unites States Coins*, 62nd Edition. Altanta, Georgia: Whitman Publishing, LLC, 2008.